2\98

D0915686

WITHDRAWN

Soul in Suspense
Hitchcock's
Fright and Delight

by
Neil P. Hurley

The Scarecrow Press, Inc.
Metuchen, N.J., & London
1993

Frontispiece Photo: In *Rear Window,* Jimmy Stewart peers in at seven apartments; he, in turn, is watched by Hitch in a cameo; we, the audience, are "voyeurs," looking at both of them. But, who is the "Absolute Gazer" who sees all, both within and outside the film?

Apologies are extended for the quality of the photos appearing on pages 64, 145, and 177. The publisher acknowledges the importance of the inclusion of these photos despite their less-than-perfect appearance.

British Library Cataloguing-in-Publication data available

Library of Congress Cataloging-in-Publication Data

Hurley, Neil P.
    Soul in suspense : Hitchcock's fright and delight / Neil P. Hurley.
        p.   cm.
    Filmography p.
    Includes bibliographical references (p.) and index.
    ISBN 0-8108-2526-0 (acid-free paper)
    1. Hitchcock, Alfred, 1899– —Criticism and interpretation. 2. Hitchcock, Alfred, 1899– —Religion. I. Title.
    PN1998.3.H58H87   1993
    791.43'0233'092–dc20   92-43921

Manufactured in the United States of America

Printed on acid-free paper

To the mentors of
Sir Alfred Hitchcock, who contributed
to his perfectionism,
his wrong-man sensitivity,
and the ironic biblical formula
of fright and delight

*   *   *

"Man does not live by murder alone
—he must have affection, encouragement,
and an occasional drink."

A toast of Sir Alfred Hitchcock
shared with his friend, Thomas Sullivan, S. J.

Never trust the artist. Trust the tale. The proper function of a critic is to save the tale from the artist who created it. —D. H. Lawrence, *Studies in Classic American Literature*

You allude to me as a Catholic . . . now you ought to allude to me as a Jesuit.—James Joyce, BBC-3, February 13, 17, and March 22, 1950.

Hitchcock's direction is not simply efficient, but so stylized that it gives these tales a symbolic significance—that of a struggle between the sacred aspect of life, which is given to us, and the impure use we make of it.—François Truffaut, *New York Times,* March 4, 1979.

If you've been brought up a Jesuit as I was, these elements (i.e., of the innocent thought to be guilty, of guilt itself and repressed feelings) are bound to intrude. If you examine my films, I dare say, you'll find very few where wrong has the ascendency. . . . My one objection to the confessional is that you say, "Father I've murdered my mother," and he says, "Yes, my son; how many times?"—Alfred Hitchcock, as quoted in *Los Angeles Times,* March 7, 1979.

Contents

Preface

Examining Hitchcock's work for the hidden influences of his early years, I was taken by James Joyce's remark: "You allude to me as a Catholic . . . now you ought to allude to me as a Jesuit." In the growing literature on Hitchcock, the Jesuit influence is a missing piece in the puzzle that makes up this complex man and his remarkable work. As a boy, Hitchcock spent the years from 1910 to 1913 with the Jesuits (Society of Jesus) at Saint Ignatius College in Stamford Hill outside London. In 1972, Hitchcock granted a transoceanic phone interview to a fellow alumnus (see Appendix I). He confirmed essentially his enduring memories of the Jesuit discipline, memories which he later shared with film critic Richard Schickel, who produced a documentary for the Public Broadcasting Service. While Hitchcock never forgot his fear of periodic punishment (three blows on the open palm), he did carry away from Saint Ignatius College a sense of reverential fear mingled with an awed sense of mystery that is evident in his early films and continues down to his last pictures.

Never does Hitchcock slam the door against hope, reconciliation, or moral regeneration. True, films such as *Vertigo, Psycho,* and *Frenzy* portray evil in an intensely stark way; nonetheless, total pessimism is not affirmed, for within the frames of the films and the lives of the protagonists are either extenuating circumstances, a support person, or a reassuring exoneration. A Hitchcock movie contains endings that point beyond the final scene, such as Barbara Harris's sly wink in the last scene of Hitchcock's last film, *Family Plot.* The imprint of his Jesuit education can be thematically seen in *I Confess, The Wrong Man,* and *The Trouble with Harry.* In his other secular adventure films, those with less religious emphasis, one can still discern unconscious residual evidence of his years at Saint Ignatius College. I refer to the "wrong person" theme and occult references to numbers and geometric forms (lines, arcs, and spirals). Later, we shall explore these "hidden sacreds," to quote mythologist Mircea Eliade. These reinforce an abiding awareness that there is a malevolent force at work in human existence and that somehow the human person can prevail. Hitchcock's films accent struggle against unjust labeling and a triumph over disorder in the world, provided the "wrong persons" do their part. Hitchcock hints at a silent, benevolent force that comes to the aid of the underdog—the "wrong person"—generally pursued, dangling, or breathlessly out of time, as with Cary Grant in *North by Northwest*. The director even hints at providential guidance. Although scenarist Ernest Lehman feels that Hitchcock was not under the influence of Shakespeare's *Hamlet,* the film confirms the Bard's conviction that "There's a divinity that shapes our ends, / Rough-hew them how we will" (*Hamlet,* 5.2.10–11).

This book's premise is that there is reflected in Hitchcock's fifty-three films the warrior spirit at the heart of Jesuit strategy, a realization that evil will make gains in inverse proportion to our human effort to struggle and strive for something greater than the self, greater than the world. Later I will explain this spirit of transcendence, this "ever going beyond" in faith and courage—what Hitchcock's Jesuit mentors called (in Latin) the *magis*. Without this valiant countereffort the evil pull of gravity would mysteriously insinuate itself into the life of nations, large cities and small towns, relationships between children and parents, husbands and wives and, yes, into sex and romance as well. Hitchcock recognized this dynamic in himself and other souls in suspense, whether on or off the screen.

The Catholic/Jesuit influence runs throughout Hitchcock's films. Take his last silent film, *The Manxman* (1929). The opening title reads, "What shall it profit a man if he gain the whole world and suffer the loss of his soul?" (Luke 9:25). Every pupil in a Jesuit school would have known this text, for it contains the warning words uttered by Ignatius of Loyola, the Jesuit founder, to Francis Xavier when they were students at Santa Barbara College in Paris in the early sixteenth

In *Notorious* Claude Rains (right) and mother (left) slowly poison Ingrid Bergman, a U.S. double agent. Though they have frightening aspects, both Nazis seem afraid themselves. (Typical Hitchcockian irony!)

century. Every pupil would also know the Jesuit motto, *ad majorem dei gloriam* ("to the greater glory of God"). The reaching for moral self-development and service to others would be a familiar theme to Hitchcock, going back to his childhood days at Stamford Hill. The following chapters will link Jesuit education to many subliminal, even occult, references not hitherto discussed in regard to Hitchcock's prodigious work.

Take *The Birds,* a film parable about the vengeance of nature neglected and abused by thoughtless humans. As a Jesuit pupil exposed to classical thought, Hitchcock would have seen the link between Aristophanes' comic satire, Daphne du Maurier's novella, and the environmental crisis in the late twentieth century. Consider that remarkable, mystical scene in *The Birds* of the gulls in the sky as the audience looks down with them on the gas station fire below and the panicky townspeople fleeing the assault of the other birds. This montage shot downward represents a God-like view, a type of ironic "third eye" viewpoint from outside our framework of time and space. Such striking vertical long shots recur often. (The French call such "top-down" shots *plongée* takes.) Look for these in *Murder!*, *Shadow of a Doubt*, *Stage Fright*, *Rear Window*, *Vertigo*, *Psycho*, *Marnie*, *Topaz*, *Frenzy*, and *Family Plot*. The *Spiritual Exercises* of Saint Ignatius have the retreatants use their imagination for such *plongée* shots in order to assume the God-like point of view. Such visual religious practices would have been part of Master Alfred's three-year sojourn with the "Jays" (British slang for Jesuits).

Any reader who invests a modicum of time and patience in

The Man Who Knew Too Much (1956) shows the panic and fear of a repentant child-kidnapping accomplice. Note the lamp light as modern equivalent of a fireplace; both signify disturbed emotions (more heat than light), as also in *Saboteur* and *The Wrong Man*.

the chapters on "The *Spiritual Exercises*" and "The Emotional Seesaw of Suspense" will appreciate the ironic third eye that Hitch used to link the foreground of crime mystery with the background of divine mystery. Religious subtexts contribute intellectual as well as emotional delight to judicious spectators of such key films as *The Lodger, I Confess, The Wrong Man, The Trouble with Harry, Vertigo, Psycho, The Birds,* and *Frenzy.*

To the end of his life Hitchcock remained in contact with Jesuits, and was close to Thomas Sullivan, S.J., who was accorded the special privilege of delivering one of the two eulogies at the director's funeral. Hitchcock was buried as a Catholic, confirming that he was a believer. Certainly, he was a churchgoer, along with his wife, Alma, a convert. Director George Cukor has remarked on how often Hitch would go to church. (Incidentally, the name "Hitch" was an endearing abbreviation used by close friends, associates, and indeed all who knew him. This book will respectfully use this sobriquet also.)

We know little of Hitch's boyhood years at Saint Ignatius College. A contemporary, Fr. Robert Goold, a Catholic priest, has stated that there was a prankish, heavyset boy who was called "Cocky" (see Appendix VI). Was that the impish Hitchcock? Possibly, for Hitch as a director was known for his puckish ways, some extreme. Some examples! While shooting *Number Seventeen* (1932), a couple are handcuffed to the banister of a rickety staircase that is about to collapse. Hitch's cameraman, Jack Cox, asked how they would escape. It seemed virtually impossible. With a sardonic grin, Hitch retorted in his Cockney accent, "Jack, the audience want them to escape." In short, the director knew that audiences were gullible and would accept any escape as plausible. Again, when he saw the lame Herbert Marshall acting spiritlessly in *Murder!,* Hitch made an aside to a crew member, "His wooden leg is spreading!" On the first day of shooting *The 39 Steps,* Madeleine Carroll was to be handcuffed to Robert Donat, whom she did not know. Hitch feigned losing the key, which resulted in their remaining manacled for many long hours—a great embarrassment. Later, on the set of *Psycho,* he tested Janet Leigh's reactions to different models of Mother Bates's dummy, surprising her often with different versions left in her trailer. In Appendix VII, Janet Leigh says, "I'm sure I had *some*thing to do with the decision as to which mother was used in the climax!" We know that the mature Hitch was ever the playful sprite, often provoking laughter in elevators—a habit which led to the scene in *North by Northwest* where everyone in an elevator is laughing inappropriately while Cary Grant remains sullen as his foreign captors and his own mother ignore his plight. In his last film, *Family Plot,* Hitch's cameo scene had him silhouetted against the frosted glass door of the Registry of Births and Deaths—very "Cocky" indeed. Fr. Sullivan knew that side of Hitch.

The quality of Hitch's images owes much to several influences: Anglo-American patriotism, German Expressionism, Freudian motifs, the contributions of Alma Reville (his wife) and, I must add, his Catholic family life and Jesuit schooling. Crucial to a deeper grasp of the Master of Suspense is the element of fear. A veteran collaborator since 1934 (*The Man Who Knew Too Much*), Albert Whitlock told me, "All of us have some fears. Hitch—he had them all!" Certainly, religious fear is evident in his films, along with other kinds of dread: entrapment, falling, the doom linked with the race against time and pursuers, and the psychosexual fears and even obsessions evident in *Spellbound, Vertigo, Psycho, Marnie,* and *Frenzy.*

For several years before Hitchcock's death in 1980, a few students of his work suspected that the great Master of Suspense was imprinting in the frames of his motion pictures a discernible psychobiography with scattered bits of evidence. These made his masterworks even more personal than those of such other auteur directors as, say, John Ford, Ernst Lubitsch, or John Huston. The most popular interpreter of Hitch as celluloid allegorist of his own life was Donald Spoto, who deciphered many clues in films such as *Vertigo, Psycho, Marnie,* and *Frenzy.* After his insightful book *The Art of Alfred Hitchcock,* Spoto published *The Dark Side of Genius,* a portrayal of the elderly director as a lonely man who was a veritable zoo of desires, suspicions, fears, and addictions (food, drink, romantic infatuation, and filmmaking). If Hitchcock's movies are dense, opaque, and complex, then so was the man. Several of his colleagues regretted Spoto's total neglect of the other side of Hitchcock, those positive qualities and strengths which they attested that he had. One of his cinematographers, Leonard South (*Family Plot*), declined to have dinner with Spoto and felt that Hitch's physical condition caused his erratic conduct at the end of his career. The director's wife, Alma Hitchcock, and daughter Patricia tried in court to prevent Spoto's controversial book from being published. Spoto's most important source was Peggy Robertson, Hitchcock's secretary, who worked closely with the director for twenty-five years and witnessed his decline. As Spoto tells it, Peggy was let go without any provision for her future. Neither Peggy Robertson nor Patricia Hitchcock O'Connell responded to my request for assistance on this study.

An ancient counsel of wisdom advises that nothing but good should be said about the dead (*de mortuis nil nisi bonum*). If there is good, it should be mentioned along with the unsavory, even when not of equally compelling interest. This is in keeping with a rule-of-thumb of the Jesuit founder, Ignatius of Loyola, who advocated a strong presumption toward charitable interpretation in order to avoid damaging reputations needlessly. Ignatius personally experienced defamation and false accusations and understood that any following of Christ as the "wrong man" would lead to similar situations of unjust attacks on reputation and even result in calumnies. (It must be remembered that the term *Jesuit* was a deprecatory label assigned by the enemies of the followers of Ignatius, much as the term *Quakers* was a derogation of the sect called the Society of Friends.) Obviously, the principles of commercial publishing are bound more by legal sanctions than by presumptions in favor of charitable interpretations. Both of Spoto's books remain as integral parts of a growing corpus of interpretations and historical analyses.

In 1983, Donald Spoto lectured on Hitchcock at Columbia University. He stressed Hitchcock's "open-ended pessimism," meaning that his films generally left room for hope, healing, and forgiveness. (Even such dark pictures as *Vertigo* and *Psycho* are not "closed" to hope though they are deeply troubled.) Having heard Spoto at Columbia, I agree with his thesis about the nature of open-ended pessimism, a felicitous and revealing term to describe the *Spiritual Exercises*. This practical manual of Jesuit asceticism seeks to enhance God's glory through personal character development and public service to spread his kingdom. Its basic strategy carries the retreatant through such despondent themes as sin, death, and hell, through Christ's public life and finally to his betrayal, passion, and death. The *Exercises* ends with the uplifting meditations of hope and joy as symbolized by Christ's resurrection.

The Dark Side of Genius leaves Hitchcock totally in the dark and subverts Spoto's own thesis of open-ended pessimism. When one shoe drops, we expect the other to fall. Like the protagonists in Hitch's films, he too was a soul in suspense, a person involved in the seesaw struggle between good and evil. To the extent we become identified with such characters, we are connecting at a deep level with the film author himself, with the recognizable spiritual dynamics of the Bible and the *Spiritual Exercises* of the Jesuits. This Catholic/Jesuit vector is missing in Spoto's biography, though it is well researched and highly readable. Hitch's life and career demand a more sophisticated treatment with multiple perspectives. Hitch was as changeable as many of his characters (e.g., *The Manxman, Secret Agent, Sabotage, Marnie,* and *Topaz*). This study may add another aspect of critical appreciation, along with biographies, interviews, feminist critiques, semiotics, Marxist interpretations, and frame-by-frame microanalyses of film texts.

For an understanding of the compleat signature of a great director, we need a holistic approach to reconcile multifaceted perspectives. One receives a complementary, and I feel, indispensable, appreciation of the Master of Suspense from his associates: Al Whitlock, Robert Boyle, Edward Haworth, Henry Bumstead, and Leonard South (who had been on his camera crew since 1951). All five were well acquainted with aspects of the dark side of his genius, and with his romantic inclinations toward actresses such as Ingrid Bergman, Grace Kelly, and Tippi Hedren. These attractions were recognized and generally overlooked by those close to him—not only because they appreciated him as a friend but

Marlene Dietrich's face pales after seeing a bloody doll held up by a boy scout, commanded by an adult to stir up her guilt. *Stage Fright* features a Hitch "look-alike" cameo!

because they understood the occupational hazards of working in Hollywood. On Hitch's seventy-fifth birthday on August 13, 1974, the Master of Suspense declared to the press that the motion picture artist "must express himself at enormous cost, the cost of entertainment." Indeed, the personal costs were great!

I was fortunate to receive a very valuable and lengthy letter from a fellow English Jesuit. At the age of ninety-one, Albert Ellis, S.J., shared with me his memories of the educational curriculum, the religious practices, and the administrative atmosphere at Saint Ignatius College during the time before World War I when young Master Alfred went there. Fr. Ellis's letter to me confirmed the marked influence that the humani-

ties and piety had on students of that era. I also acknowledge
the overseas cooperation of Paul Kenney, S.J.; Hugh Kay,
information officer for the English Province of the Society of
Jesus; Kevin Fox, S.J., trustee of that same English Province,
for giving permission to use the text of a telephone interview
with Hitch by a younger Jesuit alumnus of Saint Ignatius
College (Appendix I); and Fr. Robert Goold (a schoolmate of
Hitchcock at Saint Ignatius College) for his memories of
schooldays (Appendix VI).

Hitchcock's wife, Alma Reville Hitchcock, and their
daughter Patricia certainly could have cast great light on
Hitch's work. They have not left for posterity any interviews
or memoirs. Each chose the path of silence. This study relies
largely on what Cardinal Newman called the "illative sense,"
i.e., the convergence of bits and pieces of evidence from
Hitch's films together with an awareness of dominant Catholic and Jesuit influences as they operated on an impressionable youth. My premise is one containing mounting inferences leading to degrees of probability. Did I guard against
subjective interpretations? The reader will be the judge. I am
firmly convinced that even low-probability hypotheses will
not diminish, but rather enhance, the delight in reseeing the
films mentioned in the following pages.

A cordial letter was received from Gregory Peck (*Spellbound, The Paradine Case*). Peck thought once of becoming a
Jesuit. James Stewart, Joan Fontaine, and Norman Lloyd
shared with me memories of collaboration with Hitchcock. I
learned a great deal from Joan Fontaine over supper after her
lecture in 1978 at Loyola University in New Orleans. She
described how Hitchcock made one impression on women
and another on men. Fontaine believed strongly that Hitchcock followed a strategy of divide and conquer in her two
films, *Rebecca* and *Suspicion*. After the conclusion of each of
the films, she found that, because of Hitchcock's words and
actions, she ended by not talking to Laurence Olivier or Cary
Grant. In other words, Hitchcock separated her from her
co-stars. This was an important clue to understanding the
proprietary interest Hitchcock took in certain actresses, and
two chapters were added about the link between religious and
romantic sensibility—Chapter XII, "Asceticism, Modesty,

and Sexual Awareness," and Chapter XIII, "Toward Sexual Maturity." In Hitch's long struggle to complement his limited emotional development as a child, he gained insight on religion and sexuality which for some imperious, personal reason he incorporated into his later films. This book identifies some of the coding devices he used to cushion the shock, even at times the painful embarrassment, that audiences felt at his candor, which was oblique but not obscure—a falling short of typical British tact.

I am indebted to Glen MacWilliams, who photographed *Lifeboat;* Robert Bloch, author of the novel that inspired *Psycho;* Saul Bass, title designer for *Vertigo, North by Northwest, Psycho,* and Donald Spoto. Hitchcock spent his last days, according to writers, staff, and colleagues, in planning his fifty-fourth film, *Short Night,* a suspense thriller to be shot on location on the Russian-Finnish border (Universal Studios had shelved the project but allowed Hitchcock to indulge an illusory hope that it would be shot). It is noteworthy that art editor Edward ("Ted") Haworth believes that the film could be shot posthumously, so carefully prepared were the preproduction phase and art designs for shooting. Haworth, at Hitchcock's request, had directed the shooting of the famous runaway carousel scene at the end of *Strangers on a Train.* This is an interesting insight into Hitchcock's technique, clearly preconceptual and indicative of a logical mind. I shall return to this important point regarding the Spanish auteur-director Luis Buñuel, another Jesuit alumnus, who was also impatient with the production phase and given to preconception (cutting in his mind). Both Hitch and Buñuel needed few takes, had low shooting ratios, and sacrificed spontaneity for intellectual clarity and economy of expression.

I heartily thank Thomas Sullivan, S.J., of Loyola Marymount University (Los Angeles) for his memories of Hitch. I am also grateful to Dr. William Hammel, Ernest Ferlita, S.J., Br. Alexis Gonzalez, Professor Richard Johnson, and Dr. John Mosier, all five from Loyola University (New Orleans), and also to Dennis Trombatore of the Library at the University of Texas, for encouragement, support, and editorial advice. Warner Hutchinson, an editor and friend, assisted me in making the style more readable, especially the sections dealing with Jesuit spirituality. My thanks to Julia O'Keefe, Archivist of Santa Clara University of California, for permission to reproduce Hitch's 1963 commencement address on the occasion of receiving an honorary Ph.D. (Appendix IV).

For valuable research assistance, I am indebted to both the late Carol Epstein of the Motion Picture Academy of Arts and Sciences (Beverly Hills, California) and Charles Silver, Director of the Film Research Center of the Museum of Modern Art (New York City). Geneviève Gehl of Universal Studio's Camera Department kindly put me in touch with Leonard South, A.S.C., Hitchcock's cameraman, from whom I learned a great deal. (It was largely through South that I appreciated the close bonding of Hitch to South himself and to his predecessor, the late Robert Burks, A.S.C., both of whom showed intense loyalty to the director.) Ernest Lehman, author of the scripts for *North by Northwest* and *Family Plot,* was a source of insight and anecdotal experiences.

I thank Fran Mandarano of Xavier High School (Manhattan) for enhancing the final text through constructive criticism. Joseph McGill, S.J., and Jack Vizzard, a Jesuit alumnus, gave encouraging support. This book would never have seen the light of day had it not been for Joan Sullivan, who spent long, arduous months in proofreading, revision, and word-processing of the text, often voluntarily working extra hours. Moreover, she provided key insights into such films as *Rear Window, The Wrong Man, Vertigo, North by Northwest, Psycho, The Birds,* and *Marnie.* Reseeing these films, I was obliged, through mounting bits of internal evidence and unequivocal visual clues, to go beyond my original thesis.

Thanks too to Tom Pryor, editor of *Daily Variety,* for publishing a synopsis of the book under the same title in the 54th Anniversary Issue (October 27, 1987). My gratitude also to Tom Weaver and Bill Brent for enabling me to study more carefully on videocassette the early British films of Hitchcock (*The Lodger, Easy Virtue, The Ring, The Farmer's Wife, Champagne, The Manxman, The Skin Game, Rich and Strange,* and *Secret Agent*). Film scholar John McCabe, a Jesuit alumnus, shared with me his insight that Hitch's unique formula of fright and delight—the book's subtitle—derives from Jesuit spirituality as it infuses Jesuit pedagogy. I acknowledge Jack

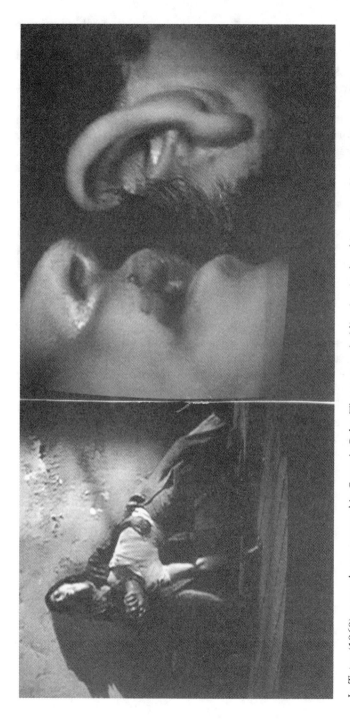

In *Topaz* (1969), a couple are tortured in Castro's Cuba. The woman, holding her husband in a Mary-Christ Pietà pose, whispers the secret into the ear of an expectant Castroite. Hitch treats "keeping" and "discovering" secrets in his fifty-three films as a human constant.

Walsh's prompt service in support of the indispensable word processing.

As the founder of INSCAPE, a nonprofit institute dedicated to educational applications of mass entertainment, I heartily thank my Board of Directors for persevering in support and encouragement. Their shared convictions about "edutainment" has sustained me through the past eight years. I also owe a debt of gratitude to the International Center for Integrative Studies (ICIS), a holistic group of action- intellectuals and professionals committed to holism in theory and practice. As a contributor to the ICIS Forum and a board member, I have enjoyed several perquisites in terms of mailing and photocopying privileges—no small help. ICIS's treasurer, George Christie, has been an unswerving supporter of "edutainment" as central to holistic thinking and tomorrow's world of interdependence through shared intelligence.

The interpretation of Hitch's work in terms of religious, and particularly Jesuit, influences is exclusively mine. I spent five years (1942–1947) with the Jesuits as an undergraduate and graduate at Fordham University (Bronx, N.Y.) and have finished more than forty-five years as a member of the Society of Jesus. Moreover, I have seen the most important Hitchcock films several times and have discussed his work at length for twenty years in the classroom, film forums, and interviews. To know the artist, study his work! To know the work, study the artist!

Neil P. Hurley, S. J.
November 3, 1992

Introduction

The theme of this book—the religious undertones and Jesuit influences in Alfred Hitchcock's films—may surprise Hitchcock fans and researchers. The entertainment aspect of these films can easily lead us to overlook the serious matters that are being treated in them. This is true of his stress on "wrong persons" involved in romantic mystery as well as crime and espionage mysteries.[1] Hitchcock had a larger sense of life's mystery, particularly of the transcendent dimension underlying our everyday existence. He was fascinated by the idea of lifting the veil slightly on the unknowable and the awesome, for he saw the ground of human experience as dark but obliquely knowable.

Spy and murder mystery stories take secrets for granted. However, secrets were for Hitch part of man's fallen nature—the urge to keep one's own trespasses private. Most of his films deal with guilt, cover-ups, people prying into the affairs of others, or passionate surprises of heroic response by seemingly ordinary people. His work is a kind of gloss on the account in Genesis of the fall from grace of Adam, who, when accused, faulted Eve, who in turn blamed the serpent. Avoiding accusation and implicating others are integral to Hitchcock's signature.

Maurice Yacowar, author of *Hitchcock's British Films*, sees the director's propensity for cameo appearances as a "maker of the film," in it but above it.[2] In essence, he is "the cocky Cockney to whom movies gave the opportunity to become a creator god, to stand apart from the fictions and the follies of his successful, complacent characters, and point—like the clown in *Blackmail*—in silent, eloquent accusation."[3] This study discloses Hitchcock's strategy of continually revealing—indeed, even of unmasking—the lack of objectivity humans have in distinguishing the innocent from the guilty.

1

This is evident in most of his films, but most especially in those about the "wrong" man or woman. In examining religious subtexts in his work, we shall recognize themes found in Scripture, in Catholic theology, in sacramental rituals, and in iconic objects of adoration and devotion (e.g., statues, rosaries, crosses, altars, confessionals, and graves). Readers may be familiar with these Catholic sources but not with the religious program of Jesuit spiritual training, especially as based upon the classical text of ascetical-mystical initiation, the *Spiritual Exercises* of Saint Ignatius. (There will be a chapter treating the basic structure and psychology of the Ignatian way to facilitate communication with God and discover his will for finding inner peace and one's life mission.) This book claims that there is a spiritual/moral impress from his Catholic/Jesuit formation that informs Hitch's fifty-three films.

Hitchcock summed up his philosophy this way: "Things are not as they seem." He believed that we are all too unaware of a bias toward evil in our natures, as if we were driving an automobile with a bent steering mechanism. Our ability to shift blame, to guard secrets, to be morbidly curious, to rationalize—these are his themes. How often Hitchcock tilted the conventional frame of reference in order to move audiences to a deeper awareness of issues beyond entertainment! (Recall in *Psycho* the distorted camera angles reflecting the viewpoint of a distressed Norman Bates as he converses with the unwitting victim-to-be, Marion Crane.) Subtly provoking the audience to the shock of recognition, Hitchcock draws us into the plot as participants rather than neutral observers. Thus, the audience does not take for granted that each of us is part of a continuum of human behavior that links saints at one end to psychopathic perpetrators of heinous crimes at the other end.

Interesting to me was the discovery—unexpected—of how Hitch portrayed the workings of disorder in countryfolk and urban citizens. After all, he did incline to films about cities—New York, London, Washington, Los Angeles, San Francisco, and Rio de Janeiro—to accent the depersonalized existence of those denizens. By contrast, he then would probe beneath the seemingly serene surfaces of small towns in northern California (*Shadow of a Doubt, The Birds*), Vermont (*The Trouble with Harry*) and Arizona (*Psycho*). The audience presumed that calm and order would not continue, nor did Hitch disappoint their expectations for mayhem, eventually revealing dark forces of disorder, criminal intent, and deviant desires behind the deceptive facades of sleepy hamlets. Hitch took mischievous pleasure in portraying normal, good citizens with a morbid interest in sensational crimes. Recall the two small-town neighbors (Henry Travers and Hume Cronyn) in *Shadow of a Doubt*, discussing, as a hobby, ways to commit the perfect crime; or Kathy, the small sister of Rod Taylor in *The Birds*, talking matter-of-factly about a man reported to have murdered his wife when she suddenly turned off a baseball game he was watching on TV.

Hitch recognized not only human frailty and horrifying sin, but also cosmic forces of disorder—recognizable themes of the *Spiritual Exercises* of Saint Ignatius. Take the scene in *The Birds* where the uneasy patrons of the Tides Café can come to no agreement regarding the sudden eruption of the birds' aggressivity. Not only does the audience experience a contemporary Tower of Babel, but the plague of attacking birds has a vengeful, apocalyptic ring to it. In the Preface I mentioned a *plongée* shot downward—a God's-eye view from the perspective of the birds flying above the burning gas station. It is a breathtakingly mystical scene with an eerie ring of biblical judgment to it. I am put in mind of a key meditation in the thirty-day Ignatian retreat: the Incarnation. The retreatant is asked to visualize three scenes: Mary's consenting to the angel's invitation to become a virgin mother; a fictional projection of a sinful world with diverse people doing different things but all in sin; and an image of a compassionate God in heaven, looking down upon the plan in motion for the birth on earth of his only Son. This triptych makes a deep impression on those who contemplate the three angles of human and divine activity and how they meet in the Virgin Mary.

Another feature of Hitchcock's cinematic vision lies between the microlevel of personal disorder and the macrodimension of cosmic threat—at the level of government ventures in the areas of espionage, sabotage, conspiracy, and concerted efforts at destabilizing enemy states. Donald Spoto points out how in *Strangers on a Train* Hitchcock links the nation's capital—Washington, D.C.—to the underworld of crime and corruption.[4] Guy Haines's apartment is in the very shadow of the Capitol; the villain, Bruno Anthony, is seen later on the steps of the Jefferson Memorial. Spoto perceptively comments, "These symbols of law and order are, of themselves, powerless to impose order on an irrational universe."[5] Hitchcock's political philosophy exposes realpolitik, the absolute—even idolatrous—nature of the state's sovereignty, as amoral and dangerous to humankind. (Hitchcock was aware of the unprecedented magnitude of nuclear weapons and treated this theme in *Notorious, Torn Curtain,* and *Topaz.*) What is the one moral lesson that can be crystallized from such other spy thrillers as *The 39 Steps, The*

Hitch's films stress secrets. We protect ours, but try to discover those of others, as Jimmy Stewart in *The Man Who Knew Too Much.*

Man Who Knew Too Much, Secret Agent, Sabotage, Foreign Correspondent, Saboteur, Lifeboat, and *North by Northwest?* If man in the singular is warped, then he is capable of even greater social harm when carrying out instructions as an agent provocateur, an intelligence gatherer, or an architect of covert dirty tricks on behalf of some sovereign government in the name of patriotic nationalism.

A specialist in spy thrillers, Hitchcock was unlike novelists Joseph Conrad, Eric Ambler, and John le Carré, for underlying his plots was deep insight. Take *Secret Agent.* Is there a more touching scene of a pet's loyalty in cinema history than the dog scratching at his master's door and whining with an uncanny sense that foul play has been committed? As we see the owner pushed from a mountain cliff, the dog's pitiful cries overlap with the next scene. Nothing more noble occurs throughout the film about espionage and the amoral survival strategems of governments locked in rivalry. The dog is a symbol of conscience, of moral outrage, a divine surrogate confirming that, in the face of such mammoth evils as the theft of state secrets, bombings, torture, and assassinations, there must be represented the principle that for every evil there must be a corresponding, countervailing good. This dynamic is derived from the Bible and runs throughout the *Spiritual Exercises* of Saint Ignatius. Not enough perceptive critical writing has been focused on the fact that, despite the accent on individual psychology, Hitch's moral irony and religious humanism extend beyond the private domain to follow the larger involvement in the twofold effects (some good and deliberate, some evil and unintended) of nation-states, cloaking their evil deeds in the name of national security (e.g., *North by Northwest, Torn Curtain, Topaz.*) If man was warped in the singular, how much more when it came to aggregates of humans working under the sanction of patriotism!

Hitchcock was not at ease with the police, the law, government, or the church. Hitch once refused a papal audience. When asked why, he replied that he would not know what to say if asked about violence and eroticism in his pictures.[6] These fears are clearly inscribed in his work, largely because earlier they were inscribed in his nervous system and soul by traumatic experiences that shaped his artistic vision. In short, he never ceased being throughout his life a "soul in suspense." Let us be specific. Hitchcock was a Catholic and died as such; he had some Jesuit and priest friends; he was patriotic, both to his country of birth, England, and to his adopted country, the United States; he was a supporter of law, order, and the common good. Yet, despite his conservative nature, Hitchcock saw the underside of even noble causes and commitments. He saw through social and political arrangements to both primordial and personal disorder, the pervasive theme of the *Spiritual Exercises* of Saint Ignatius. As for himself, he had constant reminders of his own frailties. He went on crash diets often, only to return to his usual eating habits. He knew the measure of human weaknesses alluded to in Scripture, and understood Saint Paul's boast of his infirmities: "I do not do the good I laud, but the evil I condemn."

Beneath the public image of Hitchcock as a jesting, nonserious entertainer was a conflicted man riddled with fears and insecurities, basically not a very happy individual, a man completely dedicated to filmmaking with very few outside interests. In his controversial book, *The Dark Side of Genius,* Donald Spoto related the struggle that the director had in his later years with liquor and almost adolescent crushes on younger female stars who liked him but did not love him in an amorous sense. This book suggests that Hitchcock was more serious than his public image indicates. Certainly we find a dark, pessimistic strain in *The Birds* and *Topaz,* both suggesting nuclear war. In *Frenzy,* he uses London and the "dirty Thames" (William Blake's phrase) as a dramatic metaphor for the decline of civilization through environmental pollution, public indifference, and barbaric acts of lust and anger. Hitch's most personal concerns apart from the "wrong-man" theme are contained in *The Trouble with Harry, Vertigo,* and *Psycho,* which treat death, sex, and violence along with religious allusions.

If Hitchcock himself was caught in the net of moral temptation, he also left an amazing body of sounds and images which are a monument to a complex Christian vision of human helplessness and resiliency. People are seen as frail

Hitch never drove a car and so avoided Janet Leigh's anxiety as shown in *Psycho*. He also feared uniforms.

and fraught with evil inclinations, but they rise to challenges, discover hidden strengths, and recover lost integrity. What follows will aid the reader to understand the young Hitchcock as a product of an Edwardian culture, an era of imperial ambitions and self-righteousness, and a type of Puritan-like religious training, emphasizing will. Within a short time, Hitchcock would experience the rapid changes of Edwardian England, Freudian psychoanalysis, the bold writings of James Joyce, Oscar Wilde, Havelock Ellis, Noel Coward, and D. H. Lawrence, and German filmmaking with its concern for the dark underside of human consciousness. Hitchcock was an entertainer, yes, but underneath the humor, the suspense, the romance, was a theology of sin, guilt, and redemption. Disarming audiences in order to involve them emotionally in situations of deviant behavior, he proved our affinity with evil desires (*Shadow of a Doubt* is the best proof).

We shall see that visualization, a popular therapeutic technique today, was a favorite device of Hitchcock for leading the audience gradually to identify with or against protagonists, as in *I Confess, Rear Window,* and *Psycho.* Seldom did viewers feel implicated in wrongdoing, although they would often sympathize with culprits. He takes the spectator on a roller-coaster ride of thrills, but in doing so the audience merges with the attitudes and motives of heroes and villains alike. In this sense, Hitchcock deserves to be recognized more as a moral ironist in the genre of the horror thriller.

If there is any suspense in a Hitchcock film, it is not of the whodunit variety, but rather, How can the hero or heroine (invariably flawed though innocent of the alleged crime) be exonerated—in theological terms "redeemed"? Hitchcock himself seemed fascinated by the fickleness of human life, how in one situation good appears to triumph while in another evil wins out (e.g., *Shadow of a Doubt, Strangers on a Train, Psycho, Frenzy*). Hitchcock's art consisted of narrowing the audience's vision, guiding it to details and close-ups which would make them feel the precariousness of justice, of troubled human relationships, and of paradoxical outcomes, seemingly happy but tilted toward imminent evil and disorder (e.g., *Rebecca, Suspicion*).

Having identified personally with the "wrong-man" theme, Hitch trusted neither society nor the vaunted due process of Anglo-American law which insists on judge, jury, defense attorney, and the rules of evidence. Hitchcock's technique was to induce fear in the audience by provoking those fears he himself experienced. Recall the remark of Albert Whitlock, Hitchcock's special effects supervisor, "All of us have some fears. Hitch—he had them all!"

Hitchcock was a fear-ridden child. From his earliest days, he had anxieties regarding either undeserved or excessive punishment for actions which he may or may not have committed. In short, he had from his preteen years a strong identification with and a heightened sympathy for the "wrong man." On a number of occasions he talked about the severe discipline of his early schooling. Three blows of a leather strap on the open palm was one of the favorite punishments administered by the prefect of discipline. Hitchcock also talked about a practical joke played on him when at the age of five he was locked in a cell for a short time by a jailer-friend of his father. By personally delivering the request that the jailer lock him up, young Alfred unwittingly carried out a sentence that would be executed without a trial.

We know little about his home life, his relations with his parents. There are no available photographs of him with his family. We know he feared the dark because of a childhood experience: after he had been put to bed by his parents, who went to walk in Hyde Park, he awoke and cried to find himself in a dark house without them.[7] The numerous film references to troubled parent/child relationship are very revealing. We find throughout his fifty-three films repeated allusions to unstable and disturbed family situations and shifting romantic relationships. (In *Frenzy,* the stable marriage between the Scotland Yard inspector and his wife is far from blissful, a reference perhaps to Hitchcock's own dutiful but seemingly passionless partnership in matrimony.) Since one of his obsessive themes is the lack of communication and understanding between a son or daughter and a parent, one strongly suspects that he may have yearned for greater parental acceptance and love in his own life. The images of fathers and, especially, of mothers in his films allude strongly to some biographical concern of his. Another given of life which could be seen as a type of sentence is the quality of one's parents.

Through motion pictures Hitchcock strove to cope with the strong, even exaggerated, dreads and anxieties of his youth. He seems to have cathartically purged himself emotionally by constructing situations on the screen that inspired fear in his audiences. He claimed that he understood the criminal mind through his own fantasies about ways of committing crimes. Certainly, Hitchcock read avidly about famous court trials and notorious murder cases. Was his interest morbid? Perhaps, but he agreed with the German playwright Arthur Schnitzler that the study of disease was therapeutic, a prophylaxis that could lead to both the prevention of illness and the restoration of health. Not only does every "wrong-person" film diagnose evil by bringing it out of its larval state, but the typical Hitchcock film also points to that oppositional principle of correction fundamental to Jesuit spirituality. I refer to *agere contra* ("to act against" in order to restore balance, thus offsetting disorder). In his "wrong-man" pursuit films (*Saboteur, North by Northwest*), the hero moves in a box leading to apparent doom but then extricates himself by a courage which leads to personal growth, a blissful romantic coupling, and the safety of the community or the country. (More will be discussed later about the exceptions to this pattern in that dark trinity—*Vertigo, Psycho,* and *Frenzy.*)

Hitch's shorthand emotion for sin and for disorder was fear. His whole life would be an unbroken tissue of anxiety and dread, an abiding discomfort which he tried to siphon off creatively in filmmaking. He never completely succeeded. Among the primal fears which concerned Hitch were those of space and height. He evoked claustrophobia (fear of closed spaces) by deliberately, again and again, narrowing the perceptual focus of the audience: in *Lifeboat,* through his use of confined space; in *Rope,* through continuous ten-minute takes shot in sequence; in *Rear Window,* through limited mobility and vision; in *The Wrong Man,* through somber nighttime scenes; in *Psycho,* through an extraordinary use of economy— as in the shower scene, which produced greater fear by showing less of the actual stabbing.

Hitchcock also dealt with acrophobia (fear of heights) and the accompanying fear of falling from heights. So afraid was the director of such spatially related dreads that he tried to inure his daughter Patricia to experiences of closed spaces and heights. Well intentioned, he would place her in controlled situations of fear (such as a roller-coaster ride) so that she might grow accustomed to fright. Certainly, the theme of acrophobia is identifiable in such vintage films as *The Lodger, Blackmail, Rebecca, Suspicion, Foreign Correspondent, Saboteur,* and *North by Northwest.*

The genius of Hitchcock was to use the space/height form of anxiety as a trampoline to lift the audience's awareness into the realm of the philosophical, the religious, and the spiritual. That is why the title of this book refers to Hitchcock as a "soul in suspense." Consider the experience of being falsely accused, of having one's reputation maligned unjustly. Such a situation is a form of soul-entrapment, shrinking the psychic space of the "wrong person" whose mobility and security is restricted as if he or she were an inmate in an emotional prison.

It is revealing that Hitch once remarked to a London reporter that, due to his physical size, he felt "imprisoned in an armor of flesh." He strongly intimates that in biological terms his plight is that of the "wrong man." Little comment has been made about his deep feelings as a kind of biological misfit surrounded by handsome, indeed beautiful, trim, well-proportioned stars and performers. It is hard to believe that his portly shape and irregular profile were not a constant reminder that, in the Hollywood setting of glamorous celebrities, he could not live up to those exceptional public and private standards in which the physical self was paramount. Recall that his celebrity status owed much to his profile and rotund physique. He endowed abnormal characters with sympathetic traits, appealing both to the mass public and the trusting persons within the film itself. Here humor was a disarming factor. Did he not play the witty satirist and the self-mocking tease? These were most probably defense strategies for a sensitive soul in suspense.

Crucial to this study of Hitchcock and his Jesuit religious background is the notion of falling to destruction or confinement in an unpleasant, lonely space. One can see biblical stories such as the Fall and Gehenna (or Hell) as related themes. In short, Hitchcock moved audiences to feel more than physical fear (pursued, dangling, and pressured by the clock). Thus, he effected a transition to other, less photographable, fears. I refer to missing the mark in life, what the Greeks call *hamartia,* a character defect that can lead to the moral unraveling of a life with tragic consequences for others (e.g., *Hamlet* and *Macbeth*). Resonating with the spiritual themes of the Ignatian *Exercises,* Hitchcock often treats crime as a pathetic waste, an echo of Dante's being "lost in the dark wood of error." Consider Uncle Charlie in *Shadow of a Doubt,* Bruno Anthony in *Strangers on a Train,* the murderous sacristan in *I Confess,* Norman Bates in *Psycho,* and the eponymous kleptomaniac in *Marnie.*

Alfred Hitchcock's best films are those which use sparse, even austere, means to draw us into a world different from what we ordinarily look for. In familiar and often tranquil surroundings there are sudden interventions: kidnappings, false arrests, robberies, murders, and rapes. The more lavish the film in terms of sets and location, the less Hitchcock seemed to warm up to his theme: *Waltzes from Vienna, Jamaica Inn, Mr. and Mrs. Smith, Under Capricorn, To Catch a Thief, Torn Curtain,* and *Topaz.* His most representative films in terms of expressing his deepest convictions—not necessarily in terms of box-office success—are those with simple austere settings: *The Lodger, Blackmail, Sabotage, Shadow of a Doubt, The Paradine Case, Rope, Strangers on a Train, Dial M for Murder, Rear Window, The Trouble with Harry, The Wrong Man, Vertigo, Psycho, Marnie,* and *Frenzy.* The shadow of Ignatian spirituality falls across all these films. Good and evil are blurred; persons are victims of desire and passion; spiritual rebirth takes place through prayer, love, affirmation, or courageous resolve. In *Psycho,* Marion's death unites her with her lover and her sister. Love defies the grave. Some films explore the depths of human debasement, others the heights of courageous self-betterment (*North by Northwest* certainly fits here).

In these films, Hitch peeled away the surface of everyday life to reach the deeper emotions that govern decisions and behavior. The ways he did this are technically intriguing uses of sparse cinematic means: the close-up, the tilted camera, the off-center and upside-down shot, the slow pan, the tracking shot, the zoom, rapid cutting, and doom music (i.e., Bernard Herrmann's "music of the fears"). The arrangement of these stylistic effects creates a sense of asphyxiation, of an ever-shrinking world that crowds the characters of his stories, as well as the audiences watching them.

Hitchcock's films can be categorized according to three themes: the wrong-person theme; the obsessive-compulsive theme; and the theme of guilt sharing, with a blurring of the boundaries between good and evil. The plots of these films were Hitchcock's favorites; he returned to them again and again with zest and singleminded dedication. Even though he liked to entertain his audiences, he had a personal statement to make, growing darker, denser, and deeper in insight and fright—until his last, mellow entry, *Family Plot.* His most expressionistic films were his most personal and seem to reflect the moody memories of his childhood studying under the Jesuits. (See Appendix I.) They were also a heritage of his time in Germany during the era of silent motion pictures.

The religious and educational atmosphere of Saint Ignatius College prior to World War I was heavily baroque and was congruent with the new wave of Expressionism in painting. This new art form used physical distortion, shadows, and conflicting color tones to portray externally those inner impulses of fear, anxiety, and dread which were not photographable. Considered from the viewpoint of art and cinema technique, the *Spiritual Exercises* of Saint Ignatius of Loyola are also expressionistic in mood and style. Scant attention has been paid to the nonthematic power of the *Exercises,* although its larger chiaroscuro contrasts are obvious in terms of a spiritual combat involving light and darkness, good and evil (see Chapter III). Young Alfred's experiences became, subconsciously, the scaffolding for his motion pictures, with their tight plots and concentrated emotional treatments of passion, crime, subversion, and mental disorders. Hitchcock loved to cast doubt on the law, the police, the celibate clergy, marital fidelity, small-town wholesomeness, public opinion, democracy, the family, parental integrity, and personal notions of justice. His religious motifs lend themselves indisputably to the maxim that things are not what they seem to be, a paradoxical principle which appears time and again in his fifty-three films and which pervaded the classic works of German silent cinema.

Together with Hitchcock's preference for deviant behavior, there are other religious themes: conscience, guilt, atonement, victimage, and redemption. What is particularly Ignatian and Jesuit is the growth through struggle. Hitch would have been familiar with the adage *ad astra per aspera,* a Latin version of "pain is gain." The Jesuit view is not to buckle in situations of apparent defeat. This is the case with Richard Hannay in *The 39 Steps,* Robert Tisdall in *Young and Innocent,* the second Mrs. de Winter in *Rebecca,* Fr. Michael Logan in *I Confess,* Emmanuel Balestrero in *The Wrong Man,* Roger Thornhill in *North by Northwest,* Melanie Daniels in *The Birds,* and Marnie Edgar in *Marnie.* The protagonists are more integrated both psychologically and morally at the end of the film that when we first meet them.

Hitchcock's abiding compassion is seen in such films as *Shadow of a Doubt,* with its oblique but daring look at the theme of original sin. Other films introduce moral relativity, which prevents condemnation and severe judgment of seemingly contemptible actions, as in *Spellbound, Vertigo, Psycho,* and *Marnie.* In other films, we are given glimpses of the hidden side of people with whom many identify: the patriot (*Lifeboat*), defenders of law and order (*The Paradine Case*), college teachers (*Rope*), sports celebrities (*Strangers on a Train*), detectives (*Vertigo*), professional communicators (*North by Northwest*), the wealthy (*The Birds*), scientists (*Torn Curtain*), and intelligence agents (*Topaz*).

Hitchcock was a very aware person, whether in the matter of technical advances in filmmaking or in the fields of painting, psychology, criminal lore, or public affairs. Two associates of Hitchcock, Albert Whitlock and Robert Boyle, testified to his firm grip on the process of movie production, his relentless search for perfection. Hitchcock said once, "I'm in competition with myself." He lived an intense life of the imagination and saw everyday life in terms of appearances versus reality—the ironic, slightly sardonic, view which is biblical, Catholic, and, as I will argue, essentially Jesuit. Appearances are not to be trusted; nevertheless, human nature persists in trusting what pleases the senses and provokes desirable emotions.

To anchor this pivotal point in both the Ignatian *Exercises* and Hitch's filmology, consider *Frenzy.* The audience is quick to suspect the somber, mustachioed former RAF pilot (Jon Finch) and to trust the buoyant, ever-smiling vegetable dealer Bob Rusk (Barry Foster), who waves to his mother looking out the window. Hitch recaptured London as he recalled it—the markets his father patronized, the streets and neighborhoods of his childhood, and London's Tower Bridge, Big Ben and the Houses of Parliament. Pure nostalgia, but things are not as they seem! The Thames is polluted, white- and blue-collar types make light of the series of rapes and murders, loneliness creates a market for matrimonial brokers, and false peace underlies a seemingly happy household which includes an unaware wife with gourmet aspirations (Vivien Merchant) and a police inspector (Alec McCowen) who represses his repugnance for her catastrophic cuisine.

Throughout *Frenzy*, there are repeated examples of the disorder accented in the First Week of the Jesuit *Exercises*. As a master director, Hitch draws us into the film: his films embody his personal life and relate ours to his through our vicarious identification with the characters in his plot. Indeed, Hitch is us and we are Hitch, just as a retreatant's involvement in the Ignatian *Exercises* links him with the personal insights of Ignatius of Loyola. I see Hitch as more than an entertainer—that yes—but also a spiritual communicator. Otherwise, why do we invariably identify with the Master of Suspense as he makes us co-voyeurs with Jimmy Stewart in *Rear Window,* or again, willing witnesses of the shower murder in *Psycho,* the brutal bloodletting in *The Birds,* the killing of an East German agent in *Torn Curtain,* or the rapes in *Frenzy?*

Hitch has stressed the fright side of his Jesuit training rather than the delight side. This was also the case, as I have already noted, with James Joyce and Luis Buñuel. For them and for Hitch, the disciplined regimen and the cultivation of the imagination were undeniable pluses, even when these intensely aware men reacted to the downside more than average students. Hitch was very selective in interviews and public statements; language for him concealed more than it revealed. Only a careful analysis of his films, from his British silent ones through his last ones for Universal Studios, can reach the hidden depths of his genius. An authorized biography, such as John Russell Taylor's *Hitchcock,* brings together much vital information, but, to my mind, avoids the factor of symbolic consciousness which is the most fascinating and challenging aspect of Hitch as a creative religious artist beyond the mere realm of commercial entertainment.

I do believe that in his films the more complete Hitchcock is found in the images rather than in the sounds, but especially in his very personal choices of subject matter and stars. If he saw actors as "cattle," he prized some much more than others. He was fond of Bruce Dern and once remarked teasingly, "Ah! You, Bruce, are the golden calf!" Hitch can be understood only in terms of the many signs, symbols, clues, and hints left in his work. His public utterances were discreet, oblique, and not seldom evasive.

I offer the reader this reflection: Hitch saw the world from his idiosyncratic vantage point and succeeded in winning over tens of millions to take that view seriously. The Jesuit *Spiritual Exercises* represents a highly privatized view of religious experience by a genius, Ignatius of Loyola, who eventually succeeded in imprinting his vision of open-ended pessimism on countless millions of people. Without claiming that the young Hitchcock made the full Ignatian retreat of thirty days (probably only an abbreviated three-day version), I firmly believe that the deeper portrait of the man contained in his films has roots in the Jesuit educational system.

Hitchcock's canon of fifty-three films attests to the themes of the "wrong man," moral regeneration, forgiveness, compassion, and things not being what they seem to be. Hitchcock unquestionably ranks among the six greatest directors of all time. Moreover, ten of his pictures deserve to be ranked among the 250 greatest films ever made out of an approximate 100,000 features that have been released in the century-long history of cinema. To understand Hitchcock and his world more fully, one must understand the man behind the film and the child behind the man. To do that one must understand the influence of Jesuit spirituality, Jesuit education, and Jesuits themselves on him.

For two decades, I have had a mounting conviction of the importance of Hitch's Jesuit formation on his motion pictures. What follows is the work of more than twelve years of sustained research, teaching, interviewing, and writing. The documentation has been provided as part of the unavoidable apparatus of scholarship. However, the several draft revisions have aimed at greater popularity. I understand that the reader may not be very pleased by frequent references to film titles, chapter headings, and appendixes. That is understandable. A compensating strength of this method, I hope, is to enable the reader to see a Hitchcock film again with the carefully prepared index at hand.

For fifty years I have watched the work of the Master of Suspense; I followed his advice that his films should be seen

The God's-eye view of Cary Grant in a cruciform position in *To Catch a Thief*.

at least three times. I studied *Psycho*'s motel shower scene countless times, seeing new relationships each time. Criticism of art and entertainment requires a special discipline lest subjective projections color and even distort what is in the work. In scriptural studies, *exegesis* refers to internal evidence, *eisegesis* refers to information and considerations from outside the text. I have used both. Eisegesis is valuable at times—e.g., learning that Hitch did not like eggs helps one to understand the scene in *To Catch a Thief* where Jessie Royce Landis, playing Grace Kelly's mother, puts out a cigarette in a fried egg. Attribution of intention is always difficult, nor can we take the statements of the artist or author at face value. Given Hitchcock's ironic wit and playful deviousness, this is even more true here than in many other cases. If my Jesuit background is an asset, obviously it can also be a drawback. Happily, in the free republic of letters this published interpretation will be commented on and hopefully complemented, even corrected.

While I speculate and use probability assumptions, I predicate them on what is publicly shareable *within the film*: the scripting, the images, the casting and the acting, camera style, set design, rear-screen projection and special effects, the dialogue and sound effects (even the silences), the musical score, the color coding and the editing, even Hitch's cameo appearances and his occasional ironic titles. (*Family Plot* strikes me as a biblical allegory: William Devane's diabolical villain is called "Adam-son"). Like most researchers of Hitch's work, I experienced the thrill of the pioneer explorer discovering new horizons, new territories, and new worlds that earlier investigators either did not perceive or understood in a somewhat different way.

The number of books about Hitchcock are multiplying, proving that there is a rich vein of intellectual and artistic ore to be mined in his films, more than merely well-crafted fright-and-delight examples of enticing entertainment. This book intends to share with the reader the pervasive Catholic/ Jesuit influences, dramatic and awesome at times. The films are disturbing but leave a ray of light, an awareness that the next reel may see an upturn, that the characters are not the same at the end as they were at the beginning. Like Shakespeare, Hitch gives us victories or near-irreversible despair.

Notes

1. Leslie Brill, *The Hitchcock Romance* (Princeton, N.J.: Princeton University Press, 1988), pp. 96–112. Also see my review in *Daily Variety*, December 7, 1988.
2. Maurice Yacowar, *Hitchcock's British Films* (Hamden, Conn.: Archon Books, 1977), p. 271.
3. Ibid., p. 278.
4. Donald Spoto, *The Art of Alfred Hitchcock* (New York: Hopkinson and Blake, 1976).
5. Ibid.
6. John Russell Taylor, *Hitch: The Life and Times of Alfred Hitchcock* (New York: Pantheon Books, 1978), p. 310.
7. Donald Spoto, *The Dark Side of Genius: The Life of Alfred Hitchcock* (Boston: Little, Brown, 1983), pp. 18–19.

CHAPTER I

The Man Behind the Director

A familiar maxim in the field of psychology states that the child is father to the man. Along with Chaplin, Fellini, Bergman, and Truffaut, Hitchcock is one of those film directors who often reflect the impressions of their childhood. His uniquely recognizable signature is made up of many distinctive features that can be traced to the influences of his home, school, and religious training in England.

A close friend of Hitchcock, actor and director John Houseman, wrote in his memoir that Hitchcock was "a man of exaggeratedly delicate sensibilities, marked by a harsh Catholic education and the scars from a social system against which he was in perpetual revolt and which left him suspicious and vulnerable, alternately docile and defiant."[1] Houseman paints the picture of a complex man who was introspective, observant, and wary of new situations and acquaintances. Hitchcock was rigidly reserved and cautious. Even though he went to social gatherings and had loyal friends and colleagues, he enjoyed being alone with his own thoughts. He was given more to solitude than to gregariousness, more to a predisposition to self-preoccupation which would not have been reversed by his Jesuit training at Saint Ignatius College, a boys' school at Stamford Hill outside London.

The Jesuit plan of education, called by the Latin name *ratio studiorum*, stressed analysis, reflection, and personal assimilation of the matter treated in the courses given and the lessons assigned. Insight is based on seeing how seemingly disparate events and unconnected realities link up. Certainly this hallmark of Jesuit education can be found in the writings of

James Joyce, the most individualistic writer in a century of original talents. The three years that Hitchcock spent with the Jesuits were perhaps the most impressionable years of his life, as they were for James Joyce in his years at Clongowes Wood (September 1888 to December 1891), years which for Joyce "were, in a sense, the period of his first exile."[2] The Irish and English Jesuits left on both artists "a psychological, moral, religious, intellectual, and even social impress which . . . helps to an understanding of the kind of work [they] later produced."[3] If each rebelled, it was in reluctant homage to those years of "a submissive obedient charge" and "an acknowledgment of their power and influence."[4] Such influence can be seen as well in the films of Luis Buñuel, for whom reality was not the seen but the unseen (dreams, imagination, wishful fantasy, passion, and paralysis of the will). Both Jesuit spirituality and education place a great emphasis on insight, that is, the shock of recognition, how our lives are influenced by invisible but felt forces.

To appreciate how Hitchcock's character was indelibly marked by the disciplined, even regimented, type of educational and religious formation, we have only to read James Joyce's *Portrait of the Artist as a Young Man* to obtain a partial, but personal, description of the Dublin educational environment. This would have been essentially the same environment that Hitchcock himself would experience a decade later in London. In Joyce's case, the Jesuit influence extended to the university level. Nevertheless, both artists received lasting impressions from their formative years with the black-robed sons of Saint Ignatius of Loyola. If both highlighted the fears and forbidding atmosphere, each was aware that the method of the *ratio studiorum* (distilled from the principles of the *Spiritual Exercises*) sharpened their critical powers. It is ironic that even when Jesuit education is criticized for being too restrictive, too structured, it still liberates creative energy in those who have reservations about the rigorous training they received. All three Jesuit alumni and artists—Joyce, Buñuel, and Hitchcock—fit this description. They were outspoken about the limitations and dangers of a system, but something very expansive came through, recognized in retrospect.

All three artists, despite differences of national origin, were strong individualists who rejected the conventions of their craft. Joyce created a novel mode of literary expression; Buñuel stamped his films with a disturbing surrealistic style that subverted consensus reality. First seen by audiences and reviewers as only a successful entertainer, Hitchcock won critical plaudits later with *Shadow of a Doubt, Suspicion, Notorious, Vertigo,* and *Psycho.* In short, he had an original, dialectic view of life as compounded of good *and* evil (in contrast to the simpler Victorian view of good *versus* evil). There is a subversive picture of reality in the art of these three Jesuit products. As with Joyce, Hitch and Buñuel were not in step with the crowd mentality. True, they made reputations and money by appealing to those who *go* to see a movie, but their true greatness is appreciated only by those judicious people who go to *see* a movie, and may see it more than once. Both Hitch and Buñuel were acclaimed and appreciated only later, since relatively few critics understood the single works as they appeared. These works had a coherent, distinctive point of view that sought—each in its own way—to create an order out of the disorder and drift that constitutes daily life. The artists' passionate resolve sought to deconstruct reality as socially and historically given in order to illuminate man's ambivalent nature, with its pendular swing between apehood and angelhood. Certainly, humankind demonstrates those extremes of regression and progression shown by the three image makers.

Thanks to Donald Spoto's research for *The Dark Side of Genius,* we know a great deal more about Hitchcock's early years. It is clear that he was not athletic and that he did not have many close friends. Later, in his films, he tended to distance people through camera angles. This was true of lovers when they were embracing (especially the long shot of Cary Grant and Joan Fontaine embracing on a windswept knoll in *Suspicion*). Hitchcock is one of the few world-class directors to create an intense sense of privacy and existential solitude, although not to the degree reflected by Ingmar Bergman, who acknowledged that he was influenced by Hitchcock. We can easily recognize Bergmanesque motifs in *Vertigo, Psycho, Marnie,* and *Frenzy.* Most of Hitchcock's films

Distant intimacy in *Suspicion*. Cary Grant holds Joan Fontaine. They hardly
spoke on the set. "Things are not as they seem."

affirm life and have relatively happy endings despite suspenseful anxiety, secrecy, intrigue, risk to life and romance,
and conspiracy. Yet there is a nagging incompleteness that
underlies his Hollywood-style happy endings, for in pitting
the hero against unexpected, menacing forces, Hitchcock was
reflecting a deeper struggle—conquest of self, the very
existential core of the *Spiritual Exercises* and the Jesuit
philosophy of education. I suggest that a reseeing of Hitchcock's work, especially his masterworks, will disclose discernible spiritual references hidden deep beneath the surface of
action, romance, deviance, and suspense.

Let us reflect for a moment on the themes of evil,
temptation, and pathology in his films. They are all examples
of the disoriented life that Ignatius points to in the First Week
of the *Exercises* which induces a shock of recognition in the
retreatant. He is thus enabled to see in himself a disorder akin
to the evil that Ignatius mentions in his biblical references to

Lucifer the fallen angel and to the sin of Adam and Eve. Hitchcock, as did the Jesuit founder, subtly teased from audiences their hitherto unrecognized complicity in the villainy portrayed on the screen. This seeing ourselves as God sees us was critically important to the shared ironic vision of Buñuel and Hitchcock. The power of eroticism—suggested rather than explicit—pervades such films as *I Confess, Rear Window, To Catch a Thief, Vertigo, Psycho, Marnie,* and *Frenzy.* The audience sits in a dark theater and acquiesces in love fantasies. There is also the recurring theme of abnormal, at times even criminal, states of mind: transvestitism (*Murder!*), anarchy (*Sabotage*), manic obsession (*Rebecca*), thrill killing (*Rope*), paranoia (*Suspicion*), amoral promiscuity (*Notorious*), attempted parricide (*Strangers on a Train*), childhood traumatic guilt (*Spellbound*), infatuation (*The Paradine Case*), a priest haunted by a former lover (*I Confess*), voyeurism (*Rear Window*), false arrest and mental breakdown (*The Wrong Man*), necrophilia (*Vertigo*), psychotic schizophrenia (*Psycho*), kleptomania (*Marnie*), and rape and murder (*Frenzy*). Seeing such themes in Hitchcock's early British and later Hollywood films might make one wonder what kind of psychological influences—repressions, projections, displacements—the young Hitchcock experienced. (The Freudian influences will be discussed in Chapter V and XIII.)

Hitchcock's self-conscious body image was a source of insecurity; he felt that his body was a kind of biological injustice. (He went on strict diets but could never maintain a slimmer figure.) Hitchcock saw his physiological condition as fatalism. Although fatness is not a criminal offense, it is (as corpulent persons learn) often treated implicitly as a social offense. Never physically attractive, Hitchcock was a mild misfit among those with better proportioned and more shapely figures and faces. This condition contributed to his sensitivity to the relative nature of deviant behavior and the arbitrary nature of the accepted criteria that make up social norms. His chronic obesity made him feel like a "wrong man," given the fetish for thinness and beauty.

One could speculate about Hitchcock's own view of his shape and bodily appearance from the actors he placed in his films. He had the habit of choosing the ideal type of Hollywood stars, but he portrayed them with a flaw. Consider the roles of Joan Fontaine, Ingrid Bergman, Tippi Hedren, Janet Leigh, Cary Grant, Jimmy Stewart, Farley Granger, Montgomery Clift, Gregory Peck, and Anthony Perkins. So often their roles involve a chipping away at their stereotyped star image; invariably some moral or psychic defect mars their beauty, charm, or innocence. Nor is it very hard to imagine that Hitchcock, like his audiences, may have fancied himself, say, as Cary Grant, who played four low-keyed but smoldering love scenes: the embrace on the hill in *Suspicion,* the scene on the hotel balcony overlooking the harbor of Rio in *Notorious,* the sofa romance in a Monte Carlo hotel in *To Catch a Thief,* and the hotel seduction scene in *North by Northwest.* If we, the audience, tend to identify with these romantic scenes, can we not infer that Hitchcock had the same experience before us? Beneath the director's reserve and disarming witticisms was a preoccupation with romance that was as insistent as his concern for religion. In his interview with John O'Riordan (Appendix I), a fellow alumnus of Saint Ignatius College, Hitch discussed religion. Hitch's admitted "trials over belief" certainly were linked to romance, a topic banished from his Edwardian boyhood and Jesuit upbringing.

Both Jesuit spirituality and education pride themselves on taking "this world" as seriously as the "other world." Jesuits are pragmatic idealists, even to the extent that their religious rule of life after 1540 was held suspect as too worldly. One Roman cardinal, when he heard that the new Jesuit order was eliminating the communal singing of the Divine Office, said, "Before long, they will become as dirty as chimney sweeps." Some critics would hold that this has occurred throughout the Jesuit order's existence. The point to be made, however, is that the ideal held up for Jesuits was to learn to contemplate amid activity *(contemplativi in actione)*. Jesuit spirituality strives to blend the natural and the supernatural; it tries to wed reason and faith. The goals of the Ignatian *Exercises* and the educational blueprint, the *ratio studiorum,* promote a sense of two lives—the life after death snugly contained in the Chinese box of this terrestrial life. Fr. Thomas Sullivan's letter (Appendix V) about his recollection of Hitch explicitly affirms this sense of life as "doubled," that this life is not all there is.

Jesuits have the reputation among religious orders in the Catholic church of striving to adapt spirituality to this-worldly goals. This explains the insistence upon an orderly mind trained in logic, philosophy, rhetoric, and the liberal and dramatic arts. Jesuits have had success in education in such diverse regions as China, India, and Iraq precisely because of this-worldly relevance. Similarly, Hitchcock's films are undeniably this-worldly and have universal appeal. The discipline of his early training is evident. James Stewart, in an interview with the author in 1981, said that Hitch was the best-prepared director he ever worked with. Certainly, no director ever worked more single-mindedly on his films. Each one was precision-tailored to fit his high ideals of entertainment but also to induce the shock of recognition so that the audience would feel sympathy for the deviant, the embezzler, the rapist, the killer, the saboteur.

There is a compassion in Hitchcock's films which has, strangely enough, gone unmentioned in the proliferation of close analytical studies on his work. Both Fritz Lang and Hitchcock look beyond the law-and-order issues undergirding society's stiff-willed resolve for self-preservation in the face of violence, crime, and anarchy. Lang was wont to quote his favorite Sanskrit saying, Tat Wam Asi: "There, but by the grace of God, stand I!" For Lang, any one of us might become a murderer or a villain, given certain circumstances. In *M* we have an example of a child rapist–murderer crying out to the jury of underworld types, "I can't help myself!" In *Fury,* Lang shows how simple townspeople lose reason in a mob and try to lynch an innocent "wrong man" (played by Spencer Tracy). In *The Big Heat,* Glenn Ford steps outside of his policeman's role to become a vindictive vigilante to apprehend those who killed his wife in a car bombing. Fritz Lang repeatedly quoted Gotthold Lessing's moral that the devil moves as fast as the transition from good to evil.

Hitchcock would have agreed with Lang, not only in his sympathy with the Vedanta text just quoted, but also in the immense, at times overwhelming, reality of evil as an active oppositional force. This is borne out by Hitchcock's repeated stress on the mutability of human motivation and frailty of character. In this regard, Hitchcock, though influenced by the German filmmakers of the silent-movie era, was much different from them. Fritz Lang, F. W. Murnau, and G. B. Pabst stressed fate, psychological determinism, and chance events. Free will is less a central theme in the films of these directors. It is, however, a major preoccupation of Hitchcock's pictures. Even in *Psycho,* Marion Crane repents; as for Norman Bates, he is morally beyond culpability in Hitchcock's eyes. Although agreeing with Lang, Murnau, and Pabst about the evil bias in humankind, still he believed people could undergo improvement and growth. If his view of life was dark and inclined toward pessimism, nonetheless it was in harmony with that Jesuit vision which was radically life affirming and compassionate. Again and again, Hitchcock dramatized the reversal of injustice whereby a wronged person with a sticking point proved equal to an evil that would commonly topple someone of less persevering courage. The conviction of the *Spiritual Exercises* is that, following Christ's example, one can withstand and even overcome false allegations, loss of reputation and friends, imprisonment, even possibly death. (This will be confirmed by my analysis of *I Confess* and *The Wrong Man* and also by the growth in character of such women as Tippi Hedren in *Marnie* and *The Birds*.)

Thus, we can talk about what Donald Spoto refers to as Hitchcock's "open-ended pessimism." This descriptor is certainly true of the Ignatian *Exercises*. Many of the meditations in the First Week of the *Spiritual Exercises* and the Third Week are, in cinematic terms, darkly expressionistic, such as the meditations on the fall of the angels and Adam with its consequences of travail for the man and birth pangs for the woman and possible hell in the hereafter. In the midst of these solemn considerations, Saint Ignatius proposes to the retreatant a meditation on Christ on the cross—a relief from despair. Similarly, in the Third Week, the meditations on the passion and death of Christ are followed in the Fourth Week by the joy and hope of reflections on the resurrection. In short, the resurrection, as the final note of triumph, is what film critic Parker Tyler has called "the last laugh." Jesuits have often been called laxists when it comes to granting absolution for sin in the confessional. To the allegation that a Jesuit would even forgive Satan, one Jesuit replied, "Yes, I would, if he had the necessary disposition of repentance." Within the filmic text of Hitchcock is both strict judgment and broad tolerance, a dialectical blend of high idealism and ready forgiveness. There is no doubt that Hitch was a perfectionist, seeking out of all possible camera shots the single best one.

I have seen *Psycho* at least a dozen times, studying it carefully from a Catholic and Jesuit theological viewpoint. In sharing with the reader my personal conclusions, I hope that future repeat viewings will establish that this remarkable film is drenched with irony and compassion. If one looks carefully at the two principal characters, the director's sympathy for Marion Crane (Janet Leigh) and Norman Bates (Anthony Perkins) is in abundant evidence. We know that Hitchcock is a master of enlisting audience identification with criminals, such as Joseph Cotten's "Merry Widow" bluebeard murderer (*Shadow of a Doubt*). He surpasses himself in *Psycho,* for he technically absolves Crane's burglary of $40,000 and Bates's double murder. Marion robs in passion and resolves to make restitution; Norman is psychically disqualified to be a murderer in a moral and legal sense. Thus the final scene is brilliant, for it undermines our capacity to play judge, jury, and hangman in the name of protecting life, family, and civil order. The camera is the eye of God when it allows us to view the tryst of Marion and her married lover in a Phoenix hotel room. *Psycho* brims over with horror, true, but it calls for understanding, a higher consciousness—"There, but by the grace of God, stand I!" This is the principle of Vedanta and Christianity, but it also reflects the laxism often attributed to the Jesuits.

Another reflection of the Ignatian *Exercises* and the *ratio studiorum* is preparation—putting down the high points of the meditation to be made, imagining the composition of the place where Jesus preached, and controlling the milieu (draw the shades, think congruent thoughts, do penance—fast, reduce sleep, and mortify the body as with self-flagellation with a braided cord). We know that Hitchcock prepared meticulously, making his own artistic sketches of scenes and having much of the dialogue practically memorized. Thus, the actual shooting was a technical exercise. He had a low shooting ratio and did not use much film. He knew exactly what he wanted and so did cameramen Robert Burks and Leonard South. The latter, who shot Hitchcock's last film, *Family Plot,* told me that the Master of Suspense repeatedly refused to look through the camera lens at a setup from his director's chair. He would say, "That's all right, Lenny, I know what you're getting." Actor James Stewart told me the same thing during an interview at his home. Anyone who worked with Hitchcock was impressed by his dedication, his absorption—indeed, even obsession—with filmmaking.

The method of knowing clearly beforehand what will take place in shooting scenes on the set or on location is an echo of the class *repetitio* at Saint Ignatius, where teachers provided coming attractions of lessons and drills to ensure learning. It is no surprise that both Buñuel and Hitchcock doggedly "cut" in their minds, proving their practice of preconception, that is, knowing beforehand the end result and the means to achieve it. This comports admirably with the *Spiritual Exercises,* where Ignatius (in Section 333) stresses how important it is for the retreatant to see the direction or lack thereof in his life—"beginning, middle, and end." This element of divine logic and supernatural purpose is evident in the meliorism of Hitchcock's best films, where the character of the protagonist improves as the plot unfolds.

In the typical Hitchcock film, there is a curve of ascending development. The exceptions are *Vertigo, Psycho,* and *Frenzy,* all films where Hitchcock chooses final frames which suggest that there is a void but that, conceivably (if improbably), there can be a reversal toward growth and integration. In *Vertigo,* Jimmy Stewart's Scottie is annihilated by Judy's sudden fall to death, but he does have an alternative—namely, his close friend, the mother figure Midge (Barbara Bel Geddes), who earlier had helped him to overcome his fear of heights. In *Psycho,* the telltale car is hoisted out of the murky swamp, suggesting a daylight revelation of a nefarious crime. In *Frenzy,* the "wrong man" is exonerated when the law opportunely apprehends the rapist and murderer and the audience looks at the trunk which he dragged upstairs to hide his latest victim. There is the outline of a cross on the trunk. Despite apparently doom-laden finales, all three pictures manifest a slight opening away from pessimistic closure toward hope.

Since Hitchcock's work reveals the mercurial flux of thought, word, and conduct away from and toward evil, a convex and concave image of human character emerges—a sort of blurred reflection, even a doubling which suggests spiritual myopia or blindness. The *Exercises* insists that one confront the evil within and without: the retreatant must learn to "eat one's shadow," not to project evil outward in apologetic defensiveness by denying, avoiding, or minimizing one's complicity in the mystery of iniquity.

Hitchcock likes to show the intertwining attraction of a good person to an evil person with the resulting shared-transfer of moral qualities. Examples of such psychospiritual osmosis are found in *The Paradine Case, Strangers on a Train, Shadow of a Doubt, Vertigo, Psycho,* and *Frenzy.* In the case of *Rear Window,* we have a more subtle spiritual symbiosis. Lisa (Grace Kelly) turns Jeff (Jimmy Stewart) into her own domestic ideal, while he earlier transformed her into the curious and interfering "busybody" that he himself was. Their love affair reveals a type of osmosis whereby the spirit of each flows into the other, a growing together. By contrast, in *Strangers on a Train,* the intimated homosexual attraction between Robert Walker's psychopath and Farley Granger's conflicted tennis player results in a downward pull, a study in the contagion of evil. In all these films, the evil character has an influence on the protagonist, so that we see how good people can be unhinged and turn into felons, killers, even monsters.

The use of doubling, a trait of German silent films which influenced Hitchcock, is used in the Ignatian *Exercises* for helping the retreatant to make decisions that lead away from demonic influence toward a process of divinization. The retreatant is advised to take the solid advice he or she would give a close friend, or the advice that one would wish to have followed when dying. These distancing techniques provide an objectivity which the camera as third eye can capture just as dramatically. The doubling perspective evident in Hitch's best films is aimed at shocking on the spiritual level as well.

In *Psycho,* "doubling" equals blurred identity. Janet Leigh will return the money and recover her identity.

Recall Marion Crane's conversion in *Psycho* after talking with the obviously unstable Norman Bates.

We are now in a position to appreciate Hitchcock's attitude toward actors. Deliberate in his method of preconception, he had his actors play out passively the roles assigned to them in a preconceived shooting script. He referred to them as "cattle" because they did not know which scenes, or takes, would be kept, or in what order they would appear. It is in the editing phase, where the final cuts are made, that the film takes shape for release to theaters. The actors have no part in this process. Thus, the director was the "cattleman"; he alone knew how the scenes would be juxtaposed. This style of moviemaking had one drawback, however. Although a Hitchcock movie is filled with tension, suspense, and desire, it lacks the spontaneity and vitality that characterizes the films of, say, Frank Capra, John Ford, or Preston Sturges.

There is a cool formality, at times a contrived artificiality, about Hitchcock's films. Exceptions are *The 39 Steps, Sabotage, The Lady Vanishes, Shadow of a Doubt, Lifeboat, Notorious, Strangers on a Train, Rear Window, North by Northwest, Psycho, The Birds,* and *Frenzy*—all inspired works of creative collaboration. His actors seem to be on separate planes, even when they are friends or lovers. Watch for this, especially in *Rebecca, Suspicion, Spellbound,* and *The Paradine Case.*

Hitchcock's films owe much to his formative years with the Jesuits. As a sensitive, private lad, young Alfred was initiated into an interiorized life at Saint Ignatius College—studying, reading, reflecting, and praying. He would have had constant reminders of religion: statues, crucifixes, priests in their black cassocks with rosaries hanging from their waist cinctures, chapels with candlelight and incense, prayers before and after class, sermons, retreats, talks with spiritual prefects, and mottos in Latin reminding the boys of God's greater glory and praise. Like most Catholic boys subject to early religious influences, Hitchcock probably considered becoming a priest. References to priests, prelates, ministers, and nuns in his films are too frequent to be disregarded even when they are fleeting. Look carefully for them in *Sabotage, The Lady Vanishes, Foreign Correspondent, Strangers on a Train, The Man Who Knew Too Much, Vertigo,* and *Family Plot.* In a television program produced by film critic Richard Schickel, Hitchcock explained the vivid memories and fears he had of the strict discipline and punishment at Saint Ignatius College. In such a severe setting, he developed an image of what James Joyce referred to as "the hangman God," a God who scrutinizes thoughts, intentions, and actions and who can be imagined as playing the roles of prosecutor, judge, jury, and even executioner, ready to find one out. Not all Jesuit pupils viewed their experiences this way, but a hypersensitive, imaginative student would (e.g., James Joyce, Luis Buñuel, and Hitchcock himself).

In an article that appeared in *Rolling Stone,* Hitchcock told the interviewer: "I was Jesuit educated. The only thing I learned was *fear*."[5] That interview, coupled with the Schickel interview, leaves little doubt that Hitchcock's early religious formation cast shadows that would later fall across his motion pictures. While we cannot minimize the importance of fear, conditioning, and authoritarian discipline, we must not overlook the sense of purpose—"beginning, middle, and end." This tactic enables a Jesuit-influenced person to uncover downward forces in his life rather than the Godward forces (see Appendix II). As with Scripture, so too Hitch's irony employs the principle that the first are last and the last are first, as in his "wrong-man" films.

Within the context of the Catholic faith, the Jesuit tradition was built on the belief that every human being has an ineradicable impulse to do evil, which easily leads to guilt. Indeed, anxiety and guilt provide the universal appeal of Hitchcock's movies. While he was walking along the Ginza on a visit to Tokyo, Hitchcock saw his profile on a billboard advertising one of his films and took satisfaction in knowing that people from a radically different culture and religious heritage could relate to his works. The notion of original sin, of the world being bent out of shape from the dawn of time and human beginnings, runs through Hitchcock's most personal films. It is a view that most people seem to have no problem accepting. Evil desires, guilt, secrets, morbid curiosity, and judgmental attitudes can be found in small, sleepy towns, in the largest cities, on a court bench or in a priest's rectory, and at the highest social levels. Consider:

- *The Lodger,* in which Hitchcock first raised the question of the "wrong man" and the ability of the law and its officials to make mistakes.
- *Rich and Strange,* in which he treated the link between material wealth and moral waste.
- *Shadow of a Doubt,* where we find the unlikely presence of murderous evil in a loving family in the small California town of Santa Rosa.
- *Rope,* a technical tour de force that examines the moral complicity of a professor in the murder of one of his

students by two classmates who followed the superman logic he had taught them.

- *I Confess,* in which Hitchcock questioned clerical celibacy in a murder plot involving a priest, his former sweetheart, and a blackmailer who knew of their relationship, and which possibly points to a future romantic liaison. The film is open-ended. The music stops, but the melody lingers on in the spectator.
- *Rear Window,* with the theme that curiosity, even when it invades privacy, is generally irresistible, in this case almost fatal.
- *The Wrong Man,* a quasi documentary about legal and religious victimhood, the former regrettable, the latter ennobling.
- *Psycho,* which explodes the validity of law by showing three crimes without moral guilt due to one person's repentance and another's mental disability.

England has a long tradition of detective stories, gothic horror tales, and crime writers. For the most part they have been entertaining, but as a rule they do not penetrate beneath the surface of suspense, adventure, and romance. Under the influence of such nineteenth-century authors as Dostoyevski and Poe, writers appeared who used shiver-and-shudder stories to unmask the deeper mysteries of the unseen—the interior life and invisible but felt forces that work on the human spirit. One thinks of writers such as Joseph Conrad, John Buchan, Henry James, and Graham Greene. Hitchcock also dealt with latent dreads and fears through scripts about spies, agents, criminals, psychopaths, villains, and deviants. The view of life that emerges from his films is one filled with terror and varying degrees of the abnormal. There is nothing in his early years at Saint Ignatius College, however, that would indicate his later vision. To all appearances, he was a dutiful boy, but a streak of repressed rebelliousness and hidden resentment was apparently there. Perhaps it can best be characterized as the biblical, or peculiarly Christian, sense of alienation from this world. Hitchcock's bold vision—more subtly erotic and more horrifying than that of Dostoyevski or

Conrad or Buchan—is tilted toward compassion, not cynicism. He genuinely wanted to understand—first himself, then
others whom he was relieved to discover shared similar inner
anxieties.

As we have seen, "all of us have some fears. Hitch, he had
them all!" His genius lies in the artful way he crystallized
these fears into entertainment that purged us of pity and fear
as much as did the great Greek and Elizabethan tragedies.
Hitch's use of catharsis not only emotionally purged pity and
fear but also intellectually provoked a sense of awesome
mystery, somewhat akin to that which Euripides, Sophocles,
and Shakespeare inspired. *Psycho* ends with a long academic
explanation by a psychologist of Norman's problems, but the
final scene of the dual personality—Norman/Mother—leaves
us with the conviction that the causes of the pathology are
deeper, awesomely mysterious.

One advantage of his classical humanist formation was that
Hitchcock became a moral ironist. His films can be classified
according to endings: troubled endings (*Rope, I Confess, The
Wrong Man*); dark endings (*Vertigo, Psycho, Frenzy*); and happy
endings (*Marnie, The Birds, Family Plot*). Throughout such
pictures is a rhythm of suffering and joy which is not purely
emotional but the result of moral struggle. I suggest that there
is a motif of passion and resurrection in the best of Hitchcock's work. From the German silent filmmakers, he learned
to induce psychological anguish through the use of expressionistic techniques: wind, rain, fog, shadows, shuttered
windows, mirrors, stairs, and confining situations (as in *The
Lodger*). Still, he trusted the power of human relationships,
no matter how troubled they might be, and he would accent
love as a powerful healing force.

One cannot really appreciate the images in Hitchcock's
work without recognizing the roots of his Expressionism in
his early Jesuit training. Jesuit churches, schools, and resi-
dences breathe the spirit of Expressionism. This can be seen
by visiting the baroque Jesuit churches in Germany, Austria,
and Italy. The ornate statuary, frescoes, and paintings juxta-
pose rosy-cheeked angels with conniving devils in tableaux of
heaven and hell, peopled with those either in beatific joy or
infernal pain—sharp black and white images creating the

mood portrayed by Ignatius of Loyola in the *Exercises*. The Quebec church in *I Confess* has classic baroque interiors reminiscent of Hitch's Jesuit schooldays. Through the skillful use of images, an attitude is cultivated, a point of view is built. Jesuit Expressionism takes evil very seriously, but in stressing evil, it does not overlook the grace of God by which an individual can overcome evil through personal effort.

This same attitude prevails in Hitchcock's films. He constantly shows growth through crisis and adversity. The leading characters are generally better people at the end of the film than they were at the beginning. We see this in *Murder!*, *The 39 Steps*, *Young and Innocent*, *Rebecca*, *Saboteur*, *Lifeboat*, *Spellbound*, *Notorious*, *I Confess*, *The Wrong Man*, *North by Northwest*, *The Birds*, and *Marnie*. Even where improvement is not patently evident, there is a moral lesson, a spiritual insight to be gained by watching the terrible consequences of jealousy, fear, suspicion, wealth, psychic disorders, or childhood traumas. This can be seen in *The Lodger*, *Easy Virtue*, *Blackmail*, *Rich and Strange*, *Suspicion*, *Shadow of a Doubt*, *The Paradine Case*, *Rope*, *Stage Fright*, *Strangers on a Train*, *Dial M for Murder*, *Vertigo*, *Psycho*, *Frenzy*, and *Family Plot*. Hitch said that most of his films upheld a moral order, and he is correct. Jesuit Expressionism deals with subtleties: evil lurking in unsuspected places of wealth and status; good also lurking in unsuspected places of poverty and disrepute.

An interesting study could be made of Hitchcock's films in terms of working-class settings (*Sabotage*, *Saboteur*, *Frenzy*); upper-class settings (*Rich and Strange*, *Rebecca*, *Strangers on a Train*); and contrasts between the two (*Notorious*, *Marnie*, *Topaz*, *Family Plot*). Hitchcock was familiar with the middle class through his own family and neighborhood, and his films frequently dwell upon the uneventful lives of the middle class, as well as upon the idleness and frivolity of the well-to-do. In his essay, "The Rhetoric of Hitchcock's Thrillers," O. B. Hardison holds that Hitchcock's early British films represent a contour map of the middle-class mind with helpless, ofttimes put upon females (*Blackmail*, *Murder*, *Sabotage*) and distressed couples (*Number Seventeen*, *The Man Who Knew Too Much*, *The 39 Steps*, *Young and Innocent*).[6] In

Hitchcock's later Hollywood period there is a shift to female dominance and male dependency (*Lifeboat, Spellbound, Rear Window, To Catch a Thief, Vertigo,* and *Marnie,* with the irresistible attraction of Sean Connery to Tippi Hedren's kleptomaniac).

An important internal clue is how Hitchcock made his villains upper-class gentlemen, portrayed by such actors as Godfrey Tearle, James Mason, Otto Kruger, and Herbert Marshall. The last played a good aristocrat in *Murder!* (1930), saving the heroine. But even then the director flawed Marshall's character: in two scenes he aggressively insults lower-class people. Can it be that young Alfred witnessed such coarse, snobbish treatment by those presumably socially superior? In Hitch's schooldays, upper-class students mingled with middle-class pupils as part of the Jesuit education. Hitchcock would have fallen into the group of students who were not athletes, who did not take to the playing fields in rugby, cricket, or track. He consequently was more inclined to fantasy and intellectual pursuits. Donald Spoto calls him "a loner and a watcher," studying rail timetables and shipping schedules.[7] He probably took to silent movies, but we have no documentation for that.

Master Alfred, while at Saint Ignatius College, learned very orderly and disciplined habits. Inculcated in him was a habit of preconception—a cerebral, analytical stance which inclined him later as filmmaker to edit the film in his own mind and to use a low ratio of shooting takes. Directors such as William Wyler, George Stevens, and Mervyn Le Roy sought greater safety by maximizing editing choices through the use of high shooting ratios. By contrast, Hitch followed a strategy of plot sequencing, a rule for tracking "beginning, middle, and end" as proposed in Rule No. 333 of the *Exercises.* Whereas other directors could create suspense and romantic adventure, the subtle moral drama was not present. Hitchcock's best pictures often reveal a rising moral curve in such characters as those played by Cary Grant, Jimmy Stewart, Ingrid Bergman, Grace Kelly, and Tippi Hedren. The audience naively identifies with the stars, even if flawed, and then grows with them through their heroic meliorism, their courageous confrontation with adversity (*agere contra*).

Interestingly, the title of *Psycho* was actually *Hitchcock's Psycho* in the film's credits. A puckish publicity shot with the possessive title points to a hidden meaning. With tongue in cheek, Hitchcock called *Psycho* a "fun film," although the images speak otherwise. Instead of guessing at this intention, we should heed his suggestion to study his films three times. *Psycho* has evident biographical concerns regarding Hitch's intense personal empathy for childhood traumas and unfulfilled emotional desires.

Recall that Mrs. Bates was in her son in an uncanny way. The transformation of Norman Bates was triggered by the guilt of having killed his mother and her lover. He kept alive the memory of his mother by preserving her skeletal corpse and internalizing her person in his own. *Psycho* reveals a young man living in a world of psychic fantasy, split between love for his mother and love for pretty, strange women coming to the Bates Motel. It is revealing that the Victorian gingerbread house on the hill with its turn-of-the-century bedroom was a physical replica of Freud's post-Victorian three-leveled theory: the superego corresponding to the upper room, with mother/son quarrels and parental prohibitions regarding women; the ego level of the ground floor, with its door opening into everyday, outer reality; and the id (or libidinal) force represented by the dark cellar of guilty secrets and subliminal attachments.

How personal a film is *Hitchcock's Psycho*? (Recall Bates removing the picture of Susanna and the Elders in order to peer voyeuristically at Marion Crane undressing.) Is there a psychodrama which Hitchcock may have lived, carrying parental and religious inhibitions from the past and trying to live in a liberated Hollywood of pulchritude and pleasure? I strongly recommend that the reader study *Psycho* carefully. The scene of the evening snack in the back room is filled with charged symbols. First, there are the stuffed birds, representing Norman Bates's hobby as an amateur taxidermist. The birds we see are ominous and in attack mode, with penislike beaks. There is a distant, framed picture of a naked woman with her arms wrapped around her body. As Norman talks, Marion assumes that same posture. Thus, phallic symbols are paired with female sexuality and modesty. Then we have the framed picture of Susanna and the Elders, who failed to blackmail her into sleeping with them. Beneath this picture is a peephole. The conflict of sexual desire (id) with repressed restrictions (superego) leads to the murder of Marion by repeated phallic blows of the knife. (This is a symbolic rape scene, with sexual assault blended with vengeful reprisal.) It is Norman's mother who kills his love just as Norman killed her and her lover. The imagery is as complex as it is artfully effective. Hitchcock in Mrs. Bates's chair is a prankish send-up, but beneath the humor is a web of symbolic references—parental, religious, epochal, and psychological (in terms of Freudian pansexualism, the imperious libido as determining character development).

The man behind the director was in part a child conditioned by Edwardian values and the expressionistic themes of a Jesuit education whose matrix was the Ignatian *Exercises*. As he grew into manhood and became an apprenticed director, he learned of a wider world of greater personal choices, many offered by science, technology, and the vicarious universe of experimentation in literature, drama, and motion pictures. When Hitchcock spoke of trials over religious faith in his interview with John O'Riordan (see Appendix I), he must have alluded to his post-Jesuit career in a world of accelerated advances and opportunities. The Freudian imprint in Hitchcock's films is undeniable and very probably represents his search for a countervailing corrective to the very strict Catholic values of his upbringing. He ironically practiced his own form of *agere contra* in complementing and revising his past experiences with a broader new awareness from psychology, literature, and the media, especially silent films which crossed national boundaries with the ease of the weather.

A careful study of *Psycho,* perhaps the most famous of all horror films, also gives abundant evidence of Hitchcock's abiding and deep compassion. Whatever religious fears he may have developed during his upbringing and education, he also inherited a sense of tolerance and mercy for human frailty and a respect for the regenerative powers of pardon, love, and reconciliation. In this classic horror film he seems to be asking the audience, "Who will cast the first stone?" There is a personal passion invested in what he playfully termed a "fun film." I think that he bared his own psyche; that is why his films have a classic quality about them. He wanted his audiences to realize that anything can be forgiven if the causal context is understood. No one should be condemned out of hand, for any one of us could conceivably commit a crime, even a murder without a motive. Hitchcock, therefore, not only made a personal statement in *Psycho* and in his other films, but he made a profoundly universal contribution to both psychological and religious humanism. The reader can decide whether underlying his filmology is an enduring tension between, on the one hand, his childhood in an English Edwardian culture and a Catholic/Jesuit subculture and, on the other hand, the steady expansion of his horizons on the path to fame as a world-class director. The child was, in a sense, father to the man, and the man, in turn, has become a father to all future filmmakers in terms of personal auteur statements folded into public entertainments with worldwide appeal.

Notes

1. John Houseman, *Run-Through: A Memoir* (New York: Simon and Schuster, 1972), p. 479.
2. Kevin Sullivan, *Joyce Among the Jesuits* (New York: Columbia University Press, 1958), p. 8.
3. Ibid.
4. Ibid.
5. Chris Hodenfield, "Mu-u-u-u-rder by the Babbling Brook," *Rolling Stone Magazine,* July 29, 1976, pp. 38ff.
6. This essay is contained in an anthology, *Man and the Movies,* ed. W. R. Robinson (Baton Rouge: Louisiana University Press, 1967), pp. 137–152.
7. Donald Spoto, *The Dark Side of Genius: The Life of Alfred Hitchcock* (Boston: Little, Brown, 1983). p. 20.

CHAPTER II

Hitchcock's Early Years

Artistic works reflect the background, experiences, beliefs, and convictions of the artist who produced them. It is difficult to separate artists from their work. In the case of Hitchcock, biography and filmography blend, and so it is crucial to understand the interaction. To know specific artists means to study their works not only in light of what they have said but also in light of their experiences, most especially their early experiences. Unfortunately, too many people skip lightly over the childhood and adolescent years of the biographies of famous people to reach the more exciting achievements. Although this is understandable, it neglects the significant formative influences which color and shape the later, more celebrated, years.

Alfred Hitchcock was the youngest of three children born to middle-class English parents. Typical of the family of that time, the Hitchcocks were a self-sufficient unit. The father was the lord of the home as if it were his castle; the mother was extremely devout and demanded of young Alfred that he give an account of his daily activities each evening.[1] Unprecedented economic pressures did not change the traditional habits within the home but forced the family to look outward in terms of the new challenges. Herbert Spencer complained that while both sexes needed to be prepared for society and citizenship, no care whatever was taken to prepare them for parenting.[2] The making of money was paramount in the changing industrial world of England; sex education and awareness would not have been a close second.[3]

Hitchcock's father, a fisherman, ran a grocery and when one sees *Frenzy* (1974), shot in London, the scenes of the market and the fish dinner in the inspector's home were very probably memory tributes to his childhood days. The horizons of Hitchcock's boyhood in Edwardian London were quite limited. Through imagination and fantasy he succeeded in building an alternative world to the Catholic home and Jesuit school at Stamford Hill which defined his world at that time. On the one hand there was the conservative romantic literature of Sir Walter Scott, William Thackeray, Alfred Lord Tennyson, John Keats, Lord Byron, and Percy Bysshe Shelley; on the other hand, there were the gothic novels of suspense and horror, the mystery stories which have long appealed to English reading audiences.

As a lad, Hitchcock enjoyed riding the double-decker buses (recall the scene of the boy on such a London bus in *Sabotage*). He was familiar with the British Museum (depicted in his film, *Blackmail*), the aquarium (*Sabotage*), Westminster's Big Ben (*Foreign Correspondent*), the Old Bailey Court (*The Paradine Case*), and Scotland Yard (*Frenzy*). He also explored the wharves, piers, and ships at dock in the great port city. The sea and ships played a role in three of his earliest British films (*Champagne, The Manxman,* and *Rich and Strange*), and in his later Hollywood pictures (*Foreign Correspondent, Saboteur, Lifeboat, Marnie,* and *Torn Curtain*). To understand Hitchcock's films one must understand the boy he was and the influences that shaped him, especially the metropolitan London milieu.

The industrial revolution had urbanized Great Britain more than any other nation of Europe. During Hitchcock's years at Saint Ignatius College, England had, including London, seven standard metropolitan areas—five more large urban centers than in France, Germany, or Italy. Hitchcock's filmography mirrors the urban iconography with which he was fascinated: London (six films), New York (eight films), Washington, Miami, Los Angeles, San Francisco, Baltimore, and Phoenix. England was the first country to wrestle with environmental problems (grimly alluded to in *Frenzy*). As a Jesuit graduate, Hitch went forth to a world characterized by growing general indifference to religious practices, a rise in agnosticism and atheism, and an increasing intolerance for church dogmas and standards of sexual morality. As for the liberation of women from the straitjacket of Victorian expectations, we have many daring images of women in Hitchcock's British silent films—*The Skin Game, Easy Virtue, Champagne, Rich and Strange,* and *Blackmail.* Hitch's own shift of values and perceptions must not be lost from sight.

On the eve of a revolution in philosophy, art, and morality, the lad Hitchcock was being influenced by principles which gave him an alternative view of such new trends as socialism (proclaimed by George Bernard Shaw and H. G. Wells), freethinking humanism (Bertrand Russell, G. E. Moore), and the creative ferment of the Bloomsbury Group. May the reader keep in mind that, if church on Sunday was a sacred place and time in Hitch's early training, later he would contribute to its decline indirectly as theaters remained open on the Sabbath.

No other director, except perhaps Luis Buñuel, has left such a personal record of religious, psychological, and social attitudes. Despite the reticence of Hitchcock, who was humorously evasive in talking publicly about his personal life, we do have some relevant information about his early years. As a Catholic merchant in a predominantly Protestant culture, Hitchcock's father certainly wanted his son to succeed professionally in that world without compromising the minority religious heritage handed down. It is interesting that Hitchcock's paternal grandmother left the Catholic faith, but his mother persuaded her fiancé to marry in the Catholic church. The Hitchcocks had a reserved seat in the pews of Saint Ignatius Church along with those who paid "bench rent," as it was called.

Why did the Hitchcocks entrust young Alfred to the Jesuits? Besides geographical proximity to home, there was the 300-year reputation the Jesuits had earned for intellectual excellence and religious academic training. All their schools were faithfully conducted according to the blueprint for educational strategy adopted by the Society of Jesus in 1599. The *ratio studiorum* stressed character formation more than information transfer. It could be considered a type of educational sacrament, for apart from the relative merits of the teaching staff, the stress was on a systematic set of goals and

Blackmail recalls Hitch's days as a "train boy" at Saint Ignatius College. Was the lad Hitch also this mischievous?

procedures to ensure minimum predictable and acceptable performance. Extraordinarily endowed teachers are a plus, but institutions demand measurable standards that people of average competency can meet. As with most institutional managers, the Jesuit administrators knew that better teachers and students made for a higher level of educational achievement, but they trusted the process more than the performers.

Let us look at the myriad impressions and influences that Alfred Hitchcock would have undergone from his entry into Saint Ignatius College on October 5, 1910, to his departure on July 25, 1913. There he received the customary Jesuit education with its emphasis on the liberal arts and the *Spiritual Exercises* of Saint Ignatius of Loyola. Referring years later to his youth, he recalled his strict religious upbringing and told the French film critic and director François Truffaut that such a background "influences a man's life and guides his instinct."

Fr. Albert Ellis is the source of a very complete and accurate account of the spiritual, educational, and disciplinarian atmosphere at Saint Ignatius College prior to World War I (see Appendix II). Hitchcock was a day student, one of 250 pupils. (There were no boarders at Saint Ignatius.) Daily Mass was "mildly compulsory" and was well attended. It began at 8:45 A.M. and was in Latin. During Holy Week, the Passion was read in English during the Mass. Boys from a distance— the "train boys"—were allowed to be late (unlike the discipline at such American Jesuit high schools as Manhattan's Regis and Xavier high schools). The morning prayer was recited in chapel, students genuflecting before the Blessed Sacrament. It consisted of the Our Father, the Hail Mary, the Apostles' Creed, and the Morning Offering. Then the boys filed out quietly. Each class had a homeroom with an altar dedicated to the Blessed Virgin Mary which was adorned with candlesticks, flowers, and linen altar cloth. The class remained in that one room for all subjects except for drawing, science, and woodworking. The class teacher was referred to by the English as a form master ("form" being the British term for "grade"). Whether priest, Jesuit scholastic (i.e., seminarian), or lay person, the teacher began each class with the Ignatian prayer taken from the *Spiritual Exercises*: "Grant we beseech Thee, O Lord, that all our intentions, thoughts and actions be directed toward Thee. Amen."

The number of "black robes" (Jesuit priests, scholastics, and brothers) in schools such as Saint Ignatius would have been larger than that found in English, European, or American schools run by the Society of Jesus in the late twentieth century. Vocations were more abundant at that time and the secular options not so many or so appealing as in the contemporary world. This meant that Hitchcock and his companions would have had close contact with Jesuits on both a formal and an informal basis. A Jesuit form master spent the greater part of the school day with his homeroom class. Moreover, the young Jesuits and scholastics tucked up their long black habits and played outdoor sports with the boys. They also took part in other extracurricular activities, such as drama, chess, science, debating clubs, and the Sodality dedicated to the Blessed Virgin Mary and based on a way of

Christian life drawn from the *Spiritual Exercises* of Ignatius but adapted to laymen called to live in the world.

Boys were instructed to write at the top of each page of an assignment or examination, "A.M.D.G.," the abbreviation for the Jesuit Latin maxim, *ad majorem Dei gloriam* ("to the greater glory of God"). The theme was ended with the letters, "L D S," meaning, *Laus Deo Semper!* ("Praise God Always!"). There was a daily catechism drill with a short exhortation by a Jesuit (usually a scholastic) on a theme such as devotion to the Sacred Heart of Jesus. Later I shall discuss this devotion in reference to *The Wrong Man,* where a picture of the Sacred Heart serves as the pivotal transition in helping an unjustly accused victim, Manny Balestrero (Henry Fonda), to be exonerated. (Incidentally, Hitchcock alludes to a miracle in that film, since Balestrero's Italian-born mother exhorts her son to pray, against all odds.) Religious faith is a key to this film and hearkens back to Hitchcock's childhood memories, where Saint Ignatius College abounded in faith symbols, signs, and sacraments.

Donald Spoto gives a graphic description of the twin-spired red-brick church, Victorian-Romanesque in style and containing a reredos with images of Ignatius, Francis Xavier, and Aloysius Gonzaga, the famous boy saint.[4] All around were baroque representations of angels, side altars, and votive candles sending out flickering shadows. To the side were the confessionals with their narrow doors, slightly pointed. On Fridays, the young Hitchcock and his schoolmates would be exhorted to go to confession. The opportunity was offered of going to a priest for absolution of mortal and venial sins (these latter are, according to Catholic moral theology, lighter trespasses, offenses which do not deprive the offender of sanctifying grace, i.e., a personal relation of friendship with God).

Confession through the agency of a priest is only one form of therapeutic disclosure. In the primitive church, there was self-disclosure to a small group as part of reconciliation to the larger community. The penitent practiced honesty and courage, while the recipients showed compassion and love.[5] After Constantine's Decree of Milan in A.D. 325, such group practices of integrity therapy fell into decline. By the twelfth century, the custom was confession to an unseen priest. I mention this because Hitch dedicated one film to the topic (*I Confess*). Later we shall consider this film at some length. It stars Montgomery Clift as a deeply interiorized priest and "wrong man." Moreover, the director used later pictures (*The Wrong Man, Vertigo, Psycho*) as a form of personal disclosure. Certainly, his mature films give evidence of psychic pain and a need to share intimacy as a source of relief.[6]

While studying with the Jesuits, the boy's painful shyness was evidenced by his limited circle of friends. Throughout his later life he became a "low revealer," an ultraprivate person, reluctant to share intimate knowledge for fear of rejection, ridicule, or indiscreet leaks on the part of the confidante.

God, not the law, determines guilt (*I Confess*). The acting of Montgomery Clift's priest is remarkably interiorized—more than Hitchcock expected or really wanted. Clift's role elevates the creaky plot immensely.

Thus, he inclined to the safer option of concealment. Though reserved in many ways, Hitch hid his real personality in the comic playacting of interviews, cameo appearances, and as a TV host for seven years.

Whether Hitch, the lad, found confession painful is a moot question. The social expectation, however, would have obliged him to enter the confessional box. In addition to confession, students could attend a Saturday Communion service with an economical three-pence breakfast afterward. This service was well attended, largely by Sodalists. A three-day retreat based on the *Spiritual Exercises* was offered each year, and it was a voluntary matter. It was designed to provide insight into the psychospiritual dynamics of Jesus' life, especially his teachings, death, and resurrection.

Fr. Ellis recalls a retreat given by a priest whom Hitchcock would have known, Fr. R. Mangan, whose talk on death went as follows:

> Don't be afraid of dying—just face up to it. When you get into bed at night push your feet down—though it may be cold for your toes! Say to yourself: "Well, one day I shall be *carried out* like this, am I ready now? O my God, I am sorry."

Fr. Ellis admits that though this was a frightening counsel for fourteen-year-olds, it was salutary and "very tranquillizing in action." We shall see that death was a constant theme in Hitchcock's films. The words of Fr. Mangan would have been an example of the reminder of death, its inevitability, and its association with accountability in the two judgments Catholics believe followed death—the particular judgment of the individual person and the general judgment of humankind in the aggregate. Let us remember that World War I broke out one year after Hitchcock's graduation from Saint Ignatius in July 1913. The constant reports of horror, atrocities, and death would have reinforced the memories he had of death as the "Great Interferer," a theme to which I shall return when I discuss one of his most personal and humorous films, *The Trouble with Harry*. In that film, Hitchcock shows the reappearing body of the dead man with his

Is the trouble with Harry or with Adam's fall? This is the question this black comedy (*The Trouble with Harry*) asks. Harry *Warp* (equals original sin) reappears three times as a friendly, but annoying corpse. Shirley MacLaine and John Forsythe help with the burials.

feet in the foreground and the rest of his inert body receding into the background. Shades of Fr. Mangan's sermon on death!

College activities included an open-air procession on the feast of Corpus Christi honoring the Sacrament of the Eucharist, the presence of Christ in Holy Communion. Throughout the school were many nonverbal signs of Christian piety: the long rosaries which hung down from the Jesuits' cinctures (cloth belts); crucifixes and crosses; paintings of Jesuit saints, especially Ignatius of Loyola, Francis Xavier, and Aloysius Gonzaga; the Stations of the Cross; and shrines and altars where devotions were held. In *The Dark Side of Genius,* Donald Spoto writes of a series of Lenten sermons and lectures given at Saint Ignatius on the dread of sin. The topics were "Sin and the Justice of God," "Sin and the Majesty of God," "Sin and the Christian," and "Sin and the Passion of Christ."

The emphasis on sin and the persistent condemnation of sexual sins left its mark on youth, as James Joyce recounted in his classic fictional account of life at a Jesuit school in *Portrait of the Artist as a Young Man.* Though the Edwardian age would eclipse the nineteenth-century moralistic views of the Victorian age, still Hitchcock would never be entirely free of the psychological and religious aftereffects of his impressionable childhood fears. It is interesting to see how Jesuit alumni of high schools forget the discipline—the assemblies, the "jug" (walking for an hour), the memory assignments, the obligatory Masses and prayers before class—and recall the glory days. This is usually true of the average student, but the more intellectual or artistic types keep the shadowy side of disciplinary practices in mind; Joyce, Hitchcock, and Buñuel are good illustrations of artists who saw Jesuit eduction as a mixed blessing, one which benefited them but at a price which each felt could have been less.

We can, of course, only speculate on what impressions the education, discipline, and religious atmosphere had on the young Hitchcock. Any liberal arts education in the classics leaves a lasting impression on the minds of young students. Professor Terrot R. Glover has written about the educational principles of the Greeks and Romans in forming the mentality of their citizens: "The first things you learn may shape your mind forever; it is not so much the things themselves as the way you are brought by them to think of everything you may afterwards meet."[7] Consider Jesuit education—Latin and Greek grammar, public speaking, drama, art, literature, and the basic courses in science, mathematics, English, and history. Coursing throughout this curriculum would be direct and oblique references of an attitudinal kind to Jesuit spirituality. Although it has never been documented, Ignatius of Loyola is supposed to have said, "Give me a child till the age of seven, and he will be mine forever." A little older than this, Hitch was exposed to the Jesuits from age eleven through fourteen. However, as his filmography shows, he was theirs—but not totally, and on his own artistic terms. I feel safe in stating that whenever you see a quintessential Hitchcock film, you are experiencing subtle cinematic translations of Jesuit principles of rhetoric, humanistic education, and spirituality. In *Spellbound,* Ingrid Bergman and Gregory Peck ask about rail tickets to Rome, Georgia, and Syracuse, New York. Note the allusions to ancient cities. As with the ancient Roman and Greek pupil thoroughly trained in classical thought, so too many Jesuit graduates are inclined to think along the Ignatian principles of spiritual discernment and the educational system it helped to mold.

Regarding Hitch's testimony that he was awed and frightened, Fr. Albert Ellis feels that these elements of insecurity, reverential wonder, and fear of death are part and parcel of any solid formation program which is, as he put it, "Godward." But, later in his films, Hitchcock would point to the conditioning factor in religious belief, the unconscious reflex nature of drill, memory, and obligatory practices. In the crucial final scene in *Vertigo,* he shows the devoted nun who ascends the stairs in the Dolores Mission Church tower to ring the bells. Her sudden footsteps startle Judy (Kim Novak), who falls to her death. The religious sister pays no heed to the accident she occasioned but goes on, unconcerned, to fulfill her assigned duty.

Again, in Hitchcock's final film, *Family Plot,* he shows the kidnapping of a bishop in Grace Cathedral by a couple who drug the bishop at the Communion rail with a quick injection and, in full sight of the congregation, carry him down the aisle and out to a waiting car. The parishioners do not offer to help nor are they at all suspicious. Hitchcock, perceptive and with ironic wit, suggests that these churchgoers (including a few clerics) are truly "sheep," not in the religious sense of a flock but rather of dumb, passive animals with no spark of intelligence. Hitchcock's keen sensibility made him critical of the psychological regimentation which a systematic religious education could produce. While he was opposed to mind control, he could not find a way to allay his own anxieties or fears. I shall return to this significant point.

A word about the importance of religion as a conditioning factor in his patriotic feeling. Even today many Christian believers feel uncomfortable when—on a historical visit to, say, the Tower of London or Hyde Park—the official guide speaks of the tortures and executions that took place secretly or publicly in these locations, referring to the victims as "enemies of the state."[8] Many nonconformist Protestants and also Catholics died in agonizing ways for their faith—martyrs to their co-religionists, but enemies of the state to the reigning king, Henry VIII. His chancellor, Thomas More, insisted that he was willing to die for the faith while upholding the king as his sovereign. This distinction between the king's temporal role and his religious claims did not save More from being beheaded as a traitor. So too Jesuit martyrs had no personal antipathy to the throne of England, but only to the denial of the Pope's supremacy in matters of faith.

Hitchcock would have been inculcated with this Catholic viewpoint. Most certainly he would have learned of such Jesuit martyrs as Fr. Edmund Campion, who was stretched on the rack after long confinement in the "Little Ease," a pocket dungeon in the Tower. He undoubtedly also heard of Fr. John Ogilvie, the Scottish Jesuit saint who was kept awake seven nights and seven days before being hanged, then drawn and quartered in Glasgow's public square. He would have known of recusant priests hiding out with Catholic families in Elizabethan England and celebrating Mass in hiding. These stories appealed to boys and gave them inspiring role models. On the other hand, they put a limit on unconditional patriotism. Just as the lad would have cultivated an ironic view

of his nation's own history, he very likely saw his Catholic
religion and Jesuit education in a questioning way.

Would the system of competition, emulation, rewards, and
punishment provided by the *ratio studiorum* have enthused
Hitchcock, the lad? I doubt it very much. It rather led him to
a complex feeling for Jesuits—admiration and gratitude on
the one side and nervousness and harsh memories on the
other. This is, indeed, the stuff of an ironic stance, seeing not
only the official position of an institution but comparing it to
the broader spectrum of its total performance. He would
come close to cynicism, but as in the case of Buñuel, he
preferred to use the rapier of critical wit with the button on
the point of the blade. His humor sweetened his irony and
kept it from turning into the acid of sarcasm. His trials of
conscience began early, grew more complex, and never
relented. Religion and strict educational discipline came at a
cost. It seems reasonable to conclude that his filmology would
have been substantially different without the faith and fears,
the values and views, and the will training that he received as
a child.

Hitchcock's relation to his parents was one of submissive-
ness and fear. Donald Spoto, in *The Dark Side of Genius,*
mentions Hitch's anxiety at awakening from sleep one night
to discover that his parents had gone visiting and had left him
alone in the dark. Furthermore, Hitchcock was very solicitous
toward his mother on her visits to him and his wife, Alma,
when they were successful in Hollywood. The parents did
take Hitchcock to church and seemed impressed by the
ritual—the brocaded vestments, candlelight, incense, surpli-
ced altar boys, columns, ornate carved chairs, stained glass
windows, and statues. As a boy, Hitchcock was quite introverted; he had a pronounced curiosity for railroad trains and
their schedules, boats and their navigation routes. He was also
very interested in vaudeville, theater, movies, and the life and
habits of working people, which figures among his warm,
nostalgic recollections of growing up in and around London.

It is, indeed, revealing that when he returned to London to
film *Frenzy,* after an absence of twenty years, he filmed the
produce markets, older neighborhoods, and streets stored in

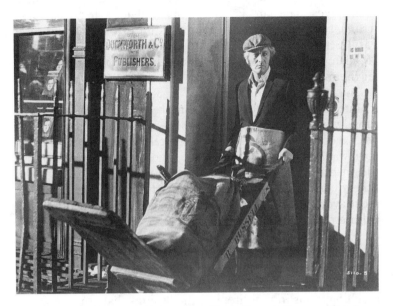

In *Frenzy,* a murderous soul in suspense (Barry Foster) disposes of his latest rape victim.

his childhood memory. The film dwells on the blue-collar class, as did many of his earlier British features. Hitchcock had no interest in games or sports and was more inclined toward creating a parallel world of fantasy. His boyhood resembles that of the young Ingmar Bergman, a Protestant minister's son with a long-lasting fear of religious mystery. An admirer of Hitchcock's films and influenced by them, Bergman too transformed religious fear and obsessiveness with women into lasting inspirational art. It is interesting that Latin directors avoid the degree of pessimism seen in the work of many Nordic filmmakers.

A word about administrative staff and faculty at Jesuit schools such as Saint Ignatius College. In general, the Jesuits have always had their talented and inspiring men who could draw out the best in impressionable youths. But there were also average Jesuits and, occasionally, problem people who, rather than being able to help youth, needed to be helped themselves. The late Fr. C. C. Martindale, a Jesuit scholar, writer, and preacher, once told an admirer of Jesuits at their Farm Street Church in the posh London district of Mayfair, "Madame, we Jesuits have our donkeys too, but we try not to let them bray in public!"

Any system, particularly one nearly 350 years old, will irritate, even alienate, some children and most especially those who are originals, that is, those who are not conforming yea-sayers. As a potential creative talent, the young Hitchcock was sensitive and, therefore, quite prone to bristle under the institutional practices of his Jesuit upbringing. On the other hand, that system with its staff—some extraordinary, most average, and a few below-average personnel—did contribute the creative stimuli which are discernible in the work of a Joyce, a Buñuel, a Hitchcock. All three had both the analytical mental skills and the artistic ability to portray in images what is basically unphotographable. What is true of James Joyce is also true of Buñuel and Hitchcock: nothing much happens in real life, but the "things that count happen inside the skull."[9] Whatever criticisms the three artists leveled at their Jesuit education, they did develop a talent for portraying the interior human drama in vivid pictures which triggered reflective thought. These are the qualities of true authorship, whether in fiction or film. I believe that Hitchcock was even more imprinted by the sons of Saint Ignatius than were his two fellow artists. In any case, behind the director is the man, behind the man is the child. His later fears and obsessive themes had their roots in country, home, church, and school.

Take as an example repeatedly given by the adult Hitchcock in interviews that he, more than many other students, experienced a type of free-floating anxiety in the face of authority figures. Hitchcock told François Truffaut that, as a child, he was a loner: "I can't remember ever having had a playmate. I played by myself, inventing my own games."[10] This posture cultivated in the boy a heightened ability to see deeply into personal and institutional relationships, marked by conditioned reflexes. Distrust of authority was engendered in him at an early age, and it plagued him to his very last days. Albert Whitlock, a collaborator for half a century, reports that Hitchcock even feared minor executives at Universal Studios, avoiding confrontation with them as if he were not a genius-director, a legend in his own time, and the third largest stockholder in the studio. He was bolder in his earlier years in Hollywood, but with failing health grew more timid vis-à-vis studio types. Fear grew progressively more acute.

Though shaped by Catholic values and points of view at a tender age, Hitchcock never claimed to be a Catholic artist. By his own admission, he never sought any label; he did not want to be known as either religious or antireligious. Unlike some Catholic artists, Hitchcock never publicly criticized the teachings, laws, or leaders of his church, but he did claim complete freedom to follow his own artistic inspiration wherever it would lead. When referring to *Rear Window*, a film about prying and voyeurism, he told Truffaut that no previous criticism of the plot would have prevented him from making the film. His love of film, he said, was "far more important . . . than any considerations of morality."

The truth of his vision *was* his morality, his religion—a position not far from that of James Joyce, whose own sense of calling as an artist was tantamount to a priestly vocation.

Notes

1. Donald Spoto describes how the young Alfred was made to stand at the foot of his mother's bed and answer detailed questions about the day's activities. Some half-century after this childhood ritual, Hitchcock recalled: "It was something she always had me do. It was a ritual. I always remember the evening confession." See Spoto, *Dark Side of Genius,* p. 18.
2. H. L. Beales, "The Victorian Family," in *Ideas and Beliefs of the Victorians* (New York: Collier Books, 1966), pp. 343–345.
3. Ibid., p. 347.
4. Spoto, *Dark Side of Genius,* pp. 24–25.
5. O. H. Mowrer, "Loss and Recovery of Community: A Guide to the Theory and Practice of Integrity Therapy" in *Invitation to Group Psychotherapy,* G. Gazda, ed. (Springfield, Ill.: Charles C. Thomas, 1968), pp. 130–189.

6. For those interested in the studies of personality development and self-disclosure in the process of "self-actualization," see Carl Rogers, *On Becoming a Person* (Boston: Houghton Mifflin, 1961); Abraham Maslow, *The Farther Reaches of Human Nature* (New York: Viking Press, 1971); Sidney Jourard, *The Transparent Self* (New York: Van Nostrand Reinhold, 1971); Valerian Derlega and Alan Chaikin, *Sharing Intimacy: What We Reveal to Others and Why* (Englewood Cliffs, N.J.: Prentice-Hall, 1975).

7. R. T. Glover, *The Ancient World* (Harmondsworth, Middlesex.: Penguin Books, 1957), p. 183.

8. See C. A. Parkhurst, *They Died for the Faith: Memoirs of Missionary Priests and Other Catholics of Both Sexes Who Suffered During the Years 1577 and 1684* (London: Catholic Truth Society, 1951); J. J. Dwyer, *The Tower of London: Notes for Catholics* (London: Catholic Truth Society, 1958).

9. Anthony Burgess, "The Task of Turning Joyce's Prose to Film Poetry," *New York Times,* January 3, 1988.

10. Quoted in François Truffaut, *Hitchcock* (New York: Simon and Schuster, 1967), p. 17.

CHAPTER III

The Spiritual Exercises

No long-term student of the Jesuits can escape the influence of the *Spiritual Exercises,* a strategic handbook of prayer, spiritual direction, and meditation.[1] The book is the fruit of a conversion by a Spanish officer, Iñigo de Loyola, a sixteenth-century soldier turned mystic. While he was recuperating from a leg injury received during the siege of Pamplona in 1521, Ignatius began reading a life of Christ and biographies of the saints, probably for lack of more chivalrous reading. He began to imagine a new type of chivalry, serving Christ and his ideals in a spiritual combat with eternal consequences for souls in suspense.[2]

The sorting out of extrapsychic influences by good and evil spirits—called by the technical term *discernment*—led eventually to a manual of techniques, meditations, and ascetical practices to find the will of God and the peace that such an exercise of God-directed liberty produces. This combat spirituality anticipates modern game theory in the sense that it assumes a spiritual adversary called by Saint Ignatius the "enemy of human nature," an interesting descriptor compared with such names as the Devil, Satan, Lucifer, and Beelzebub. Hitchcock makes reference to demonlike characters. Take Joseph Cotten's Uncle Charlie in *Shadow of a Doubt.* Arriving in the train amid curls of black smoke, he represents the dark nature of man, which Carl Jung calls the "shadow." One writer sees this Jungian metaphor as referring to the "bestial side of man, experienced historically as that peculiar guilt known as 'original sin.' "[3] When projected outward, the "shadow" becomes the Devil. In *Shadow of a Doubt,* niece Charlie thwarts Uncle Charlie's attempt to kill her; he falls into the path of an oncoming train. She will live on, wondering about her affinity to a murderous uncle. Original sin is dramatically implied. What Hamlet called a "mole of nature" that can unravel a personality unaware of a "particular defect" is the "shadow" that falls across many of Hitchcock's suspense thrillers, particularly his later, dark classics, such as *Vertigo, Psycho, The Birds,* and *Frenzy.* Ingredient to his canon of films is evil, but not only as an absence of a quality within the tragic or victimized person, but also as a positive energy. An accidental false step over a precipice is different from a step into a trap planted to kill. Hitch never subscribed to the excuse, "The Devil made me do it." Rather he saw, as did Saint Ignatius, a suprahuman force doing mystical battle with humans aided by equally powerful agents of good (angels and divine graces). Souls in suspense struggle valiantly not to become "wrong persons" in a spiritual combat in which the defeat has eternal and irreversible consequences. Later I shall address his dark motifs of hell, agents of evil, and symbols of infernal influences. Hence, the concept of souls in suspense is grounded in the challenges to human free will in terms of a destiny within this world and beyond.

The chief purpose of an Ignatian retreat (whether three, eight, or thirty days) is to dispose the subject to read the life signs, thus discovering God's will in all things. The key to the Ignatian *Exercises* is trying to seek a better way (called in Latin *magis*). One must look to find. Ignatius was firmly convinced that the good stands in the way of the better, that the better must be earnestly sought for the sake of perfection (the *magis*). It is intriguing to note that Hitchcock would advise his cameramen that, among the many possible camera positions, there was one "best shot."

This perfectionism presupposes an active adversarial force that moves against the protagonist, whether he acknowledges it or not. This is, obviously, a different situation from the scientist who tries to learn the secrets of nature but can be assured that nature will not try to deceive him if he finds the correct path of inquiry. It was Albert Einstein who said, "The Lord God is subtle, but malicious he is not." Hitch's films do not assume the posture of the scientist merely looking for information, but that of a combatant who must reckon with a serious rival. Thus, the Ignatian-trained person learns to live with an alert eye for whatever leads to choices and courses of action, to personal moral development, service to others, and indirectly the glory of God. Of course, Hitch's picaresque films of a falsely accused "wrong man," being pursued and questing for vindication, are not recognizably spiritual. However, one will discern growth in all directions— a moral strengthening of purpose and character, the blossoming of a solid romance, and a satisfying, just resolution which prevents harm to the community or nation.

As with the Jesuit retreatant, so too the Hitchcockian protagonist seeks first to survive and then to thrive, to grow in character and thus assume a look that is closer to that which we recognize in the Christ of the Gospels. This two-pronged reaching for the *magis* through minimizing spiritual loss and maximizing spiritual gain is the foundation of the *ratio studiorum,* the Jesuit plan of pedagogy which seeks to train character, emotions, intellect, and will. The pupil is inculcated with the discriminating criteria for seeking and choosing the better, not merely the good. Hitchcock probably never made the full thirty-day retreat, but he and his classmates did make three-day retreats and were constantly exposed to Jesuit influences, motivations, and the example of highly disciplined religious and lay staff. As a child he could not have known the technical structure and rhythmic dynamics of the spiritual manual for discerning God's will by rooting out disorder (*agere contra*) and following Christ as a way of spiritual growth. However, for three impressionable years he was immersed in a learning environment and religious atmosphere permeated by the spirit of the Ignatian *Exercises.* The authority figures— the rector, the headmaster, the prefects of religion and discipline, and many teachers—were Jesuits. In those days, Jesuit priests studied for seventeen years, and the seminarians who taught Hitchcock would have completed seven years' training. In short, the daily discipline, chapel duties, days of recollection, overnight retreats, classwork, school assemblies, extracurricular activities, and even after-school punishments—all these constituted an immersion pedagogy whose double purpose of information transfer and character formation were distilled from the *Spiritual Exercises,* the core spiritual vision of Ignatius of Loyola.

Let us look more closely at this famous book of the Ignatian *Exercises,* which is a book not really to be read but to be pondered, prayed over, and assimilated into one's private life. It has been said that this spiritual path has produced as many holy men and women as the number of printed letters in its bound contents. This process of discernment regarding the positive and negative influences on one's imagination, memory, intellect, and will has, incidentally, intrigued secular persons curious to unlock the power of the Jesuits as educators, missionaries, and influential trendsetters. W. Somerset Maugham once submitted to a Jesuit retreat to learn about the methodology. His novel *Ashenden* deals with deceit, cover-up, and assassination, attracting Hitchcock to use it as the basis of his 1936 movie, *Secret Agent.*

The *Spiritual Exercises* is based on motions of the spirit, a tug-of-war between good and evil forces with certain powers of intercommunication with embodied spirits such as humans. Classic religious writers use the term *spiritual combat,* personally experienced by Iñigo Loyola. How uncanny that this particular event has held the seeds of a shareable universal method for narrowing down the domain of freedom so as to attune it to a faith criterion, namely the will of God. Note that the soul in suspense, perplexed as to future decisions, is not psychically determined by the good and evil spirits. Ignatius, following the teachings of the Bible and the Catholic church, stresses the autonomy of the will in us human souls in suspense. I benefited in delight and greater understanding from this spiritual frame of reference in such films as *I Confess, The Wrong Man, Vertigo, Psycho, The Birds, Marnie, Topaz, Frenzy,* and *Family Plot.* The Jesuit dynamics of motivation and decision making are discernible even when clothed in a legal, psychological, or even psychoanalytic drama. As a child of the twentieth century, Hitchcock would have had access to greater intellectual resources for a more sophisticated and broader understanding of the spiritual combat than Ignatius of Loyola, who lived in a time of less complex organizations and moral issues. Note that I do not say a deeper awareness, but merely one that draws on the wider horizons of knowledge regarding the behavioral sciences and biblical and theological research. Critical for human happiness is a sense of direction, and that means both guidance and discernment. The Ignatian *Exercises* requires the spiritual director as indispensable for helping the retreatant find God's will. Ignatius first mastered self through awareness of the divisions and distractions within him and then learned progressively to apply this knowledge to directing and aiding others.

The reader familiar with Hitch's filmology will understand the importance of direction. His classic period—from *Strangers on a Train* (1951) through *Marnie* (1964)—stresses lost souls, (human agents of evil) and stalwart good characters undaunted by victimhood. In *Strangers on a Train* and *Psycho,* he casts the two villains against type, using Robert Walker and Anthony Perkins, who each came from a past of positive roles. This induces in the audience memory-investment complexity. The viewer experiences crossed emotional wires, trying to reconcile the previous image of the good guy with the now-deranged role. Hitch adds more complexity by showing each villain as wanting to kill a parent or spouse. There is deep psychological and motivational mystery here. How responsible are these two killers? Hitch seems to point to an Absolute Judge who alone will be able to resolve these complexities. In addition, Hitchcock deepens the notion of evil so that the protagonist must react with great courage to overcome the evil with which he is confronted. In addition to themes of guilt and psychologically disturbed individuals, he also treats the pathology of amoral national security policies by nation-states. The challenge of attaining a balance in life and not being tipped toward disorder, even self-destruction, is a common theme in Hitch's work. It greatly contributes to the uniqueness of his film signature. The pattern is remarkably isomorphic in terms of the Ignatian vision.

After recovering from his battle injury, Ignatius went to Manresa, where he lived in a cave for a year. There he gave himself up to prayer and severe ascetic practices, such as fasting, abstention from pleasure, and the infliction of discomfort and even pain. He believed that through these practices (mortifications), he could become a better and holier man. He merely applied to the psychospiritual stirrings of others what he felt—deep consolation when reading of heroic service for God and desolation when thinking about worldly, often vain, pursuits. Ignatius wondered during his conversion, "What is this new life which is beginning for me?" He felt called to help other souls in suspense to reflect on the inner life and the rhythm of desolation and consolation in order to effect a profound change in religious consciousness.[4] From his mystical experiences at Manresa, Ignatius learned that things are not as they appear. Key to all recovery therapies is the principle that as one withdraws from the causes of disease, one feels bad but is getting better. The

I Confess treats "impossible love" relations. Here Anne Baxter, playing a married woman, gazes admiringly at her former boyfriend, Father Logan (Montgomery Clift).

sufferings of Hitch's protagonists prepare the way for betterment (meliorism). This dynamic underlies the *Spiritual Exercises*: first, to recognize the malady—symptoms and root cause; next, to find the cure or antidote; then, to submit to the healing procedures—however repugnant, however long, however costly; and, finally, to enjoy the fruits of restored health. This medical analogy comports with the psychospiritual process of diagnosis, prescription, remedial processes, and recuperation. Study a Hitchcock film with a "wrongperson" theme and see the moral, romantic, and patriotic benefits that result—e.g., in *The 39 Steps, Young and Innocent, Saboteur,* and *North by Northwest.*

Consider the fruits of the rhythm of sin, repentance, and regeneration as outlined in the Jesuit *Exercises*—Christ's Incarnation, life of service, wrongful accusations, trials, death, and resurrection. Is there not a parallel in, say, the conversion of Cary Grant's Roger O. Thornhill (a Calvary symbol) in *North by Northwest?* He begins as a hollow character, a Madison Avenue adman, whom his secretary calls a "liar," and ends as a patriot who has converted an amoral undercover agent (Eva Marie Saint). Take the Kansas cornfield scene and the crop-dusting plane's attempt on Thornhill's life. Notice the obvious cross symbols: the crossroad and the two wooden posts shaped as crosses. These symbols are typical in Hitchcock's canon of motion pictures. Where did this penchant for such religious symbolism come from? In great measure from the Ignatian *Exercises,* which pervade not only the constitution and governing structure of the Society of Jesus, but also its educational plan, the *ratio studiorum.*[5]

Studying as a young boy under the direction of the Jesuits at Saint Ignatius college, Hitchcock was exposed to the influence of the *Spiritual Exercises* in terms of pastoral care and practices of piety, administrative policy, and the program and ideals of Jesuit education. He became imbued with the dynamics of the *Exercises,* which encourages and predisposes the participants to strive for greater transcendence in their lives—to move beyond the limits of ordinary experience and to attain greater spiritual awareness and freedom from moral disorder. The psychology underlying the *Exercises* is that the good stands in the way of the better, just as evil stands in the

In *The Man Who Knew Too Much* (1956), cymbals represent angel wings—the angel of death. The Jesuit *Exercises* use "death" as the ultimate test of authenticity. "What would I have wished to have done in life as I lie on my deathbed?"

way of the good. It is clearly a struggle spirituality, not a quiescent nor passive way toward closer union with God. It stresses powerful, adversarial forces that are overwhelming if one does not resist the darkness and personal weakness that conspire to keep human potential undeveloped at all levels.

An underresearched topic in the burgeoning cottage industry of Hitchcock research is the ability of his most sympathetic protagonists to rise to exceptional challenges. Hitchcock begins exactly where Saint Ignatius does—with the surface appearance of order in families, communities, and society and the chaos which percolates beneath the surface, intermittently erupting. Neither the Master of Suspense nor the Master of Spirituality ever gave short shrift to moral and spiritual disease. Each had a surgical instinct for probing into the dynamics of human nature, not to wound but to heal. Hitch's films and the Ignatian *Exercises* have been equally criticized as being pessimistic, even paranoid, and inclining almost by some bias of temperament of the author to a chronic critique of what behavioral scientists accept as the norm of human behavior in a statistical universe of case studies. Neither Hitch nor Ignatius would have agreed with the democratic process of polling as a way of determining what is desirable for the individual and society. In this sense, many avid fans of Hitchcock are not aware that he is in deep disagreement with the assumptions underlying their view of the human condition.

Take one of Hitchcock's own favorite films, *The Trouble with Harry*. One critic sees the film as prelapsarian, a fable

In *Family Plot,* Hitch's last film, childhood Jesuit memories returned—of graves as "Godward" reminders of the "Great Crossover."

about Vermont folk in a pre-Adamic state of relative bliss with no fear of death.[6] Harry Warp's body is found in lush autumnal leaves in the woods. His body disappears and reappears three times. No one seems perturbed; he is taken for granted, even by a playful youngster with a toy rifle. I think that Hitch's background would have disposed him to make this tongue-in-cheek satire on the meaninglessness of death to many people who live in complacent comfort. The great crossover cannot be a fright to those who do not believe in a hereafter. Does that mean that the Vermonters are heathen or indifferent to death? No, not at all! It merely suggests that death in America is commonplace and therefore discounted in personal terms. It is not Hamlet's intimidating "undiscover'd country from whose bourn / No traveller returns," but an incident, something that occurs without very serious thought to what follows. I read into the film a jibe at complacency, an attempt through quiet humor to stimulate gently the shock of recognition about Hamlet's macabre musings on the difference it makes "to be, or not to be."

Hitch's Jesuit background helps us to see *The Trouble with Harry* in the light of eternity. Recall the scenes of Harry Warp's feet, always forward and seen large in frontal perspective. This recalls the meditation on death which Fr. Mangan gave to his students. Perhaps Hitchcock was satirizing that spiritual lecture. Perhaps. However, his own last days in the office, on the set, and with associates reveal a man keeping active and not facing career retirement, the antechamber to that final phase of the pilgrimage in which we "shuffle off this mortal coil." *The Trouble with Harry* is an undervalued film, one that has a Jesuit imprint and a cocky denunciation of the secularization of a solemn event that saints and the Bible attest to as solemn—*memento mori*: "Thou are dust and to dust thou shalt return." I cannot accept the thesis that this film is a return to a time before Adam's fall. The insignificance of the characters, their faces, their priorities, gives no such evidence of divinized immortal creatures instead of dethroned kings and queens in exile. Not a few of Hitch's ardent followers would be uneasy to find the depth of the honest differences that separated him from them.

One point which is important and is not meant as irrever-

ent: Motion pictures afforded Hitchcock a pictorial sophistication to record dramatically concrete images of the human
condition which was denied to Ignatius in the age of movable
type. Not that a thirty-day retreat under guided direction is
not more effective than three hours in a movie theater, but
the ability to return to a Hitchcock film and ponder the
subliminals—the remarkable interactions between people
and their consciences and God—is something no one has
thought of in exactly the same way since Carl Dreyer's
breathtaking *Passion of Joan of Arc* (1927). That Hitch was
impressed by Dreyer's film is borne out by the tribute to
Dreyer in the prison cell scene of Nora Baring in *Murder!*
(1930). An edifying film about a saint's martyrdom is one way
to photograph the action of God on earth, but there is another
way—to use secular plots and invest them with conversions.
For every heroic Fr. Michael Logan (*I Confess*) there are
countless persons working out their destinies in more prosaic,
less dramatic ways. To take a Madison Avenue huckster (Cary
Grant) and give him a little of the look of Christ is a brilliant
coup—which is what Hitch did in *North by Northwest*. (And
the title, taken from *Hamlet,* is not fortuitous.) Indeed, Hitch
was ever under the spell of cosmic mystery, that poignant
legacy of Hamlet to Horatio, "There's a divinity that shapes
our ends, / Rough-hew them how we will."

A breakthrough by Hitchcock in terms of application of the
Ignatian *Exercises* to modern life is his elevation of the
diagnostic power of active spiritual warfare (good spirits
versus evil spirits) to institutions and nations. The Jesuit
retreat is geared to individuals and runs the risk of ignoring
that in the twentieth century—more than before—persons
are creatures of powerful influences from complex organizations, some of them with resources outweighing small, poor
nations. With *North by Northwest, Torn Curtain,* and *Topaz,*
Hitchcock used the Ignatian principle of "beginning, middle,
and end" to accent the fatalistic purposelessness and waste of
patriotism and nationalism, those time-honored sanctions for
evil which "sugar o'er / The devil himself" (*Hamlet*). In effect,
he applied astutely a powerful personalistic strategy of spiritual combat to international realpolitik with stunning results,
not necessarily as movie fare but as fodder for thinking

seriously about the amorality of global affairs in terms of divine accountability.

Consider three of Hitchcock's mature films. At the end of *North by Northwest,* the U.S. agent and the (presumably) Soviet spy master are on friendly terms, indifferent to the tragedies that have just transpired. (Little has been made by commentators of this sardonic touch by an indignant but discreet Hitch.) In *Torn Curtain,* Paul Newman slowly kills an East German agent, finally thrusting his head into an oven with the help of a strong peasant. The allusion to the Nazi gas chambers passed by many film critics. At the end of *Topaz,* after a slew of suicides, murders, and political tortures, the Cuban missile crisis is terminated as we see a man throw a newspaper with its headline about the crisis into the trash can. Life is insignificant; it has no worth, no value—but Hitch knows better and shows the no-exit nature of world politics as practiced in terms of self-interest, violating all the principles of the First Week. As a Jesuit I feel confident that Hitch knew that many double agents, spies, and practitioners of intrigue, dirty tricks, and cover-ups were trained by Jesuits and probably made Ignatian retreats—privately.[7] This awareness would not have been lost on his keen sense of irony.

Hitchcock transformed what he once learned into his own Hitchcockian spirituality, a type of cinematic *Exercises,* to serve as a powerful diagnostic tool for raising consciousness and *that* in the hands of an artist/entertainer with access to countless millions of viewers who, unlike pupils, were not unwilling, captive audiences but eager ticket buyers. Hitch paid tribute to his Jesuit role models, teachers, confessors, and retreat masters with this revealing testimony: "If you've been brought up a Jesuit as I was, these elements are bound to intrude. If you examine my films, I daresay you'll find very few where wrong has the ascendancy."[8]

Hitchcock's experience with Ignatian spirituality was in a received tradition which, since the five hundredth anniversary in 1991 of Ignatius of Loyola's birth has been revised and liberated from misinterpretations and glosses due to scholarly scrutiny.[9] A number of themes that run through the *Exercises* find their way into Hitchcock's work. The Christ theme, which is central to the *Exercises,* crops up in Hitch-

TOP: In *The Birds,* Rod Taylor is "pursued and out-of-time." Attacked by gulls, he flees, while protecting a scared little girl. Note the touching Pietà pose, a key motif in Hitch's film signature. BOTTOM: *Frenzy's* Pietà scene has barmaid Babs (Anna Massey) caring for her lover, Richard Blaney (Jon Finch). His friend, Bob Rusk (Barry Foster) has committed sex crimes attributed to Blaney, who is jailed. Rusk will rape Babs, who dies a lonely death, lacking the tender care shared with Blaney.

cock's films in the person of the "wrong man," the one unjustly accused who courageously assumes imputed guilt. As we shall see, the parallel with Christ is too strong to overlook. Furthermore, the number of cross symbols is impressive and must be seen in the light of earlier, Ignatian influences. Hitchcock's *Manxman* (a silent picture), *Mr. and Mrs. Smith* (a romantic comedy from 1941), and *Family Plot* (his last feature) each have a scene with a cross or a crucifix. Hitch consciously seeded his films with religious symbols—biblical, but especially Christian.

In the *Exercises,* human beings are seen as fickle creatures subject to quick shifts in mood and behavior. *Family Plot* takes on an entirely new meaning if one sees it as a celluloid tract on the mutable motivation of all the characters—their ability to change identities, to appear other than they really are, and to deceive others. Hitchcock's films also deal with swings of mood that range from the terrifying to the consoling. Unpredictable emotional shifts add dramatic power to such films as *Strangers on a Train, Vertigo,* and *Psycho.* If one applies the review of life to Hitchcock's protagonists, retracing each life in terms of beginning, middle, and end, the viewer will quickly recognize how the happy ending grows out of the Ignatian principles of *agere contra* and meliorism.

However, Hitch can also leave an audience dangling with the sense of incompletion. The ending seems blissful (often to satisfy the Motion Picture Production Code). In reality, the emotional dynamics of a given scene deny the facile felicity which the verbal text promised but which the visual text subverts (in, for example, *Suspicion, I Confess,* and *The Wrong Man*). Retreatants are confronted by the *Exercises* with dark forces of evil and guilt. The popularity of Hitchcock's films can be found in his skillful portrayal of these same forces—they are generally far more interesting to people than the theme of goodness—nonetheless, the good generally prevails.

The *Exercises* shows that spiritual health and moral development depend on understanding disorder, distress, and spiritual decline. A discerning study of unfulfilled potential and backsliding can lead to valuable lessons in terms of retracing one's religious experience. Thus the awareness of beginning, middle, and end can help one recognize the serpent's tail ("by their fruits, ye shall know them"). Ignatius believed that the study of spiritual illness could lead to spiritual recovery and future prevention of sin, mortal and venial.

The Gospels see victory in victimage, a reversal of the world's values. Ignatius encouraged his disciples, similarly, to recognize injustice and stand up to it, to right wrongs, to suffer valiantly, to be open to love and service, and to sacrifice for it—all for Christ's sake. In this way, they would be triumphant in the end despite the overwhelming odds of organized evil. A militant spirituality, the *Exercises* is essentially a personal guide to neutralizing the interdependent web of such malevolent forces as greed, power, and lust for reputation and status. It is not a question of the person

Young and Innocent (1937)—"Wrong Man" Derrick de Marney loves Nova Pilbeam (right). Together they find the real killer. Jesuit moral? The good (a bit of trust) stands in the way of the better (a lot of trust)!

putting forward his best moral foot. It is rather a case of game theory, of avoiding the snares and traps of lurking adversarial powers, seemingly innocent but competing for an edge at the expense of the unsuspecting victim. The sanctions for and shields of evil must be recognized, if God's greater glory is to be realized.

Hitchcock's films replay these same themes. They are concerned with moral education—suffering through crisis, purification through enlightenment and reconciliation—in Hollywood's terms, the classic happy ending. Hitch was committed, as was Ignatius, to the principle that a study of moral disease was a step toward health and happiness (e.g., *North by Northwest, The Birds, Marnie*). It is noteworthy that the happy endings in these three mature films are ironic; they insinuate future trouble, further temptations and imperilment. There is often an upward spiritual journey as well as a horizontal story line with a chase plot. The Jesuit path contrasts with an enlightenment spirituality, such as that of Eastern mysticism and the visions of Teresa of Avila and Francis of Assisi, or a service type of witnessing such as that of Vincent de Paul and Mother Teresa of Calcutta. Instead it fosters a warrior mentality, a stance of courageous resistance that characterizes the heroes and heroines in Hitchcock's best films. Note the marked moral development of Cary Grant in *North by Northwest* and of Tippi Hedren in *The Birds* and in *Marnie*.

Hitchcock always let a ray of hope shine through even his most despondent works. If we are shocked by Jimmy Stewart's "vertigo" and Anthony Perkins's "psychosis," then we must be reminded that Scottie Ferguson can always return to the ever-loyal Midge (Barbara Bel Geddes) and that, if Norman Bates is non compos mentis, the discovery of Marion Crane's car may well clear her sullied name. Both *Vertigo* and *Psycho* are masterful examples of how Hitchcock deprofanizes the world as ordinarily seen through periodicals, mass media, and daily conversations, thus sorting out malevolent influences from those which are benign. Above all, appearances alone must not be trusted. After all, even the devil can sing sacred hymns—do we trust the singer or the song? The test for Ignatius of Loyola is the final outcome, the serpent's tail which is seen last.

To see Hitchcock's films as mere mystery or suspense thrillers without this religious subtext is to miss why Hitchcock's films are distinct from other suspense thrillers. Compare the character and acting of Anthony Perkins in the original *Psycho* with the sequels, which beg tragic believability, lack psychospiritual mystery, and merely offer shock sensationalism. The director's viewpoint goes beyond moral irony and humanism with its implicit theology of human existence as a combat zone, where the odds are stacked against the protagonist. Hitchcock hints that to initiate moral effort is to invite mysterious guidance from on high. Again, he agrees with Hamlet: "There's a divinity that shapes our ends, / Rough-hew them how we will."

Indeed, there seems to be a providential wind at the backs of such determined protagonists! For example, in the remake of *The Man Who Knew Too Much* (with Doris Day and Jimmy Stewart), darkness over the disappearance of a small son turns into light. The resolution of this thriller subverts the fatalistic resignation in Doris Day's rendition of "Que Será, Será" ("Whatever will be, will be"). Neither Ignatius of Loyola nor Alfred Hitchcock would subscribe to that stoic principle of grudging acceptance of blind destiny. Hitchcock's brilliance is to provide a biblical foundation of trust in life in seeming entertainment contexts involving handsome, available bachelors, pretty women, and nefarious political plots. I agree with O. B. Hardison's statement that Hitchcock's thrillers point to the salvation of the hero or heroine "not by reason or works but by a divine thrusting on."[10] However, I disagree that Hitch's theology is one, like the Calvinistic City of Man, in which "the few Elect muddle through."[11] Anyone can be equal to any challenge, no matter how great, provided he or she trusts in inner resources and a happy outcome. Ignatius used the expression *instrumentum conjunctum cum Deo*, "a partnership with God," or to quote Teresa of Avila, "God and I as a majority."[12]

I hope that this summary of the *Spiritual Exercises* may cast some appreciative light on the complex meanings and allu-

In *Psycho,* the gnarled dead tree, a surreal cross symbol, stands for Norman Bates, a psychically twisted victim.

sions to such themes as the "wrong persons," troubled endings, and meliorism in Hitchcock's films. His message sympathetically vibrates with the spirit of the Ignatian *Exercises*: the person acts on mutable motives, often influenced by emotions and with little thought of dark forces at work. History, the press, and scholars are baffled by the fact that so many people swing in an arc of behavior from the most godlike to the most subhuman. Hitch squarely faced this irrepressible fact, as did the Greek and Elizabethan tragedians and men like Saint Paul and Saint Ignatius, who grasped the dynamics of our bent nature, inclined to evil which is theoretically abhorred, but too often embraced or acquiesced in.

I am moved each time I see *Psycho,* particularly the scene in which Norman Bates watches his victim's automobile sinking in a swamp. Suddenly, it stops. He's visibly disturbed, but we, the audience, share his concern and have a strange, even perverse, partisan interest in the disappearance of the telltale car. Hitchcock implicates the viewer with the psychopath—"There but for the grace of God go I." This compassionate and ironic note runs throughout the Ignatian *Exercises*. Whatever the offense, it is pardonable. We cannot fall out of God's love. Study the last scenes of *Psycho*: the psychiatrist's diagnosis of Norman/Mother Bates, the scene of Mother's voice talking through Norman's straitjacketed body and the raising of Marion Crane's sunken car from the murky swamp. These scenes invite awe at the mystery of good and evil and deny the viewer grounds for judgments. These scenes brim with reverent unknowing. By introducing mystery, Hitchcock de-profanizes the daily chronicle of crimes and passion in the press.

As does the Ignatian *Exercises,* so too Hitchcock's films may assist audiences to track the moral decline of his screen characters and their reform (meliorism). This ability is not only a plus for enjoyment but adds moral insights. Sin distorts our powers of self-assessment; it should not be seen as a poor grade on some heavenly report card. No, sin is self-effacing. It impedes our moral vision, as tinted glasses filter out some colors. Take *Strangers on a Train,* with Bruno Anthony as the tempter and Guy Haines as the tempted. Or *Psycho*. In terms of Catholic moral psychology, no serious (mortal) sin is ever committed, despite embezzlement and four murders (including Mrs. Bates and her lover). Considerable psychic determinism is at work in Marion Crane's state of passionate desperation. And total lack of responsibility is obvious in Norman Bates, a homicidal schizophrenic. Public menaces? Assuredly. Hell-bound souls in suspense? Hardly, Hitch would imply and I, a Jesuit, would concur. It is very difficult to incur eternal damnation. Some theologians (such as Karl Rahner) believe that no one is in hell—not even Judas—though they affirm hell's existence.

No other director in film history has used cinematic techniques to relate moral allegories and religious parables through entertainment narratives based on suspense, mystery, romance, and adventure. It is said that auteur directors keep making essentially the same film. This is true of Hitch, due to the mold of spiritual humanism in which his imagination, mind, and will were shaped at an early age by his Jesuit mentors. The *Exercises* postulates a spiritual battleground with us souls in suspense in the cross fire between two antagonistic—and invisible—agencies of good and evil, each of which can influence us intrapsychically. In the Master of Suspense's best work we see evidences of open-ended pessimism with powerful evil forces virtually overwhelming the protagonist and his or her lover. (*North by Northwest* and *Marnie* are relevant case studies.) Unjustly beleaguered people prevail with God's aid *and* persevering courage and trust. The reader will recognize in future viewings of Hitchcock's films the subtextual dynamics of limited dualism, meliorism, *agere contra,* and above all the biblical and Ignatian foundational belief in open-ended pessimism. There is a paradox in Scripture, the Ignatian *Exercises,* and Hitch's fifty-three motion pictures: the kite soars higher in the face of a contrary wind. No other director has seeded his work with so many secular Christ figures, Pietà scenes, cross symbols, and troubled happy endings which point to the continuing spiritual drama of the romantic couple or the homeland made safe, for now, from enemy agents.

The "wrong-person" motif is closely related to the secular transfigurations of the Christ. Hitchcock's filmology would be niggardly without these mutually supporting references.

The director's penchant for internal mind games has a correlate in the Ignatian *Exercises*: the mystical use of geometric designs (such as spirals and lines) as well as the esoteric, often biblically based, use of numerology. If Ignatius altered the way Catholics and others viewed God as an intimate presence in their daily lives, at the core of their being, then his Jesuit sons have kept alive that vision, not only in retreats but also in a pedagogical system based on it. Jesuit spirituality implies the willingness of God to communicate through signs that are felt internally and must be tested over time. It is, basically, an unspoken language.[13] The Jesuit educational system is a kind of sacrament, working independently of the personal gifts and individual characteristics of the staff, though these cannot be discounted. Although Hitchcock worked with a wide range of diverse collaborators in his over fifty years of filmmaking, his films bear his stamp indelibly. I would argue that this stamp owes not a little to his childhood Jesuit training. Is it too farfetched to see his filmology as a kind of mass entertainment sacrament? Not if we see his films at least three times, to employ the trinitarian figure he himself used.

Notes

1. For over twenty-seven years I have used a valuable French edition of the manual of Ignatius: Saint Ignace de Loyola, *Exercises Spirituels* (Paris: Desclée de Brouwer, 1960); English references include *The Spiritual Exercises of St. Ignatius*, Louis J. Puhl, trans. (Westminster, Md.: Newman Press, 1951); and David L. Fleming, *The Spiritual Exercises of St. Ignatius: A Literal Translation and a Contemporary Reading* (St. Louis: Institute of Jesuit Sources, 1978). Valuable reference books include William V. Bangert, *A History of the Society of Jesus* (St. Louis: Institute of Jesuit Sources, 1972); Robert Harvanek, ed., *Proceedings of the Institute on Contemporary Thought and the Spiritual Exercises of St. Ignatius Loyola* (Chicago: Loyola University, 1963); and Karl Rahner, *Das Dynamische in der Kirche* (Freiburg: Verlag Herder, 1958), of which a translation by W. J. O'Hara is entitled *The Dynamic Element in the Church* (New York: Herder and Herder, 1964).

2. Interesting and dependable lives of Ignatius Loyola include James Brodrick, *St. Ignatius Loyola: The Pilgrim Years* (Farrar, Straus and Cuddihy, 1956) and *The Origin of the Jesuits* (New York: Longmans, Green, 1941); Leonard von Matt and Hugo Rahner, *St. Ignatius of Loyola: A Pictorial Biography,* John Murray, trans. (Chicago: Henry Regnery, 1956); Hugo Rahner, *St. Ignatius Loyola: Letters to Women* (New York: Herder and Herder, 1960); and Hugo Rahner, *Ignatius: The Man and the Priest,* John Coyne, trans. (Rome: Centrum Ignatianum Spiritualitatis, 1977); W. W. Meissner, M. D. *Ignatius of Loyola.* New Haven: Yale University Press, 1992.
3. Richard Woods, *The Devil* (Chicago: Thomas More Press, 1973), pp. 79–80.
4. This moral awakening of Saint Ignatius bears a strong resemblance to a later film of Hitchcock, *Shadow of a Doubt,* a personal favorite of his. In that film, there is the same shock of recognition of complicity in moral disorder, of being a child of the rebellious Adam. The audience experiences the deepening and troubled awareness of Teresa Wright (as niece Charlie) as she realizes her spiritual as well as blood affinity to her Uncle Charlie (Joseph Cotten), a serial killer of wealthy women. I see this film as permeated with the spirit of the First Week of the *Spiritual Exercises.*
5. See Ruth Tiffany Barnhouse, "The Spiritual Exercises and Psychoanalytic Therapy," *The Way,* supplement 24 (1975), pp. 74–82; Daniel J. Fitzpatrick, "Ignatius Loyola and Modern Religious Education: A Study in the Pedagogy of the Spiritual Exercises," *Dissertation Abstracts* A 37 (1976), 1476; and Robert Newton, *Reflections on the Educational Principles of the Spiritual Exercises* (Washington: Jesuit Secondary Education Association, 1977).
6. Leslie Brill, *The Hitchcock Romance* (Princeton, N.J.: Princeton University Press, 1988), pp. 283–291.
7. Since the 1950s there has been a disproportionate number of Catholic college graduates (a large number from Jesuit colleges) recruited by the FBI and the CIA, a number higher than the percentage of Catholics in the total population of the nation.
8. Quoted by Charles Champlin, ed., "AFI Tribute: A Homage to 'King Alfred,' " *Los Angeles Times,* March 7, 1979.
9. See Josef Stierli, "Ignatian Prayer: Seeking God in All Things," in *Ignatius of Loyola—His Personality and Spiritual Heritage, 1556–1956: Studies on the 400th Anniversary of His Death* (St.

Louis: Institute of Jesuit Sources, 1977), pp. 135–163. See also Morton Kelsey, *Discernment: A Study in Ecstasy and Evil* (New York: Paulist Press, 1978); Heinrich Bacht, "Good and Evil Spirits," *The Way* (London), No. 2 (1962), pp. 188–195; Jacques Guillet et al., *Discernment of Spirits* (Collegeville, Minn.: Liturgical Press, 1970); *St. Ignatius' Own Story as Told to Luis Gonzalez de Camara,* William J. Young, trans. (Chicago: Loyola University Press, 1968); and *The Spiritual Journal of St. Ignatius of Loyola,* William J. Young, trans. (Rome: Centrum Ignatianum Spiritualitatis, 1979).

10. Hardison, "Rhetoric of Thrillers," op. cit., p. 143.
11. Ibid.
12. See Gaston Fessard, *La Dialectique des Exercises Spirituels de Saint Ignace de Loyola* (Paris: Aubier, 1966); and Joseph Conwell, *Contemplation in Action: A Study in Ignatian Prayer* (Spokane: Gonzaga University, 1957).
13. Regarding Ignatius Loyola's development of a language of reciprocal God-to-person address, I refer the reader to a provocative communications study of *The Spiritual Exercises* by a linguistic analyst, Roland Barthes, "Loyola," in *Sade, Fourier, Loyola* (New York: Hill and Wang, 1976), pp. 38–75.

CHAPTER IV

The Wrong Man

If we had to choose the single most often recurring theme that runs through Hitchcock's films, it would be that of the "wrong man." I have identified twenty-one films with five variations on this theme.[1] The first variation deals with persons unjustly condemned and sentenced to prison or killed for a crime or action committed by another: *Blackmail, Murder!, Secret Agent,* and one of Hitch's last films, *Frenzy.* The second variation includes plots in which the audience suspects someone of being the culprit but finds out later that it was wrong (*The Lodger, Stage Fright, Spellbound, To Catch a Thief*). In the third variation, the leading character is innocent and awaits the inevitable, just outcome of the plot (*Downhill, The 39 Steps, Young and Innocent, Saboteur, I Confess, The Wrong Man, North by Northwest*).

The fourth variation deals with five films about "wronged" women, either with unconventional life-styles or under a legal cloud. In *Easy Virtue,* a society woman (Isabel Jeans) is stigmatized by the press, gossips, and in-laws, ending in two tragic divorces. *Notorious* starred Ingrid Bergman as an alcoholic whom federal agent Cary Grant loves and converts into a double agent serving the U.S. In *Psycho,* a thief (Janet Leigh) repents, resolves to make restitution, but dies as the victim of a stabbing. *Marnie* features Tippi Hedren as a kleptomaniac whose childhood trauma is greatly healed by the loving patience of her mother and her husband. In *Family Plot,* spiritualist Madame Blanche (Barbara Harris) narrowly escapes an undeserving death at the hands of totally evil Arthur Adamson (William Devane). The fifth category has one sole entry—*Suspicion.* Does Cary Grant intend to kill his wife, Joan Fontaine, or is she excessively paranoid? Unlike the novel, the film *Suspicion* leaves a doubt. The personal importance of the twenty-one "wrong-person" films to Hitch has not been acknowledged and deserves more reflective study by critics and scholars.

All too little has been written about the spiritual implications of the "wrong-man" theme, the notion of an undeserved fate which an innocent victim resists as totally unjust. Chapter VII, "Christ Figures—Overt and Covert," discusses Hitchcock's use of Christ as the prototype of the "wrong man." We cannot overlook Hitchcock's exposure in his impressionable years to the religious insistence that Christ died instead of us, the leitmotif of the Third Week of the Ignatian *Spiritual Exercises*. Fr. Albert Ellis described the religious devotions and practices used when Master Alfred studied at Saint Ignatius College prior to World War I (Appendix II).

In those days, Jesuit students were exposed to dark Lenten sermons and recurring exhortations touching on First Week topics of the *Spiritual Exercises* regarding sin as related to divine justice and God's majesty and to the Passion of Christ as unmerited. The latter meditation portrayed Jesus as an innocent victim who died voluntarily for the sins of humankind. The preoccupation with sin was linked to the Third Week, dedicated to the Passion. If the emphasis in the First Week stressed that Christ died for all, the Third Week accent was on Jesus as a surrogate victim for each of us. The reader will recognize here, as Hitch did later, a case study of the "wrong-man" theme.

Critically acclaimed, *The Lodger* was a brilliant application of the "wrong-man" theme with a Christic reference. A mysterious, foreign-looking lodger (Ivor Novello) is attracted to a lady in the boardinghouse where they live. Her fiancé, who is a detective, finds a map in the lodger's room with markings that are unmistakably linked to the scenes of certain murders. Subsequently, the audience discovers that the lodger was analyzing the case as an amateur sleuth in order to find ways to trap the killer. He escapes arrest and is pursued by an angry mob eager for quick vigilante justice, even though he is innocent. The alleged killer narrowly escapes death and is exonerated, but only after the crowd harasses him unmercifully.

We have here a clear case study of the "wrong man"; the innocent lodger was apparently willing to take the law into his own hands in pursuit of the real killer. Ironically, therefore, his life becomes endangered by the actions of a mob bent on private justice without any due process under law. Hitchcock's films bear reseeing in order to benefit from his multileveled meanings and inferences. The theme of punished innocence returned with *Downhill* (1927). Again Ivor Novello plays the victim of injustice, this time as a schoolboy expelled for supposedly stealing at school. Enraged, the young man's father summarily rejects his son, who goes to Paris and falls in love with an actress. Later there is a reconciliation in England. Expressionistic techniques gave an artistic sheen to the picture; moreover, Hitch used dream sequences, experiments tried by such directors as Jean Renoir, Abel Gance, René Clair, and Luis Buñuel.

The motif of the "wrong man" was a personal one to the director. Hitchcock keenly felt that being fated to fatness was an arbitrary sentence, not merited. In short, he felt like the "wrong man." Furthermore, news items constantly gave proof that society misperceived felons, while family members rejected loved ones for unfounded reasons. Hitch began to recognize how pervasive the "wrong-man" reference was in actual life. Personally chagrined by the bias against obesity, the hypersensitive Hitch became so chary of society's propensity to impute unproven guilt that he even began to blur culpability, especially in cases where self-interest created a conflict between love and duty.

Take *Blackmail* (1929), England's first sound picture. The film was a sharp departure from the crime films of Hollywood, such as Josef von Sternberg's *Underworld*. Hitch went for the complex gray areas of intention. A flirtatious young woman is invited to the studio of an artist, who makes advances. She stabs him and is not apprehended. Her fiancé, a policeman, protects her. Another man is accused, guilty of other crimes but not this one. The guilt she feels recurs, especially in the memorable sound sequence in the kitchen when a woman says, "Please pass the bread knife." Hitch and his sound engineer amplified the word "knife" so that it beats on the perpetrator's conscience like waves on the ocean's shore.

With this film Hitch realized that he had an additional device to penetrate the psychic interior of both the screen characters and the audience. *Blackmail* ended with a spiritual lesson: the Catholic distinction between the internal forum of conscience (where guilt resides) and the external forum of legal conviction (where imprisonment or execution results). The woman and her detective boyfriend see the picture of a laughing clown, painted by the dead artist, who appears to be mocking them from beyond the grave. Clearly, we have an instance of the "last laugh," an ironic reminder that there are psychospiritual laws we do not break but which, when violated, break us. The coquettish lady will never have inner peace, says Hitch. Pounding in her imagination will be the word "knife" and the image of the derisive clown sharing the secret of her guilt.

It was, however, with *Murder!* (1930) that the director made a breakthrough with a saintly "wrong-woman" type. Norah Baring plays Diana Baring, an actress falsely accused of murder. Herbert Marshall plays an actor and juror at her trial. Convinced of her innocence, he strives to exonerate her, and even visits her in prison. He is put on the trail of a suspect—a sensitive, nervous trapeze artist and transvestite named Handel Fane. (Hitch knew how to treat controversial, even daring, themes.) The police await the culprit as he performs on the trapeze; he espies them and falls to his death. We are not sure whether he was unnerved or preferred to die rather than to face humiliation and jail. The film is discrete and compassionate. Hitchcock wins sympathy for the circus performer: "There but for the grace of God go I." Guilt is attenuated through the acting and Hitch's camera language, pleading for tolerance, for a respect for nuances. Motion photography is superb for that, provided the filmmaker knows how to evoke subtleties.

The "wrong woman" in *Murder!* is notable because of the Rembrandt-like chiaroscuro scene of Diana in prison. Hitch paints with light and shadows as did the Dutch master; the interiority of Diana is felt by the viewer, especially when she is visited by Herbert Marshall, who sits at one end of a long table to talk to the prisoner seated far away at the other end. Always quick to learn from others—especially the Scandinavian, German and Russian filmmakers—Hitch was impressed by *The Passion of Joan of Arc* (1928), the silent masterpiece of Danish director Carl Dreyer, who cast a cabaret entertainer, Maria Falconetti, in the role of the warrior-saint, the Maid of Orleans. That was one of the greatest "wrong-person" trials since Socrates, and Hitch related to it in both substance and style. The acting is unparalleled and occupies a special niche in the history of screen performance. (The accompanying still testifies to the power of the close-up. Hitch employed this power in three remarkable close-ups of women suffering agonizing passion as innocent victims of inexplicably dark forces in *Psycho, The Birds,* and *Frenzy.*)

As far as I am aware, Hitch seldom acknowledged sources of inspiration and imitation. The indebtedness of Hitchcock to Dreyer's classic speaks for itself. Falconetti's Joan is the prime analogue for those innocent feminine types who have more than a little of the look of Christ. The chasteness of Dreyer's Jeanne d'Arc is captured by Norah Baring in *Murder!* and later would be translated to the screen in *Psycho*'s shower scene, the vicious bombardment of beaks upon Tippi Hedren in *The Birds,* and the rape and murder of Barbara Leigh-Hunt in *Frenzy.* I shall return to this theme in Chapter XI, "Spiritualizing Horror." This spiritualization includes a compassion for such miscreant deeds as sexual perversity. Hitch's penchant for understanding, and through such comprehension, for being disposed to pardon erotic excesses, must be included within the topic of the "wrong person." Any concern for the mystery of biblical revelation must deal with degrees of accountability and the gradations of guilt. These topics were in the forefront of Hitch's cinematic attention. Not many theologians or biblical scholars have treated the bold theme of Christ's androgynous nature and the feminine Christ-figure types in literature and the popular arts.

Returning to the "wrong-man" theme as a spiritual analogue of the Christ, we see that *I Confess* and *The Wrong Man* are

In *The Wrong Man,* Henry Fonda plays bass, suggesting Hitchcock's body outline. Recall his cameo in *Strangers on a Train;* he boards a train with a double bass.

Hitchcock's two most explicitly Catholic, indeed Jesuit, films. In *I Confess,* Fr. Michael Logan (Montgomery Clift) is falsely accused of murder. Although a motive was present, Fr. Logan is presented from the outset as innocent. It is he who hears the killer's confession, thereby being prevented by the seal of confession from defending himself.

Both these films—*I Confess* and *The Wrong Man*—are explicitly religious in nature. Study each film carefully, and you will start to recognize the supernatural frame of reference pointing to Hitchcock's preoccupation with Christ as the "wrong man." Both films deal with crimes that are seen not only as illegal but also as spiritual offenses. In each film the criminal is aware that an innocent man is suffering unjustly for crimes that are at the same time illegal and sinful.

The larger context of the films supports the interpretation

of the "wrong man" as a Christ reference, for both Fr. Logan (*I Confess*) and Emmanuel Balestrero (*The Wrong Man*) are not only legally wronged, they are saintly, long-suffering types, unambiguous parallels to the victim Christ. Each film has narrative signals alluding to Christ: either the Way of the Cross or an image of the Sacred Heart. Other films treat the same "wrong-man" theme, but more obliquely, for innocence is only partial.[2] Since the law does not prosecute religious or moral offenses unless they are also in violation of statutes or ordinances, it is important to distinguish in Hitchcock films between the legal domain (the external forum of behavior) and the spiritual realm (the internal forum of intentionality which evades conclusive evidentiary proof).

A parallel can be seen between *The Lodger* and *Suspicion,* in which Hitchcock used a happy ending uncalled for in the novel upon which the film was based, because he claimed that the audience would never accept Cary Grant as a murderer. Thus the revised screenplay made the wife, Lina McLaidlaw (Joan Fontaine), seem paranoid, a creature of exaggerated fears, leaving Cary Grant's Johnny Aysgarth as a sympathetic type of the "wrong man." Hitchcock would have preferred to use the novel's ending in which Johnny kills Lina with a glass of poisoned milk. In the book, Lina asks Johnny to post a letter in which she states her suspicions, thus incriminating her husband should she die by murder. The unknowing Johnny grins smugly as he deposits the letter in the mailbox—an ironic ending. Hitch revised the story to give Grant's character the appearance of a playboy, irresponsible and untrustworthy. Circumstances lead Lina to suspect that her husband is a murderer and that he is plotting to kill her. The suspense is Hitchcock at his best. In the final scene we see the couple riding in a car on a winding road atop a perilous promontory. Suddenly Lina's door, facing the cliff side, swings open. She panics as he reaches out. At first she is horror-struck. Her husband abruptly stops the car. The previous clues point to Johnny as a bad guy, a villain.

The audience is left wondering if her fright may not have led him to look for a less cruel way to dispatch her. The lobby posters publicizing the film read, "Each time they kissed, there was the thrill of love, the threat of murder!" More than one woman in the audience has felt that *she* would not choose to return home with such a husband. The ending is unsettling. One has an eerie sense that there could be a next time, that Johnny is looking for the opportune moment to commit murder. Hitchcock uses images, sounds, and music to undermine the literal meaning of the final scene.

On the surface, the character Grant plays is a type of innocent victim. But is he really? Hitchcock suggests two levels—a physical one of conduct and a more hidden one of motive and desire. The latter is equivocal, the former is univocal. If Lina sees her husband as a potential wife-killer, then Johnny Aysgarth could qualify as a "wronged" man but hardly as a Christ figure.

To the distinction between the executed deed and the intended purpose, Hitch added the motive of desired result, though independent of immoral or criminal intent. Consider *Strangers on a Train*. Bruno Anthony (Robert Walker) is a playboy with psychic conflicts and obvious homosexual leanings. On a train, he approaches a tennis celebrity, Guy Haines (Farley Granger), and suggests a murder-exchange plan. Bruno offers to murder Guy's wife if Guy agrees to murder Bruno's father. Although Guy refuses to take Bruno seriously, it is clear that Guy would be happy if his wife were out of the way. Bruno thinks he has a bargain and strangles Miriam Haines at an amusement park. He brings her shattered glasses to Guy as proof and insists that the companion murder be executed.

Hitch's Jesuit training in Latin very likely acquainted him with the expression *cui bono?* (in whose interest is an action?). Hitchcock suggests that Guy was culpable in terms of this principle. Since, willy-nilly, he is unjustly enriched, we may ask whether Guy is a classic "wrong man" worthy of exoneration. A long shadow of doubt is cast across his status as perfectly innocent, because he enjoys greater bliss now that he is free to marry a senator's daughter. The ending recalls *Blackmail* with its haunting feelings of guilty discomfort.

Using this key moral distinction between intention and deed, Hitchcock often probes beneath the surface of actions and studies a person's motivation and feelings. The moral irony of his films depends on an awareness of that distinction.

Through it, a difference can be established between what is photographed and what can be concluded by the audience from the subtle images and clues planted by the Master of Suspense.

Consider the final scene of *Spellbound,* a Freudian suspense thriller. When discovered by psychiatrist Ingrid Bergman, the culprit, Dr. Murchison (Leo Carroll) points a gun first at her (as she leaves the room), then at the screen—that is to say, at us in the audience. (An oversized pistol was employed to magnify the menace.) Hitch definitely wished to have the spectators identify with the "wrong person." We, the audience, feel our innocence and resentfully recoil from being arbitrarily "killed" without judicial procedure or motivation. Here Hitchcock mingles fear with black whimsy, the formula of fright and delight learned from his Jesuit mentors.

The tables are quickly turned as Hitchcock makes us feel like psychological accomplices in the doctor's suicide. Carroll points the revolver at his head and pulls the trigger; a Technicolor red frame appears to give us, the audience, the sensation of blood. For a split second we feel relief that he killed himself and not us. This unusual twist on making each member of the audience feel like the "wrong person" dates back to 1903 when a similar scene was first used in *The Great Train Robbery.* This scene is a precious use of preconception, extremely self-conscious, and generates less real emotion than intended. Hitch could sometimes be too subtle, and at other times indiscreet.

The most complex type of "wrong" character in Hitch's filmology is, to my mind, Cary Grant's adman, Roger O. Thornhill, in *North by Northwest.* Recall Cary Grant's role in *Suspicion* as Johnny Aysgarth. His wife suspected him, not of infidelity, but of murderous designs. The film's ending is ambiguous. Is he the "wrong man" or not? Hitch purposely leaves the question open. If, in that film, Cary Grant is under a small black cloud of moral inauthenticity, Hitch leaves no stone unturned in *North by Northwest* to present Thornhill as unscrupulous, rudely insensitive, and a perceived liar (in the opening scene in a taxicab, which Thornhill has mendaciously wrested from a gullible pedestrian, his secretary flatly faults him with being a "liar"; in the penultimate scene on Mt. Rushmore, Eve [Eva Marie Saint] calls him "liar").

Can this scoundrel, dedicated to the principle of the permissible lie, be the "wrong man"? Yes, when he is mortally imperiled for being George Kaplan, a decoy planted by a U.S. intelligence agency and pursued by a foreign spy ring. (Hitch does not specifically mention the country, but the reference to Glen Cove hints that it was the Soviets, who at the time had a mission in that town on northern Long Island, New York. Hence, I shall be referring to the spy ring, headed by James Mason's Vandamm, as crypto-Russian.) True, Roger Thornhill is portrayed as an egotistical "taker," but his moral flaws swiftly recede in our memory, eclipsed by the cruel threat to his life and country. Suddenly, Cary Grant's character is catapulted into the domain of international crime and

In *North by Northwest,* Cary Grant, the "wrong man," drops from a blank fired by Eva Marie Saint. "Things are not as they seem!"

conspiracy, an astronomically higher immorality which shrinks his shortcomings to negligible peccadillos. If our sympathies were earlier with the victims of Thornhill's scams, now they are squarely on his side when contrasted with dirty tricks and assassination.

North by Northwest is full of allusions generally overlooked by viewers and critics. A subliminal key to understanding the meliorism of the picture is that Thornhill's initials are R.O.T.—as printed on his matchcover. During the dining car scene, Eve, a tease, asks Thornhill what the "O" stands for as he offers her a match to light her cigarette. He replies, "Nothing." This is a trenchant clue to his character. The plot and Thornhill's persona have two levels: first, corruption in the business world of consumer advertising, and second, the callousness of the foreign and domestic covert operators on both sides of the Cold War. (In a policy conference, the Professor [Leo G. Carroll] is called "callous" by a colleague and admits to it readily.) The risk of life and reputation spurs Thornhill on to reach deep inside himself for strengths and degrees of courage his calling had not hitherto demanded of him. He is improving morally, developing spiritually, all the while facing death.

At first, he is bitterly disappointed with Eve, who sets him up to be assassinated in the Kansas cornfields. Those immortal scenes of nerve-tingling suspense, with Grant's Thornhill surviving a menacing crop-dusting plane and an onrushing oil truck, establish him as a secular analogue of Christ. As transformed—even religiously transfigured—he can now drop his defensive stance and begin a moral offensive in terms of redeeming his country and the morally compromised woman to whom he is obviously attracted. He is in love with her but angrily disenchanted: not only has she callously jeopardized his life, but she is, in his mind at least, a tool of the crypto-Russians. He discovers her in the company of Vandamm at a public auction, where the latter bids for and acquires the pagan statuette containing state secrets which can be used against U.S. national security.

Eve is seen in a red dress, not the black garb of earlier

scenes. Is she a scarlet woman? Thornhill's bitter diatribe cuts her to the quick. He alludes to her giving her all, even her body, to the cause. This suggests political prostitution, and the astute biblically trained viewer might link her red dress with the Book of Revelation (17:4–7): "I saw a woman sitting on a scarlet beast . . . arrayed in purple and scarlet . . . and drunk with the blood of the saints and the martyrs of Jesus." She is obviously touched, despite an understandably angry response. Since she is an agent for the U.S. government, we presume her repentance for subordinating love (Thornhill) to duty (national security). He saves her soul. Later, he learns she is a double agent working for the Professor and fears for her life at the hands of Vandamm. With a chivalrous spirit, he rescues her in another classic scene on Mt. Rushmore, pulling her to safety from her precarious, dangling position.

One other distinction should be made in Hitchcock's films— that between the *"wrong"* man and the *"wronged"* man. The "wrong" men generally end up cleared of any blame and are stronger for the experience. The "wronged" men, however, suffer the lasting consequences of evil inflicted upon them, e.g., Henry Fonda's Manny Balestrero remains "wronged" due to the earlier mental stress on his wife (Vera Miles). Within the "wrong-man" theme of Hitchcock, therefore, is the sacred notion of a victim. Any unjust suffering implies victimage, which in turn calls forth one of several responses: bitter resignation, active vindictiveness, conformity to a higher mysterious plan of divine providence, or a letting-go motivated by the therapeutic principle of positive thinking as the path to inner peace.

An excellent case study of this distinction is that of the falsely accused Richard Blaney (Jon Finch) in *Frenzy*. The entire film deals with the betrayal by a friend, Bob Rusk (Barry Foster), a sick rapist and killer of women. He attacks and strangles Blaney's former wife in her matrimonial bureau and later a co-worker at the pub where Blaney once was employed. Imprisoned for the crimes committed by his "mate" Rusk, Blaney ingeniously escapes, as eager for personal revenge as for exoneration. He enters Rusk's room, prepared to bludgeon the blanketed figure in the bed, when he is shocked to find Rusk's latest victim. A Scotland Yard inspector arrives; both hide as they hear heavy thuds and footfalls on the stairs. Rusk enters with a steamer trunk to use as a makeshift coffin to cart the body away. The inspector surprises him and says, with typical British understatement, "Why Mr. Rusk—you're not wearing your tie." (Rusk had used his tie to garrote his victims.) The scene spells out Blaney's instantaneous exoneration, but leaves him with a sense of emotional loss, an unexpressed anger, and a dubious future. In short, he is wronged and will need time for complete healing to overcome his disorientation. Shades of Henry Fonda's "wrong man!"

Recall that earlier I mentioned that Hitchcock's self-image disposed him to see himself as a type of the "wrong man." Since Hitchcock's films were so personal, so carefully planned, and so full of subliminal meanings, one might ask, What response did he make? I cannot say. I believe that he had a theological conviction about false labeling, that integral to the primeval disorder of original sin is the inclination to judge unjustly by superficial circumstances and physical appearance. At the same time, I find it supremely ironic that, while resenting the general bias against obesity, he himself saw beautiful blond women as irresistibly desirable, passing over other tests of character. He should have been more consistent in his understanding that beautiful women are not necessarily as they appear.

It is noteworthy that Hitchcock cast his own daughter, Patricia, in three significant minor roles as a comely but witty foil for Jane Wyman (*Stage Fright*), Ruth Roman (*Strangers on a Train*), and Janet Leigh (*Psycho*). One comment on Janet Leigh's volatile short-lived role in *Psycho*. We first meet her as the "wrong woman" in an affair with a married man. She steals money to finance his divorce. Now she becomes in the legal sense a "wrong woman," motivated by passion. When she repents and turns "right," she dies in the shower, morally and physically cleansed. Now she becomes a spiritual victim and again a "wrong woman." In effect, she passes through three different phases of Hitch's "wrong-person" theme: moral, legal, and theological. This observation invites sustained reflection. Indeed, *Psycho* merits a triple viewing, as Hitchcock recommended for many of his more personal pictures.

That Hitchcock flawed his leading men's characters is a clue to his own sensitivity to the principle that things are not as they seem. Cary Grant looks different in *Suspicion, Notorious,* and *North by Northwest* than in Howard Hawks's *Only Angels Have Wings* and *Bringing Up Baby.* In the Hitchcock films, Grant is a negative-type personality. Take *North by Northwest.* Audiences accepted, all too gullibly, the insufficiently motivated leaps in character development of a basically shallow man. Hitchcock exploits Cary Grant's Teflon-coated screen persona: he cannot be willfully drunk; he cannot die; he cannot murder. However, he can be lazy; he can lie; he can be a philanderer. These "minor" vices seem forgivable. Or take Jimmy Stewart, who also looks much different in Hitch movies than as the "golly-gee-whiz" characters he played in Frank Capra's classics, *Mr. Smith Goes to Washington* and *It's a Wonderful Life.* In *Rope,* he's a Nietzschean philosopher; in *Rear Window* he's a voyeur; in *Vertigo* he's a necrophiliac. Hitch's understanding of human nature and mass visual communications brought him to the point in his Hollywood career where he could secure audience identification with his personally perplexing concerns and compassionate ethic through the judicious employment of intensely attractive box-office stars. Even Joseph Cotten's bluebeard killer in *Shadow of a Doubt* is a far cry from his role in *Citizen Kane.*

Hitch knew he was casting Cary Grant, Jimmy Stewart, and even Joseph Cotten against type. Hitch "wronged" established good-guy types, then made them "right" through struggle. This reflects his Jesuit years at Saint Ignatius College and the religious meditations on Christ's suffering and death as necessary to make sinners "right." Indeed, things are not as they seem. A sensitive, overweight schoolboy would have identified with that, especially when put in jail for a short period by his father's jailer friend (as a jesting lesson to teach him to behave) or when punished with the leather thong by the Jesuit prefect of discipline. The "wrong-man" theme is deeply imprinted in the frames of Hitchcock's films and in his own psyche.

Notes

1. The twenty-one films are *The Lodger, Downhill, Easy Virtue, Blackmail, Murder!, The 39 Steps, Secret Agent, Young and Innocent, Suspicion, Saboteur, Spellbound, Notorious, Stage Fright, I Confess, To Catch a Thief, The Wrong Man, North by Northwest, Psycho, Marnie, Frenzy,* and *Family Plot.*
2. See Neil Hurley, "Soul in Suspense: Catholic/Jesuit Influences on Hitchcock," *Daily Variety—54th Anniversary Issue* (October 27, 1987), pp. 140ff.

CHAPTER V

Mysticism of Spirals and Lines

Hitchcock used the elements of time and space to heighten suspense and to focus on the inner world of his characters; he borrowed forms and allusions from geometry and arithmetic, using them with the skill of an architect. The education he received at Saint Ignatius College, with its stress on logic and Jesuit spirituality, prepared him for this type of balanced expression, using asymmetry to denote disorder and chaos. The *Spiritual Exercises,* the Jesuits' handbook of spiritual direction to seek God's will, is divided symmetrically over a four-week period, with the daily programs arranged with deliberate geometrical precision. The formal meditations always follow the same pattern and sequence:

- three preludes, or introductory points, designed to help the participants enter into the spirit of the meditation;
- an examination of conscience, aimed at discovering personal weaknesses;
- three points focusing on some aspect of the life of Christ; and
- a conclusion, consisting of a spiritual lesson drawn from the meditation and an appropriate resolution.

There is a consistency, both arithmetically and structurally, that permeates Hitchcock's work, particularly his silent films, which reveals a preoccupation with balance and geometrical forms. The director was conscious that he had "a rectangle to fill."[1] Maurice Yacowar has inventoried the many geometric allusions in Hitch's pioneer stage of apprenticeship. Take *The Lodger,* with its triplets and triangular references: the title, with its illumination effect of a triangle; the Avenger's "A" with the omitted bottom legs; the traced triangle of the search map; and a love triangle—Joe, Daisy and the lodger. There are also circular objects: the handcuffs, the stage of concentric circles, and the spiral staircase. In *Downhill* (1927) Ivor Novello plays a schoolboy who falls from social grace, tracing a descent similar to that of the series of engravings by Hogarth called *The Rake's Progress*. He marries a well-to-do woman. The boudoir shows a triple set of neo-Gothic arched doors recalling the classy prep school from which he was expelled and also suggesting a triptych of linked church doors.

It is, however, with *The Ring* that Hitchcock manifests dramatic influences traceable to religious symbolism and Ignatian rhetorical devices. Yacowar is extremely thorough in his analysis, pointing out that though the "three basic images in the film are the rectangle, the circle, and the arc," nonetheless "the film flows as an easy narrative with none of these shapes obtrusive."[2] There is a triangle: a circus midway fighter, Jack Sanders, who challenges all comers; his girl, Nelly, who sells tickets; and an Australian professional heavyweight champion, Bob Corby, who knocks down Sanders. Nelly is attracted to Corby. (Women in Hitch's early films—*The Lodger, Champagne, The Manxman, Blackmail, Rich and Strange*—have heads that are extremely easy to turn.)

One has no trouble proving intent in reviewing such objects as upward arching swings, the swingers' panoramic view, the barker's drumlike mouth in close-up, the clown's mouth in a target game, the fighter's water bucket, the merry-go-round, the fortune-teller's ring of cards, Corby's conspicuous yawn when the parson says "till death us do part," the fallen button, champagne glasses, rounded furniture, a circular box of chocolates, the nightclub's round tables, and the bass drum. Yacowar goes on to note arcs—a horseshoe, a gypsy's pendant earrings, a wishbone—but then highlights the wedding ring and the coiled bracelet, "emblematic of serpentine temptation and the fall from innocence."[3] (François Truffaut agrees that the bracelet is a clear reference to the serpent in the Genesis account of the Garden of Eden.)

In *The Manxman* Hitchcock uses odd rock formations, angular and rough, to overshadow lovers who must meet in secrecy. Betrothed to another, Kate goes in search of her true love, Philip. Leaving the inn, she walks along a coastal promontory beneath a cloudy sky. We see her lover framed within an irregularly shaped opening in the crags. Odd geometric shapes mingle with circles and arcs discernible in the sky, the rocks, and the water's ebb and flow. It is a mystical and delicate scene with "seven shots in a row where the lovers are overwhelmed by the rock formations," reduced in comparative size by the majestic, indifferent fortress of nature all about them.[4]

A good example of Hitchcock's genius for balanced expression can be found in *Vertigo*. The opening scene and the recurring use of circles and spirals are sense-related symbols aimed at making the audience lose the security of boundaries. As the film opens, we see a woman's face. The camera moves in first to her lips, then to her eyes, which glance anxiously left and right. As the camera moves to a focused shot of the right eye, catching a small tear on the lower lid, a psychedelic pattern emerges as the audience seems to enter the pupil with a spiraling movement. This technique of spiral movement from exteriors to interiors, used a number of times in this and other films, creates vertigo, or a disordered state in which individuals or their surroundings seem to whirl dizzily.

We saw that Hitchcock's symbolic use of circles and arcs abounded in *The Ring* (1972). A generous use of geometric references through camera movements and visionary allusions mark *The Wrong Man*. A key scene depicts the innocent victim (Henry Fonda) being thrust into a prison cell. The camera rotates to convey to the audience the vertigo he feels at bearing an unjust sentence. Thus, circles and spirals help change the way Hitchcock wants his audience to look at reality. Odd camera angles also create moods of anxiety—even agony, as in the final scene in *The Wrong Man*. Circular staircases, peepholes, binoculars, photographic lenses, and other eye motifs are found in *Suspicion, Notorious, Strangers on a Train, Rear Window, I Confess, The Wrong Man, Vertigo, Psycho, Topaz,* and *Frenzy. Family Plot* shows Bruce Dern steering a brakeless car down a steep, spiraling road. Barbara

I Confess opens with Hitch in a hellish cameo scene. The crosses suggest a cemetery.

Harris's awkward but humorous physical reactions humanize the horror of the dizzying, circular, and uncontrolled fall.

Hitch inclined to circular patterns in his film plots:

- *The Lodger* opens and closes with a flashing neon sign advertising hair dye ("Tonight Golden Curls").
- *Downhill* symbolizes the moral descent of Roddy, a disgraced schoolboy, who is restored to grace in the last scene as we see him back at the school where the film opened.
- *Easy Virtue* opens with a downward view of the part in a British judge's powdered wig, as he sleepily presides over a divorce trial. The next-to-last scene repeats the shot.

- *Champagne* begins and ends with a suspicious, mustachioed man leering through a tilted cocktail glass of champagne.
- *The Manxman* opens and closes with sailboats carrying fishermen on the Irish Sea.
- In *The Skin Game,* the first shot shows three men chopping down a tree in a grove; the last shows a tree being toppled.
- *The Man Who Knew Too Much* begins with a snowy ski slope and ends with a sloping roof at night.
- *The 39 Steps* stresses circularity (start and finish) by showing Robert Donat in a vaudeville theater.
- *Sabotage* begins and ends with people leaving a movie theater in London.
- *Young and Innocent* opens with the music of "The Drummer Man." After the drummer man, a murderer, confesses, we hear not only the music but also the ironic lyrics:

> I am right here to tell you, mister,
> No one can, like the drummer man!

- *Strangers on a Train* begins and ends with Guy Haines (Farley Granger) on a train, meeting someone who strikes up a friendly conversation.
- *I Confess* returns to the opening confessional scene, with Fr. Logan (Montgomery Clift) hearing the confession of the murderer, Otto Keller (O. E. Hasse), who now, with his last breath, is truly repentant, unlike his earlier attitude.
- *North by Northwest* has a subliminal circularity in the monumentality of the office tower at the beginning and Mt. Rushmore at the end, with Bernard Herrmann's discordant musical score and the very early reference to Cary Grant's adman being a "liar" repeated at the end.
- In *Torn Curtain,* the story begins and ends in Scandinavia, although the main action takes place in Central Europe.
- *Topaz* opens and closes with the very same scene: a May Day parade.

Let us now analyze *Shadow of a Doubt* in terms of multiple levels of balance and parallelism. Throughout, the film corroborates that the sweet country girl Charlie is the moral twin of her nefarious Uncle Charlie, who is defined as a demonic presence by the smoke of both the train and the cigarette hanging over him at the rail station of Santa Rosa. William Rothman in *Hitchcock: The Murderous Gaze* sheds much light on patterns reflected back and forth between the two Charlies. Three trenchant visual clues establish a balanced relationship binding the niece and uncle together as doubles (the doppelgänger theme).

The first clue shows Uncle Charlie reclining on a bed in a seedy Philadelphia boardinghouse and then cuts to niece Charlie lying on her bed in her California hometown. Each is

Vandamm (James Mason), symbol of evil, with Eve, and a fallen Adam, adman Cary Grant (*North by Northwest*). The tired Grant carried the film. He looks strained.

pensive and in apparent need of completion through the other. He telegraphs that he is coming, and she is overjoyed. The second clue is provided upon his arrival at the railroad depot. Upon seeing each other, they eagerly hurry forward: matching frontal shots of each link one with the other in terms of frame composition and facial expression. We see Uncle Charlie, with three-piece suit, tie, fedora, and cane, hurrying forward with a broad smile. Also seen frontally is Charlie, coming from the opposite direction; she is dressed plainly and is also smiling. Their warm embrace anchors the symbolism of a union which will grow progressively darker as the film unfolds. The third clue turns up in the penultimate scene where Uncle Charlie forcibly keeps his niece on the moving train as he departs from Santa Rosa. Viewers hold their breath as he opens the train door and we see the blurred landscape and rails moving by swifter and swifter. Somehow—and a bit implausibly—Charlie turns the tables on her uncle and shoves him out the door. Rothman gives strong visual proof that perhaps Uncle Charlie intended his death at her hands, thus consummating a forbidden relationship of incest implied by many phallic symbols which Rothman points out in the course of the film. I agree with Rothman that Charlie grows into a woman with lost innocence and awareness of her complicity in a moral kinship with her murderous uncle. Certainly, before she expels him, their feet are seen intertwined in a suggestive sexual union—two persons in one flesh.

Circular plot development suggests harmony and completeness, so that disorder is more shockingly revealed when seen against it. Both Jesuit spirituality and Hitchcock's films use a point/counterpoint dialectic of good mingled with evil (as contrasted with Victorian morality—good versus evil). Thus, when Hitchcock wanted to give his audience a brutal shock, he denied its expectation for harmony, order, and circular satisfaction. *Easy Virtue* (1927) is a fascinating instance of circularity, exceptional in that the maligned woman sinks further in terms of social disrepute at the end, which concludes with her second unfair divorce. Or, take *Frenzy*: we believe that Richard Blaney (Jon Finch) is guilty of a sexually motivated murder because the first time we see him he is putting on a telltale fraternity tie pin like the one used to garrote a woman. In *Sabotage,* a small boy unwittingly carries a bomb onto a bus. The audience knows it will go off at 1:45 P.M. We expect a happy intervention. It never comes. The boy, a matronly woman with a lap dog, and the other passengers are blown to bits. In his zeal to convey the ruthlessness of terrorists, Hitch frustrated the audience's normal desire for a happy resolution. *The Wrong Man* also lacks a neat Hollywood ending—though exonerated, the husband (Henry Fonda) must care for his mentally disturbed wife (Vera Miles) following her breakdown caused by his false arrest and imprisonment. Following *The Wrong Man,* Hitchcock became bolder in portraying shocking scenes of innocent suffering and disorder in *Vertigo, Psycho, The Birds,* and *Frenzy,* films which deny circular completeness and leave the audience panting for some rosy resolution.

Seen as a whole, Hitch's motion pictures together provide the deep psychic satisfaction of struggle rewarded (meliorism) and the happy ending (secular version of the resurrection). True, the Ignatian *Exercises* induce the shock of personal recognition, lowering the barriers of self-serving interests and defensive ego concerns—in short, all those rationalizations which veil departures from conscience and the norms of biblical revelation. However, the *Exercises* pushes beyond the void: the First Week meditations on the sins of the fallen angels, on Adam and Eve, and on one mortal sin by a hypothetical person who dies suddenly. By contrast, Hitch startles precisely by destroying symmetry, circularity, and a desire for a happy ending, as in *Torn Curtain* with its flame-engulfed opening scene under the credits. As the *Exercises* progresses psychologically in a rhythm of desolation and consolation ("Rules for the Discernment of Spirits"), so too Hitchcock's films must not be looked at in terms of single scenes and independent movies but placed within the total context of his fifty-three pictures.[5]

In the First Week of the *Exercises,* Saint Ignatius proposes the "Examen of Conscience" to review one's life in order to assess religious fidelity. The examination consists of a general review of one's spiritual life and a particular examen regarding a dominant fault to be diminished or eradicated by the principle of opposing it with the contrasting virtue. What is relevant to this study is the fact that the book of Ignatian *Exercises* diagrams a method for recording progress made either against a sinful habit or in cultivation of a specific virtue. There are different strategems ("Additions") to help the process of sanctification. The first is touching one's breast each time the fault is committed or the virtue is practiced. The second advises using lines as a standard of comparison for measuring progress or decline, whether on a daily, weekly, or monthly basis. Horizontal lines can be spaced to represent a ladder image for visually charting spiritual progress or lack thereof:

————

————

————

————

Among Hitch's fifty-three films, the image of ascent and descent is a recurring motif, from *The Lodger* down to the last scene in *Family Plot*. One can alternatively place vertical strokes, one after another, every time the fault or virtue is incurred. Now the image for examining conscience illustrates a "picket fence" motif:

||||||

I presume that Hitchcock would have been familiar with the ascetical visual practices of the descent-and-ascent model and the horizontal marks. Later, as an apprentice engineer and art designer, Hitch dealt professionally with similar geometrical graphics. The ladder design and the picket-fence motif cannot be ruled out as influences on several moody expressionistic themes in *Number Seventeen, Foreign Correspondent, Suspicion, Spellbound, Notorious, Strangers on a Train, Vertigo, Psycho, The Birds,* and *Frenzy.*

Let us consider the nefarious uses of geometrical visuals. In *Hitchcock: The Murderous Gaze*, William Rothman repeatedly refers to what he terms the "parallel-vertical-line" motif, whereby there is in a scene a type of "picket fence" pattern, generally signifying imprisonment. I am indebted to Rothman's study for pointing out this striking and unsettling motif in the five films he chose to analyze: *The Lodger, Murder!*, *The 39 Steps, Shadow of a Doubt*, and *Psycho*.[6] In addition to these films, the picket fence motif (either slightly tilted to the right or vertically upright) is discernible in *Spellbound, The Wrong Man*, and *Torn Curtain*. A referral to the Ignatian *Exercises* will confirm that geometrical visual aids are a psychological incentive to improve one's moral character and to come closer to imitating Christ.

We should also consider the use of arcs, lines, and drawn figures for uplifting, hopeful moods. We must not lose sight of the fact that the Ignatian *Exercises* has an architectonic balance, complementing the darker themes of the First Week by offering hope in the Second Week's consoling meditations on Christ's person and mission. So too Hitch's dark films offer thin rays of hope. *Psycho* ends with a scene of the demented Norman Bates, obviously innocent of conscious evil (a scene not of judgment but rather of pity), followed by the hauling up of Marion Crane's car, which had been sunk by Norman. Coming out of the bog into the sunlight, the murky car symbolizes the inevitable revelation of the mystery of iniquity. Hitchcock points to a mystery that is omitted by the unconvincing explanation of the psychiatrist.

Then there is *Vertigo*: the final scene shows a distressed Scottie Ferguson with no hold on rationality. Following Judy's death, is he exorcised of his obsessive infatuation? We can only guess. He might possibly turn to Midge, symbol of a more diffuse type of nurturing love. Unlike so many Hitchcock films in which the lead characters can and do develop personally, the protagonists of *Psycho* and *Vertigo* inhabit a moral limbo. Wounded and desperate to be healed, they seek relief in their fantasies. We learn nothing about their childhood backgrounds. How did Norman Bates and Scottie Ferguson get that way? As we know very little of their distant past, so too we cannot predict their future. What we miss in both films are the bright rays of psychological reintegration through romantic solidarity found in *The Birds, Marnie,* and *Family Plot*—all marked by an ascending line of personal development. All Hitchcock scenarios focus on dark, menacing forces and then relieve the audience's anxieties by moral and legal vindication, as in the "wrong-man" films, by a deepening of individual character, by a blissful man-woman bonding, or by courageous sacrifice on behalf of the security of the community or state.

If generally the trajectory of Hitchcock's films is upward and melioristic, *The Wrong Man, Vertigo,* and *Psycho* run contrary to that directional thrust. The last chapter, posited *Frenzy* as a question-mark film, hinting at a possible happy ending in the future. Hitch's work, despite its dominant expressionistic style and substance, is in essence hopeful. The Hollywood happy ending is part of his film signature, but with an idiosyncratic twist that repeatedly clouds the final scene with a hint of future trouble, the reopening of Pandora's box. Despite the seeming triumph of chaos, Hitchcock consistently affirms man's potential to prevail against even the greatest odds. *The Wrong Man* raises the eternal question, "Why me?" *Vertigo* asks, "Is there only one real love made in heaven?" *Psycho* poses the query, "Do children bear the sins of their parents?" And *Frenzy* emphasizes that "passion" is part of "compassion." Following his Jesuit mentors, Hitch was interested in searching questions, confident that, when correctly posed, they would lead to valuable answers. Important was the quest based on an unswerving pursuit of evidence and the implications for a searching mind.

We should contrast *North by Northwest* with *Saboteur,* in which the movement is from west (Los Angeles) to east (New York City). Whereas *Saboteur* ends on a strong patriotic note, *North by Northwest* spoofs Mt. Rushmore—the national memorial in the Black Hills of South Dakota on which are carved gigantic faces of Washington, Jefferson, Lincoln, and Theodore Roosevelt—as a public relations stunt on behalf of great men. In fact, Hitchcock wanted Cary Grant's Thornhill to sneeze inside the nose of one of the presidents, but state and federal officials disapproved. There is no ethical back-

In the last scene of *Family Plot*, Barbara Harris, a spiritualist, winks at the audience, a more reassuring "last laugh" than the perverse smile on Norman Bates's face in *Psycho*.

bone to Roger O. Thornhill nor is there in *North by Northwest* that basic conviction which seventeen years earlier ran through *Saboteur*, with its defense of those democratic freedoms embodied in the Statue of Liberty.

In *North by Northwest*, Hitchcock reflected America's self-doubts in the intense Cold War years of the 1950s. It was an era of dirty tricks, double agentry, and blurred moral boundaries, the world of Graham Greene's and John le Carré's burned-out espionage types. Significantly, Hitchcock uses open spaces to indicate the new order of expediency and treachery: the murder in the U.N., the cornfield scene, the final Mt. Rushmore sequence. The use of space is different in *Saboteur* (1942). There is a more expansive sense of America in the cross-country pursuit and the death plunge of the villainous agent (Norman Lloyd) from the Statue of Liberty, a patriotic finale.

One of Hitchcock's favorite techniques was to create a feeling of rootlessness. Traveling horizontally in space and dangling vertically are dramatic suspense mechanisms for gaining audience attention—they indicate anxiety and the need for being anchored and at rest. Space is a psychological stratagem in the Ignatian *Exercises* also. The First Week involves three falls: Lucifer (the fallen angel); Adam; and the man dying, having committed one mortal sin. In the Second Week, we have the meditation on the plain of Babylon (Lucifer speaks to his minions) and the plain of Jerusalem (Christ calls his disciples). These are contrasted spaces and causes—even location signifies good versus evil.

Also in the *Exercises* are the contrasts of Christ's birth ("below the earth at Bethlehem") and death ("above the earth on the cross at Calvary"). Spatial contrasts—vertical and horizontal—are found throughout the *Exercises* and also in Hitchcock's films, suggesting not conscious causality but subliminal influences. Spatial dislocation and geographical discontinuity are evident in the Ignatian *Exercises,* where the retreatant is told to contemplate Jesus traveling, constantly, from town to town. Both *Saboteur* and *North by Northwest* show involuntary nomadism due to false labeling, thus setting up conditions for reviewing one's life and taking stock of priorities and purpose.

The dangling motif is shorthand for suspense, anxiety, danger, and the insecurity of spatial location. In *Psycho,* Hitchcock takes a place of comfort, the shower and turns it into a tiled sepulcher. The terror is mediated in a reversal of expectations of Marion Crane and the audience by means of revealing geometric touches. The reversed directions of the spraying water is seen falling from above and then hitting the upturned face of Marion standing in a rapturous pose. She is morally cleansed by virtue of her resolution to return the stolen money. The water brings more than physical purification; it is spiritual as well. The shower scene is the first time we see her relaxed, not under stress.

We go from falling water to falling knife to falling body. Marion Crane passes from victimizer to repentant thief to victim. The falling water turns to blood, as if to indicate the process of an involuntary sacrifice. We watch the victim's left hand slowly sliding down the tiles. Leaning against the wall, she then slides down into death. She reaches out for us—but we recoil. Seeking final support from the shower curtain, she rips it from the hooks and falls forward over the edge of the tub.

The next cut shows the downpour of cleansing water, then a close-up of Marion's blood spiraling down the drain. In one of cinema's most stunning lap dissolves, the spiraling blood becomes Marion's eye—the eye of a sacrificed animal—with the camera spinning outward from it. Something has gone out of control; the linear direction of the plot has been upset. We experience a disordered state of vertigo, with a helpless feeling and disgust before the force of evil.

The spiraling movement at the beginning of *Vertigo* is in the reverse direction; the movement is from outside the face to within the eye. *Psycho* should be seen as the companion film to *Vertigo,* since both treat better than Hitchcock's other films the nagging anxieties of sex, guilt, and death. Falling, running, and circling are the motifs of direction and geometrical design that Hitchcock used to point to what cannot be photographed or registered by a soundtrack.

There are circular staircases in both films. In *Psycho* the Bates's house has three floors, with the cellar the repository of dark secrets. In *Vertigo* we see the hills of San Francisco; there are constant references to heights and spirals. The audience and the characters experience the dizzy sensations of vertigo several times because of the use of techniques such as making a room spin around. Something similar happens in the final scene of *Strangers on a Train,* when Hitchcock puts us on a merry-go-round gone out of control. In *The Wrong Man,* Henry Fonda's Emmanuel Balestrero is put in a prison cell; the camera's clockwise spinning motion induces a feeling of chaos, suggesting the victim's Gethsemane-like agony. Through the centrifugal camera movements symbolizing disorder in *Strangers on a Train* and *The Wrong Man,* the audience experiences gratuitous horror, the thunderclap surprise of life being balanced precariously on a pinhead. In Hitchcock's best films, he is accusing the audience, shocking

In *Vertigo*, James Stewart rescues Kim Novak from San Francisco Bay—a veritable Pietà scene. This classic film is unsurpassed for tracing maniacal love from hypnotic origins to tragic bitter conclusion.

the viewers with the recognition that the potential for evil and dread lies in the depths of us all.

The beauty and symbolic links of Hitchcock's art and religious outlook can be missed by not paying attention to the feelings of danger from falling downward or swinging from a height. Dangling is a metaphor for the human condition, precarious and labile; it is not mere theatrical entertainment. In the early *Number Seventeen,* for instance, we see a man and woman handcuffed to a railing that collapses, leaving them suspended in midair. Such examples of physical danger can easily be seen to signify a fallen and sinful world. Hitchcock used heights and suspension as symbols of a conviction about the human race, described by John Henry Newman as implicated in some terrible "aboriginal calamity." This seems to be the sense of metaphysical imbalance with which we are left at the end of *Shadow of a Doubt, Strangers on a Train, The Wrong Man, Vertigo, Psycho, The Birds,* and *Marnie.*

Marnie ends on a note of hope, but the hope is a conditional one. The audience is led to believe that the same situations of peril could develop again. The gulls may return to the town they menaced in *The Birds;* perhaps the inner city Baltimore neighborhood will produce another Marnie. At the end of *Marnie,* the long street with a ship moored at the pier at the end seems to be a dead end; but it turns out to have a right and a left exit. The car that carries Mark and his recovering kleptomaniac wife to a hopeful tomorrow turns right—there is an exit which was heretofore unseen. This left/right escape route was a deliberate design and, I submit, suggests a cross, the horizontal axis of exits crossing the long, seemingly dead-end street and depicting a tau cross. In any event, the finale was carefully thought out in terms of subliminal effect. It offers a pleasing, optimistic note in a film with streaks of pessimism, suspicion, sexual innuendo, and cat-and-mouse strategies.

Regarding *Marnie,* why did Hitch choose this plot out of countless others? Though the reasons are not patent, speculation is inviting. Mine would revolve around three probable motives: (1) the mystery of childhood, the haphazard nature of it all, especially why one has the parents one has; (2) Hitch's interest in love across social boundaries, since he himself acquired success and wealth without having been born to it, and thus empathized with Marnie's acquired upper-class status, and; (3) the value of psychoanalysis to probe and cure psychic trauma together with a context of affectionate affirmation and strong hope. To support this last observation I appeal to a significant scene showing the distraught kleptomaniacal wife of Mark Rutland (Sean Connery) as she lies tormented in an ornate, canopied double bed. Having carefully studied this pivotal scene, I recognized two candles adorning a boudoir table in the background. Closer to the camera is a dressing table with two objects very similar to chalices. Furthermore, a cross is outlined on the door. This atmospheric set reminded me of the "Additions" which the *Spiritual Exercises* employs to condition the subconscious and create a congruent mood for the lessons to be imparted. The reader can judge whether we do not have a crossing over of sexual and sacred symbolism—a Mass chapel and a connubial chamber. (In his only romantic screwball comedy, *Mr. and Mrs. Smith,* Hitch has a crucifix on Carole Lombard's dresser in her spacious bedroom.)

The scene represents a breakthrough in communications between Mark and Marnie. He plays the amateur psychoanalyst, engaging her in free association. She taunts him with the caustic remark, "You Freud, me Jane!" Her instant responses to the cascade of his random topics reveal bits of evidence from her past. After she unreflectingly utters, "Washed in the blood of the Lamb," she becomes hysterical and he embraces her.

What follows answers for the audience questions that were raised in the early scenes. Our first sight of Marnie is of her back as she walks on a railroad platform; the camera cuts to her purse bulging with stolen money. Her criminal compulsiveness has sexual origins. On a stormy night in Baltimore, Marnie, as a preteen, killed a sailor, a client of her prostitute mother. Her traumatic memory of blood is reawakened either with the sight of the color red or when it rains and thunders. Her crimes are limited to stealing money (a phallic symbol) from the vaults of wealthy executives, thus avenging the victimization of herself and her mother by men seeking sex in exchange for money.

Mark Rutland, an aristocrat, has a chauvinistic attitude of possessiveness toward his wife.[7] He senses that she is emasculating rich men by putting their stolen money in her purse (a female genital symbol). The film definitely has a complex Freudian design with an overlay of Ignatian spirituality. Her reversal of moral direction follows the shooting of Forio, her favorite riding horse. She insists on firing the fatal shot herself. Here again we have a typical Hitchcockian blending of the sexual with the sacred. A living thing Marnie loves is wounded and must be exterminated. Later, when she tries to rob the Rutland safe of money belonging to her patrician husband, she finds she cannot take the neatly bound packet of bills—even when Mark catches her and tries to force her hand into the safe. This is a splendid instance of reversal of direction, or *agere contra*.

Marnie is cured by the passion of a suffering animal with which she is deeply identified. Are the rocking movements of her steeplechase horse, bounding over high hedges and wooden fences, a subliminal sexual allusion? Certainly the scene is long and seemed significant to Hitch. In any event, she is on the upward path of regeneration. The therapy culminates when Mark accompanies her to meet her mother, Mrs. Edgar (Louise Latham), in her humble Baltimore home. The revelation of Marnie's scarred childhood surfaces and the three persons, at first very nervous, become mellow and look toward a future of reconciliation and forgiveness. As Marnie and Mark leave, girls are seen singing a ditty on the street: "Doctor, Doctor, I am ill, send for the Doctor over the hill." Is Hitch indicating that there will always be traumatized children such as Marnie who yearn for healing? She trusts Mark and is no longer under that biblical curse, *Vae soli* ("woe to the solitary man!").

An underrated film, *Marnie* deserves to be ranked with three other female-identity-crisis films—*Blackmail, Shadow of a Doubt,* and *The Birds*—all showing progress through struggle.[8] *Marnie* merits study as a subtle motion picture, dense with symbolism and very personal to Hitchcock. His architectonic sense of visual composition, form, and geometric patterns is discernible. First we note seven scenes marked by the color red. Then we see the upward ascent (a Second Week conversion) in the free-association session with Mark in her bedroom. Christ's Passion in the Third Week is echoed symbolically in Marnie's grief at Forio's death at her hand. The family reconciliation qualifies as a happy ending, a type of resurrection. We see the port with its ships, a deliberately artificial backdrop to remind the spectator that it was, as Hitch was wont to say, "only a movie." The sudden right turn is an escape exit we did not expect. The scene recalls the ending of *The Birds,* with the reconciled family leaving the site of the fierce attacks by birds, now seen calm and cooing with a glowing sunset in the distance.

Jimmy Stewart has said that of all the directors under whom he worked, Hitchcock was the best prepared. He, as did James Joyce and Luis Buñuel, worked out a form of language to express his emotions and visions. Each sowed hidden meanings into the thematic surfaces of their art, challenging audiences and readers to see connections, to probe more deeply into the subtext. Whatever the criticisms of their Jesuit days, all three owed to their Ignatian-inspired formation the means of using sight as a creative stimulus to insight.

Symbolism runs throughout the work of all three—an impish, seemingly irreverent way of unmasking reality and its chameleonlike changes of form. Nevertheless, there are recurring signs of a respect for mystery and the force of intellectual light as a beacon capable of dispelling confusion, disorder, and sham. With Joyce and Buñuel, Hitchcock ranks as a demystifier of the conventional reality in daily, pedestrian experience and registered by the senses without further analytical pondering. The widespread use of circles, spirals, lines, and directions gives support to the thesis that Hitchcock knew what he was doing, if only instinctively, as the result of a learning process which stressed order, harmony, and purpose through spatial, geometric, and patterned imaging techniques.

Indeed, order is the objective of the *Spiritual Exercises* of Ignatius. Even photos of Hitchcock in his habitual conservative suit reveal his passion for order. To what degree did the strict Jesuit formation at an early age contribute to the architectonic style of patterned visual design and abrupt contrapuntal intrusions of disorder—at times personal, at times circumstantial, at times political, and on occasion cosmic? Certainly, there are numerous provocative parallels suggesting strong influences, if not outright causality.

In *The Films of Alfred Hitchcock,* Robert A. Harris and Michael S. Lasky observed that "for him *content* has never been as important as the accent on *technique* to make the content more interesting."[9] His early Jesuit training would have exposed him to a variety of rhetorical patterns of imagery adopted from both Jesuit spirituality and educational psychology. There, and in his filmology, we find clear evidence of two types of persuasion, one based on fear and the other based on hope. Similarly, there is present also a cyclical balance of fright and delight in terms of architectonic style: numbers, lines, circular repetitions, and unexpected chaotic reversals (as in the contrasting diagonal composition of the shower water and the opposing knife thrusts in *Psycho*).[10] Order and disorder make up Hitchcock's nervous, but fascinating, signature. The alternation of fright and delight in the Ignatian *Spiritual Exercises* and Jesuit pedagogy is a recurring and discernible pattern throughout the silent and sound films of Alfred Hitchcock.

Notes

1. Maurice Yacowar, *Hitchcock's British Films* (Hamden, Conn.: Archon Books, 1977), p. 29.
2. Ibid., pp. 59–60.
3. Ibid., p. 61.
4. Ibid., p. 94.
5. See "Rules for the Discernment of Spirits," in *The Spiritual Exercises of St. Ignatius* (Anthony Mattola, trans., with an introduction by Robert W. Gleason). (Garden City, N.Y.: Doubleday/Image Books, 1964), pp. 129–134.
6. The page references in Rothman's book are *The Lodger* (49), *Murder!* (59), *The 39 Steps* (139), *Shadow of a Doubt* (196, 211, 230), and *Psycho* (250, 265, 302, 306, 325, 331).
7. Michele Piso, "Mark's Marnie," in *A Hitchcock Reader,* Marshall Deutelbaum and Leland Poague, eds. (Ames: Iowa State University, 1986), pp. 288–303.

8. See Kay Sloan, "Three Hitchcock Heroines: The Domestication of Violence," *New Orleans Review* (Winter 1985), pp. 91–95.

9. Robert A. Harris and Michael S. Lasky, *The Films of Alfred Hitchcock* (Secaucus: Citadel Press, 1976), p. 1.

10. Rothman, *Hitchcock: The Murderous Gaze,* pp. 240ff.

CHAPTER VI

Mysticism of Numbers

Numerology is an esoteric science, going back to the ancient cultures of the Hindus, the Arabs, the Sumerians, the Egyptians, the Chinese, the Israelites, and the Phoenicians. The Greek philosopher Pythagoras founded a school in the late sixth century B.C. to use mathematics for deepening human knowledge with respect to divine laws governing the universe. Numerology presupposes an unmanifested unity (oneness) which binds together the immense plurality of apparently individualized entities. I am inclined to see a remarkable, even exceptional, note of unity in the final scene of *The Birds*. Hitch did not wish to use the almost obligatory title, "The End," to close the picture, but he was overruled. In the distance, we see a mild, very peaceful sunset; the birds seem content; the Brenner family and Melanie Daniels cautiously leave in a scene of loving solidarity which is unprecedented for Hitchcock. *The Birds* is an impressive fable about cosmic unity and its precariousness—to my mind a stunning contrast to his dualism, fragmentation, and intimations of division and pluralities. Things are not as they seem.

In short, unity is the precondition for the unfolding of numbers and their various meanings. In Chapter III, "The *Spiritual Exercises*," I spoke of "limited dualism," the difference between good and evil and the rivalry between them. Both the *Spiritual Exercises* and Hitch's filmology address themselves to this duality. Donald Spoto is excellent on this point in *The Dark Side of Genius*.[1] Spoto convinces me that the film *Shadow of a Doubt* mirrors the deep dualism Hitch felt within himself perhaps more keenly than the average person. After the death of the villainous Uncle Charlie

(Joseph Cotten), his alter ego niece Charlie (Teresa Wright) says: "He didn't trust people. He seemed to hate them. He hated the whole world. He said that people like us had no idea what the world was really like." To that, the detective (MacDonald Carey) responds: "It's not quite as bad as that. But sometimes it needs a lot of watching. It seems to go crazy every now and then. Like your Uncle Charlie." *Psycho* would later reprise this theme.

I accept Spoto's perceptive list of dual themes and dual camera insinuations throughout this remarkably disturbing but inspired film. I would add that Hitch's dualism at times seemed absolute, as did the Victorian and Puritan interpretative models, but that—deep down—his was the limited dualism of the Jesuit training he received. In that model evil is not discounted nor underestimated, but a countervailing good is postulated to match whatever the evil is, no matter how towering or taxing. I prefer to see Hitch not in terms of the two tragic Charlies (as Spoto seems to do), but rather in the two father figures, Herbie Hawkins (Hume Cronyn) and Joe Newton (Henry Travers). Both men discuss murder and the perfect crime, not recognizing the "Merry Widow" killer at a table in the same room. Like Hitchcock, both men are imaginatively and mentally involved, but not in terms of practical commitment.

I credit Hitch with irony, while admitting that he was a complex, troubled person. His work reflects his imagination more than does his life. His presence in his films must be part of his biography, for the secrets are there as well. His pictures often connect as well as contrast polar opposites: woman and man, child and parent, day and night, poor and rich and, finally, the national ideologies based on "us" versus "them" (as in his spy thrillers).

Psycho, to my mind, is a masterly study of duality, with *Vertigo* a close second. The scene in the Bates Motel front office is charged with paired symbols: two framed pictures, two candles, two stuffed birds and two personalities existing in one body and talking with a split, psychotic mind. Hitchcock's films reveal a keen interest in the subject of numerology (e.g., the number seven in *Spellbound*). Certainly, triadic references occupy a critical role in his work. Three refers to the Father, the Son, and the Holy Spirit. *The Lodger* (1920) begins with a shot of a woman's face silently screaming; three intermittent titles flash, "Tonight golden curls!" A search for the killer begins with a careening police van with two bobbies in the front seat. Seen from the rear, their backs look like the moving pupils of two eyes, the impression given by the two oval windows on the back door. In *Blackmail,* an artist is stabbed to death by a young woman resisting his advances. We see the portrait of a laughing clown. Her boyfriend, a policeman, shields her from a blackmailer. The clown painting appears three different times, a symbol of their pricked consciences. We have here two of the earliest uses of the sacred number three.

Rich and Strange (1932), a personal favorite of the Master of Suspense, studies a wealthy couple on a luxury cruise. The marriage becomes strained. The film features three telltale scenes in which the husband shows signs of nausea. Perhaps Hitchcock and his wife, Alma, made such a pleasure trip on which he became seasick (we know that she did on one occasion). At the end of *I Confess,* Fr. Logan (Montgomery Clift) absolves the dying, repentant Judas figure, solemnly making the trinitarian sign of the cross. The sacred number three recurs in the Ignatian *Exercises*: the meditations include three preludes and three points, i.e., highlights from Christ's life. In Chapter III, I referred to three mystical degrees of spiritual progress: the purgative, the illuminative, and the unitive. Whether Hegelian, Marxist, or Ignatian, all dialectic is essentially triadic, resting on thesis, antithesis, and synthesis (a composite result of the first two stages). The Ignatian *Exercises* is dialectical: first, original innocence (the sinless angels and Adam and Eve); second, the negation of that innocence through a fall; and last, a recovery of lost innocence through a regenerative faith in Christ's death and resurrection. As for Hitch's dialectic (thesis, antithesis, and synthesis), it goes like this: first, someone is charged with complicity in crime; second, this precipitates flight, anxiety, and peril; and last, the crime is solved and the accused is exculpated. *Frenzy* follows this triadic rhythm; by contrast, *Psycho* and *Vertigo* are notable exceptions to this dialectic, leaving the audience

In *Vertigo,* James Stewart embodies Hitch's fears about death, love, and religion. Look for three crosses, an example of the mysticism of "the triadic," as a recurring symbol.

perplexed and unfulfilled. The audience's unease is linked to the lingering, acute disorders of the protagonists as Hitch deliberately withholds the expected emotional release of the Hollywood-style happy ending. Both *Psycho* and *Vertigo* are special cases of impossible-love pathology, themes to which Hitchcock felt drawn. Uneasy but artistically brilliant works, the films deal with inverted relationships of withdrawal from possessive women (Barbara Bel Geddes as Midge in *Vertigo;* Mother Bates in *Psycho*) and impetuous acts of falling in love with beautiful women. There is no triadic balance, no normal relationship to women as either caring or affectionate creatures. I shall show in Chapter XIII that Hitch evolved beyond these two precarious studies of romantic introversion.

Psycho's three-storied Victorian mansion symbolizes the Freudian id (the basement), ego (the ground floor), and superego (Mother Bates's upper room). Norman lives in the attic—beyond reality.

There is no fulcrum to support the overexerted imaginations of Scottie Ferguson and Norman Bates. Both films lack the dialectic balance of the Ignatian *Exercises* because they have no triad of disorder, countervailing effort, and healing. Rather, they exhibit only the negative state of the First Week of the Ignatian *Exercises*: alienation, lack of direction, and hellish despair and shock. The failed love relationships in both films represent falling, in romantic and spiritual terms as well. The Ignatian *Exercises* and the rules of the society of Jesus pay but scant attention to the Sixth and Ninth Commandments. Both these commandments, however, are central to the work of Hitchcock. Integral to Hitchcock's film signature are allusions to a fallen world; unlike the Ignatian *Exercises,* but following its dynamic, Hitch studies the *dis*-ease of impossible loves. These manqué relationships are seldom treated in cinema so often as are falling in and out of love. Love is not only a many-splendored thing, it has the ability to punish in a variety of psychospiritual ways.

Like *Psycho* and *Vertigo, Frenzy* paints a picture of a fallen world which keeps falling. However, unlike the two earlier studies of mental illness, the third film points the audience beyond the purgative way toward the illuminative path. Too few critics have seen that *Frenzy* subtly hints at spiritual hope. I see a triadic pattern in the exoneration of Blaney as the "wrong man," accused of and arrested for the rapes and murders committed by his friend Bob Rusk. After Blaney escapes from prison, he finally meets the police inspector, who has also tracked Rusk to his lair. Both hear muffled thuds. In typical Hitchcock fashion, this dramatic, although

In *Frenzy* Jon Finch views his split mirror-image, a dark trinity of his troubled "wrong man" self.

improbable, scene mixes sex with religion. Rusk enters with a huge black steamer trunk to cart away the strangled woman, whose nude body lies under the blanket. Startled by the sight of Blaney and the inspector, he surrenders without resistance. The camera cuts to the coffinlike trunk; the audience, if attentive, can discern the outline of a cross on its lid. (Critics have overlooked Hitch's penchant for subliminal references to the cross, going back to *The Manxman* [1929]).

Why the symbol of the cross, faint but discernible? Can it be interpreted in any other way than as a deliberately planted clue? The allusion certainly provides *Frenzy* with a hesitant line of ascent (unlike the gloomy descent in *Psycho* and *Vertigo*). Will Blaney be healed? His former wife and a dear woman friend have been murdered. He seems alone. I interpret the last scene not as a resurrection symbol, but as an ambiguous happy ending. Each viewer must fill in the blanks of a cross allusion that is unmistakably there. We are clearly in the realm of relative, subjective interpretation, but once again Hitch smuggles in a faint narrative signal, perplexing as to his meaning and provocative as to ours.

Frenzy presents us with a triad: unjust accusation; aborted revenge; and an open future relatively unencumbered by the past. *Frenzy* surpasses both *Vertigo* and *Psycho* by evidencing Hitchcock's understanding that the depth of evil needs to be tempered by hope and faith. Again, the Master of Suspense proved to be ahead of where critics and film analysts believed him to be. Giddiness and loss of perspective is as central to *Vertigo* as later it will be to *Frenzy*.

There are also triadic patterns of a biblical nature, suggesting innocence, fall, and redemption. This could signify the celebrated happy ending (though, with Hitch, they could be ironic and even ominous). Examples can be found in *Blackmail, Sabotage, Notorious, The Paradine Case, I Confess, The Wrong Man*, and *Frenzy*. Donald Spoto makes an interesting observation regarding *Shadow of a Doubt*. He points out that Hitchcock alluded to his own dying mother "in the unseen and ill Mrs. Hawkins, of whom characters speak with concern three times."[2] There is also a mystical aura surrounding the three falls in *Vertigo*. In *The Wrong Man*, the falsely accused Manny Balestrero (Henry Fonda) possesses a rosary, which

appears in three separate scenes. Again, it is hardly coinciden-
tal that in *The Trouble with Harry* the dead body is dug up
three times. Is this an indirect reference to the resurrection of
Christ? Harry's body is treble trouble, an uninvited guest, like
Banquo, at nature's autumnal feast. Harry's corpse teaches us
much about the Vermont villagers, their fears, avoidances,
and desires. Surnamed Warp, Harry does not fit into their
predictable daily lives. In *Psycho*'s shower scene, Marion
Crane holds the attacker's arm as it spirals three times. Her
defense is futile.

The number three runs through the Bible, the *Spiritual
Exercises* of Ignatius, and the Christian imagination. In the
films of Hitchcock, one can argue convincingly that number
mysticism is present. Take *Foreign Correspondent*: the Dutch
diplomat, Van Meer (Albert Basserman), speaks lovingly of
birds on three distinct occasions. The references to birds here
and in *Sabotage* are, decidedly, not fear inspiring, unless we
consider the murderous Disney cartoon character in "Who
Killed Cock Robin?" Again, take *The Wrong Man*: in three
different scenes, the innocent victim is flanked by two persons
who are either authority figures or those suspicious of him.
Curiously, *North by Northwest* often shows the "wrong man"
(Cary Grant) flanked either by foreign agents or by police.

Consider the numbers thirteen and seven:

• Although he never completed it, the very first film
  Hitchcock worked on was called *Number Thirteen,* the
  most awesome of all superstitious numbers.
• In *The Lodger,* Hitch's first authentically personal film,
  the stranger uses the knocker on the front door of a
  boardinghouse marked with the number 13.
• In *The 39 Steps,* we have a multiple of thirteen ($3 \times 13 =
  39$).
• The pursued "wrong man" of *Young and Innocent* visits a
  flophouse to look for a tramp who has his overcoat. The
  number on the man's bed is twenty-six, posted in large
  numerals. Again, a multiple of thirteen.
• In *Strangers on a Train,* Hitch makes his appearance
  playing bridge in a train car. A close-up of his cards shows
  he is holding thirteen spades.

- In *Torn Curtain,* Michael Armstrong (Paul Newman) is instructed to turn to page 117 of a book to discover a clue. The page number is a multiple of thirteen: $9 \times 13 = 117$.

Seven is another mystical number. Significant in almost every culture, seven is used frequently in both the Old and New Testaments, where it means totality, fullness, completeness. The number seven is revealingly present in both Hitchcock's British and his Hollywood films. Here are some pertinent examples.

In *Secret Agent* (1935), a casino scene has the roulette wheel stopping at the number seven, shown in a dramatic close-up.

In Hitch's charming British romantic suspense thriller, *Young and Innocent* (1937), the title is borne out by the number of daylight scenes. Erica (Nova Pilbeam) matures through romance with a falsely accused murderer-on-the-run, young Robert Tisdall (Derrick de Marney). She grows in sympathy with the accused, comes to like him, and finally helps him to exonerate himself by identifying the real killer. This takes place in seven locations:

(1) On the open road, he is ready to help her, a Girl Guide whose car has stalled. Once she learns of the charge against him, she trusts the police, of whom her father is the local supervisor.

(2) Later, she witnesses the police arrest Robert in a mine shaft, and she grows sympathetic.

(3) At home, her father disapproves of her growing affection for Robert and banishes her to her bedroom. There she assumes a fetal position on the bed, only to see Robert's shadow after he climbs in her window. He has escaped, and she is now willing to help him.

(4) They hide out in a mill, a romantic locale (as in *The Manxman*), and love begins to bloom.

(5) Their flight together leads to a roadside café, where a group of truckers get into a fight. They leave the donnybrook to move on.

(6) Erica brings Robert to her cousin's birthday party, where children play blindman's buff. By introducing

Tisdall to her family, she runs a risk. Her aunt becomes suspicious.

(7) With the help of a kind hobo who once met the killer, the three set out for a grand hotel to locate the guilty man, a drummer who plays with a jazz band in the ballroom. There the culprit sees the police, actually in pursuit of Robert; the drummer, feeling trapped, confesses to Erica, thus creating the happy ending.

The seven milestones of Erica's independence from her father and her growing romantic interdependence with Robert are clear. Three of Alfred Hitchcock's Hollywood films are also marked by seven related events (*Spellbound, The Trouble with Harry,* and *Marnie*). I wish to add two other key pictures which I interpret as prudent applications of the seven motif (*Vertigo* and *The Birds*).

In *Spellbound,* a victim of amnesia (Gregory Peck) acts rather normal but is troubled whenever he sees parallel lines, such as a fork on linen or railroad tracks or stripes on a bathrobe. The mystery clues, which are psychological teasers, occur exactly seven times. Explicitly deliberate, Hitchcock always puts more in a film than one single viewing can detect. This is true of *Spellbound,* a highly contrived, so-so Hitchcock entry despite its star cast. However, attention must be paid to its subliminal elements.

Mystical reference numbers, such as seven, exert a subliminal influence, felt but not consciously understood. There are passing references to seven in *Foreign Correspondent* (1940). Edmund Gwenn points out tourist attractions to Joel McCrea from a church tower; if we add these verbal allusions to the pictorial landmarks, they total seven: London Bridge, Big Ben, Saint Paul's Cathedral, Saint James's Park, New Scotland Yard, Buckingham Palace, and the Houses of Parliament. In one scene, the hotel room assigned is number 7. In another, there is reference to a treaty clause—that's right, clause seven. Probably an unintentional use of the number seven comes in the final scene of *Notorious* and adds to the mysterious, off-center mood. Claude Rains has just been left behind by Cary Grant and Ingrid Bergman; he must now return to face his angry mother and two disaffected Nazi

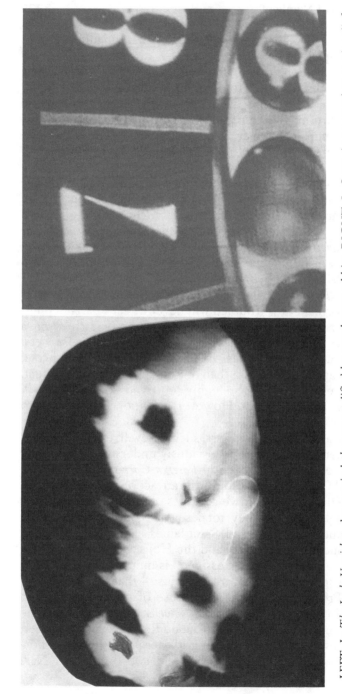

LEFT: In *The Lady Vanishes*, the mystical *three* exemplified by cute bunny rabbits. RIGHT: In *Secret Agent*, another comic relief scene as the casino roulette wheel shows a lucky *seven* to be the winner.

associates. He must climb six steps to a concrete terrace and then to the final step—the seventh—to face a harsh destiny. The walk must seem very long to him, and the number seven is appropriate for this scene, even if not a conscious device.

The number seven is also key to the plot of *Spellbound*, with its unusual dream-recollection scene designed by Salvador Dali in his surreal style. Hitchcock told François Truffaut that he wanted an artist like either Dali or Chirico to provide that disjointed dream-association sequence with "long shadows, the infinity of distance, and the converging lines of perspective."[3] The dream features a card game of twenty-one, the reference being to the famous 21 Club in New York City. Obviously, the number twenty-one is a multiple of seven. The seven motif refers to the anxiety of the traumatized hero, John Ballantine (Gregory Peck), upon seeing parallel lines (e.g., ski tracks), thus triggering negative subconscious associations. As a child Ballantine assumed guilt when his small brother was impaled on a picket fence. The number seven blankets the plot, suggesting that the laws of the psyche are associated with visible signs. The dream sequence plays on the theme of trust and strongly suggests that love is an infallible healer. Death and love are recurring themes in *Spellbound* and, as we shall see, in *The Trouble with Harry* and *Vertigo*. That Hitchcock would use seven intentionally seems to be undeniable, because he employed versions of the same strategem in four other movies.

The Trouble with Harry is a very underrated picture. When it first was released, critics saw it as substandard Hitchcock fare. We must look for deeper meanings in a film which the director judged to be one of his favorites. Cinematographer Robert Burks lightens Hitchcock's usually dark settings with gorgeous Technicolor scenes of a Vermont countryside awash in autumnal colors. Putting aside his preferred expressionistic style (characterized by shadows, fog, rain, night scenes, and single-source lighting), Hitchcock lulls us into complacency—and then cleverly involves us willy-nilly in a film noir. It has been argued that *The Trouble with Harry* was a pastoral, laid-back film, a sort of throwaway comic-relief film after *Vertigo* and *North by Northwest* and before *Psycho* and *The Birds*. It is, however, a subtle, disturbing treatment of anxiety, guilt, and fear—themes which are major ingredients of Hitchcock's best work. The lightness of the photography and the simple, folksy nature of the Vermont villagers should not blind the viewer to the fact that the inevitability of death is the theme.

In the *Spiritual Exercises,* death is a pivotal theme, for the retreatant is alerted to the death of Adam and Eve, one's personal extinction, and then Christ's death with its cosmic relevance for those with faith in his redemptive self-sacrifice. Death is the touchstone for ultimate authenticity. It is significant that Martin Heidegger, the noted German philosopher of phenomenology, spent a year in a Jesuit novitiate and derived from his thirty-day Ignatian retreat the conviction that death is the proving ground for integrity so that, in a sense, each moral decision is a rehearsal for death. Every choice implicates us in death as the ultimate frame of reference and must be viewed in a Christian context as the primary radical ground for decision making. Hitchcock adds to this the unexpressed thought that we are all guilty of not being innocent and therefore that everyone's death is a reminder of our own. Harry Warp is Everyman— commonplace, good but "warped."

There are seven visits to Harry's corpse. Interestingly enough, Hitchcock shows us the body feet first. We meet a spinster who invites the portly Captain Wiles (Edmund Gwenn) for blueberry muffins at the side of the body. The "trouble" is not so much with Harry as with the complacency of the visitors and their dismissal of death, an unrealistic reluctance to have their placid lives upset in any way. Death, the "Great Interferer," is not allowed to interfere. What an illusion! The humor is nervous, not escapist in any sense. Hitchcock is not only a master of suspense but also a master of black (or gallows) humor. In *The Trouble with Harry,* each scene builds on the incongruity of mortals who miss the point of the single most obvious fate. Thus Hitchcock manages to focus the attention of the audience on death. The death of others is an "I/It" relationship—distant from the self. In contrast to this objective, cool perception of death is that subjective "I/Thou" relationship—more vibrantly existential and intensely personal. Ignatius in his *Spiritual Exercises* has the retreatant place himself or herself on a deathbed, imagining what decision a dying person would like to make on the verge of stepping off into eternity. Ignatius' concept of death as personal encounter with one's real self in diaphanous revelation is an example of what psychologists call "hot cognition" (i.e., "I/Thou"). It is this perception of death which moved Martin Heidegger, and it coincides with Hitchcock's ironic, at times black humor, version of death. *The Trouble with Harry* plumbs the immeasurable ocean of philosophical and theological depths such as death, judgment, and the venture into that unknown particular destination which crossing over from life through death implies.

Death is, in a natural sense, the completion to life. Thus the seven motif can signify a finish, that which is completed. The number is expressly there; so is death, personified by Harry's corpse with his big feet standing out for us to see, a reminder of our own inescapable horizontal destiny and, as mentioned earlier, of Fr. Mangan's exhortation on death given to the boys at the Jesuit school.

Vertigo also makes use of the mystical number seven, but less explicitly. In this deeply psychological film, in which Scottie Ferguson (James Stewart) is buffeted about by emotional forces he neither controls nor understands, seven distinct examples of the disordered state of vertigo can be identified. They are effected by blurring the boundaries of life that provide security:

(1) Space—physical falling (the roof scene) and acrophobia, the fear of heights.
(2) Time—the Spanish ancestral references to colonial times.
(3) Antiquities—falling back into prehistory (the scene with the giant sequoia trees).
(4) Social and personal interactions—fear of the overprotective mother figure, a symbol of the limits on personal independence and growth; Midge (Barbara Bel Geddes) is such a symbol, offering Scottie security, warmth, and predictable domesticity without risk or adventure.
(5) Psychology—infatuation with Madeleine and Judy (Kim Novak).

(6) Philosophy—Scottie Ferguson as a hard-nosed Anglo-Scottish detective with a tough-minded empirical bias. In other words, Scottie has the legal or police mentality, which is open to evidence, what is sense-verifiable, but closed to mystery. He suffers from the unknowable, that which lies beyond what the senses register.

(7) Religion—guilt, anxiety, and surrender to the mystery of death, which is the opaque veil that keeps us from knowing what lies beyond the grave. The Dolores Mission Church is central to the plot and frames Scottie Ferguson's romantic passion and anger at being deceived.

When I first applied the seven motif as a possible interpretative key to a deeper understanding of *Vertigo,* I had a more expansive appreciation of the film and its author. Undeniably, sexual infatuation is the principal type of giddiness treated in this remarkable film. Still, there are other modes of decenteredness in the mysterious fallen world we inhabit. I have mentioned that Hitch was panphobic. If he had all the fears, then can we not presume that he was susceptible to all the forms of vertigo? A reseeing of the film will be rewarding, if one looks for the other centrifugal forces mentioned above.

The film is a modified version of a mystery novel by Boileau and Narcejac called *D'Entre les Morts.* Hitchcock used physical vertigo as an entertainment trampoline to catapult the audience's emotions to other, less photographable, levels of insecurity and boundary blurring. It is apparent that the seven examples of vertiginous anxiety mentioned above are in the film. *Vertigo* makes audiences feel adrift—without map or compass—on a sea of fears and insecurities; boundaries and definitions of situations swim without direction or hope. The use of the seven motif in this mystical masterpiece strongly suggests, I submit, that Hitchcock intended this mystical number as an example of infinity, the unnumbered dreads that make up the existential angst of fallen humankind with its fate flawed by fallibility, human fickleness, and frequent felonies of every variety.

William Rothman, in *Hitchcock: The Murderous Gaze,* holds us in debt for his analysis of the shower scene in *Psycho,* arguably the most subliminally loaded scene of emotional communication ever filmed. Rothman reproduces seven enlarged frames of the spiral motif: the first three frames show us the blood-drenched water flowing into the drain, then the open drain in close-up and third, a slow rotating camera shot of the victim's right eye filmed in extreme close-up (the eye appears to peer out from the shower drain, suggesting Norman's peephole).[4] The fourth frame enlargement continues to rotate Marion Crane's eye as it spirals clockwise in the fifth frame (the slow rotary motion is a visual coup which creates in the audience emotional stirrings of a living Marion). The sixth frame characterizes the visual advance to a fuller view of her eyebrows, eyelashes, stationary pupil, and nose. In the seventh frame, the camera pulls back still further and gives us a floor-level view of Marion's mouth, partly open and pressed down to the white porcelain tub. The scene shifts to the shower head, spraying water. Rothman presents us with seven distinct imaging modules that build the mingled feeling we have of a personalized confrontation with death as the Great Interferer. Of course, Hitch did not shoot this scene with the number seven in mind; nevertheless, Rothman's analysis has subliminal numerological relevance and is eminently worth mentioning.

Now let us examine another classic Hitchcock motion picture. *The Birds* presents us with seven ominous scenes of birds attacking human beings. Each scene advances not only the plot but also the moral development of a self-centered socialite:

(1) Driving up from San Francisco, Melanie (Tippi Hedren) crosses Bodega Bay in a boat after leaving the lovebirds at the home of Mitch Brenner (Rod Taylor). She is attacked by a gull and has a bleeding, if slight, head wound.

(2) The attack of the birds at the children's outdoor party. This scene inspires acute fear because of the innocence of the boys and girls.

(3) The visit of Mitch's mother, Lydia (Jessica Tandy), to the feed dealer who was pecked to death by birds. The fear spreads since the threat is coming closer to the family through friends and neighbors.

(4) The birds invade the Brenner household. Now the threat is focused on the family itself and its guest, Melanie.

(5) The outdoor scene of the birds gathering behind Melanie, who does not at first notice them on the jungle gym where the children climb. Melanie warns the teacher, who has the children leave quietly. The birds pursue them and attack Melanie, locked in her car.

(6) The gas-pump explosion outside the Tides Café and the frightful attack on Melanie in the telephone booth (suggesting that she is an encaged human bird). This is a striking example of Hitchcock's empathy with the winged creatures and the retributive nature of the feathered thunder they create in their descent from the skies.

(7) The final assault of the gulls on the Brenner home and on Melanie alone in the attic.

Again, as in *Spellbound, The Trouble with Harry,* and *Vertigo,* we have the themes of fear and love, sex and death, hurt and healing. It is curious, indeed, that the seven motif, clearly a biblical allusion, is employed again and again to link these themes together as recurring cyclical experiences repeated endlessly, the number seven suggesting infinity.

Tippi Hedren also starred in *Marnie,* where the seven motif figures thematically. In *Marnie,* seven red impressions appear on the screen, referring to the blood of the sailor (Bruce Dern) killed by Marnie (Tippi Hedren). They serve as a traumatic memory teaser for her subconscious. The impressions occur during the following scenes:

(1) When Marnie visits her mother in Baltimore.

(2) Asleep in her mother's house, where she hears thunder and tapping on the window, and sees the shadowy figure of her mother.

(3) The spilling of red ink in the office where she works.

(4) At the racetrack, where she is startled by the red spots on the jockey's silk blouse.

(5) When a tree felled by a storm crashes into Mark's (Sean Connery) office.
(6) At the hunting meet, where Marnie spots the scarlet jacket of the burglar.
(7) In a flashback scene, when we learn that the crimson shirt had been bloodied by Marnie, who struck the sailor, a client of her prostitute mother, with a poker.

It is no coincidence that Hitchcock used the seven motif as a recurring mystical reference in five of his most psychological, and indeed most personal, films: *Spellbound, The Trouble with Harry, Vertigo, The Birds,* and *Marnie.* I would add *Psycho,* since I discussed William Rothman's seven static photo enlargements on the classic shower scene. Numerology has its role, for there are digits (e.g., nine) signifying "crisis-decisions," major turning points in consciousness.[5] Recall Marion Crane's handwritten letter determining the exact amount of money she intended to restore. She tears up the calculation and throws it down the toilet (where later it will be found by her lover, played by John Gavin). Her shower is a cleansing experience—she obviously enjoys it as more than physical euphoria; it is the beginning of a new life. She has let go, and she is ready for another phase of her life (recall that she said that the tryst in the hotel would be the last). Marion trusted to fate but now has found an inner peace. Yes, numerologists can shed some light on reality, a belief which Hitchcock accepted along with Ignatius.

Hitch's last film, *Family Plot,* was first titled *One Plus One Equals One.* It was then changed to *Deceit,* and finally to its present title. A smooth chase-suspense mystery, the film is a veritable labyrinth of criss-crossing plots and historical guises, ruses, and subterfuges. Thus, only repeated viewings, sustained study, and pen and notepaper can bring the dedicated viewer to the fullest appreciation of this mellow swan song by the Master of Suspense. If the plot is built on addition, division, and multiplication, then the intriguing scenario by Ernest Lehman, the splendid casting and acting, plus Hitch's low-key use of camera tricks and lighting make a remarkable architectonic unity.

The plot contrasts two young couples, neither married. George Lumley (Bruce Dern) and Blanche (Barbara Harris) are tricksters: she is a crystal-gazing spiritualist; he is a cabdriver who digs for information to make credible her psychic revelations to clients. Arthur Adamson (William Devane) and Fran (Karen Black) collect jewels as ransom for kidnapped hostages. Romance seems to take a backseat to the pursuit of dishonest gain, and Blanche obviously has sexual needs left unfulfilled by George. This is a departure for Hitchcock, deft at spicing sex with adventure throughout his fifty years of directing. We have four individuals coupled in crime: one + one + one + one = four. So dedicated are they to antisocial scheming and deviant behavior that they really never get to know one another.

Certainly, that is the case throughout for Arthur and Fran. However, in the case of Blanche and George, there is a decisive, life-threatening experience which magically melts them into a unity. With their car leaking brake fluid due to villainous impairment, they suddenly find themselves speed-ing along with no brakes and a stuck accelerator, forcing George to use the steering wheel as his only control. In this classic scene, Hitch frightens the audience with oncoming vehicles, steep precipices, and sharp turns in the road, but he also introduces humor as Blanche is tossed around, even upside down, tangling and encumbering the ordinarily cool George. The hair-raising scene terminates with the car leaving the road, bumping along over a slightly sloping terrain, knocking down a sign (clearly a cross symbol), and finally turning over on its side. Rather than heightening the suspense, Hitch remains playful, with Blanche stepping on George's face as she extricates herself; he carefully pulls himself out from under, and the two wonder how it all happened.

I note a remarkable transformation in George's attitude following the desperate descent and the miraculous escape from what seemed inevitable doom. Hitherto, he had re-mained cool, indifferent, and even insulting to Blanche's amorous advances; now he kisses her on the cheek and puts his arm around her. One plus one equals one. Their closeness contrasts with the dramatic duality of the second couple, Arthur and Fran. More fitting for them is the axiom, one plus one equals two. Furthermore, they both dress in dark (usually black), conservative clothes, while George and Blanche dress in lighter colors; Blanche (meaning white) drives an ivory-toned car.

Barbara Harris is easily the most individuated person of the four—lively, upbeat, outreaching, and unified. She is a medium, a self-styled bridge of communication between the living and the dead. True, she is a psychic in a confidence game, but she evolves beyond that in the course of the film. When she meets the evil Arthur Adamson, she tells him the truth about his inheritance. Here, Hitchcock/Lehman insinuate the marvelous possibilities that could have been realized by the "son of Adam" had he not chosen to set fire to his stepparents' home, thus killing them and passing for dead. Guilt plays a role in the film, troubling the rich, elderly Julia Rainbird, who seeks peace by trying to locate her sole-surviving heir, a lost nephew, namely Adamson (originally Edward Shoebridge). Out of fear, Adamson drugs Blanche and carries her to the secret room, just mentioning to Fran that the diamond is hidden in the chandelier.

I find the remainder of the film wonderfully intriguing, for Blanche, following her rescue by George, locates the diamond. George now believes that she has authentic powers of clairvoyance and is a "spiritualist" in the full sense of the word. Is she? Did her subconscious mind grasp the words spoken by Adamson about the location of the diamond? It seems clear she was unconscious. Is she now the possessor of a higher spiritual awareness, a channel of that great ocean of consciousness that is pure unity, the unmanifest? Ordinarily, such unity of consciousness is achieved by specially endowed persons—saints and mystics. If we study the opening and closing scenes of *Family Plot,* we see that the crystal ball beneath the opening credits shows an insubstantial, emerald-colored reflection of changing shapes, an undifferentiated unity. The chandelier in the final scene is a dazzling symmetry of finite facets of reflected crystal light.

What Hitchcock intended in terms of conscious awareness

I cannot say, but possibly astute eavesdropping led Barbara Harris to gain conscious knowledge of the location of the diamond secreted in the glistening chandelier. I offer a mind-teasing fillip from the last book of the Bible, the Apocalypse, as related to the last film of an inspired director. In Chapter 21, we find references to three gates at each of the four points of the compass of the heavenly Jerusalem, a city whose wall had the names of the twelve apostles of the Lamb and also twelve gates guarded by twelve angels, and on the gates the names of the twelve tribes of the sons of Israel. Dense imagery, to be sure. That archspiritualist John the Evangelist recounts a visit by one of the seven angels who came in the spirit and "carried me away to a great, high mountain, and showed me the holy city, Jerusalem, coming down out of heaven from God, having the glory of God, its radiance like a most rare jewel, like a jaspar, clear as crystal" (21:10–11).

Is there any significance in such a linkage? Is it purely subjective? Or are Hitchcock and Lehman painting on celluloid a neobiblical allegory? Barbara Harris's knowing wink is the most apt commentary. I see, in my mind's eye, Hitch coaching her in his ironic, puckish way. Sensitive to biblical themes, I find a tantalizing parallel in the way that Hitchcock's camera stays with the blessed couple, George and Blanche, just as the Old Testament followed the genealogy of the children of Adam's son Seth and disregarded the offspring of Cain. *Family Plot*'s son of Adam, Arthur, and Fran are left in their own tight, secret room, and we learn no more about them. They remain alone with one another in a type of Sartrean no-exit situation. *Family Plot* is a provocative and complex parable about the species and not merely about the Rainbird clan. More than the genial entertainment described by most critics, the film is, I find, a quasi-mystical allegory inviting sustained reflection and even spiritual contemplation.

Notes

1. Donald Spoto, *The Dark Side of Genius,* pp. 327–331.
2. Ibid., p. 290.

3. François Truffaut, with Helen G. Scott, *Hitchcock* (New York: Simon and Schuster, 1967), p. 118.
4. See Rothman, *Hitchcock: The Murderous Gaze,* pp. 307–309.
5. Lynn M. Buess, *Numerology for the New Age* (Marina del Rey, Calif.: DeVorss, 1978), passim.

CHAPTER VII

Christ Figures—Overt and Covert

The abundance of subtle clues and subliminal allusions in the work of Hitchcock adds solid reasons why his work will live and even grow in appreciation. Take a silent film: *Easy Virtue* (1927), a minor film with a major Christomorphic allusion.[1] The finale shows us a liberated woman (Isabel Jeans) leaving a courthouse after a notoriously scandalous divorce case involving a jealous aristocrat. The cameramen cluster about at the foot of the steps to take photographs for their tabloid papers. As a feminist with free ways, she is resented by many of her social class. Looking down at the *papparazi,* the badly maligned victim throws her arms sideways in a cruciform posture, she cries out (in a title card): "Shoot, there is nothing left to kill!" She is a martyr of social hypocrisy.

Throughout his career in England and in Hollywood, Hitch employed, obliquely but discernibly, "hidden sacred" symbols such as crosses. Take *Notorious* (1946). We meet a U.S. secret agent Cary Grant at a Miami party with a dissolute Ingrid Bergman acting as the hostess in a teasing striped blouse. Behind them is a lighting fixture clearly giving the impression of a cross. Later she will serve her country, risking her life as a double agent in Brazil, and escape with Devlin's help in a top thriller. Victimization is a common theme in Hitchcock's pictures, though not all qualify as transfigured Christ figures.

As another instance of a surprising cross allusion, take *Mr. and Mrs. Smith* (1940), a frothy screwball-type romantic comedy with Carole Lombard and Robert Montgomery. Reviewing the film some fifty-two years after my first viewing upon its release, I was astonished to spot a crucifix on a dresser in the bedroom where Lombard sleeps and Montgomery,

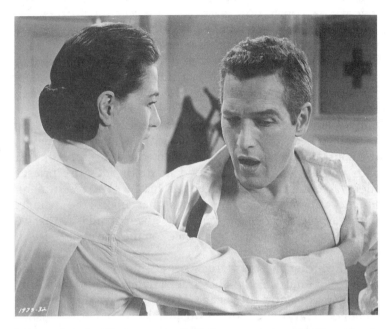

In *Torn Curtain,* Hitch uses the Red Cross symbol as a hidden sacred, uniting red for Communism with Christianity, an ironic visual.

unshaven and in pajamas, observes her from a distance.[2] In *Mr. and Mrs. Smith,* can Carole Lombard be a female after-image of that Christ who was treated *as if* he were not the expected one? Farfetched, I agree, but so is that purple patch of religious passion in the corner of our eye. Was Hitch smuggling Christian symbolism past the studio's watchful eye and, as would a schoolboy, deriving some forbidden pleasure? Why such a continuous pattern of Christic themes, mostly subtle but often enough also manifest? The cross emblem especially is an indirect narrative signal which, I have discovered, links "wrong persons" to parallel Christ figures thinly disguised in secular appearance.[3]

The two most overt examples of this type of Christ figure are found in *I Confess* and *The Wrong Man.* In *I Confess,* Montgomery Clift plays Fr. Michael Logan, a Canadian priest from Quebec. Before entering the seminary, he had been in love with a woman now married to a successful attorney. Fr. Logan was being blackmailed by a man who saw the two together (before he became a priest) leaving an abandoned house where they had been forced to spend the night due to a sudden storm. The church sacristan, Otto Keller, murders the blackmailer, Vilette (who had caught Keller stealing). Keller then confesses the crime to Fr. Logan, who later is himself accused of being the cassock-garbed figure seen leaving the scene of the crime. Hitchcock contrasts the agony, the court trial, and the humiliation of the tight-lipped priest with the suffering and trial of Christ. Besides the priest's silent acceptance of injustice and his lack of resentment, Hitchcock gives important clues that make the parallel unmistakable. Three clear signals are given to indicate that we are dealing with a Christ reference, or the spiritual sense of the wrong-man theme:

First, during the murderer's confession to Fr. Logan, the background music is the Dies Irae, a hymn traditionally sung during masses for the dead. The theme of the hymn is Judgment Day, the day of the divine trial when perfect justice will be dispensed. It is obviously not referring to the upcoming trial of Fr. Logan.

Second, there is a scene in which the priest walks on a hill in Quebec in the shadow of outdoor stations of the cross. The camera angle from above frames Fr. Logan alongside a foreground picture of Christ carrying his cross. Both are examples of the "wrong man"; both are making their way of the cross because of a betrayal; and both will experience a resurrection.

And third, in the courtroom, as the priest stands trial, the camera focuses on a huge wall crucifix. The meaning is unmistakable: Fr. Logan will be tried and unjustly convicted for the crime of another—not only a serious crime, but a serious sin as well.

Hitchcock returned to this theme in *The Wrong Man,* a story based on a true account of misplaced blame. As mentioned in Chapter IV, "The Wrong Man," Henry Fonda plays Christopher Emmanuel Balestrero, a bassist at the Stork Club. A nightmare begins when he is unjustly arrested as a holdup man. Seven distinct narrative signals link him with Christ, the "wrong man" of the New Testament:

(1) Balestrero has two names. The first, Christopher, means "Christ-bearer" in Greek; his middle name, Emmanuel, means "God-with-us" in Hebrew. Both are obvious references to Jesus.

(2) The detectives wait for him in the car in the wee hours of the morning, and Manny is approached by them on his return from work at the Stork Club. The detectives constantly call him "Chris," an ironic reference to the scene where Jesus is apprehended at night.

(3) The two detectives are extremely self-righteous, modern Pharisees. They keep insisting that the innocent man has nothing to fear, that the police want to be fair because "that is our way." However, they deny him the right to tell his wife where he is or to get a lawyer.

(4) The rosary, an object of devotion to the Blessed Virgin Mary, is featured in three scenes, one of which shows Manny with his lips moving in prayer. It is ironic that the bailiff takes all of Manny's valuables but says, "You can keep the rosary."

(5) On the wall of the Balestrero home is a picture of Christ with his heart exposed. Devotion to the Sacred Heart of Jesus,[4] well known to Catholics, has found some of its most ardent advocates among the Jesuits and is a classical part of Jesuit spirituality. The crucial scene of Manny's praying lips as he gazes at the picture hints at a miracle. Hitchcock dissolves through the picture into a scene of attempted robbery and the apprehension of the real felon.

(6) When Manny is put in his prison cell and sees its austerity, there is a close-up of him wringing his perspiring hands. Hitchcock's camera rotates to convey the sense of giddiness. This seems to be a clear narrative signal alluding to the Gospel account of Christ's agony in the Garden of Gethsemane.

(7) In a scene at the police station, Balestrero stares at the apprehended look-alike robber with a silent expression of mingled pity and indignation. It is the sort of

knowing look that Christ had when Peter denied him three times.

The Christ parallel is unmistakable; however, the happy ending is unconvincing—a mere title telling the audience that, after two years, Rose was reunited with her husband and two boys. We see a scene of the four strolling along Collins Avenue in Miami. This ending is somewhat hollow. Lacking any resounding note of resurrection, it is a true Hitchcockian troubled ending.

Hitch seems to aver that, for the vindication of every wrong person, another one takes his or her place. I am reminded of Luis Buñuel's *Viridiana,* in which a man releases a small dog roped to a horse-drawn cart only to see another dog trotting on a leash fixed to a pony cart going in the opposite direction. This ironic stance seems to suffuse the final scene of *The Wrong Man.* Unconvincing is the disclaimer of happiness with the reunited family or four after Rose's two years in a sanatorium. In effect, Rose Balestrero seems a symbol of unredeemed victimhood, unmoved by Manny's reassurance that her two boys are praying for her. It seems there are two wronged persons, one an overt Christ figure and the other a failed Christ figure.

I sense a turning point in Hitchcock's filmography and personal life in this film. My letter to him suggests that Hitchcock did not want to talk about this point (Appendix III). Perhaps the trials of conscience which he mentioned in his interview with the alumnus of Saint Ignatius College (Appendix I), had to do with living with fears, with his panphobic temperament, and not with what he considered sentimental rhetoric and easy grace. Watch carefully the last scene of *The Wrong Man,* with its tilted angle shots and decentered camera setups. I see Hitchcock's fears surfacing. Was he commenting obliquely on his own marriage, as he apparently did with the scene of the unappetizing dinner in which the Inspector's well-meaning wife serves him an unappetizing stew in *Frenzy?*

The title—*The Wrong Man*—gives away the plot, because Hitchcock identifies with Balestrero. The film has marvelous bits of aural Expressionism: Bernard Herrmann's edgy "music of the fears" and a dozen scenes with the roar or background noise of subways or elevated trains. In fact, the mounting volume of mass-transit noises accents the deterioration of Rose's mental state. In the first meeting with the lawyer, Frank O'Connor (Anthony Quayle), there are three sound signals of an elevated train: the first associated with Manny, the second with Rose, and the third with O'Connor as he encourages the couple to obtain witnesses to prove Manny was elsewhere on the dates of the thefts. In the next meeting with O'Connor, it is clear that Rose needs a doctor. The lawyer asks her to verify her husband's alibi. She looks blankly ahead as an elevated train roars in the background and departs with a shrill whistle. I see an allusion to hell here. At the same time, O'Connor rises from his chair and circles leftward to observe Rose from behind as she grips her right arm in anxiety. This is called a sinister pan, a counterclockwise camera movement as a sign of impending danger. The film's plot broods with the idea that what the detectives call "the normal routine" is deeply disordered and threatening, especially to defenseless citizens.

In addition to these saintly Christ figures, we have more implicit instances of the wrong man as oblique examples of the Jesus character. Less explicit than *I Confess* and *The Wrong Man,* several female Christ figures suggest themselves to the prepared mind on guard against overinterpretation. Take the early sound film, *Murder!* (1930): a falsely accused woman (Norah Baring) is sent to prison after four undecided members of a jury are persuaded one by one to vote guilty. The woman conducts herself in prison in a dignified, even saintly, manner; she neither complains nor is embittered. Hitchcock effectively employs chiaroscuro lighting effects to convey the weight of the offense that besets a female Christ-like victim. The shadow of the gallows warns of impending death; the guards walk rigidly and are dressed in somber garb; the cell is forlorn. The spectator could sympathize with an innocent, pretty woman who accepts her fate calmly. Was Hitch inspired here also by Carl Dreyer's *Passion of Joan of Arc?* I firmly believe so.

Although *Murder!* presents us with one clear Christ figure in the person of the convicted woman, we might be tempted to consider the possibility of another. The same film has a curious allusion to "the dangling man," the actual killer, who is a double victim of society—branded as a half-breed and as a transvestite. A trapeze artist, he is trapped during his act and looks down at the menacing sight of the crowds and the detectives, hostile and waiting for their prey. The prejudices of society, thematically emphasized in the plot, make us wonder about the circumstances of the crime, which might have lessened his guilt and made him a victim, too. (Hitch found sexually ambiguous persons fascinating, as we see in his oblique references to lesbianism in *Champagne* and homosexuality in *Secret Agent, Rope,* and *Strangers on a Train*.)

Psycho takes on a whole range of subtle theological implications when seen against the backdrop of Hitchcock's dramatic irony. This is the device he often used to arouse suspense, giving the viewer more information than the characters themselves possess (e.g., the famous bomb sequence in *Sabotage*). It is this subtle use of dramatic irony in *Psycho* that allows us to see Marion Crane as more than a wronged person.

Like Fr. Logan, Emmanuel Balestrero, and the heroine of *Murder!,* Marion Crane is a Christ figure. The converging bits of evidence keep adding up. This is supported by a scene in which Marion talks with Norman Bates (Anthony Perkins). She is standing beneath an oval painting of three women with wings, the central figure of which appears to be flying up to heaven. The implication seems to be that Marion is a type of angel-woman. Moreover, the peephole Norman uses to watch Marion undress for her shower is hidden by a framed painting of the scene from the Old Testament of Susanna and the two elders who perjured themselves to accuse her of seduction when she refused their sexual advances.

This scene is an example of Hitch's care for details and deliberately planned camera positions. The viewer must not take for granted Hitch's attention to the two paintings nor the other decorative elements in the room, which include stuffed birds with phallic beaks. In addition to the location of the birds, attention must be given to the upward, decentered angle of Norman Bates's talking head. The highly charged

RIGHT: *Psycho* ironically ends with a lawyer's pompously wordy explanation challenged by a higher mystery. Note the light fixture as a cross. LEFT: In a cell, a straight-jacketed Norman Bates further confounds viewers with Mother Bates' smile superimposed on her son's mad face.

scene constitutes a multisymbolic omen that is the crucial hinge for Marion Crane's change of mind.

A brief, stimulating, although speculative, comment on *Psycho*'s reference to Christology: As Christ had a divine and human nature combined in one personality, so too Norman Bates lived with a similar dual tension. As Christ's freedom was conditioned by an external necessity, the will of the Father, so too Norman's liberty was restricted by his mother. Listen carefully to the psychiatrist's speech, very much like a theologian's discourse on the Incarnation: two natures in one person. Was the cruciform lighting fixture on the wall to the audience's left intended by Hitchcock as a subliminal embed, a tantalizing cross symbol?

Study carefully the scene of the psychiatrist entering the room and you will see the outline of a cross. With this subconscious sacred reference, the ensuing scene assumes a higher theological irony. The cross is obedience to a higher will and this, basically, is the link with the disturbing, yet poignant, final scene of a schizoid Norman Bates. Mrs. Bates's voice is heard speaking, while Norman smiles with glazed eyes, protesting that she would not "harm a fly." Is Norman saying sardonically, "Mother made me do it—and mother is good"? In my letter to Hitchcock, I referred to James Joyce's "hangman God." This thought returns to me each time I see the final scene of *Psycho*.

If one pairs the psychiatrist's facile explanation with the reincarnated mother, there is discernible an inverse Christian theology. On the one hand, Marion Crane is a scapegoat; her boyfriend (John Gavin) finds the fragment of her torn statement in the toilet bowl; the number $40,000 is legible. This offers hope for the vindication of her reputation, as does the retrieval of her car with the remains of the stolen $40,000 wrapped in newspaper. There is a resurrection of sorts in her public exoneration. I do not believe it is strained scholarship to point out that her determination to return to Phoenix is also a resurrection note. The Arizona capital is named after the mythical bird that comes back to life from its ashes, seen as a pagan foreshadowing of the resurrection by the early Christians.

It is obvious to me that Hitch is pointing the film beyond the final frame, as he does in his next film, *The Birds*. The internal projector of the viewer continues to supply the mental screen with taunting possibilities. Is it not interesting that the telltale paper scrap is lifted from the toilet much as the car in the final scene is hoisted from the swamp? Secrets come to light, Hitchcock seems to say, even those buried in the deep subconscious. Out of sexual desire and fantasy come deep religious meanings.

Is Hitchcock suggesting that darkness and evil are necessary conditions for coming to divine light? Norman Bates is, in a sense, the Great Interferer who provokes Marion Crane to thoughts of restitution and conversion (she is scared straight). In the mother guise, Norman is the instrument of making the repentant Marion a type of martyr, for Hitch's ironic combination of sex and atonement is "passion" in the fullest sense. That is why both Marion and Norman supply much Christomorphic food for thought to the theologically prepared mind.

After World War II, Hitchcock studied captured Nazi footage of the atrocities committed in German concentration camps, however, his planned documentary on this subject was put aside. Is there a symbolic link between this project and *Psycho,* which stressed the innocence and helplessness of the victims? The shadow of the Holocaust seems to lie across *Psycho.* Moreover, Hitchcock was influenced by a mass murder on a Kansas farm. Like the serial murderer, an eccentric recluse, Norman Bates had to kill as a reverse form of atonement. Many serial murderers kill under some dictate of a "higher force." Certainly, Marion is a scapegoat in Norman's attempt to appease his mother.

As in *The Wrong Man* and other works, there is a film within a film in *Psycho.* If the protomessage is escapist horror, the subordinate message is definitely biblical:

First, the need for psychological cleansing. This can be seen in the Norman/Mother Bates schizophrenic personality, which seeks ceremonial purification by eliminating all elements of threat.

Second, the choice of a scapegoat, or person who carries the blame for others. The availability of Marion as the victim makes the act of sacrificing her convenient. And that act has the effect of placing her close to the source of the holy.

And third, the victim seen as a Christ figure. Marion is offered up, as was Christ, on an altar of prudery and pharisaism. This is clear from the moral scolding we hear the mother deliver to her son:

> No! I tell you no! I won't have you bringing strange young girls in for supper. By candlelight, I suppose, in the cheap, erotic fashion of young men with cheap, erotic minds.

This scolding is hypocritical because the mother had her own illicit love affair. Marion stole for love; whatever she is, she is not a prude, not corseted in Victorian morality with its fears and guilts. *Psycho,* considered by some an exploitation film,

has many levels of symbolic meaning—it is fraught with
themes of terror and splendor.

In many films, the director hints at Christ figures in terms
of an undeserved death or mortal threat and the abandonment
or loneliness of the scene. Hitch makes the audience feel the
eerie isolation of a potential victim despite the closeness and
even availability of police, neighbors, and loved ones.

- In *Blackmail,* an artist is stabbed by a woman resisting
  rape. The camera cuts to a London bobby patrolling the
  streets, unaware of the crime being committed close by.
- In *North by Northwest,* Cary Grant is completely alone
  and defenseless in a Kansas cornfield, desperately elud-
  ing the mortal threat of a crop-dusting plane.
- In *Psycho,* a concerned highway patrol officer advises
  Marion to avoid further driving in the nighttime rain. As
  a result, she seeks refuge, at the cost of her life, at the
  Bates Motel.
- In *The Birds,* there is a tantalizing hint of a female Christ
  figure in Suzanne Pleshette, a schoolteacher who dies
  from wounds inflicted by the birds while protecting her
  young students. Furthermore, Tippi Hedren is, to my
  mind, a full-fledged candidate due to her entrapment in
  an attic with hostile seagulls, one of Hitchcock's most
  moving scenes. I will devote more attention to this in
  Chapter XI, "Spiritualizing Horror."
- In *Frenzy,* a rape and murder is committed in broad
  daylight while two women pass by and chatter mindlessly
  on the street below (a comment on urban indifference
  and on the famous victim Kitty Genovese, a secretary
  who screamed for help but was murdered in public even
  though over thirty people in nearby apartments heard her
  cries).

In these scenes, Hitchcock brings us close to the loneliness
experienced by those who die alone. It is a contemporary
theme of existential solitude. It also has indirect resonances
with the loneliness of Christ, who died surrounded by a few
friends and his mother but was deserted by so many others.

North by Northwest, a spectacular Hitchcock success, is a

complex film made up of subplots, ironic allusions, and dense symbolic meanings. (Does the title refer to Shakespeare's *Hamlet?* What is its significance, apart from the plot's geographical movement?) Let us look carefully at the memorable scene of the crop-dusting plane in pursuit of Cary Grant stranded in an open cornfield in Kansas. A close reading of this fascinating segment of pure cinema reveals a subliminal religious code punctuated by identifiable cross icons. Roger Thornhill (Cary Grant) has been betrayed, dispatched by double agent Eve (Eva Marie Saint) to meet the nonexistent George Kaplan. (He is always about to appear, but he never comes, this mysterious person with a Jewish surname.) Thornhill waits patiently for Kaplan. Will he come? What will he look like? What message will he deliver? The suspense grows as Thornhill's patience declines. Instead of Kaplan, however, a crop-dusting monoplane appears at a low altitude. We soon learn that it is on a lethal mission—to eliminate "R.O.T.," Roger O. Thornhill. If he was the "wrong man" up till now, he is now being sentenced without any real defense, witnesses, or trial by his peers. The truth is, he is an expendable embarrassment to the two powers at loggerheads in the film: the United States on one side and its unnamed rival on the other.

Let us pass the scene through a sensitive religious filter. The scene opens with a long establishing aerial shot. It shows a crossroad, and the cross is unmistakable. Cut to an impatient Thornhill, waiting for Kaplan. When he looks screen right, we can see in the distance a signpost strongly suggesting a cross. When the chase begins between the mechanical bird in the sky and its defenseless prey, one with hardly any refuge, the suspense mounts ever higher. Shots are fired at a low altitude. The plane's gunner has no accurate aim, but let us not ask why, for we are as grateful as is Thornhill, who can now hide in the tall corn. After the plane flies overhead, he dashes for safety to the main road to hail an oncoming vehicle. While running he passes a cross, a signpost, in the foreground. An oil truck swiftly approaches. Thornhill runs toward it, waving his arms frantically in cruciform motion. The truck screeches to a halt. Thornhill falls unharmed under the truck between the front wheels. Again his arms are outstretched, suggesting a horizontal crucifixion. At that moment the crop-dusting plane crashes into the truck perpendicularly; flames go up. Both machines, the oil truck and the crop duster, would probably suggest a fiery tau cross if seen from above. Hitch spared us an example of infernal irony; what a marvelous scene that might have been.

A commercial hit, *North by Northwest* contains more depth than the public and most critics have grasped. There is a discernible crossroad emblem and two signpost crosses, as well as the outstretched arms of desperate Cary Grant. Scenarist Ernest Lehman does not agree with this interpretation. Am I overreading the Hitchcock/Lehman screen sequence and investing an overactive religious imagination into merely neutral matter? I ask the reader to judge. Happily, video cassettes of the film can be rented cheaply to enhance any close study of an entertainment which is also a spiritual allegory. My own conclusion is unequivocally that Hitch deliberately planted Christocentric clues in the famous corn-field scene.[5]

Marnie lacks the narrative signals found in *I Confess, The Wrong Man,* and *North by Northwest.* Nonetheless, we can detect an undertone of guilt and reconciliation, with tempting parallels to a secular passion and romantic resurrection. We saw that in *Murder!* Hitchcock dealt with a killer who was a double victim of society, branded as a half-breed and as a transvestite. Marnie (Tippi Hedren) is a kleptomaniac who steals from wealthy men. In a twisted way, she—like the trapeze artist in *Murder!*—is a societally wronged person. Attracted to her because she is pretty and needs help, wealthy Mark Rutland (Sean Connery) tries to help her understand her irresistible impulses. In anger, Marnie shouts a reference to her early religious upbringing, mentioning being washed in the blood of the Lamb.

In the previous chapter ("Mysticism of Numbers"), I discussed *Marnie* and the seven red impressions that appear on the screen and their reference to the blood of the sailor she had killed with a poker in an attempt to protect her mother. Admittedly a passing reference, the mention of the "blood of the Lamb" must, nevertheless, be linked to the bloodstained shirt of the murdered sailor that haunts Marnie throughout the film. It is the recognition of that bloody scene from her childhood that liberates her from her thieving habits.

In Chapter V, I mentioned the last scene in *Marnie*: the long street that we thought was a dead end, with No Exit, that turns out to have two side streets (forming a tau cross, an emblem of redemptive love) leading away from the seedy neighborhood where Marnie was reared. Marnie's future happiness is tied in with the symbol of regenerative love, the ancient Greek cross. Washed in blood, Marnie is saved through a therapy that avoids the tragic sacrifice that Marion Crane had to endure in *Psycho*. I am inclined to see Marnie as a thinly veiled Christ figure. First, there are suggestive references to the redemptive symbols of water and blood— the pool on the ship, the ocean voyage itself, the references to rain and storms, the seaport of Baltimore, the earlier allusion to being washed in the blood of the Lamb, and the final scene with Mark driving Marnie away from the ghetto neighborhood with its traumatic associations and turning the car alongside the Baltimore waterfront, opening a sudden exit leading to a new life. Second, the happy ending suggests Marnie's resurrection. I have mentioned that Hitchcock often and in a masterly, even poetic, way desecularized them, turning victim-type dramas into subplots of a hidden-sacred nature.

Take *Frenzy*, with its memory-searing rape scene in which a sexually motivated killer attacks a woman who runs a matrimonial bureau. In an uncanny scene, the woman, realizing what is taking place, becomes interiorized. The audience sees a gold cross on a chain around her neck and hears her quietly recite a Psalm. The Master of Suspense combines active resistance to the unloving rapist with complete surrender to a loving Providence. I encourage the reader to study this scene. On the surface it is repugnant; but after a detached reflection, it is a brilliant insight into Christ's Passion. (In the Austrian Tyrol there is a church with Stations of the Cross designed by an artist who is a woman; the tenth station shows Christ being violently stripped of his garments by leering Roman soldiers, as if they were about to commit a rape.)

In a study of this sort, one must practice brinkmanship, careful not to fall into the abyss of overinterpretation. There

Hitch contrasts sexual passion and religious devotion in *Frenzy*. A rape-murder victim, Barbara Leigh-Hunt, is also a female Christ figure. Dying, she whispers a Psalm.

is a provocative spectrum of clues, analogies, and nuances, both overt and covert, with varying degrees of subjective interpretation. Can an argument be made for a latent Christ figure in Canada Lee's cameo in *Lifeboat* (1943)? The black seaman exhibits calm reserve and is free of the panic and passionate prejudices of his restless, white co-survivors. With moving dignity, he prays a psalm. Brief though the role, I incline to a probable Jesus surrogate and, as Hitch knew, a "wrong man" in the society of World War II.

Interestingly, a still photo I own of *Rear Window* reveals a dimly outlined cross on a courtyard window. It appears when Raymond Burr's Lars Thorwald is pushing Jimmy Stewart's L. B. Jeffries out of the window before he breaks his second leg. To the right can be discerned the distant cross. Does this religious symbol portend a crucifixion scene? Will Jeffries grow out of a voyeurism that comes from professional conditioning and use his training as an observant photographer "seeing" for the good of others?

After fifty years of seeing and studying Hitchcock's fifty-three films, I note a blending of the sacred and profane in subtle ways. In addition to internal evidence indicating a character having "a little of the look of Christ," there are repetitive themes which could be meaningfully applied to the Great Carpenter in the Gospels: "the dangling man," "the pursued man," "the wrong man," and "the helpless victim." All desperately seek human understanding in their marginal roles as alienated, if not criminalized, by society. In *Psycho,* the bleeding Marion Crane (Janet Leigh) extends a pleading hand to us *as if* we might help. In *Vertigo*'s dark ending, a cruciform Scottie Ferguson (James Stewart), hands disconsolately apart, looks down from the Dolores Mission tower. He sees a dead Madeleine/Judy (Kim Novak), who had just been surprised by the arrival of a nun coming to ring the bell. Scottie had just berated Judy for acting *as if* she committed suicide as Madeleine. Obsessively in love with a woman who was part of a cover-up plot, Ferguson may repeat his earlier mental breakdown. One could argue that Christ too was psychologically shattered by a betrayal. At least there is a provocative parallel here. Indeed, it is open to speculation whether the mantle of Christ fits the shoulders of Scottie Ferguson. The finale is one of Hitchcock's most poignant—less mystical than *Psycho,* but with more dramatic impact than *Frenzy.* (That picture's last scene ends with a closeup of a coffin/trunk with a visible cross deliberately positioned for the audience's consideration, and, I submit, its mystification.) An "open-ended pessimist," Hitchcock never closed the door on hope, but left a thin ray to shine through dark tragic endings.

There is manifest in Hitchcock's vintage films a pervading Christ-consciousness, secularized in terms of popular entertainment but revealed, whether overtly or covertly, in the obsessive motif of the wrong man, first portrayed in *The Lodger* (1926). An innocent man is threatened as a scapegoat for a guilty person who, in the film, is never caught. It is interesting that Hitchcock would identify himself with one of the mob flailing at the helpless Christ figure, suspended by handcuffs from an iron picket fence. Hitchcock would have remembered his earlier Jesuit training and the image of Jesus as the "wrong man" as presented in the *Spiritual Exercises* of Ignatius. In short, the intuition behind the cameo role is not only that Jesus died for each of us, but also that, in a real sense, we caused his death. I am inclined to see this scene as a type of self-irony, pregnant with spiritual insight and a remarkable shock of recognition. Hitchcock was never free of guilt and, I feel, took more of it unto himself than he had to.

In an interview with a graduate of Saint Ignatius College (Appendix I), Hitchcock remarked: "A Catholic attitude was indoctrinated into me. After all, I was born a Catholic." James Joyce counseled that, more than a Catholic, he was a Jesuit— in sensibility if not by vows. This too can be said of Hitchcock. For a deeper understanding of Hitchcock's signature as artist, entertainer, and man, one must appreciate the Jesuit legacy of convictions, memories, and emotions from his formative years.

Beneath the sinister surfaces and black humor are, consequently, profoundly religious and metaphysical issues: the mercurial nature of human motivation; the swimming boundaries of guilt and innocence; the unintended evil consequences of good intentions; the ironies of justice, institutional religion, and fervent patriotism; the recurrence of Christ figures in secular form; and the troubled happy endings which subvert the audience's desire for easy, even consoling, resolutions to the knotted problems of life. These themes reflect deep personal concerns in Hitchcock. To an alumnus of Saint Ignatius College he admitted that he had "trials over belief," religious anxieties among them.

Behind Hitchcock's favorite motto, "Things are not as they seem," is the "wrong-person" theme, at times thinly disguised male or female Christ figures. This theme is deeply imprinted in the frames of Hitchcock's films as it was in his own psyche. There is a strong presumption that Hitchcock's realization of Christ's suffering and death as undeserved, even as Christ dying for "me," personally and existentially (and not for the abstract faceless "us"). This, in the mind of St. Ignatius of

Loyola, establishes Christ as "the wrong man." A large number of Hitchcock's pictures give evidence, cryptic but consistent, of his abiding interest in the Gospel theme of Christ's passion and death, given primacy in the meditations of "the Third Week" of the Ignatian *Exercises*. Master Alfred was exposed for three years (1910–1913) to these religious exercises of the imagination, mind and will, while a student at Saint Ignatius College outside of London. May I cite another Jesuit alumnus, James Joyce, who aptly wrote something applicable to the artist, Hitchcock, in *Finnegans Wake* (No. 192):

> "O, you are excruciated, in honour bound to the cross of
> your own cruelfiction!"

Hitchcock has left us six world classic films with Christomorphic "wrong persons" featured or alluded to: *The Lodger, Vertigo, North by Northwest, Psycho, The Birds,* and *Frenzy*. Indeed, creative fiction—and motion pictures are included—contribute to an understanding of life as well as draw upon it for a source of inspiration and substance. The films of Sir Alfred Hitchcock document this in a brilliant and impressive way.

Notes

1. See the thorough analysis of *Easy Virtue* in Maurice Yacowar's *Hitchcock's British Films* (Hamden, Conn.: Archon Books, 1977), pp. 53–57.
2. A friend, Tom Weaver, supplied me with a 16-mm copy of the film to view. We both were equally surprised by this purple-patch discovery of a cross in a lighthearted comedy.
3. For literary allusions to the Christ figure, see Theodore Ziolkowski, *Fictional Transfigurations of Jesus* (Princeton, N.J.: Princeton University Press, 1972). See also my article, "Christ-Transfigurations in Film: Notes on a Meta-Genre," *Journal of Popular Culture,* Vol. 13, No. 3 (1980), pp. 427–433.
4. The heart of Christ—symbolizing the love of Christ for his church and for all of humankind—has been a focus of Catholic devotion since the eighteenth century. The devotion can be

traced back to the Middle Ages and is based on the writings of a number of mystics and visionaries, such as Bernard of Clairvaux (1090–1153), Bonaventure (1221–1274), and Margaret Mary Alacoque (1647–1690).

5. Surprising that in the growing literature about Hitchcock and his work, scarcely any allusions (down to 1991) have been printed regarding his virtual obsession with fictional transfigurations of Christ, whether male or female. As an example, I cite the very valuable and best-selling 1976 critical study (laden with rich insights and hidden motifs)—*The Art of Alfred Hitchcock* (Hopkinson and Blake). Author Donald Spoto makes not a single reference in terms of cues or clues to the recurring Christomorphic pattern, largely subliminal, and so critically essential to understanding the director's full *auteur* signature.

CHAPTER VIII

Dangling, Pursued, and Out of Time

In order to understand better the three motifs discussed in this chapter, I should address the issue of the popularity of crime, mystery, and suspense literature in England after 1870. More than any other Western country, the fiction of England was bathed in the gothic imagination—a glorification of evil—best illustrated in Mary Wollstonecraft Shelley's *Frankenstein*. It seems ironic that a proliferation of moody melodrama through penny dreadfuls should exist in a society which boasted material prosperity, moral progress, and economic security for many. It was the age of laissez-faire, bringing with it what John Stuart Mill characterized as "the new consciousness of living in a world of change." The full spectrum of the transformation of effects due to England's industrial revolution affected art, entertainment, and the popular imagination. Referring to the "mood of doubt," British scholar Humphry House wrote, "We are in a position to begin to understand the depths of psychological disturbance which the whole change of human tempo . . . brought on."[1]

Hitch would have been critically sensitive to the surface order and Pollyannaish spirit of the late Victorian age. Surely, he was more attracted to Charles Dickens's gritty realism than Thomas Macaulay's flowery rhetoric. He distrusted the easy optimism of those many voices preaching progress: Dickens and such other writers as Matthew Arnold were inveighing against child labor, overcrowding, long work hours, vice, disease, and penury. In *Hard Times,* Dickens wrote, "It was a town of real brick, of a brick that would have been red if the smoke and ashes had allowed it; but, as matters stood, it was a town of unnatural red and black like the painted face of a savage . . . out of which interminable serpents of smoke trailed themselves forever and ever." Such graphic prose reeked of an expressionistic style that Hitchcock would later find in German silent films.

I strongly believe that Hitch's developing cinematic imagination drew on literary examples to make audiences feel the precariousness of human existence, what Professor House has called, "The Mood of Doubt."[2] Anxiety and worry hung in the air during the Victorian era. Not only did they worry about sex, money, empire, and social status, but they even worried about the speculative question of the immortality of the soul—is life worth living at all? Life became suspenseful; the new world of factories, new towns, and commuting raised frustrations and a confused sense of Whither the future? The gothic imagination was a spice flavoring the tasteless aspects of urban-industrial existence. In a world of denuded human feeling, it is logical to expect a turn toward escapism and purgation through cathartic forms of fear and vicarious forms of sensationalism. Dangling, pursued, and out of time were tactics that Hitch experimented with and developed in order to make himself and the audience feel alive. It is no surprise that the lurid tale of Jack the Ripper would have gripped the English imagination and later formed the basis for Hitch's silent classic, *The Lodger* (1926). The Victorian imagination was a split one: beneath apparent order were volcanic forces of sin, crime, and even horrible deeds.

The popularity of Hitchcock's films is closely linked to the skillful way in which he plays upon the emotions of the audience. A viewer ends up sharing the anxiety of someone hanging from a cliff, or racing against a deadline to avert a disaster, or being pursued. The audience is kept in a state of excitement and tension because it identifies with characters in danger—those dangling precariously: a man hanging handcuffed from an iron railing while an angry mob clamors around him (*The Lodger*); a trapeze artist nervously swinging beneath the big top while detectives wait below to arrest him (*Murder!*); a man and woman tied to the railing of a rickety staircase that collapses, leaving them in midair (*Number*

Seventeen); and an escaping couple involved in the collapse of an abandoned mine (*Young and Innocent*).

These scenes from Hitchcock's earlier films prepared the way for some of the most thrilling incidents in his later Hollywood films. In *Foreign Correspondent,* an American reporter (Joel McCrea) spying on foreign agents in a Dutch windmill tries to escape down a narrow winding staircase. The sleeve of his coat gets caught on one of the revolving wheels of the mill. He manages to remove the coat, but it continues to dangle from the spinning wheel until it is noticed by the agents, and the reporter is caught.

In *Saboteur,* an innocent man, Barry Kane (Robert Cummings), flees his defense job in southern California when he is wrongly suspected of sabotaging the factory. In New York, he picks up the trail of a foreign agent named Fry (Norman Lloyd) and prevents him from blowing up a newly dedicated warship in the Brooklyn Navy Yard. Afraid he will be found out, Fry pursues Kane to Liberty Island. As they struggle on the crown of the Statue of Liberty, Fry slips over the edge. Kane tries to pull him up, but Fry's sleeve tears and he falls to his death. Actually, audiences sympathized with Fry, the villain. Perhaps Hitchcock intended this!

Giddiness produced by being suspended from a height reached its most eloquent, even mystical, expression in *Vertigo*. The peril of falling from heights makes Detective Scottie Ferguson (Jimmy Stewart) acutely acrophobic. The film begins with Stewart looking down from a great height, dangling from a rooftop in pursuit of a criminal. The risk of falling was a physical tactic of suspense to describe impending dread or pervasive anxiety. Hitch's use of dangling scenes not only entertained through vicarious thrills, but also was his commentary on the existential plight of persons on the knife-edge of life. He used fear of heights as negative delight and to provide cathartic insight into fear, and the precarious nature of human existence confronted by such mysteries as romance, family history, religion, guilt, death, and the beyond. Thus, dangling situations are metaphors alluding to souls in suspense.

The climax of *North by Northwest* is played out on the

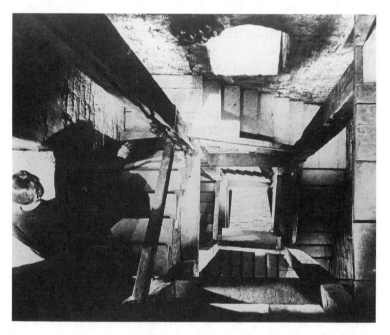

We, the audience, are made to feel Jimmy Stewart's vertigo cinematically: while the camera moves back, the lens zooms forward. In *Blackmail* (1929), Hitch experimented with a boom shot down a long staircase.

carved stone faces of Mt. Rushmore, the national monument in the Black Hills of South Dakota. Roger O. Thornhill (Cary Grant) sees his love, Eve (Eva Marie Saint), hanging precariously from a rockface and pulls her up. Hitchcock cuts to a scene in which Thornhill is in a train berth pulling Eve up to join him.

In Hitchcock's so-called hunter-and-hunted films, the suffering inflicted on the hero, or "wrong man," generally has three results: the personal growth and development of the hero; a romantic commitment to a woman from whom the hero was previously estranged; and greater national security. It is in these films that Hitchcock used the device of pursuit.

In *The 39 Steps,* after Richard Hannay (Robert Donat) learns about a plot against England, he is suspected of

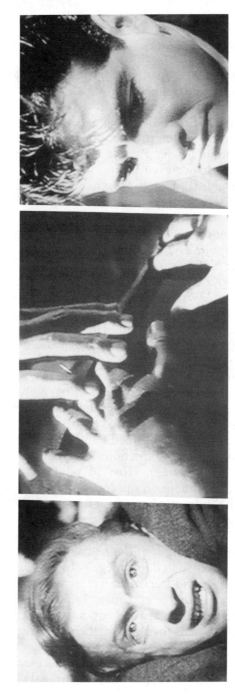

As the *Saboteur*, Norman Lloyd (left) falls from the Statue of Liberty, as Robert Cummings's out-stretched hand (right) tries to pull him up. Barely touching, their fingers recall Michelangelo's Sistine Chapel painting of God's creation of Adam.

murdering a woman agent. Fleeing, he searches the north English countryside to locate the culprit, a man missing a finger. He meets a beautiful blonde, Pamela (Madeleine Carroll). She becomes a fugitive by circumstance; handcuffed together they flee to a country hotel where they register as husband and wife. Pamela is uneasy about sharing a room. Both are handcuffed; ironically, the proprietress thinks they are lovebirds. Things are not as they seem. There are two pursuits—a suspense-filled "wrong-man" one of physical escape and hiding; the other of a reluctant courtship by an apparent criminal wooing the right woman under the illusion of his guilt. The double pursuit cleverly climaxes in one of cinema history's most delicious endings. In a theater Hannay shouts out to the stage performer with the fabulous retentive memory, "What are the 39 steps"? Through automatic reflex, the man blurts out the secret plans he is to carry out of the country that same night. He is shot; the spy ringleader is apprehended; Pamela accepts Hannay.

The finale has three levels of dense activity. In the foreground we see the backs of the two reunited lovers—she holding his handcuffed hand in her velvet-gloved one; Mr. Memory is in the middle ground being tended to; and in the background, are the dancing girls who have come onto the stage to calm the alarmed audience. There has been growth (meliorism) in all directions. The pursuit of "wrong men" in Hitch's films are mirrors of pilgrimage with descent and ascent dependent on the courage of the unwitting victim and the faith, however hesitant at first, of the woman encountered during the pursuit. This is the plot of *Young and Innocent, Saboteur,* and *North by Northwest.* Redemption through country-hopping is at the heart of *Notorious,* a subtle thriller about a dual search for integrity by FBI agent Cary Grant and a flawed Ingrid Bergman, willing to be a sacrificial pawn in a patriotic undercover caper. Pursuit is not a mere lateral displacement in space, but a spiritual struggle and self-discovery with love as a cathartic catalyst. There are more examples.

Robie (Cary Grant), a falsely accused jewel thief in *To Catch a Thief,* is pursued relentlessly by the gendarmes through the marketplace and streets of the Riviera and is finally cornered on a rooftop during a costume ball.

In *North by Northwest,* carefree Roger O. Thornhill (Cary Grant) is kidnapped in Manhattan's Plaza Hotel and is caught in an international plot. He meets Eve, an attractive blonde. Her name indicates she is a temptress. By flirting with Thornhill, she succeeds in winning his confidence and sending him on a wild-goose chase to Kansas where he narrowly escapes death on the open plain. The use of horizontal space to highlight peril is matched in the penultimate scene with vertical space and risk to life. Later, Eve, a double agent, helps Thornhill foil the spy ring. At the end of the story, Roger and Eve fall in love, and a national danger is averted. Obviously, the Master of Suspense realized that imperilment scenes of dangling, pursuit, and deadline pressures enhanced romantic attraction. *North by Northwest* gingerly turns imminent death by pursuit and dangling into matrimonial bliss.

In *Torn Curtain,* scientist Michael Armstrong (Paul Newman) pretends to defect to the East Germans; in reality, he had been sent by the United States government to secure a vital formula. After killing a suspicious official at a farmhouse, he is hounded by the authorities. Discovered in a theater with his fiancée, Sarah Sherman (Julie Andrews), he escapes by screaming "Fire!" and the race is on again, this time in the midst of a frightened crowd. He escapes, but only after the audience is convinced that he has been killed when the basket he hid in was fired on.

Family Plot has Julia Rainbird (Cathleen Nesbitt) hiring the spiritualist Blanche and (unknown to her) Blanche's accomplice and lover, George Lumley (Bruce Dern) to seek out her long-lost nephew, Edward Shoebridge. William Devane plays the nephew (now called Adamson) who realizes he is being pursued. He thinks Blanche and George have discovered his illegal activities and has them followed by his henchman, Maloney, who attempts to kill them by sabotaging their car. Maloney is himself killed during his second murder attempt.

Hitchcock deliberately created anxiety and suspense in his films, suggesting that things are not as they seem. Horror may wear a bow tie; an innocent glass of milk may contain poison;

a loving husband may be a bluebeard, murdering one wife after another; a young man running a motel may be a schizophrenic sex maniac; a savage rape and murder may take place at midday in an office or an apartment, as passersby idly chat on the street below. Just as the wrong man is pursued in *The Lodger, The 39 Steps, Young and Innocent, Saboteur,* and *North by Northwest,* so too innocent objects and places often turn out to be sources of doom, making justice, peace, and stability extremely unpredictable.

In addition to dangling and pursuit themes, Hitch used the race against time. In *Sabotage,* a young boy is asked to deliver two tin reel-cans of motion pictures to the post office. Inside one of the tins is a timebomb set to go off at 1:45. The boy is detained on the way, distracted by the pageantry of the Lord Mayor's parade in London. The audience grows nervous for it knows of the deadline. The lad boards a double-decker bus. The conductor lets the boy on reluctantly, for the former thinks that the latter is carrying flammable material. It is, of course, explosive. The boy plays with the small dog belonging to another passenger who is seated behind the driver. Hitchcock periodically cuts to a large public clock to heighten the tension. Only the audience knows that the timebomb is ticking away. Hitchcock stretches the hours, then the minutes, and then the final seconds in an incredible sequence of dramatic suspense. The bomb finally explodes. Film viewers were horrified over the death of three innocents—the boy, the elderly woman, and her pet puppy. Later, Hitchcock had doubts about the scene since audiences resented the deaths involved.

In *Notorious,* U.S. agent Devlin (Cary Grant), with his ally and lover, Alicia Huberman (Ingrid Bergman) acting as lookout, searches for important evidence in the wine cellar of the Nazi agent, Sebastian (Claude Rains). The audience is aware that the wine is running out at the party upstairs and the couple could be discovered at any moment. In a slightly comic cameo appearance, Hitch is seen drinking wine at the serving table in a rapid fashion, creating a sense of urgency—at this rate, the wine will run out and the secret in the cellar will be disclosed. It is a nerve-racking moment as we identify with the two agents and their precarious situation.

In *Frenzy,* Jon Finch, as the wrong man, risks his life to escape prison. We share his breathtaking anxiety as "dangling, pursued, and out of time."

Collapsing time is an advantage cinema has over theater, which cannot so easily change the sense of time. Years can be made to pass by showing calendar pages falling; months can pass by showing the change of season. In *The Ring* (1927), Hitch builds a quick temporal interval by showing a shower of rice coming down, thus indicating the lapse of time between a wedding and the reception scene to follow. It is an economical device to push the clock ahead, one of cinema's great advantages.

Hitch's brief appearance in *Rear Window* shows him pushing the hands of a clock forward. He is seen with a relaxed countenance, looking at a composer seated at a piano. Reflecting on this cozy cameo scene, I saw that Hitch, as the director, determined the pacing of the plot. There is a remarkable resemblance to the classic rescue scene of the southern belle held captive by the Union soldiers in Griffith's

The Birth of a Nation. Rear Window builds to a dramatic climax when the killer (Raymond Burr) enters Jimmy Stewart's apartment. The rapid intercutting does not follow the normal passage of time, but hastens the heartbeat of the audience. Just as in *The Birth of a Nation,* so too in *Rear Window* we are emotionally invested in the rescue. Neither Griffith nor Hitchcock disappoints the audience's expectations.

There is a subtle, if unintended, spiritual message behind the melodramatic race against time. Hitchcock was aware that the great timebomb in every human life is death, as in the horrifying explosion of the bus in *Sabotage.* The race against time is one in which all of us are involved. Hitch's Jesuit education exposed him to the *Spiritual Exercises* and impressed on him the key meditation on death as a penalty for the Fall and our inevitable shared destiny. The dramatic effects Hitchcock achieved in his pictures strongly depended on the imminence of death by means other than natural causes.

Take one suspenseful scene in *Foreign Correspondent.* Joel McCrea is on the tourist's lookout platform of the cathedral tower. Edmund Gwenn has been contracted to eliminate him. When no one is around, the would-be assassin rushes with hands extended at the camera (that is, the audience) to push McCrea to his death. Cut! People collect around a broken body on the street; when we next see Joel McCrea, we know that somehow Gwenn has died instead of his intended victim. The subjective camera shot of Gwenn's murderous look and out-turned palms makes us feel the shadow of death. Thus we have a preview, a kind of substitute experience of that unique and unrepeatable event. We are pursued by death. We never see the pursuit, of course, but that is why Hitchcock was so effective—he could make his audience feel what cannot be directly photographed. The contest with the clock is such that the clock actually becomes the killer.

Hitchcock referred to something similar in his comment about the cymbalist in *The Man Who Knew Too Much.* The cymbalist, playing for the orchestra in Royal Albert Hall, is "unaware that he is the instrument of death." "He doesn't know it," Hitchcock said, "but in fact, he's the real killer." When he clashes the cymbals, that is the signal for the assassin to shoot the diplomat. So, too, the ticking clock can be viewed as the killer. We are all, in a philosophical sense, in a race against time. In Hitchcock's films, meanings reverberate, pointing beyond the concrete scene to more philosophical, even religious, concerns, ones associated with personal fears with which audiences invariably identify.

In *Strangers on a Train,* the final scene shows the killer, Bruno Anthony (Robert Walker), struggling with Guy Haines (Farley Granger) on a runaway carousel. The ticket taker, an elderly man, courageously volunteers to crawl under the madly spinning merry-go-round to reach the brake. Hitchcock cuts from the two men struggling to the man on his knees, trying not to be struck by the platform revolving above his head. This scene was fraught with danger when shot, and Hitch resolved that he would never again expose a person to such risk.

Years later, in *The Birds,* Hitchcock had Tippi Hedren exposed to the beaks of attacking birds in the famous attic scene where the audience witnessed that peculiar obsession of Hitchcock, blood and blondes. The scene is intense; it is a race against time. Chase melodrama is as old as the movies, but Hitchcock elevated it to a metaphysical plane by giving it a universal anxiety beyond that of a particular film character in danger. The audience personally senses peril—a risk to limb and most often to life, but also, at times, to one's reputation (*Easy Virtue, Murder!, The Wrong Man*) or, to psychic trauma and madness (*Vertigo, Psycho,* and *Marnie*).

For one with a Catholic sensibility such as Hitch, the belief in an afterlife would be an added dimension of imperilment, as Hitch indicates in *I Confess.* There the theme of the risk of mortal sin, possible eternal damnation, for a violation of the seal of confession is the motivational piston that drives the engine of the plot (and, understandably, makes the film less interesting for those not initiated in the Catholic faith). Two people, Mr. and Mrs. Keller, die to exonerate Fr. Logan (Montgomery Clift), but belief in an afterlife turns such sadness into religious consolation for those who understand Logan's actions in sacramentally reconciling them to the God of their faith before they expire. Again, this subliminal and highly unusual type of happy ending would be lost even on many nonreflecting Catholics.

Dangling, pursuit, and racing against time are mechanisms Hitchcock used to create suspense, but they are more than suspense tactics. Hitchcock exposes us to a brief moral education, one that demands trial and suffering, the risk of being caught and executed even though innocent, and the insecurity of not knowing whether things will end well or badly. Dangling, pursued, and out of time are metaphors for the dark consequences of a fallen and deeply disordered world, one in which happiness and harmony are never guaranteed and are only possible on the condition of personal responsibility, a courageous will to face the challenges of discontinuity in human life and not to be awed by the seemingly absurd but rather to cooperate with the mysteries of existence.

In the next chapter I shall examine Hitch's use of Expressionism to create suspense. He is rightly identified with melancholy and moody themes. Closer study of his signature, however, reveals that he folded into the frames of his films—even the earliest—the classic concerns of the species regarding the meaning of life. True, he was reflecting his own fears, his own anxieties, his own romantic yearnings, his own deep need for expression. Nonetheless, he touched profound chords of empathy in all of us, perhaps more than other film directors. For Hitchcock did not indulge in a merely fashionable existential scream of protest against the given order of things, as did Jean-Paul Sartre, but rather spelled out in images a struggle ethic implicit in biblical faith and, most pointedly, in the Ignatian *Exercises*.

Taking advantage of a remarkable new technology, motion pictures, the Master of Suspense tried to communicate the brooding doubts, mercurial moods, and exhilarating new opportunities for prosperity and pleasure that have characterized the twentieth century. Beneath all the myriad changes that have taken place since Hitch's birth has been an explosion of consciousness incomparable in world history. If we are more secure from natural disasters, the vagaries of cosmic events, and acts of God, we are still heir to the psychological and spiritual insecurities that Hitchcock has tried to deal with through such photographable suspense devices as dangling, pursued, and out of time. We must reassess this genius of both light and darkness if we wish to grasp the breadth and depth of his film signature.

Notes

1. Humphry House, "The Mood of Doubts," in *Ideas and Beliefs of the Victorians: An Anthology* (New York: E. P. Dutton, 1966), pp. 75–76.
2. Ibid., pp. 76–77.

CHAPTER IX

Techniques of Expressionism

The term *Expressionism* describes a technique used in the visual and literary arts in which the representation of reality is distorted to communicate inner feelings and emotions. It aims at creating a psychological or spiritual effect rather than at recording external events in logical sequence. Thus, we feel the brooding presence of evil and disorder even when we cannot hear or touch it directly. Hitchcock used the technique to suggest risks and dangers and to hint at the adversarial forces of good and evil that lie behind what is trusted and familiar. Although feelings of determinism, even cynicism, can be communicated through the devices of Expressionism—implying that human beings are powerless to change events—Hitchcock's films are not fatalistic, since, with very few exceptions, they suggest that adversity creates an opportunity for the hero or heroine to achieve greater understanding and deeper character development.

In this respect, his films differ from those of Fritz Lang, Otto Preminger, Billy Wilder, Michelangelo Antonioni, and Ingmar Bergman, whose works cannot be justly qualified in terms of "open-ended pessimism." Hitchcock's pictures can be seriously related to the images and meditation scenes from the *Spiritual Exercises* in that they use stark expressionistic devices to motivate the retreatant or audience to follow a passion-death-resurrection pattern. This pattern is especially evident in *I Confess, The Wrong Man, North by Northwest, The Birds, Marnie,* and even, although subtly, in *Frenzy* and *Family Plot.* Let us analyze the element of Expressionism in the *Spiritual Exercises* of Ignatius of Loyola.

If we fan out the four "Week" divisions, we find an alternating pattern of darkness, then light, again darkness, and once again light. The solemn themes of the First Week deal with the misuse of godly attributes in creatures: the fall of the angels (Lucifer and his cohorts) and that of Adam and Eve in the Garden of Eden, and the hypothetical case of a man who suddenly dies in a state of deliberate mortal sin. The subsequent meditations are equally gloomy: a review of the personal life of sin by the retreatant, followed by meditations on death, the final judgment, and Hell. During this week, the retreatant is advised to shun happy thoughts by avoiding sunlight and practicing austerity with fasting, less sleep, and fleshly chastisements. Obviously, *Expressionism* is the most apt descriptor.

The mood changes as the Second Week introduces a meditation on Christ as king, beckoning volunteers to follow Him, even by actual poverty, to attract others to the imitation of Christ and the greater glory of God. (Contained in this major meditation are the principles of the *magis* and *agere contra*—the spirituality of struggle leading to meliorism.) Throughout the meditations and reflections, emphasis is placed on the attractiveness of Jesus and the joy of embodying His preachings. At the end of this Week, an Election is made, a life-transforming decision with practical consequences for a faithful following of the Lord.

The Third Week treats the passion and death of Christ, a theme which is dark, even when consoling. Again, as in the First Week, self-denial is encouraged to help the retreatant to grasp that Christ died *for each individual* (here we recognize the "wrong-man" theme). Long expressionistic shadows fall across the inner world of the retreatant in the contemplation of the betrayal of Jesus, his four unjust trials, the way of the cross, death by crucifixion, and descent from the cross. Obviously, the Fourth Week, dealing with the resurrection and ascension of the Lord to heaven, is uplifting and joyously impressionistic. The retreatant puts aside mortification and dark thoughts to rejoice with the miraculous victory of the Lord over death. We see, therefore, that the *Spiritual Exercises,* with its unmistakable geometrical symmetry, is a kaleidoscope of, first, inky shadows, and then, bright lights.

A distinguishing characteristic of Expressionism is the use

of shadows. In all of Hitchcock's films, dramatic effects are created in nighttime scenes or by emphasizing details of nature. Hitchcock learned from the German silent films how to suggest hostility, danger, and moody mystery, as in *The Lodger* (fog), *The 39 Steps* (mist), *Spellbound* (snow), *Lifeboat* and *Psycho* (rain), and *Marnie* (thunder and lightning). Shadows cast by moonlight, streetlights, or fire arouse suspicion and destabilize the audience.

In his most expressionistic film, *The Wrong Man*, the audience feels trapped along with the man falsely accused—there is no escape. Throughout the film, Hitch made extended use of the jarring sounds of New York City subways and elevated trains to convey a subconscious premonition of urban chaos through the intermittent cycle of infernal metallic noises. Critics missed this brilliant use of aural Expressionism crucial to a deeper understanding of Hitchcock's personal emotional message. Only close attention to the soundtrack can provide an appreciation of Hitch's intention to subvert our trust in the normal routine of home life, work, and the commuting journey. The film is saturated with irony; for example, a detective tries to reassure Manny Balestrero that the "normal routine" of crime investigation is eminently fair, not realizing that it will create a nightmare for this "wrong man" and his family.

Related to the use of shadows and ominous sounds, but different as a technique, is single-source lighting. A narrow focus of light highlights a person or object while plunging the rest of the picture into shadowy darkness. The most memorable example of single-source lighting is in *Suspicion*, where John Aysgarth (Cary Grant) brings a glass of milk to his wife (Joan Fontaine). Hitchcock had a light bulb placed inside the glass to make it the principal focus of attention. Other examples include the lit windows of the Bates mansion in *Psycho* and the shadowed wall in the room of Mrs. Bates. These effects provide an eerie atmosphere, confirming our suspicion of the presence of evil.

Shuttered windows, bars, broken mirrors, and shattered glass are other devices of Expressionism. Shuttered windows seen at night set the mood in *The Lodger, Blackmail, The*

39 Steps, The Lady Vanishes, Psycho, and *Marnie.* The face of a scared rapist-murderer is framed by a window with a broken pane in *Frenzy;* the scene suggests psychological imprisonment. A similar mood is created in *Strangers on a Train,* when we witness a strangling through the broken lenses of the victim's eyeglasses. Later, Guy Haines (Farley Granger) is shown the broken lenses of his murdered wife's glasses by Bruno Anthony (Robert Walker). Haines joins Anthony, the murderer, behind an iron rail fence. It is night, and the light from a street lamp casts shadows. The setting hints at moral guilt—both men seem to be behind prison bars—and the effect of the broken lenses and the shadows is unsettling. Clanging jail doors and unsympathetic jailers also unsettle the audience in films such as *Murder!, The Paradine Case, The Wrong Man,* and *Frenzy.* Broken teacups indicate distraction and escape in *Young and Innocent* and signal chaos in *The Birds.*

Staircases, usually winding, are a classic technique of Expressionism inherited from the silent movies and appear frequently in Hitchcock's films:

- In *Suspicion,* John Aysgarth climbs a staircase to bring the glass of milk to his wife.
- In *Foreign Correspondent,* an American reporter (Joel McCrea), spying on foreign agents in a Dutch windmill, tries to escape down a narrow winding staircase.
- In *Saboteur,* winding stairs lead to the top of the Statue of Liberty, where a struggle takes place and the foreign agent falls to his death.
- In *Strangers on a Train,* Guy Haines climbs a spiral staircase to visit Bruno's father. A huge guard dog waiting at the top of the stairs heightens the feeling of danger.
- In *I Confess,* Ruth (Anne Baxter) descends an outdoor spiral staircase to embrace an eager Michael (Montgomery Clift) prior to his entering the seminary for priestly studies.
- In *Vertigo,* steep stairs in the mission church create a destabilizing atmosphere, producing in the audience the claustrophobia that Scottie Ferguson (James Stewart) feels.

Germanic expressionism in *Strangers on a Train*—stairs, shadows, brooding camera angle, a revolver, and a menacing Great Dane.

An important device in Hitchcock films, staircases hint at the uncertainty of existence and dangers that lie unseen. They also suggest that there are secrets to be learned. This can be seen clearly in *Psycho,* where the Victorian home of the Bates family has three levels connected by stairs. In *The Wrong Man, Psycho,* and later *Vertigo,* the director employed aural and visual expressionistic techniques to lead the audience on the descent into hell, much as the Ignatian *Exercises* does in an imaginative manner of meditation. Expressionistic techniques also hint at the adversarial forces of good and evil that lie behind what is trusted and familiar. This is sometimes referred to as expressionistic dualism, suggesting that people are other than what them seem.

Interesting is the idea of the doppelgänger (the alter ego, or another person who resembles us in what we are or could become). Hitchcock became familiar with this concept in the German silent-film studios where he made two films at the beginning of his career. Hitchcock returned again and again to this theme, in *Shadow of a Doubt, Strangers on a Train, Vertigo, Marnie,* and *Frenzy.* In *Psycho,* Norman Bates's schizophrenia (Norman/Mother) is an extreme instance of dualism—two people with an overlapping psychic identity. A dualistic motif appears so often in fact that one suspects Hitchcock himself had thoughts of being other than who he actually was. The desire for another identity is not hard to imagine in a man of his physical appearance. Perhaps through his films he managed to become someone else in the characters he created. Through motion pictures, directors as well as audiences can vicariously lead other, sometimes more interesting, lives.

Mention should also be made of music as an important device of Expressionism since it can prepare an audience for unknown dreads and chilling surprises. Hitchcock built upon the tradition of mood music at Universal Studios to make ample and effective use of what was cleverly called "music of the fears."[1] He also used the talents of Hollywood's noted composers for the background music. Franz Waxman, Dmitri Tiomkin, and Bernard Herrmann were among the outstanding composers who worked with Hitchcock. *Psycho* provides the most brilliant example of such music, succeeding in taking soundtrack music out of the category of a mere auditory prop and elevating it to the category of cinematic art. Try to imagine the shower scene and Marion's death without Bernard Herrmann's accompanying musical score, "dissonant glissandos" and violins bowing faster than Mrs. Bates's knife.[2] (Herrmann used only the string section of his orchestra. At first, Hitch wanted no music at all.) The scene is both a marvel of sound and a masterpiece of visual editing. Herrmann succeeded in meeting the first job of a composer, namely, "getting inside the drama."[3] In Paramount's *Vertigo,* there is more music than spoken dialogue. The audience is made to feel Scottie Ferguson's lingering memories of Madeleine.

Hitchcock used the techniques of Expressionism to

heighten suspense and fear. We have considered shadows, nighttime scenes, single-source lighting, shuttered windows, prison bars, fences, broken mirrors, shattered glass, ominous signs of nature (fog, rain, snow, thunder, and lightning), staircases, the doubling of characters (doppelgänger), and evocative sound tracks. According to veteran co-workers, Hitch had an amazing grasp of moviemaking and would never settle for anything less than the best ("There is only one best shot and a thousand other possible shots," he was quoted as saying). The heavy, at times oppressive, expressionistic atmosphere of almost all his major films stands in sharp contrast to his humor and humanity. It is known, however, that he reacted quickly in the face of opposition and to the demands of authority figures.

Evidently the Expressionism used in his films reflected Hitch's own inner anguish and torment. With a vivid imagination and what seems to be an acute state of emotional insecurity, he was attracted to such beautiful actresses as Joan Fontaine, Ingrid Bergman, Grace Kelly, Eva Maria Saint, Janet Leigh, and Tippi Hedren. His films showed romance as dark, passionate, and teasing. The love scenes are filled with longing and desire. Donald Spoto's *Dark Side of Genius* documents Hitch's personal turbulence in this regard, and close colleagues of Hitchcock remarked to me about his inordinate attraction to many of his actresses, quite noticeable to keen observers of human nature. Nevertheless, those who knew him considered him not only a genius but a feeling and faithful person as well. Expressionism was the style suited to his sensitive nature so aware of dissonance in life, the principle of anarchy. Bernard Herrmann's music was eminently congruent with Hitch's style, as it was with that of Orson Welles, the actor and director. This study offers evidence that Hitchcock was also a master of psychoreligious phenomena in ways that brought this-worldly concerns together with other worldly considerations. This spanning of time and eternity, of reason and faith, of nature and grace, of action and contemplation is an essential ingredient of the Ignatian charism and classic Jesuit spirituality in its deepest expression.

We should not be surprised at Hitchcock's preference for

Cary Grant felt Hitch did not know how to direct comedy in *North by Northwest*. Eva Marie Saint enjoys his antics.

TOP: *Stage Fright* presents reverse feminine sides: Jane Wyman as Eve and Marlene Dietrich as a post- "Blue Angel" Charlotte (which rhymes with "harlot"). BOTTOM: In *Family Plot,* Barbara Harris and Bruce Dern survive a spine-tingling drive on a steep mountain road in a car with no brakes. Having smashed into a wooden cross, they emerge (in a comic scene) with him carrying her away—Pietà style, thus reaching the dénouement.

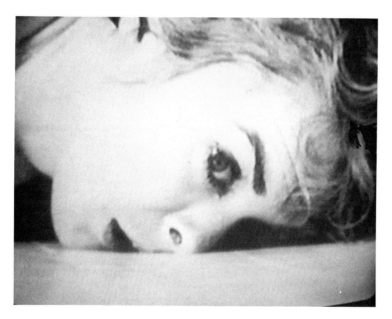

TOP: No scene in film history is as rich in psycho-spiritual terms as *Psycho*'s shower scene. Guilty of theft, Marion Crane repented and pledged restitution of the stolen funds. As Marion reaches out to us, we are both implicated and also made to see her as Christ-like, washed in innocent blood. BOTTOM: Marion Crane's direct stares again implicate the audience, now as voyeurs, as passive "thrill seekers."

Marnie (Tippi Hedren) steals from rich men. The money is a phallic symbol, while the purse is a Freudian-type female symbol.

In *North by Northwest,* a crop-dusting plane almost kills Cary Grant, pursued and out of time, but now, after the dénouement, having a clear cause and a "sticking point."

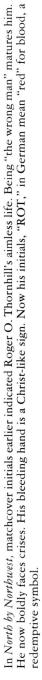

In *North by Northwest*, matchcover initials earlier indicated Roger O. Thornhill's aimless life. Being "the wrong man" matures him. He now boldly faces crises. His bleeding hand is a Christ-like sign. Now his initials, "ROT," in German mean "red" for blood, a redemptive symbol.

TOP: In *Notorious,* love purifies the self-interest of Cary Grant and Ingrid Bergman, deepening their romance and character. (A case study of moral betterment or the *meliorism* of St. Ignatius of Loyola.) BOTTOM: In *The Birds,* Tippi Hedren's "cruciform" suffering placates the vengeful birds and unites her and her lover's family.

TOP: In *The 39 Steps,* Robert Donat is handcuffed to Madeleine Carroll. This "love-on-the-run" film was inspired by Capra's auto motel scene with Clark Gable and Claudette Colbert in *It Happened One Night.* BOTTOM: In *The Wrong Man,* the Sacred Heart of Christ is a central icon, suggesting a miracle. A distraught Mrs. Balestrero (Vera Miles), double-imaged, angrily faces husband Manny (Henry Fonda), who is also doubled.

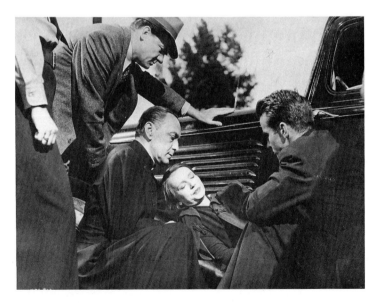

TOP: In *The Birds* (1963), Hitchcock reversed the roles of birds and people. In the opening scene, birds are in cages. At the end, the humans are seen trapped by birds. BOTTOM: In a Pietà scene from *I Confess,* the sacristan's wife, Alma, is shot for revealing her husband as a murderer, thereby exonerating Montgomery Clift's priest. (Was Hitch sending a crypto-message to his wife, Alma? Probably, since Hitch changed the name of the woman in the novel.)

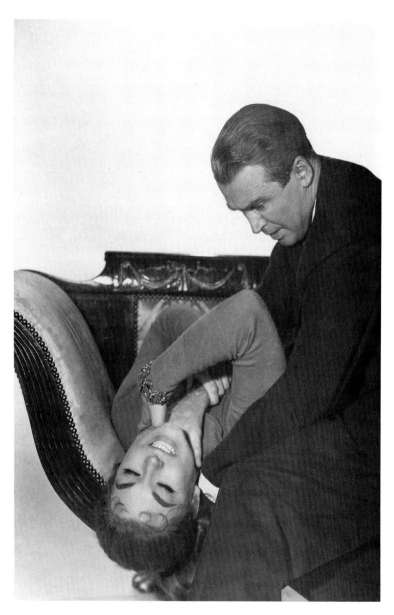

Vertigo suggests a recurring Hitchcock motif: men incline more to strangle women (*The Lodger, Strangers on a Train, Dial M for Murder, Frenzy*), while women tend to stab men (*Blackmail, Sabotage, Dial M for Murder*).

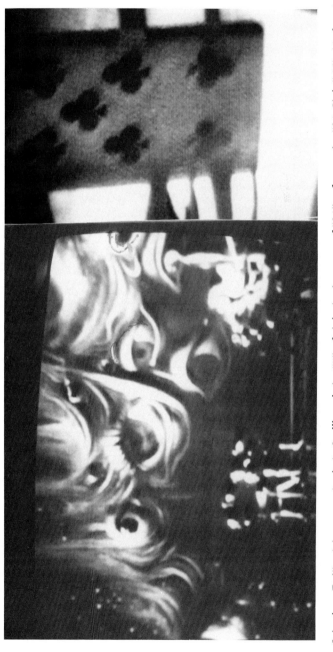

In Salvadore Dali's nightmare episode in *Spellbound*, the "7" of clubs in the game of "21" refers to the "21 Club," Hitch's favorite New York City nightclub; the "7" surreal eyes connote "life is a stage" with onlooking spectators.

In *Shadow of a Doubt,* the innocent Charlie (Teresa Wright) causes the death of her murderous Uncle Charlie (Joseph Cotten), who tried to kill her. Is she now like him?

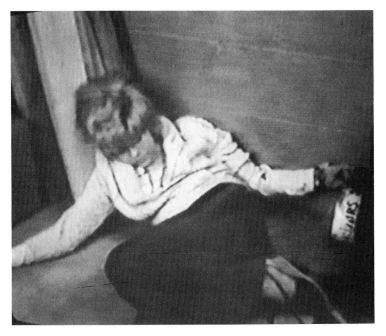

Madame Blanche (Barbara Harris) is attacked by *Adam*son. Her name means white, in contrast to his black eyes, hair, mustache, and clothing.

In *The Lady Vanishes*, Margaret Lockwood plays Iris Henderson. Note her initials on a scarf within a circular symbol, half "S"-shaped. Roman Catholic Mass vestments have a stole (scarf) and a dress-like robe, the chasuble, with IHS inscribed on it (Latin initials for Jesus Christ Savior).

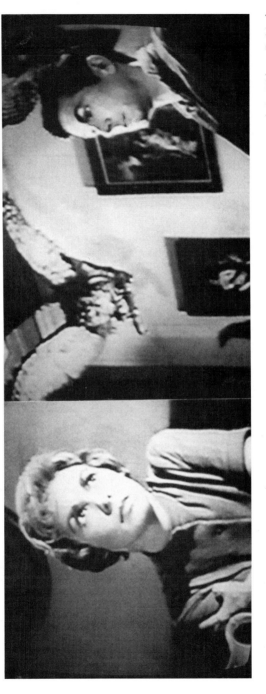

Anthony Perkins (right) says: "We all go a little mad sometimes!" The painting on the left shows Susanna and the Elders. Behind it is a peephole to the guest room. His guest, Janet Leigh (left) holds her arm exactly as Susanna in the picture.

Dial M for Murder shows a lively Grace Kelly in red; later, her dress becomes black. Escort Robert Cummings watches her gentle farewell to husband Ray Milland, planning her murder.

Underlying this cameo is Hitch's motto: "Man does not live by murder alone; he must have affection, encouragement, and an occasional drink."

what the eye takes in rather than what the ear picks up. Hitchcock learned a great deal from such German filmmakers of the silent era as Fritz Lang, Carl Mayer, and F. W. Murnau, who had a marked influence on him. In 1924, he spent nine months at the UFA Studio in Munich working on an English film, *The Pleasure Garden.* There he learned that the mobile, or "unchained," camera has the power to free the human eye from bodily limitations and make it float through space—looking down from heights, moving up the face of tall buildings, and peering through windows. It is rewarding to study *Rear Window, Vertigo, Psycho,* and *Frenzy* for an appreciation of Hitchcock's skillful use of the camera and his editing techniques, for that is how he "directed" audiences. That was his chief concern; he directed his audiences more than he directed the actors. He generally accomplished this by making the audience identify with a morally ambiguous situation, objectively wrong but subjectively plausible and, perhaps, legally justifiable.

The clearest example of the Hitchcock technique for involving the audience in the gray areas of moral conduct is *Rear Window* (1953). L. B. Jeffries (James Stewart), a photographer, is recovering at his Greenwich Village apartment from leg and hip injuries. Despite the presence of the romantic Lisa Fremont (Grace Kelly) and a visiting nurse (Thelma Ritter), Jeffries is bored and spends his time peering through binoculars into the apartments across the courtyard. The audience gradually identifies with Jeffries and his temptations to voyeurism, to looking at life through a lens. Viewers never feel disgusted with themselves for doing this; they accept the view of the world they receive from the "rear window." Hitchcock once remarked:

> I'll bet you that nine out of ten people, if they see a woman across the courtyard undressing for bed, or even a man puttering around in his room, will stay and look. No one turns away and says: "It's none of my business." They could pull down the blinds, but they never do; they stand there and look out.[4]

He admitted to the French film critic and director François Truffaut that he was primarily interested in providing "a real index of individual behavior." At the heart of his moral or ethical vision is a realism about temptations to lust, theft, murder, and neglect of duty. The camera eye invites us to identify with the story and its characters through direct emotional involvement. *Rear Window* is a masterpiece of ironic subtleties and the lives of "quiet desperation" which can be led even in an exciting neighborhood such as New York's Greenwich Village. The characters are flawed, frail but eminently forgivable. An exception, of course, is Thorwald (Raymond Burr), the wife-murderer, whose appearance Hitch modeled on David O. Selznick. The likeness is striking, and Hitch coached Burr to imitate personal mannerisms of the producer.[5]

The Lodger was Hitchcock's first film to deal with the wrong-man theme. As we saw in Chapter IV, "The Wrong

Man," a mysterious lodger keeps in his room a suspicious map containing references to the scenes of a crime; later, we learn that he was doing his own sleuthing in order to entrap a notorious killer. Hitchcock's visual use of Expressionism leads the audience to suspect the lodger when he first arrives at night, wearing a muffler wrapped around his neck. The camera's eye sees the shadowy figure as the villain, but things are not as they seem. Jealous that his fiancée has eyes for the suave, handsome Continental-looking man, the detective is anything but impartial. In this he resembles the attorneys, judges, and law enforcement officials in *Easy Virtue, Blackmail, Murder!, Sabotage, The Paradine Case, Strangers on a Train, I Confess,* and *The Wrong Man.*

For example, in *The Paradine Case,* a British attorney (Gregory Peck) not only defends but is in love with a woman accused of murder. The judge (Charles Laughton), himself married, has wandering eyes for other women. Hitchcock suggests that humans who administer the law are fallible and that society's procedures for justice are very dubious. The film used multiple cameras to obtain diverse points of view in the dark, formal setting of the English courtroom. The film's mood is heavy and unrelieved (diminishing the dramatic effect, I think). Everyone in the film has some emotional vested interest which undercuts the idea that the ritual of law (very solemn in England) is really unbiased and essentially fair.

In *Strangers on a Train,* the psychopathic Bruno Anthony is an uninvited guest at a Washington social affair. His menacing presence and maniacal manner changes the party into a macabre event. First, Bruno asks a dignified judge at the party how he can sit down to dinner after sentencing someone to death. The suggestion is that official role-playing hardens a person's reactions to personal and societal needs. Then Bruno tries to demonstrate how to strangle someone. The guinea pig is a society matron, whose eyes bulge when he forgets where he is as he imagines the killing of Miriam Haines, his real victim. Hitchcock uses expressionistic camera angles, close-ups, and lighting to unbalance the audience's emotional states.

Even in *I Confess,* Hitchcock leaves us with a nagging doubt about the relationship that had existed between Fr. Logan

(Montgomery Clift) and Ruth Grandfort (Anne Baxter). As we saw earlier, prior to her marriage and his entrance into the seminary, they were forced to spend the night in an abandoned house due to a sudden storm. Though they are innocent of the murder of the blackmailer who had seen them coming out of the house, it is insinuated that Fr. Logan felt a deep sense of relief over the demise of someone who could embarrass the woman he once loved. Reason goes along one path; feelings go along another. This is not an exception, Hitchcock implies, even for the saintly.

In *The Wrong Man,* Manny Balestrero (Henry Fonda) fingers his rosary during his trial for armed robbery. We see his lips move in silent prayer. Hitchcock cuts to the dangling crucifix at the end of the rosary in order to increase anxiety and distrust of the legal system. Hitch has Manny gaze around the court in mute astonishment. He sees the prosecutor smile as an aide whispers an apparently humorous remark into his ear. Manny watches another legal functionary doodle on a piece of paper. He looks at the jury and notices bored and inattentive faces. Two court offices chatter idly nearby. When he looks to the back of the court, where the visitors sit, he observes a well-dressed woman in the first bench putting on her lipstick. This is a remarkable scene, reminiscent of the trial of Longfellow Deeds (Gary Cooper) in Frank Capra's *Mr. Deeds Goes to Town* (1935). In that scene, Deeds observes the strange, nervous habits of several people in the courtroom and cites these idiosyncrasies to prove that his own eccentricities do not legally disqualify him from inheriting $20 million.

Whereas Capra's scene is comic and impressionistic, Hitch's camera makes Manny's observations more melancholy and expressionistic. Since he is praying, his is the eye of God. The camera's eye makes us see with Manny's eye, suggesting that there is a higher witness to the process of human justice, not only Balestrero (Christopher, "Christbearer"). The Flemish painter Jan Breughel (1568–1625) composed a famous painting with the Crucifixion in the upper right-hand corner and the rest of the canvas filled with diverse people engaged in their own disparate kinds of activities. oblivious to Christ's sacrifice nearby. This painting resembles

Hitchcock's scene of the normal routine of the judicial process.

Hitchcock chose to leave his audiences in moral ambiguity and used mood-inducing sight and sound techniques pioneered by the Germans in the silent era of the 1920s. Hitchcock learned the artistic devices to depict souls in suspense. The German directors, scriptwriters, and actors combined to make viewers feel insecure in deciding whether characters are actually good or bad, whether justice has been achieved, whether there would be a happy ending. Take F. W. Murnau's *Last Laugh,* the set of which Hitch attended while it was being shot in Munich. This expressionistic masterpiece takes the audience on a roller-coaster ride of uncertainty. At first, Emil Jannings's hotel doorman is joyous, then despondent (having been demoted to toilet attendant), then happy again when restored to his old position. Hitch's "open-ended pessimism" swung from very dark endings through troubled happy endings and, occasionally, to sunlit happy endings, such as in *The Man Who Knew Too Much.*

An apt example of Expressionism which is muted but moody can be found in Hitch's unprecedented use of color. As Hitchcock grew older and watched Cold War issues intensify, he became more moralistic about world affairs. He raised his sights beyond individuals to issues without neglecting the psychospiritual laws applied in his more personal dramas. Concentrating on sociopolitical problems in *Torn Curtain, Topaz,* and *Frenzy,* he attempted to diagnose the *dis*-ease of the twentieth-century Western world. All three films use color coding, have religious and mythic allusions, and refer to the darker themes of the First and Third Weeks of the Ignatian *Exercises.*

Frenzy is a superior Hitchcock entry, made in London after an absence of about twenty years. The chromatic accent is on the color brown to underscore subconsciously the thematic disorders in the environment, in human relationships, in marriage, and at the pathological level of murderous crime. The film opens with a shot of a helicopter flying over London Bridge and the Houses of Parliament. The Thames is seen as brown. Cut to a riverbank where Sir George, Minister of

Health, is giving a speech about environmental protection to a standing audience. The speech moves inspiringly, with the rhythms and colorful nouns and adjectives that the English language so comfortably accommodates. Though Hitchcock did not write the speech, it shows his preference for the elegance of that classical style which marked those privileged to receive the kind of humanistic training Hitchcock would have received at Saint Ignatius College:

> When I was a lad, a journey down the rivers of England was a truly *blithe* experience—bliss was it in that dawn to be alive, as Wordsworth has it. Brook lime and flag iris, plantain and marsh marigold rioted on the banks; [water shrews sang by the mossy alder stumps], and kingfishers swooped and darted about, their shadows racing over the brown trout [jumping from the clear waters to snap at the mayflies that danced away their short lives just out of reach]. Well, ladies and gentlemen, I'm happy to be able to tell you that these ravishing sights will be restored to us again in the near future thanks to the diligent effort of your government and [your] local authority. All the water above this point will soon be clear! Clear of industrial effluent. Clear of detergents. Clear of waste products of our society with which for so long we have poisoned our rivers [and canals].
>
> Let us rejoice that pollution will soon be banished from the waters of this river and that there will soon be no *foreign bodies*. . . . Let us today welcome back those water creatures which so delighted us as children—the tadpole, the crested newt, and the stickle-back.[6]

Suddenly the crowd's attention is drawn to the washing up on the shore of a woman's nude body with a fraternity tie wound around her neck. Her murdered corpse is a pollutant which dwarfs the issues rhetorically raised by the Minister of Health. The scene resembles the image which opened *Young and Innocent*. Both films have a female body washed ashore with an item of menswear suggesting an erroneous clue to the murderer: a raincoat belt in *Young and Innocent* and a necktie in *Frenzy*.

The pace picks up as Hitch cuts to media pollution, with the placards of the London tabloids clamoring sensationally: "Who is the 'neck-tie murderer?'" The suspect is a former RAF pilot, Michael Blaney (Jon Finch), who is fired from his job in a pub. We meet another pub worker, Babs Mulligan, a sympathetic, comely Cockney. She overhears the calloused conversation between a lawyer and a doctor. The latter refers to the shocking crimes as "a good juicy series of sex-murders," likely to draw tourists to London to see the fog, the Tower of London, and the "ripped whores." This is another example of civilized degradation—the pollution of gentlemanly conversation. Having seen the brown Thames, we now have the allusion to the brown ale of the pub. Later, Scotland Yard's Inspector Oxford (Alex McCowan) is served a brown fish-soup by his wife (Vivien Merchant). Moreover, "Bob Rusk," the name of the rapist-murderer, suggests brown, twice-baked dough.

One of Hitchcock's most chilling scenes is that of Rusk's tying up Babs's corpse in a sack of brown potatoes and loading it onto the back of a lorry. Later, he is struck by the thought of his missing stickpin with the initial "R"; he frantically returns to the truck, fumbles to find the telltale pin in her stiff fingers. He must break the fingers to retrieve the piece of evidence. An aural link occurs when Mrs. Oxford breaks the brown breadsticks at the dinner table. There are critics who see the scene in the truck as imitation pearl, a faded echo from earlier Hitchcock thrillers. I do not agree. Yes, the motif is one he used before (Robert Walker fishing for the cigarette lighter in *Strangers on a Train* and *Psycho*'s Anthony Perkins anxiously hoping Marion Crane's car will sink). But, as an ironist, even a satirist, of human nature, Hitchcock comes through as wanting to prove his point about the audience's affinity with amorality as gullible, easily led spectators with no "sticking point," no true moral direction.

Returning to *Frenzy* and its monochromatic thread of coffee-colored Expressionism, we follow Blaney's ingeniously planned escape from a prison hospital after being falsely sentenced for his friend's crimes. He purposely falls down the stairs to gain entry into the infirmary. His blood is seen as a brownish stain. Another taunting clue is the fact that Blaney's name may derive from the Middle English word "bleine," an infected sore, blister, or pustule. Again, the color brown is implied as an association with a blemish or infection. The Expressionism is not classic light-and-dark Expressionism but rather something in between, darker than gray. Unquestionably, the repetition of brown serves as a shorthand for the pollution of nature, friendships, fulfilling marriages, attractive women, and the public safety by the *dis*-eased serial murders. Notice the variety of impure uses of what should be held sacred.

Hitchcock saw color as a refinement of the cinema techniques of montage or cross-cutting to awaken in the audience awareness of ideas and moral issues. Hitch would have known of the pioneer work of the great Russian silent film directors, (e.g., Sergei Eisenstein, Vselevod Pudovkin) and their experiments with visual montage of sharply contrasting images. Beginning with *North by Northwest* and continuing through *Frenzy*, Hitch adopts color as a type of psychospiritual "Addition" to affirm, even heighten, the audience's mood regarding disorder and corruption, themes of the Ignatian First Week. *Frenzy*'s anger was also fueled by the disloyal double-agentry of Blunt, Maclean, and Philby! As in *North by Northwest*, Hitch saw England as under Hamlet's "antic disposition"—"mad" and heading "north-northwest." For different reasons, both the United States and Great Britain are collective symbols for the theme of the soul in suspense. As in *Psycho, The Birds,* and *Topaz,* Rusk's rape and murder of Blaney's ex-wife is another bravura aesthetic coup, a Freudian interpretation of Good Friday.

In a Hitchcock film, there is a great deal of thought invested in the plot and its audiovisual embodiment. Expressionism is an integral part of psychoreligious treatment of human existence, as the Ignatian *Exercises* attests so definitely. Hitch's heavy moods are not fatalistic and closed, mechanistically propelling people forward like mechanical toy soldiers. Rather, the director allows for change, conversion, and compassion. Even in *Psycho,* there is understanding and a ray of hope.

Whatever we think of Norman Bates in *Psycho,* he cannot

be judged. He is as innocent as his victim, Marion Crane. Both are criminals, but in the internal court of spiritual justice they are not guilty. Hitchcock's passion for reality and his Catholic upbringing made him see the social world of law and order framed against a psychological and moral, or ethical, world. In two Hitchcock films the details of the deaths are left unclear: *Blackmail* (was the rapist seduced?) and *Sabotage* (did Verloc run into the extended knife?). Wedded to expressionistic techniques, Hitchcock averted rash judgments, preferring to provoke reflection and balanced conclusions.

The claustrophobic closed set of *Rope* reeks of an expressionistic atmosphere. The audience wonders about the undeniable influence that a college professor (James Stewart) has exercised over the two (presumably) homosexual "thrill" killers. The professor was convinced that "murder is a crime for most men, but a privilege for the few." Can we blame the two students solely and exclusively for their admittedly callous crime?

Take the swank Expressionism in *Dial M for Murder*. Doesn't Ray Milland's wife (Grace Kelly) give undue attention to another man (Robert Cummings)? Doesn't the jealous husband have provocation for resentment, if not for revengeful murder? Expressionism blurs motives, suggesting invisible forces at work. (Again, the *Spiritual Exercises* of Ignatius deal explicitly with other-worldly agents of light and darkness.) Our reactions seem to confirm Hitchcock's suggestion that the audience is not reluctant to identify with evil intentions and fantasies. We are no better or worse than the people we are watching, although we may feel superior (as with the temptation of Jimmy Stewart's photographer in *Rear Window*). When we react to a scene in Hitchcock, we are, unknowingly, affirming his view of human nature, its contradictions, its disorder. Too much daylight (*Shadow of a Doubt*), too much sunshine (*The Trouble with Harry*), too much affluence and prosperity (*North by Northwest*) suggest fear, unhappiness, and denial of the reality of life as a combat zone where we as souls in suspense engage in a psychospiritual struggle.

As a great moral ironist, Hitchcock seemed to enjoy

Rope—both scenes feature "thrill-killers" Farley Granger (right) and John Dall (left). The murdered student in center has a cross symbol on his lapel. Note the bottle as a phallic symbol, a clue to homosexuality. (Yes, the three candles are intentional!)

dwelling on the human capacity for evil; he was also quick, however, to bring out the human ability to respond to love. In most of his films, crisis and danger serve to awaken the main characters from moral slumber and complacency and to bring about their personal growth and character development. Hitchcock's moral irony has spiritual and ethical overtones traceable to his Jesuit education, combining rigorous discipline (fright) with highly motivated personal achievement (delight). From the Jesuits he learned distrust of appearances and, especially, the notion that justice was unattainable in this world. His films caution us not to overtrust either perceptions or institutional pretences (the law, the press, government, and even religious institutions). He does this by depicting the representatives of these agencies at work and allowing the audience to draw their own conclusions. Recognizing that downward forces in life must be resisted in order to avoid the spread of disorder and chaos, Hitch always offered a message of courage and hope in his suspense and irony.

Expressionism suggests suprahuman forces at work on the individual. Saint Ignatius teaches that there are three thoughts: one from the invisible good spirit, one from the invisible evil spirit, and the autonomous thought of the person who is the battlefield for the contest of malevolent and benevolent inspiration. As with Ignatius, Hitchcock accents evil to elicit the will to triumph—the growth (*magis*) through counter-efforts (*agere contra*). Again, this is evidence of that "open-ended pessimism" which undergirds the *Spiritual Exercises*. Attention must be paid and moral effort must be made. So Hitchcock seems to be saying to us (or perhaps even warning us). The study of evil through expressionistic moods of seductive desolation and negative mood-empathy can be a valuable strategem for healing, for meliorism. The medical and psychiatric professions know that patients must retrace their disorders and subjectively feel corrective pain at the same time that they are getting objectively better. The spiritual life is no different. Health results from the correction of abuse and misuse—corrections seldom without personal cost to the one being healed.

Notes

1. John Broeck, "Bernard Herrmann: Music of the Fears," *Film Comment,* Vol. 12, No. 5 (September/October, 1976), pp. 56–60.
2. Ibid., p. 59.
3. Ibid., p. 56.
4. Truffaut, *Hitchcock,* p. 160.
5. Leonard J. Leff, *Hitchcock and Selznick* (New York: Grove/Weidenfeld, 1988).
6. From scripts of *Frenzy* at the British Film Institute and dialogue of the film as screened at the Library of Congress. Brackets indicate statements omitted in the film as screened but present in the scripts.

CHAPTER X

The Soul in Suspense

Hitchcock's suspense is not of the whodunit type. The uncertainty does not lie in identifying the criminal but rather in how justice is achieved, how the "wrong person" is vindicated and the real culprit apprehended. Only three of his films— *Murder!*, *The Paradine Case,* and *Stage Fright*—can be described as classical suspense mysteries in which the audience discovers only in the final scenes who perpetrated the crime and why. Most of Hitchcock's plots are based on dramatic irony, that is, the spectators are given clues and information which the story's characters do not have. If we know, as in *Sabotage,* that a young boy is carrying a timebomb on a bus, then whenever we see the clock's hands moving, we feel anxious for the lad and the other passengers.

Or take *Young and Innocent.* The police are pursuing a young man falsely accused of murdering a woman. Halfway through the film, we learn that the murderer is the victim's husband, a man whose eyes twitch. While fleeing from the police, the falsely accused young man meets a pretty woman; they fall in love; she believes his claim of innocence. Searching for the murderer, the couple enters a hotel. Moving high on an elevated crane, Hitchcock's camera follows them through the lobby into a large ballroom and begins to move down past the dancing guests to the bandstand. It zooms toward a drummer made up in minstrel blackface, focusing on his blinking eyes. A daring and memorable scene in cinema history, the shot provides the audience with knowledge that the couple has yet to learn. In effect the camera plays the "eye of God." Hitchcock is probing beneath physical appearances and disclosing inner states by suggesting what the human eye would not ordinarily see, as in the interior crises of *Vertigo*.

In this is a dimension of suspense that is hardly alluded to in studies of Hitchcock's art. His work has recognizable theological themes, cloaked in the entertainment guises of adventure, romance, horror, humor, and such deviant behavior as robbery, espionage, kidnapping, and murder. Early in his moviemaking career, Hitchcock discovered that the camera has the power to provide viewers with intimate knowledge; it can make them bearers of state secrets, witnesses to silent killings, and trusted recipients of information about people's motives and most hidden desires. Hitchcock understood well the lexicon of film grammar: parallel cutting, editing, close-ups, and camera mobility (the pan, the tilt, the dolly shot, the boom shot, the use of the zoom lens). The spectator was empowered to see human beings in many situations—alone, with a confederate or a paramour, in public or hidden from view, even that of the audience (who never do see the actual murder in *The Lodger*).

As a moral ironist, Hitchcock recognized the fickleness of human motivation and did his best work in the gray areas of doubt, suspicion, and complicity. Critics and students of his work have commented on the masterful way in which he treated the themes of social deviance and psychic instability. But none of them has recognized that the core of his obsession with crime and horror is fundamentally a religious pursuit with psychological groundings, what I would refer to as the soul in suspense. I firmly believe that Hitchcock's early religious experiences were reexamined and revised by his learning later of the new ways of probing the subconscious by psychoanalysis. Sigmund Freud's writing constituted a real revolution. Hitchcock saw its possibilities for the silver screen. When the German filmmaker G. W. Pabst made the unusual *Secrets of a Soul*, Hitchcock was impressed by the power of the camera to probe dream states and the horror of discovering a tragic event.

It is illuminating to study the reaction shots of faces upon viewing a dreadful scene. By such close-ups, Hitch magnified the lineaments of facial panic and cemented a bond with the viewer of both sympathetic compassion and antipathetic revulsion. In other words, the audience was brought into the screen's rectangle and thus also emotionally marked as souls in suspense. Understanding this psychological rhythm helps one to appreciate the meaning of several films that were either box office failures or not very popular, even though they numbered among Hitchcock's favorites.

Take *The Lodger,* a story full of the suspense created by an attempt to find a killer terrorizing women in nighttime London. (I treat this film's plot at greater length in Chapter IV, "The Wrong Man.") A jealous and overprotective inspector is assigned to the case, and he suspects an innocent but quietly suspicious-looking man. Hitchcock leads the audience to identify with the inspector; like him, it is quick to convict the "wrong man." In a sense, Hitchcock is X-raying the motives of the audience. By showing the fickle mood swings, he affirms human fallibility and cautions humility. The instinctive reactions of the audience invariably prove the director's abiding conviction about the mercurial nature of human feelings, judgments, and behavior. Again, let us not forget that Hitchcock's portly body and unattractive appearance made him ever conscious that people are not necessarily how they look.

In *Rich and Strange,* the Hills are an attractive young couple who have just inherited money and go on a voyage. The film, one of Hitchcock's favorites, depicts the emptiness of their lives, which are cushioned by easily gotten wealth. Despite exotic ports of call, the Hills find very little personal fulfillment. Their wealth is viewed with suspicion and—as in the *Spiritual Exercises* of Saint Ignatius—is presented as the first step toward inauthenticity and pride, unless corrected by detachment and attitudes of humility (the oppositional principle of the Ignatian *agere contra*—to go against forces of disorder). The film did not do well at the box office, but Hitchcock liked it and believed it had qualities of which he felt artistically proud. Not a few of Hitchcock's later suspense films have lessons about wealth and fame being corrosive of character and weakening moral resolve. Such films include *Rebecca, Suspicion, Notorious, Strangers on a Train, Dial M for Murder, To Catch a Thief, North by Northwest, Psycho, The Birds, Marnie,* and *Family Plot.*

Nor should we overlook the several pictures which dealt not so much with the upper classes or the powerful but with the greater social realism: street scenes (*The 39 Steps*); flophouses (*Young and Innocent*); country inns (*Jamaica Inn*); factories and dentist offices (*The Secret Agent,* the first version of *The Man Who Knew Too Much*). It is interesting to note that these films were released between 1934 and 1939. It was during his later American period (1940–1976) that he began setting his films in upper-middle-class and wealthy surroundings. I believe that he always drew a connection between social station and the inner life, realizing that the one shapes and molds the other.

His films frequently suggest that a person risks inauthenticity in direct proportion to his or her wealth, status, and authority. This reflects a central conviction of Saint Ignatius, who explicitly alerts the retreat director and the retreatant about the debilitating effects on the soul of power, fame, and riches. (The Jesuit tradition never condemns wealth or authority as evil per se but warns how it can erode character and lead to social injustice.) In short, Hitch realized (as did such spiritual masters as Francis of Assisi and Ignatius of Loyola) how wealth induces a special kind of fear. As Hitchcock grew successful and wealthy in Hollywood, he used more affluent surroundings in *Rebecca, Mr. and Mrs. Smith, Saboteur, Notorious, The Paradine Case, To Catch a Thief, North by Northwest*. Rich persons of status and influence changed for different reasons than poorer people. The mutability of character, Hitch understood, had a relationship with status, wealth, and influence.

Consider *Sabotage* (1936), a superbly crafted study of London's blue-collar class. Untypically, Hitch presents three souls in suspense, a saboteur, Verloc (Oscar Homolka), his American wife (Sylvia Sydney), and her teenage brother (Desmond Tester). Verloc, the owner of a neighborhood theater, is an anarchist bent on subversion. Verloc's wife is shocked to learn that her kid brother died in an explosion: Verloc had asked him to deliver a timebomb to a post office by 1:45 P.M. The boy tarried out of curiosity to see the Lord Mayor's parade. Few scenes in a Hitchcock movie are so poignant as the lad playing with a puppy belonging to a friendly dowager on a bus. The director cuts from the tender scene to the public clock as the fateful hour approaches. It is a case of dramatic irony: we, the audience, know what is happening. We are the souls in suspense, not the unknowing victims-to-be. The bus is blown up as the clock strikes 1:45. Our suspense is ended, but not our desolation or resentful discomfort. Why was this permitted in an entertainment picture?

The subtlety of *Sabotage,* an underrated film, lies in the inadvertent death of a child, a pet dog, and a kind elderly woman. (Hitchcock learned from Sergei Eisenstein, who, in *Battleship Potemkin,* imperiled a baby in a runaway carriage bouncing down the Odessa Steps.) Verloc is one of Hitch's more complex characters, with hardly a true villainous streak in him. He is a reluctant saboteur, a man with compassion who is disinclined to take the lives of innocent people. Hitchcock brought this out in the scene where Verloc meets a contact at the aquarium and recoils at the details of blowing up a government building, his next assignment. We are made aware by the close-up of Verloc's face that this is a task he finds eminently repugnant, that he had never anticipated such a commission on behalf of his fatherland. We have a quick portrait of a divided man, caught in the iron vise of conscience. It is a sublime form of suspense—the soul in suspense. The scene makes the perceptive viewer ask, What makes this man tick? What are the reasons for his activities? Hitchcock gives no clues, no answers. He never simplifies the human condition, seeing humankind as a moral battlefield with good and evil struggling for supremacy. Rather than facilely solving the mystery of human motivation, Hitchcock takes us into an area of ambiguity, taking satisfaction in leaving his audiences with muddled or suspended judgments.

Another example of souls in suspense is the scene in *Sabotage* where Verloc visits his fellow conspirators in the pet shop. It is a light scene, providing comic relief, until the proprietor remarks to Verloc about a friend of theirs, a lady in trouble, "She must carry her cross. Everyone must carry his cross." (I an inclined to see this marvelously witty and sympathetic man as an Hitchcockian reference.) The dialogue is not without its allusion to Verloc, who must carry the cross of his hateful assignment. Although the film seems to have a happy ending, the final scene leaves the audience with a feeling of uncertainty. Verloc is stabbed to death by his wife who learned that her brother died carrying the timebomb planted by her husband. When their theater residence burns down, it appears that she is safe from any suspicion of having killed him. The police inspector, although he knows the wife is implicated in the murder, is relieved, for he is now free to marry her. What can the audience expect regarding the future of a couple who harbor this terrible secret? Did the wife murder Verloc or, as one could plausibly argue, was he responsible for his own death? In the death scene, Hitchcock showed Verloc approaching his wife; she holds a carving knife in her trembling hand. She is nervous, and the scene is not clear, for Verloc almost seems to run into the blade. Did she really murder Verloc? Will she and her lover be found out? These same nagging doubts end *Blackmail, Murder!, The Paradine Case,* and *I Confess.*

Saboteur (1942) is an apt study of souls in suspense. Robert Cummings is accused of sabotaging a war plant; he enlists a woman (Priscilla Lane) to help him. They become lovers on the run and share fear. The real culprit (Norman Lloyd) is trapped in Manhattan's Radio City Music Hall. Firing into the crowd, he kills a man. (The audience, unaware, keeps laughing.) Finally, cornered atop the Statue of Liberty, the villain pleads for Cummings to help. He tries, but the saboteur falls to his death, thereby earning audience sympathy. How often Hitch lured the audience unwittingly into identification with a malefactor.

In *Shadow of a Doubt,* we are moved by the intense feelings Uncle Charlie (Joseph Cotten) has toward the parasitic women who were his victims. "Silly wives," he declares, "and what do these women do? You see them in the best hotels, wasting their money, drinking their money, losing at bridge, smelling of money, proud of their money and nothing else." The Bible and the Jesuit *Exercises* warn against riches, but without bitterness. This terrifying scene portrays Uncle Charlie as an avenging angel.

In *Strangers on a Train,* the audience holds its breath as Bruno Anthony (Robert Walker) reaches down the sewer grate to recover the cigarette lighter of Guy Haines (Farley Granger), which he needs to link the latter unjustly with the murder of his own wife. Forgetting the purpose of his mission, we are relieved when he retrieves it.

In *Marnie,* we hope that the charwoman does not hear the falling shoe as Marnie (Tippi Hedren) tiptoes in stocking feet out of the office with stolen funds. It turns out that the woman is deaf.

In *Frenzy,* we forget that we are rooting for a rapist and murderer as he frantically tries to recover the telltale tie clasp from the rigid hand of his latest victim.

In these and other ways, Hitchcock proves that human desires and motives are not to be trusted; they are too mutable, too chameleonlike. Hitchcock constantly anchors the audience's identification with deviants. The spectators' uncritical sympathy spurs them to root for the villain to escape. The audience repeatedly proves that Hitchcock's view of human nature is valid and objective. Things are not as they seem. Hitchcock is saying this of the audience as well as of the characters within the film; he revels in the gray areas of human motivation.

A splendid example is *The Paradine Case.* This film is only incidentally about the perils of courtroom justice. It is much more a story about respectable, upper-class men and women and the emptiness of their lives. The audience is shown clinical case studies of souls in suspense, people with no direction, no navigational map. Charles Laughton plays the role of a judge with moral frailities (which will be discussed in Chapter XIII, "Toward Sexual Maturity"). Hitchcock shows us that the judge, the defense attorney, and the defendant share moral fallibility, however relative the degree of gravity. The director does not permit the reflective viewer to indulge in a black-and-white ethical judgment, but teases out of him or her a sophisticated response—always leading to compassion and to pardon. The fact remains that Hitchcock's signature is as theological as it is psychological and sociological. Like his educational and religious mentors, Hitchcock tried to direct people away from simple judgments toward a posture of understanding and even forgiveness. The pivotal presupposition of the Ignatian *Exercises* is a benign interpre-

In *Rebecca,* Joan Fontaine and Laurence Olivier are married lovers. Never seen, Rebecca is his first wife.

tation of the deeds, words, and actions of others, which forms an integral part of Hitch's signature: his obsession with the gray areas of doubt. *Tout comprendre, c'est tout pardonner* (To understand is to pardon).

In *Rope,* the camera takes us into a New York City apartment where we witness a young man being strangled to death by two classmates. One of their college professors, Rupert Cadell (James Stewart), has taught them that a person can sometimes claim exemption from the moral order. "Murder is a crime for most men," he maintains, "but a privilege for the few." The film deals with another gray area: shared guilt. Who is more guilty, the person who teaches an idea, or the person who carries it out?

In *Strangers on a Train,* Bruno Anthony (Robert Walker) is willing to murder the wife of Guy Haines (Farley Granger) on the condition that Guy murder Bruno's father. In the highly dramatic scene where Bruno is standing behind an iron grill

A thief, *Marnie* (Tippi Hedren) fears discovery when her shoe drops. We hush with her. Relax! The cleaning woman is deaf. (In 1929, *Blackmail*, nervous guilt plagues Anny Ondra, who stabbed an over-flirtatious artist.)

fence in the shadows, with Guy opposite him, both are seen through the prisonlike bars of the massive fence. Complicity is clearly symbolized. The two men are linked by faith in an evil deed—one by perpetrating a murder, the other by reaping its fruits. Intention, deed, and benefits are blended into one complex action. In this scene, and repeatedly throughout the film, Hitchcock reminds us how tainted are our motives, acts, and judgments.

In *I Confess,* Fr. Michael Logan (Montgomery Clift), falsely accused of murder, protects the seal of confession at the expense of his reputation and life. (The plot outline is treated in Chapter VII, "Christ Figures—Overt and Covert.") The film ends with the awareness that Ruth Grandfort still loves Fr. Logan and that he knows it. Is it possible that Hitchcock used a lying flashback about the night the couple spent together? Recall that in *Stage Fright* he patently deceived the audience. A partial flashback made it seem impossible for a man to commit a crime that later we learn he did commit. I doubt that Hitchcock intended a lying flashback in *I Confess,* but the film does not prove sexual innocence, but merely suggests it.

In *The Wrong Man,* a bass player at the Stork Club, Emmanuel Balestrero (Henry Fonda), is falsely accused of a robbery that was committed by a look-alike. (The plot was detailed in Chapter VII.) Hitchcock immerses us in a series of police arrests, interrogations, and the indignities involved. The film presents a married couple who live in such sympathetic vibration with one another that the husband's misfortune affects the wife inwardly even more than it does Manny. Like a tuning fork, she reverberates with his depression, but even when he is exonerated she is still deeply disturbed. The last scene is one of Hitch's darkest in terms of isolation and alienation, foreshadowing his next film, *Vertigo.*

Hitchcock clearly suggests that injustices cannot be remedied in this world. In the moral order the scale of human justice is a poor balancing device. Professor Cadell in *Rope* and Guy Haines in *Strangers on a Train* go free, even though the latter benefited from one crime, while the former influenced another intellectually. Similarly, Fr. Logan and Emmanuel Balestrero are recipients of uncalled-for sorrow. Hitchcock saw the fate of the human soul dangerously perched between good and evil but not always shaped by personal decisions. Humankind seems to be driving an automobile with a bent steering mechanism. Perhaps this explains Hitchcock's use of autos out of control on steep precipices (*Suspicion*) or due to an intoxicated driver (*North by Northwest*) or because the break and steering mechanisms have been tampered with (*Family Plot*). This vehicle the human race is driving does not seem to arrive at its planned destination, and yet Hitchcock does not embrace fatalism but continually hints that man may prevail.

As I have already mentioned, Hitchcock's obsession with crime and horror is fundamentally a religious pursuit with psychological groundings. He blended two frames of reference into a psychospiritual viewpoint. By recognizing the fickleness of human motivation, Hitchcock made a distinctive contribution to cinema art in the domain of psychospiritual attitudes and quicksilver patterns of mood motivation (consolation and love as contrasted with fear and anxiety). The uniqueness of Hitchcock's signature on a film is the power he concedes to evil without allowing it any ultimate victory. The soul of man prevails but only when moral struggle is present. Hope is there, but it must be activated by human initiative. Hitchcock seemed to take satisfaction in presenting the soul in suspense—dangling, in a race against time, and often the victim of mercurial emotional swings which have no essential constancy. Implicit throughout his work is the existence of a higher frame of reference, some absolute standard of justice, morality, and happiness against which we can measure our imperfect and evil-prone world. In an important tribute to Hitchcock, François Truffaut credited him with a unique film style coupled with symbolic significance, "that of a struggle between the sacred aspect of life and our impure use of it."[1]

Note

1. François Truffaut, "Hitchcock—His True Power is Emotion," *New York Times,* March 4, 1979.

CHAPTER XI

Spiritualizing Horror

Current events confirm film critic Richard Schickel's observation that more and more our world is becoming "a Hitchcock world," one where sudden horror and destruction haunt humanity. Hitchcock has brought to the horror genre a style and substance which comports with what was inculcated in him at Saint Ignatius College, a religious humanism based on the binomial formula of fright and delight.

At the heart of this rhythmic pedagogical principle is the biblical accent on spiritual influences—good and evil—both within and without the human person. The *Spiritual Exercises* of Saint Ignatius affirms not only benign but also malevolent disembodied spirits, as do the Old and New Testaments. Jacob wrestled with an angel of light, and Job was tested by afflictions allowed by God and presumably mediated by lesser spiritual agencies. Moreover, the fall of Adam left his descendants with the strong inclination to evil, a darkening of the mind and weakening of the will. The First and Third Weeks of the Jesuit blueprint for learning to find God's will through a personal existential relationship deal with dark, expressionistic themes which would have left an impress on the sensitive young Hitchcock. I refer to such disorders as crime and sin, shame and guilt, death and hell—all subjects which are treated in his fifty-three films. Nor should we overlook those Christocentric themes of victimhood and sacrificial regeneration. It is interesting to chart the evolution of Hitchcock's religious signature from *The Lodger* (1926), with its theme of a "wrong man" suspended by handcuffs from a railing and jeered at by an angry crowd, to *Family Plot* (1976), with a protagonist called Adamson (son of Adam). I shall return to a fuller discussion of *Family Plot* in the last chapter, but permit me to remind the reader that in *The Lodger,* Hitch not only joined the "wrong-man" motif with that of the Christ figure, but included himself in the frenzied mob molesting the innocent Christ surrogate, dangling, pursued, and out of time. In his next three films—*Downhill, Easy Virtue,* and *The Ring*—the young director kept to the themes with a wronged schoolboy, a publicly and unjustly maligned society lady, and a boxer whose fiancée (later wife) is seduced by another pugilist. Written and directed by Hitchcock, *The Ring* has a critical scene where the formally dressed fighter-husband (Carl Brisson) and his cronies impatiently await the errant wife at the fighter's apartment. Not only does Hitch show the champagne going flat during the long wait, but perceptive viewers can see shadows of a cross on the wall cast by a strange-looking lighting fixture (shaped somewhat like a tau cross) behind his restless buddies, rough but loyal.

Hitchcock's later British successes were adventuresome and, at their best, exposed the injustices of police procedures and court trials. He began with his first Hollywood movie for David O. Selznick, *Rebecca* (which won the Academy Award for best picture of 1940). He introduced the dark, brooding presence of the spectral Mrs. Danvers (Judith Anderson). She never walks into a room but is suddenly pictured standing there as if preternaturally transported. The following years would reveal the director intensifying the presence of evil, beginning with *Strangers on a Train* (1951) and continuing through *Frenzy* (1972). No more Iago-like psychopaths are found in Hitchcock's extensive dramatis personae than Robert Walker's character in *Strangers* and Barry Foster's in *Frenzy.*

A careful study of Hitch's ability to spiritualize horror is evident in *Notorious.* A close analysis reveals the two main characters to be flawed, ennobling themselves at the end after Cary Grant allows the woman he loves, Ingrid Bergman, to enter a loveless marriage with a German agent (Claude Rains). In Chapter VII, I referred to the crosslike lamp fixtures in *Notorious*'s early party scene in Miami, a crypto-sacred clue pointing forward to the personal and political disorders to follow. (The accompanying still will give the reader the chance to assess this subliminal sacred clue.) Is Hitchcock forging some strange link with original sin? Does the average viewer fully fathom the betrayal felt by Claude Rains, a Nazi agent but nevertheless genuinely in love within a curious, one-sided marriage of political expediency? Love and duty are brought into conflict, as they will be again in *North by Northwest*.

Furthermore, *Notorious* carries forward recognizable Ignatian themes of the contagion of evil from Hitchcock's earlier (and his own favorite) film, *Shadow of a Doubt*. Cary Grant's Devlin is unscrupulous, if not like Joseph Cotten's villain, a bluebeard. Indeed, Hitchcock has the audience identify with Cotten's Uncle Charlie, who considers the world a pigsty. His niece (Teresa Wright) often reminds him "how alike we are," and after his death, Uncle Charlie is eulogized, perhaps hypocritically, by a representative of the small town as "truly one of us." It is significant that Hitchcock wanted Thornton Wilder, author of *Our Town,* to write the screenplay for *Shadow of a Doubt,* a film which represents Hitchcock's searching spiritual X-ray of the small, quintessentially American village.

Notorious treats moral disorder, betrayal, and opportunism as an integral part of foreign policy. (Recall that the CIA did not exist at the time.) Praised for its writing, acting, and directing, *Notorious* has a nasty feel to it. If one watches the film without letting the seductive images, the brilliant camera work, and bravura acting lull the viewer into a hypnotic state of passivity, one finds the regeneration of Grant and Bergman hardly credible in terms of prior motivation. The lead personalities change too quickly into morally sensitive creatures after giving the impression of being celluloid windup dolls with the director turning the key in their backs. Study the very last scene, one of Hitchcock's most brilliant and overlooked trophies of genius. Do our sympathies not lie with Claude Rains? Another director would have cut away from the Nazi villain, stranded and branded by his waiting mother and his disaffected servants of the swastika. Instead, he would have focused on the escaping romantic couple and their rosy future together, much as Hitch did later with the honeymoon scene on the tunneling train in *North by North-*

west. But the characters played by Cary Grant and Ingrid Bergman are flawed deliberately by the director, leaving us with unresolved emotions and evoking a miasmic mood of restless dissatisfaction. Why are audiences not repelled by Grant's dutiful delivery of his beloved into the arms of an enemy agent? The *shadow* of original sin without a *doubt* falls across this complex film, a neglected study in the spirituality of horror. I encourage the reader to study the two early scenes with the obvious references to the cross symbolized by the lighting fixtures behind the heads of the two stars.

In this and other films, Hitchcock revealed the world's moral axis to be badly tilted; one has the feeling that it could easily topple. If *Shadow of a Doubt* and *Notorious* indicate Hitchcock's shadowy fears about human nature's fallenness, this somber theme will grow even darker in *Vertigo, Psycho,* and *Frenzy.* In these last three films is an imbalancing quality similar to the pervasive darkness of *Shadow of a Doubt* and *Notorious.* We saw earlier Hitchcock's indebtedness to the Ignatian *Exercises* in terms of meliorism, *agere contra,* and an untroubled happy ending (the entertainment equivalent of the Gospel account of Jesus' resurrection, as critic Parker Tyler astutely pointed out[1]).

The theme of open-ended pessimism becomes more sharply etched on his celluloid frames. Certain movies apparently have a no-exit finale: *Vertigo, Psycho,* and *Frenzy,* all amply discussed elsewhere. As the evil is portrayed in ever blacker tones, the audience's requirement for a matching force of good becomes more imperious. I detect in Hitchcock's films, beginning with *I Confess* and *The Wrong Man,* a biographical reference, so that Hitch not only appears in person in his cameo scene, but also in spirit as the wronged and tormented protagonist. Disorder, whether at the personal, marital, or sociopolitical level, demands therapeutic antidotes (*agere contra*).

In Catholic theology, a distinction is made between medicinal grace which heals a spiritual wound or a moral malady, and sanctifying grace, associated with redemptive victimage and altruistic suffering. Hitch stands on a pinnacle of the horror film genre because of his stylistic and religious touches. His struggle spirituality embodies the conflict of grace and demonic force in the characters who carry the plot forward. Whether happily resolved or uncomfortably open-ended, the conclusions of his films in his mature years had a recognizable spiritual core. The fright increases in terms of mental anguish and near-despair. However, Hitch always rallied to return with a film that bespoke compassion, reconciliation, and a promise of peaceful happiness—but always on the condition of some act of redemptive sacrifice.

If Hitch leaned, from time to time, to undiluted pessimism, the bulk of his fifty-three films evoke the foundational principles of Jesuit spirituality with its shuttling back and forth from harsh themes of darkness, remorse, and passion to the more reassuring ones of light, consolation, and resurrection. Indeed, his last years mirror that struggle against a closed type of absolute pessimism. Certainly, *Family Plot* was an entertainment film with humor, romance, and suspense but no doomsday insinuations. The world around the aging Hitchcock was caught up in permissiveness and a liberalizing of traditional morality. Add to this Hitch's growing awareness of his own mortality and the closing of a brilliant career. These inclined him to form negative views; nonetheless, he never abandoned that compassionate spiritual vision of hope, forgiveness, moral struggle, and ultimate triumph. I submit that there is a convergence of themes, expressionistic style, and religious narrative signals which argues for a concordance of his spirituality of horror with the fright-and-delight strategy of the Jesuits, as embodied in the *Spiritual Exercises,* which stamped the Jesuit order through its constitution and its education rule-book.

No better proof of this exists than Hitch's treatment of an unusual plot, verging on science fiction, in *The Birds.* A possessive mother, Mrs. Brenner (Jessica Tandy) makes an effort to know and like Melanie (Tippi Hedren), who loves her son, Mitch (Rod Taylor). The final scene shows Mrs. Brenner with her arm around Melanie. The pose is intensely maternal, even Madonna-like. In *Marnie,* Hitchcock stressed how Marnie's mother (Louise Latham) wants to bring up her daughter "decent." Realizing the force of childhood trauma, Marnie (Tippi Hedren) herself says, "I'm a cheat and a liar and a thief, but I *am* decent." The power of rationalization, to defend one's deeper self from incrimination, is strong in us. To a greater or lesser extent, each of us feels at times like the "wrong man" or the "wrong woman." When we feel this way, then we should, according to the motivational dynamics of the Ignatian *Exercises,* feel closer to Jesus, the "wrong person" par excellence.

The reader should note that *The Birds* has an affinity with a brilliant poem by the English Jesuit, Gerard Manley Hopkins, a British writer who describes in *The Windhover* a type of bird that, though buffeted by strong winds, soars higher and higher. In the first eight lines, Hopkins describes the upward flight in function of the windhover's struggle, and the final six lines draw the analogy with Christ. The meliorism of this religious poem, inspired by the Ignatian *Exercises,* is dramatically evident in *The Birds,* a masterpiece of fright and delight.

Nor should we overlook the reversal of horror in two terrifying examples of false accusation. *I Confess* explicitly counteracted the horror through religious faith, especially in the allusion to the outdoor Way of the Cross and the courtroom scenes with the large crucifix on the wall. *The Wrong Man* invokes divine providence as coming to the rescue of Manny Balestrero (Henry Fonda), falsely accused of a theft. The picture of the Sacred Heart of Jesus, a Jesuit devotion, is key to the film's denouement, for Manny's prayer in front of it leads to the arrest of the real culprit, exonerating Balestrero and effecting a symbolic resurrection. The victimage signified is a response to Hitch's earlier references in the film to hell in terms of subway and elevated train noises and the metaphorical flames of hell implied by a picture of tonguelike flowers above a table lamp. I submit that this is a strategy for spiritualizing horror.

This same strategy is at work through the many other allusions to religion and religious faith. Hitchcock liked to show nuns in fleeting street scenes, as in *Sabotage* and *Foreign Correspondent.* The role of a fake nun in *The Lady Vanishes* (she wears high-heeled shoes with her habit) is central to the plot. We see a nun in the murder enquiry of Scottie Ferguson in *Vertigo;* then later we meet the dutiful nun whose forbidding appearance frightened Judy into losing her balance, thus causing her death; unperturbed, the nun says "God have

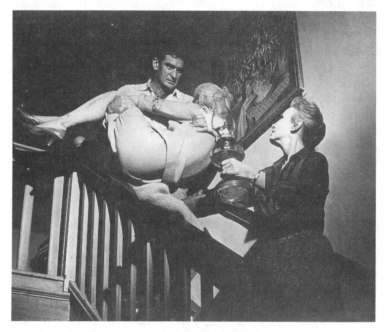

In *The Birds* Hitch stresses "love therapy," as Rod Taylor rescues Tippi Hedren, bleeding from a gull attack. (Shades of Michelangelo's Pietà!) Mother Jessica Tandy holds a lamp. Yes, crisis knits families as the final scene shows.

mercy," as she begins to toll the bell in the mission tower. Furthermore, after the bloody attack by birds, the bandaged head of Tippi Hedren resembles a nun's coif (*The Birds*).

Male clerics make their appearances, too. Apart from the dominating figure of Fr. Michael Logan in *I Confess*, there are the parson in *The Farmer's Wife*, the minister at the end of *Strangers on a Train*, the fake Anglican priest at Ambrose's Chapel in *The Man who Knew Too Much*, the pastor greeting his flock after Sunday services toward the end of *Shadow of a Doubt*, and the kidnapped bishop in *Family Plot*.

Biblical allusions—the Garden of Eden, Eve, the serpent, the apple as a symbol of forbidden fruit—can be found in *The Pleasure Garden, The Ring, Stage Fright, North by Northwest,* and *Frenzy*. Hitchcock's last silent film, *The Manxman* (1928),

In *The Lady Vanishes,* Hitch shows that danger often causes people to grow. This is proved in the cases of Dame May Whitty (left), Margaret Lockwood (center), the fake nun who converts; Michael Redgrave, who finds love; and the helping Naunton Wayne, the charming cricket fan.

opens with the title: "What shall it profit a man if he gain the whole world and suffer the loss of his soul?" As we saw earlier, this was the scriptural quote used by Saint Ignatius to convert the rather worldly Francis Xavier when they were in Paris together.

Other symbols of religious value include cathedrals, churches, chapels, confessionals, statues, an outdoor Way of the Cross, wall crucifixes, the rosary, Pietà scenes, and Christomorphic allusions (such as Cary Grant's outstretched arms while looking down from a roof in *To Catch a Thief*).

A profound Catholic and Jesuit imprint on his work is found in the moral flaws he depicts in likable and seemingly average people of all social classes. No one is innocent in the angelic sense; all are guilty of not being innocent. Take his five rather apocalyptic films with strong intimations of hovering death and guilt: *Shadow of a Doubt, Strangers on a Train, The Trouble with Harry, The Birds,* and *Frenzy.* There is no place to hide except in a faith which reconciles harsh realism with trust in a caring Providence, which responds to the initiative of those exerting courageous moral effort. Having previously dealt with *Shadow of a Doubt, Strangers on a Train,* and *Frenzy,* let us now consider *The Trouble with Harry* and *The Birds.*

The Trouble with Harry (1956) works at a number of levels: first, simple entertainment, in which playful humor is introduced into a highly fantastical story about a corpse that appears, disappears, and reappears; second, a study in free-floating guilt; and third, a story of the intrusiveness of death into a peaceful and quiet part of rural America. Hitchcock always tried to demystify the countryside and remove the attraction for rural America so deeply rooted in literature and the popular arts. He wanted to show that behind this enchantment with nature and the thirst for simplicity and innocence is a longing for a Garden-of-Eden type of existence that does away with sin, death, guilt, and punishment. The escape valve of such a paradise concept recalls those travel ads which counsel, "Get away from it all!"—as if one could leave one's problems behind.

Death is the touchstone for a reality behind reality. To ignore it and long for a Garden of Eden attests to the consequences of corruption and sin, namely, the need to escape. Indeed, death is the Great Intruder in *The Trouble with Harry*: Hitchcock used Harry's body as a symbol for death. The film seen in this light turns out to be a parable about the imbalance between nature and humanity, and it foreshadows *The Birds.* Both films imply the biblical point of view that human beings are disturbers of natural cosmic order because they behave as fallen creatures in a fallen world. Original sin is seen as disrupting the whole of nature. I mentioned earlier the triple appearance of the corpse and the seven visits to the body. Hitchcock's use of the mystical numbers three and seven strongly suggests that he was aware of the religious nature of death, that dying was not terminal but a crossover incident, leading to a transformed conscious-

Hitch's comedy *The Trouble With Harry* highlighted the common sense of false security. A bright Autumn, fallen leaves, and romance make death seem such an uninvited visitor to complacent country folk. With wife, Alma (lower left), Hitch directs Edmund Gwenn and Mildred Natwick.

ness (a Christian would say "resurrection"). While we chuckle through *The Trouble with Harry,* the film is buoyed up strangely by a deeply felt free-floating anxiety. The fears of the rural residents are only mirrors of their disorder. *The Trouble with Harry* was relished in France but not savored in America. The black comedy is highly sardonic in its sharp contrast of pervasive guilt found, surprisingly, in a bucolic atmosphere marked by Americanism, averageness, and apple-pie goodness. For Hitchcock, wholesomeness suggests lack of wholeness.

In *The Trouble with Harry,* we see the tragic consequences that follow from disrupting the delicate balance of nature's forces and the human need for justice—not just legal justice, but total, perfect justice. Death, the Great Interferer, makes way for judgment, the redressing of moral imbalances. The film reflects a preoccupation central to Jesuit spirituality—namely, the awareness of psychic, social, and cosmic disorder.

The Birds (1963) echoes this theme. It gives us another view of the imbalance in nature and humankind. The setting is Bodega Bay in northern California, where Hitchcock again destroyed the illusion of rural bliss. One might wonder why he spent three tedious years putting together a special-effects film. *The Birds* falls somewhere between a horror film—such as *Frankenstein*—and a science fiction film—such as *The Invasion of the Body Snatchers*. It seems to me that he invested his time for a purpose beyond that of mere entertainment. He was filming *The Birds* in the early 1960s, when the war in Southeast Asia was spreading, though relatively unknown in terms of serious media awareness. Is it completely unreasonable to see the birds in this film as symbols for death from the sky by airplanes or nuclear missiles? Is the retribution of crimes against nature in *The Birds* only philosophical (every action brings a corresponding reaction), or can it be seen as supernatural (the Last Judgment)? After all, the gas-pump explosion and the panic that follows are seen from the air, from the perspective of the flying birds. It is a detached view. The perspective is provocative, triggering free associations. It could be the view from the eye of an all-seeing God.

In *The Birds,* one should recognize by now the director's suspicion that a placid, pastoral milieu is a surface sign of underlying unrest in terms of escapist fantasy, boredom, seething passions, deviance and, yes, even murder. There is a Spanish proverb which says, in effect, that small towns can be big hells. This is true of the northern California towns of Santa Rosa in *Shadow of a Doubt* and Bodega Bay in *The Birds*. The theme of a primeval disorder from *Shadow of a Doubt* is given an expanded, cosmic frame of reference in *The Birds*.

In a documentary produced by film critic Richard Schickel, Hitchcock said explicitly about *The Birds*, "Don't mess around or fool with nature." He saw a revenge theme at work, since birds are eaten, shot at, and put in cages. He implied that indifference to nature and taking it for granted are signs that human beings may be tainted by original sin. What strikes the viewer as complete disorder is really Hitchcock's way of depicting injured nature as trying to restore itself. Again, we recognize the Ignatian preoccupation with imbalances and the attempt to correct them, restoring and repairing the natural order when it is violated morally or spiritually.

In *The Birds,* too, a reference is made to ancient Greek religion (as I noted in *The Trouble with Harry*). The Greeks of 500 B.C. (the age of Pericles) recognized that the forces of justice always triumph. In an article that appeared in *The New Yorker* (April 29, 1974), Penelope Gilliatt drew the following connection:

> In *The Birds* the characters who play out the revenge are the birds themselves, those creatures who for millennia have been used for food and quill pens and ladies' hats; they terrorize the heroine in a telephone booth when she is caged like a canary, and swoop down the chimney as if they were the Eumenides.

The Birds' kinship to Aristophanes' classic should come as no surprise to those with a liberal arts education. Would Hitchcock have been familiar with the ancient Greek belief in the Furies—the Eumenides—those goddesses of vengeance and justice who hounded their victims to restore cosmic balance? He would have been familiar with the notion of fate and retribution at the heart of the ancient Greek idea of justice. As Aristophanes' satirical comedy, *The Birds,* humanized horror, Hitch added his own apocalyptic perspective of a world with billions of souls in suspense.

The Birds ends on a note of unambiguous compassion: crisis brings people closer together and strengthens their characters. Though not developed thematically, religious faith is implicit in *The Birds.* The birds are mysterious agents of the universe, operating on the principle of *agere contra,* which could be thought of as a type of cybernetic feedback in terms of modern communications theory. The three adults courageously confront the rebellion of nature and become more responsible, less egoistic, at the end.

A word about Hitchcock's symbolic references to hell, unquestionably the most disconsolate meditation in the Ignatian *Exercises,* a pivotal reflection in the First Week. It is noteworthy that, as a pioneer filmmaker in England, Hitch borrowed from the forlorn iconography of Gehenna, the Old Testament name for that unthinkable place of eternal punishment. *Downhill* (1927) describes the steady spiritual decline of a wronged schoolboy, Roddy (Ivor Novello), who shoulders the blame to avert a school chum's loss of a scholarship. The film is divided into three titled sections: "The World of Youth"; "The World of Make Believe"; and "The World of Lost Illusions." The young man leaves home when his father, not believing Roddy's assertion of innocence, calls him a liar.

Hitch points forward to the infernal regression of Roddy, filming his back as he descends an escalator in the Underground and sinks from view. His affair with a leading lady of the stage ends in their separation. His fortune squandered, he is ejected from the flat they shared and is seen descending in the elevator. In France, he becomes a gigolo, receiving fifty cents for each dance with a lonely woman or the young date of a wealthy old man. He sinks into penury, living in the dockside area of Marseilles, until two blacks and a seaman help him to recover and return to England. Following Christ's Parable of the Prodigal Son, he is welcomed back by his stern father and returns to the sheltered world of upper-class manners and comfort. This film indicates Hitch's interest in the imminence of that chaos which lies just beneath the surface of a complacent, civilized life-style.

In *The Ring* (1927), discussed in Chapter V ("Mysticism of Spirals and Lines"), Hitch accents the futility of romance when lovers overinvest sentiment into such material objects as rings, bracelets, and other emblems that represent feelings of the human heart. The scenes of loneliness are in sharp contrast to those of romantic delight and victory in the boxing quadrangle. If love promises expansion, its disappointment brings deflation and, in marriage, Hitch would suggest, heavy restrictions of responsibility. The serpent's image on the bracelet is the key to a suggested foretaste of hell, even in this life.

In *The Farmer's Wife* (1928), the theme of romance and marriage treats what Maurice Yacowar calls a "satiric vision of the decorum that hovers on the brink of disaster, of a world where courtship breeds dissension, confidence humiliation,

and the hero's simple, earnest attempts to connect alienation."[2] Here we see a pattern of order decomposing into
unraveling chaos, themes which will recur with a dramatic
vengeance in *Psycho, Vertigo* and, in a more qualified way, *The
Birds.* If hell is radical instability, life on earth, Hitch implies,
has passing mirror images of it contained in the fickle
pilgrimage of the species.

Champagne (1928) echoes the moral of *The Farmer's Wife*:
the upper class is insulated from the black-and-white character of life below, and happiness disappears like the bubbles in
a glass of flat champagne. Chaos lurks close by in the image of
the Passenger (whom Yacowar refers to as the Vile Seducer).
He takes on different forms—now delight, now fright,
representing a sinister force that can pull people down with
their own unwitting complicity. Behind the champagne froth
is the hiss of molten lava. As Sartre defined hell as "other
people," this film, curiously, has no endearing characters.

An example of the deft use of acoustic atmospherics is
found in *The 39 Steps,* where Hitchcock employs grating
sounds to raise audience anxieties and suspense. Similarly,
cacophanous music and noise occur in later films to suggest
the infernal (e.g., Herrmann's discordant score which opens
and closes *North by Northwest*). In three patriotic films about
the Allied cause in World War II, Hitch used lively swing
music to indicate disorder, alienation, and even torture. In
Foreign Correspondent, a Dutch diplomat kidnapped by the
Nazis is cruelly interrogated concerning state secrets. An
intense, hot spotlight is focused on him, and American swing
records are played loudly. In *Saboteur,* the opening scene of
Robert Cummings going to a defense plant has a soundtrack
of jazzy rhythms, suggesting the impersonality of assembly-
line work and the appetite for gratifying distraction. Again in
Notorious, an early scene shows a Miami party with loud dance
music punctuating flirtatious conversation by a tipsy hostess,
Ingrid Bergman. These three films indicate Hitch's resentment of swing music as infernal. The jazz trade magazine
Downbeat (January 7, 1960, p. 16) commented on Hitchcock's distaste for America's native musical expression.

In *The Wrong Man,* the soundtrack contains a strategic use
of back-channel acoustics: the rumbles of the subways and

Torn Curtain's hellish crowd scene has Julie Andrews calling to Paul Newman. His false "Fire" alarm was their only means of escape. (Curiously, the ballet they were attending was inspired by Canto V of Dante's *Inferno*.)

elevated trains of New York City. These grating noises are amplified in critical scenes to underscore the distress of the accused (Henry Fonda) and his wife (Vera Miles). The unmistakable reference to hell is an external metaphor for the internal despair of Fonda and his mentally ill wife. The slamming of the cell door and Fonda's frightened-gazelle eye peering through the slit conveys Dante's message above the portals of his *Inferno*: "Abandon hope, all ye who enter!"

Also Dantesque are the two scenes of fire in *Torn Curtain*. The opening credits appear over a Technicolor scene of red flames breaking out on a ship at sea. The scenes in Eastern Europe show a drab gray world of regimented communism, oppressively colorless and moodily monotonous. Later in the

A dignitary (Albert Basserman) is tortured by loud swing music in *Foreign Correspondent*. (Hitch had no tolerance for jazz or swing!)

film, Paul Newman avoids pursuit in a theater where a ballerina dances amid make-believe papier-mâché flames. Again, there is a reference to Dante's *Inferno* and the Red hell of what Hitchcock presumably viewed as suffocating state socialism.

We do not know to what extent Hitchcock drew on memories of his Jesuit education in creating these scenes. But it is clear that his use of jazz, swing music, jarring mass-transit sounds, and fiery visual motifs point to the concept of hell as a theme of this director, as was seen in *The Wrong Man*.

Following sacred Scripture and the Ignatian *Exercises,* Hitchcock never underestimated evil in terms of suffering or unnatural crimes. The greater the evil, the greater the counterbalancing good. Although Hitchcock is admired and studied, his fans do not seem to understand his respect for evil, as evidenced in such dark masterpieces as *Shadow of a Doubt, Vertigo,* and *Psycho.* Hitch's greatest portrayal of horror, almost mystical in artistic power, is found in the three innocent redemptive victims: the female Christ figures in *Psycho, The Birds,* and *Frenzy.* These pictures portray ordinary mortals as overwhelmed by the onslaught of evil. As in that of Shakespeare, so too in Hitch's work we have recurrent rays of hope and regeneration. Hamlet, Othello, Macbeth, and Cleopatra die tragically, aware of their failings but with an exalted sense of their worth and station. Similarly, in the work of Hitchcock, the seesaw battle tips now toward disaster, now toward survival. The end of *The Birds* is clearly hopeful, although ambiguous. In Hitchcock's films, as in the plays of Shakespeare, humans work out their destinies when there is some trust in the larger purpose. Faith seems to reduce the odds, as demonstrated in Hamlet's majestic affirmation of supernatural assistance: "There's a divinity that shapes our ends, / Rough-hew them how we will."

Throughout his work, the Jesuit-influenced director pointed to the triumph of will over adverse circumstances, the paralysis of fear, and the desire for flight—as in *The 39 Steps, Young and Innocent, Notorious, Lifeboat, Saboteur, Spellbound, I Confess, The Wrong Man, The Man Who Knew Too Much, The Birds,* and *Marnie.* These films confirm the thesis of open-ended pessimism, a theme also evident in Shakespeare's plays. I believe that the reputation of the Master of Suspense will continue to grow as his signature becomes better understood. His principal characters evolve, or when they do not—as with the villains in *Shadow of a Doubt, Strangers on a Train, Psycho,* and *Frenzy*—we suspect an extenuation of motive because of pathology. Generally, however, Hitchcock's protagonists succeed in growing because of and despite the evil threats around them. This recurring plot dynamic resonates, as we have seen, with the Jesuit principles of *agere contra* and meliorism in terms of personal integration, romantic bonding, and greater security for the community or nation, often interlocking themes of a typical Hitchcock happy ending (even when tenuously temporary).

Notes

1. Tyler discusses *Suspicion* as a "false ending." He analyzes the happy ending in terms of Christ's resurrection in his insightful volume, *The Hollywood Hallucination* (New York: Simon and Schuster, 1944).
2. Maurice Yacowar, *Hitchcock's British Films* (Hamden, Conn.: Archon Books, 1977), p. 75.

CHAPTER XII

Asceticism, Modesty, and Sexual Awareness

The Roman poet Horace wrote in one of his Epistles that you can drive Nature out with a pitchfork, but she'll keep coming back. In a poetic sense, he echoed what Freud would call the dynamics of repressed erotic impulses in human attitude and conduct. Freud's "pansexualism" did not allow for sublimation by siphoning off sex urges in play, art, or work. In this chapter, I wish to consider the evidence in Hitchcock's filmography of the widening sexual consciousness released in the period during and after World War I. The relaxation of morals in the 1920s was due to the influence of bold literary works (James Joyce, D. H. Lawrence, Havelock Ellis), the women's movement, new media (radio and film), and America's general waywardness due to the disrespect for the prohibition of liquor (the Jazz Age).

A word about school discipline and the distancing among the pupils which Hitch experienced at Saint Ignatius College as a "train boy" (London commuter). The boys were deliberately kept occupied on the assumption that an idle mind is the devil's workshop. Those favoring athletics were gregarious by nature; others more introverted had more solitary pursuits. As a lad, Hitch enjoyed the sights of London and studied shipping and rail schedules. We know his attitude toward the strict surveillance by the form masters and the prefects of discipline. The college reflected aspects of seminary life. In a womanless world, boys were protected from "particular friendships," the seedbed of homosexuality. General sociability was encouraged so long as the students remained chums or pals. Ordinarily, the strict regimen of a private school such as Saint Ignatius was not seen in ascetical terms. But the school bells and presence of black robes in the corridors, cafeteria, and chapel could make for a lonely crowd, people who were alone even when together. The cascading events after Alfred's graduation from Saint Ignatius College can be fully appreciated when contrasted with the strict schooling and religious training he received at the Jesuit preparatory school.

Even though Hitch as a lad was not a boarder, his school days were lived out in an all-male world which avoided and minimized the facts of sexuality. The corseted morality of Edwardian and Catholic worlds before World War I would not have heavily accented the verse of Genesis which said that God created the world and saw it as good. From James Joyce's *Portrait of the Artist as a Young Man* we have some indication of the relation between Jesuit religious formation and adolescent curiosity about sex in this period. The unstated assumption was that women were at least a distraction, often a temptation, and in some cases dangerous. The dress code for Edwardian ladies showed them fully clothed—beribboned hats with wide brims and loose-fitting ankle-length dresses with tight lace collars. On the one hand, women were seen as temptresses and often even active predators; on the other hand, they were put on pedestals and idealized as Madonna types, proper mothers, and wives. Certainly the women portrayed in the films of D. W. Griffith and Charles Chaplin represented the ideal.

During Hitchcock's last year at Saint Ignatius, motion pictures were beginning to deal with bolder treatments of sex. Though there were no stars such as Mae West, Brigitte Bardot, or Marilyn Monroe, spectacles were imported into London from America: *Traffic in Souls* and *The Inside of White Slave Traffic,* both released in 1913. In *The Celluloid Sacrifice: Aspects of Sex in the Movies,* British film critic Alexander Walker wrote: "By 1914, therefore, all the apparatus existed and was ready for the idea of sex-appeal, as one now understands it, to be incarnated on the screen and projected so forcefully that it would change the sort of expectations that people took with them to the nickelodeons."[1]

The progenitor of sex appeal was Theda Bara, portrayed as an aggressively sexual woman in Empire dresses, wearing a jeweled diadem with a tall tuft of feathers. Her pathbreaking

film was released in 1915—*A Fool There Was*. As a play, it was
a hit at New York's Liberty Theater. William Fox bought the
screen rights and remolded a tailor's daughter from Cincin-
nati, Theodosia Goodman, into the image of a sex siren.
Hollywood publicity projected her image as brimming with
baleful eroticism, decked out in heavy jewelry with whorling
beads and, on one occasion, metal chains against bare flesh—
suggesting perversion. During the next five years, the world
became familiar with her mesmeric malevolence in her vamp
portrayals of Carmen, Du Barry, Camille, Salome, and
Cleopatra. Hitchcock would have been aware of Theda Bara
and may even have had the opportunity to view this femme
fatale, a "comic caricature of the libido," who felt suffering as
well as supplied it.[2] Bram Stoker's novel *Dracula* appeared
while Hitch was a student at Saint Ignatius College. Theda
Bara, as vamp, and the vampire character of Dracula "created
a vogue for the vampire type of woman who sucks the love
and life out of a man."[3]

We must remember that even the most strictly controlled
educational environment cannot hermetically seal off the
leisure-time activities of student "day-hops." There is the
appeal of forbidden fruit when strong prohibitions are in-
voked by moral guardians, be they parents, educators, or the
clergy. The Gospel Parable of the Prodigal Son touches on
this by inviting meditation on the reasons for the younger
son's leaving home. Perhaps he lived in a valley and saw the
traders riding over the hills past his father's farm and then
watched them ride away back over those same hills. The
obvious nagging question would be, What lies beyond those
ridges? We do not know specifically what Hitchcock learned
from movies and legitimate theaters, but surely he knew of
Picadilly Circus (see an early scene in *The Lodger*). He would
have seen the publicity displays with their inviting ads. The
desire to know more about taboo subjects becomes stronger
when the opportunities to learn are near. Like James Joyce,
Hitch must have had prodigal fantasies. His Jesuit mentors
knew the Latin adage, *Nulla ignoranti cupido* ("Knowledge
precedes desire"). The explosion of means to obtain vicarious
experience was never so great as in the early part of this
century, which accentuated the retreat into privacy that the

church embarked on in the previous century with the rise of rationalism, Marxism, modernism, romanticism, and new interpretations of the Bible. The Index Librorum Prohibitorum was the Catholic church's list of prohibited books that could be read only if special ecclesiastical permission was granted. Whereas books as private reading experiences could be regulated, the Catholic church has never fully succeeded in classifying and censoring the newer audiovisual media of motion pictures, radio, records, and television. (This is not to say that the church did not exercise great influence, for the Legion of Decency in America did contribute to the establishment of the Motion Picture Production Code in Hollywood.)[4] In the face of expanding secular influences on the public, particularly the working class, the church saw a decline in moral and religious influence.

As part of its later teaching, the church preferred not to use the term "mass media," but rather "social communications." The hope was to sensitize the faithful to the fact that they should bring critical awareness to such subjects as sex which were being treated profanely in the entertainment media. Once alerted, it was hoped, they would avoid the dangers of indiscriminate and passive receptivity. In Catholic countries (such as France, Italy, and Spain), the church made contact with movie producers, directors, and actors, the majority of whom were baptized Catholics. In England and the United States, however, predominantly Protestant nations, the Catholic church adopted as coping strategies censorship, theater boycotts, and pledges to abide by the classification system. In short, the Anglo-American Catholic church sought, understandably, a solution through withdrawal of patronage. In the eyes of most non-Catholic filmmakers, however, this seemed like a type of fortress mentality. This background casts some light on the dilemma of an adolescent with an active imagination trying to straddle the disparate worlds of home, church, school, and the ever-expanding realm of exciting experiences carried by the new sight and sound media.

It is important to understand that Jesuit spirituality historically evolved beyond Saint Ignatius' original vision. The Ignatian ideal for Jesuits is that they become *contemplativi in actione* ("contemplatives in action"). The danger is turning away from that ideal, either toward activism or toward pure contemplation. In the *Spiritual Exercises* provision is made (No. 333) against lapses from resolutions by reviewing one's life in terms of "beginning, middle, and end." This retrospective technique—a flashback—discloses the nongeometrical deviations from one's straight-line plan of amendment. Jesuit spirituality stresses means and ends. Not only individuals but organizations can lose clear sight of the ends over time. French scholar Joseph de Guibert presents the case that, in the nineteenth century, Jesuit spirituality lost its balance to become prominently one of introversion.[5] In effect, the order became "world shy," as institutional apostolates substituted a quasi-monastic stability for the original Ignatian ideal of mobility and responsiveness to the pope's priorities. From 1540 to 1770 the Jesuits were immersed in worldly activities and even politics—so much so that they were disbanded by a papal bull of suppression. When restored in 1815, the order, like a person recovering from a nervous breakdown, became cautiously conservative and introspective when contrasted with the previous two hundred forty years.

The young Hitchcock was trained by products of the introspective school, marked by private piety, strong will training, and intellectual skills. Jesuits are considered very cerebral and analytical, a considerable strength, but one that could lead to aloofness from practical matters. Following his strict Edwardian and ascetical Jesuit childhood, Hitch rapidly changed from 1915 to 1930, due to the liberalization of thought and morals regarding sex, marriage, and women. No longer were the English or the Catholic laity corseted by puritanical morality.[6] Consider the abrupt worldwide changes that his generation suddenly experienced: experiments in art and literature and new developments in broadcasting and photography. Nevertheless, Hitch carried forward certain deep convictions about the sacred—God's merciful forgiveness, humankind's bent nature, the mystery of death and the beyond, and some awareness of sex and love as having divine origins.

What occurred to him was similar to the transformation in artistic vision of two other artists—James Joyce and Luis Buñuel—who also went beyond the cautionary pedagogy of

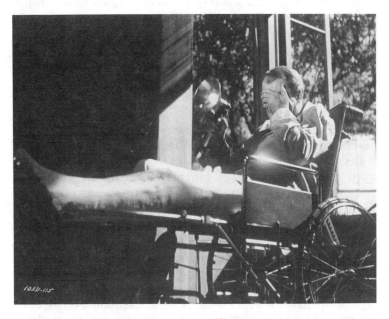

In *Rear Window,* James Stewart peers into seven apartments with his telephoto lens. Here he is alone with the murderer, and blinds him with camera flashes. As Stewart spies on Hitch in his cameo, the latter turns to stare back. A higher spectator may be watching both!

their Jesuit guardians. A telltale clue would be the strict "modesty of the eyes" as a protection for purity. This means one's eyes must be downcast, especially with women and those of a higher station. However, mass media were opening the eyes and ears of the entire world. Take Buñuel's surrealistic film *Un Chien Andalou,* which shockingly showed the slitting of a woman's eye with a razor (actually the eye in the close-up was that of a cow). Not only Buñuel, but also Joyce and Hitchcock were exponents of Joseph Conrad's creed: "My one objective is to make you see." If that was also the goal of Ignatius, then the three artists (Jesuit alumni) had much greater means of dramatization at hand to probe beneath the surface of reality (things are not as they seem). The three artists knew the writings of Sigmund Freud. All three experienced in their early years at school sexual repression, exaggerated fear of women, and excessive scrupulosity regarding the six and ninth Commandments—and all this in an atmosphere of exclusively male companionship. Buñuel jokes in his autobiography that no Chinese pagan could derive nearly the erotic pleasure that one Catholic could from a single forbidden sexual fantasy.[7] There is a common mold of priorities, prohibitions, and principles that each artist carried forward into his aesthetic work. None divorced sexuality from the sacred, although they were perceived by some as irreverent and even blasphemous.

Let us look specifically at evidence to clarify further. If we trace the development of Hitch's imagination through his early days in advertising and as a journeyman director of silent films, we are struck by the repeated theme of liberated, even frivolous women, in *The Pleasure Garden, Downhill, Easy Virtue, The Ring, Champagne, The Manxman,* and *Blackmail.* These films cast great light on the nature of Hitch's imagination and future direction in Hollywood. He admitted his predilection for the theme of "blood and blondes." *The Lodger* (1926) opens with a blood-curdling scream and a newspaper headline about the violent death of a blonde. The linkage between red blood and golden-tressed women carries a psychoanalytically charged meaning. Twenty-eight films out of fifty-three treat blondes.[8] However, not all of these connected blond hair with blood, but merely with physical desire (e.g., *Spellbound*). Also, in *Vertigo* Kim Novak played a dual role, as did Tippi Hedren in *Marnie*: both films showed women changing their hair color from blond to brunette and back again. The Master of Suspense had come a very long way from his Jesuit days. If he retained many religious principles from the Ignatian *Exercises,* he supplemented them with wider secular interests in romance, courtship, marriage, and even such entertainment spices as double entendre, male flirtation, female teasing, and intimations of sexual dalliance. Recall Ingrid Bergman's loose woman at the outset of *Notorious.* Hitch shows her drunk and daringly dressed. On the wall is a cross symbol—a portent of future redemption. Hitchcock blended the sexual and the sacred in a truly astonishing, if compulsively troublesome, manner.

The director was very devoted to his wife, Alma Reville, who worked with him on his films till his death. Yet, Hitchcock casts doubts repeatedly on marriage (e.g., the farmer and his wife in *The 39 Steps,* the cynical marriage in *Notorious,* the triangle in *Dial M for Murder,* the marital strains in *The Wrong Man,* the detective and his wife in *Frenzy,* the supper scenes in *Family Plot*). A longtime friend of the director, Fr. Thomas Sullivan testified that Hitch would say to him and other trusted friends that he had been a married celibate for nearly three decades. While his imagination was active as befits a director of entertaining films, his own inner drama was made up of emotional conflicts and fantasy projections, incubated by the austere environment of his Edwardian Catholic upbringing and richly sated by the proliferation of the literary, cinematic, and psychoanalytic revolutions of the age. No wonder he suffused filmmaking with thought and profound psychospiritual insight, but at a high personal cost. Romance and religion were for Hitchcock not separated into hermetically sealed compartments.

Consider how Hitchcock dealt with deviant eroticism, a theme that would have been eyebrow-raising (if not hair-raising) in the world of taboos in which he was reared. Hitch surely received many warnings regarding sex, marriage, divorce, and family life from his parish church and Jesuit school. The value of sex was generally avoided, if not denied altogether. It was certainly minimized, thus eclipsing its God-related origins and its purpose. Unlike the church after Vatican Council II, Catholics before World War I heard more about original sin and man's fallen state than about the power of Christ's resurrection to restore his total personality, including his sexual nature. As did many other Catholics, Hitchcock synthesized his own creed with Catholicism as the core, but with personal convictions the church would seldom publicly endorse. Keeping this in mind, the reader will gain added insight into that masterpiece, *Rear Window.* Sexual themes and marriage references abound in this film as in no other of Hitchcock's. A close reading of this classic will bring to the

surface a surprising number of doubts about the stability, the
felicity, and the anticipated fulfillment of marriage, particularly in the depersonalized context of a metropolis such as
New York City. Among the couples in the Greenwich Village
apartment complex, the most ideal relationship is that of
Jimmy Stewart and Grace Kelly, comparatively more promis-
ing than most other tenants. And yet, Hitch's final scene
leaves us with a question mark. Is the best yet to be between
the society lady and the world-traveling photographer, or has
it already taken place? We wonder!

Despite Hitch's sense of moral irony and skepticism
regarding male-female bonding, there is more than ample
internal evidence in his total corpus of images which testifies
to a mingled sense of reverent awe and abiding curiosity
regarding sex and death. A study of Hitch's late middle period
in Hollywood, after *The Wrong Man,* will disclose a mounting
preoccupation with the psychospiritual facets of those time-
less topics—*eros* (love) and *thanatos* (death). This interest
never showed a sharp decline, although his last film, *Family
Plot,* reveals a greater trust, indeed, a deeper mellowing, in
terms of forgiveness, compassion, reconciliation, and a general acceptance of life's mystery. Unlike most Hollywood
films about death (war, gangster, western, and horror genres),
Hitch's films do not insinuate that this life is all there is: his
religious beliefs suggest not closure, but rather an unfamiliar
continuity beyond and greater than that Shakespearean description of life as a "brief candle." Study *Frenzy*'s final scene
and see how Hitchcock subtly points beyond the horizon of
death with the cross outlined on the trunk-coffin dragged by
the killer so that he can cart away his latest rape and murder
victim.

It is fascinating to analyze how Hitchcock blends religious
themes from the Bible and the Ignatian *Exercises* with the
more modernistic concerns of D. H. Lawrence and Sigmund
Freud, from *Spellbound* and *Notorious* to *Topaz* and *Frenzy.*
Both Lawrence and Freud believed that Christianity deem-
phasized romantic love in an unhealthy way. (I refer to the
common preachments and procedures at the parish level and
not to the theological ideals imparted from the professor's
podium.) Lawrence saw sexual love as an integral element of

religion; he condemned casual sex, as does Catholicism, for denying the full value of a genuine interrelationship between men and women. Cinematic evidence indicates that Hitchcock moved toward Lawrence's conviction regarding marriage as a sexual communion that contributed to moral cleansing and personality development, as shown in *The Birds* and *Marnie*. In the latter, unilateral sex is shown as deficient, while reciprocity and trust (achieved at the film's end) creates a fuller relationship, more honest and happy—a shadow of the divine. People, in Hitchcock's view, must transcend their loneliness and complete one another. *Marnie* is a film which deftly mingles Christian, Lawrentian, and Freudian ingredients, producing, I believe, an advance in Hitch's total understanding of love as a healing power.

It is noteworthy that Hitch's later films reflect an intense spiritual struggle in matters of romance, whether extramarital or not. Like Ingmar Bergman, Hitch has made very personal statements of self-doubt and even agony in terms of impossible-love relationships. However, Hitch's complete signature inclines much more away from *Vertigo* and *Psycho* with their themes of sexual frustration. These films should not be judged merely as single entries, but within the broader context of such previous films as *Rear Window* and *The Man Who Knew Too Much* and such later films as *North by Northwest, The Birds,* and *Marnie*. Hitch's signature wavered at times, indicating fluctuations due to personal mood and creativity. His signature, I would argue, is more richly varied because of his darker classics. In this he invites comparison with Shakespeare. One gains a deeper appreciation of Hitch's genius by not forgetting his age's preoccupation with sheltered childhoods, environments of sexual modesty, cloistered campuses and churches, and some harsh taboos which presumed that sexual ignorance was tantamount to moral innocence. All of these assumptions regarding human sexual dynamics gave way within a short space of time. By 1920, there suddenly broke upon the world a convergence of revolutions expanding human consciousness in unprecedented ways, involving the permissive postwar morality, greater artistic liberty, the new mass media (radio, cinema, pictorial journalism, phonograph records), the women's

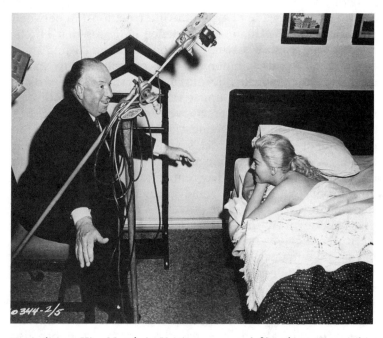

Hitch directs Kim Novak in *Vertigo,* a personal film about "impossible love." The perils of romantic illusion plagued Hitch as three favorite stars had surprisingly short careers with him: Ingrid Bergman, Grace Kelly, and Tippi Hedren.

movement, and urban growth (in 1920, the United States census showed more people in metropolitan areas than in rural). This chapter has sought to make the reader familiar with the hunger for direct and vicarious romantic and sexual experience that was created by the high, thick walls of asceticism, modesty, and puritanical strategies in the teenage years of Alfred Hitchcock. *Nulla ignoranti cupido.* Never in human history has so much sexual knowledge been disseminated to so many people within such a short span of time. Hitchcock pondered his life experiences and the exploding opportunities for vicarious experiences following World War I. He saw silent film as a medium more powerful than the theater, broadcasting, and tabloid journalism. If he is ranked as one of the three greatest directors, then it is crucial to understand his fascination with how human beings make impure use of the sacred. Make no mistake: he saw the sexual as an integral part of romance and marriage as a "sacred," hidden perhaps but irrepressibly of divine origin.

Notes

1. Alexander Walker, *The Celluloid Sacrifice: Aspects of Sex in the Movies* (London: Michael Joseph, 1966), p. 19.
2. Ibid., p. 26.
3. Ibid., p. 20.
4. My thanks to Jack Vizzard, who worked for over twenty years with Joseph Breen, the head of the Motion Picture Production Code. A Catholic, as was Breen, Vizzard attested to the fact that the code staff was predominantly Roman Catholic, on the premise that other countries (such as India) would accept the strict moral interpretation of those in tune with the church's standards.
5. Joseph de Guibert, *La Spiritualité de la Compagnie de Jésus: Esquisse Historique*, Via dei Penitenzieri, Vol. 20, (Rome: Institutum Historicum Societatis Jesu, 1953), pp. 169 ff., 588 ff.
6. Historian Samuel Hynes described the sea changes that took place during the years of Hitchcock's early maturity: "No aspect of human life changed more in the transition from Victorian England than the way Englishmen thought about sex" (*The Edwardian Turn of Mind* [Princeton, N.J.: Princeton University Press, 1968], p. 171).
7. Luis Buñuel, *My Last Sigh*, translated by Abigail Israel (New York: Alfred Knopf, 1983), passim.
8. *Easy Virtue, Champagne, The Manxman, Blackmail, Rich and Strange, The 39 Steps, The Secret Agent, Young and Innocent, Rebecca, Mr. and Mrs. Smith, Suspicion, Saboteur, Spellbound, Notorious, The Paradine Case, Stage Fright, I Confess, Dial M for Murder, Rear Window, To Catch a Thief, The Man Who Knew Too Much* (1956), *The Wrong Man, Vertigo, North by Northwest, Psycho, The Birds, Marnie, Frenzy.*

CHAPTER XIII

Toward Sexual Maturity

Having pointed out that Hitchcock in his developing years had to make the transition from the vanishing Victorian era to the more liberated Edwardian age, we can better understand his growth regarding womanhood in all its variety, the male-female relationships with which he had to deal in his own courtship of Alma Reville, as well as the inescapable romantic-couple scenes in the screenplays he was to direct. It is noteworthy that Alma Reville contributed to the scenarios of a good number of his British silent and sound pictures, thus helping her fiancé, later husband, toward a mature appreciation of the relations between the two genders.

Hitchcock's actresses in the 1920s were either bouncy flapper types, such as Betty Balfour, with her Cupid's bow lips and rolling eyes (*Champagne*), and the flirtatious Lilian Hall Davis (*The Ring*), or stately, aristocratic types, such as the elegant blondes Isabel Jeans (*Easy Virtue*) and Joan Barry (*Rich and Strange*). His later films starred more reserved British leading ladies: Edna Best (*The Man Who Knew Too Much*), Madeleine Carroll (*The 39 Steps, Secret Agent*), Margaret Lockwood (*The Lady Vanishes*), and Nova Pilbeam (*Young and Innocent*). These frosty feminine types contrast sharply with the casting alternatives whom, in Hollywood's sound period, Hitch had at his command. One of the advantages of the large studios was the exhilarating choice of women stars and ingenues available. When we look at the pictures he made from 1940 on, we can notice the difference between the type exemplified by Laraine Day, Carole Lombard, or Priscilla Lane and, say, Joan Fontaine, a demure British-type lead. True, Ingrid Bergman was a Nordic star, but like Garbo she had been Americanized. No doubt that the director was more closely identified with his actresses than with such male stars as Joel McCrea and Gregory Peck. Any study of his growth toward sexual maturity must factor in his irresistible inclination to select women who, though reserved and dignified, exuded a wisp of sexual abandon. Take *Rebecca* and Joan Fontaine's role as a slightly neurotic shrinking violet with a strong, one-sided romantic dependency upon her husband (Laurence Olivier). Or consider Fontaine's part in *Suspicion*: in the opening scene she is asked by a charming stranger (Cary Grant) to let her hair down, and when she does, the difference is dramatic.

In sharp contrast with Joan Fontaine's two roles (one an Oscar-winning performance), we have the three Ingrid Bergman roles *(Spellbound, Under Capricorn, Notorious)*: they reveal an equivocal personality, vulnerable to the attentions of handsome but flawed men. In *Spellbound,* she plays Dr. Constance Petersen, drawn to the director of the mental hospital, Dr. Edwardes (Gregory Peck). She boldly enters his living quarters at night on the pretext that she is looking for a book in the library living-room. When he finds her, she melts in a way we would expect of a schoolgirl smitten by puppy love rather than a mature woman who is a professional psychiatrist.

Another pertinent example is *The Paradine Case,* an intense study of impossible love. Gregory Peck plays Anthony Keane, a barrister who, though married, is irresistibly attracted to his client, Maddelena Paradine (Alida Valli). She pleads innocent of the charge that she caused the death of her husband, an older man. Seeing her husband in the throes of sexual obsession, Gay Keane (Ann Todd) feels helpless. But, just as the barrister is infatuated with his client, the judge (Charles Laughton) is infatuated with the barrister's wife. In an ironic scene, the judge bestows undue attention on Gay at a party, fixing looks at her neckline and bosom. He evidently is eager to seduce her. To emphasize the precariousness of human justice, Hitchcock links the adulterous clues with a transition cut to a statue of Lady Justice blindfolded, holding the scales in her hand. The director insinuates that the human representatives of justice are myopic, prejudicially compro-

A plain Joan Fontaine will soon let her hair down. In *Suspicion,* she and Cary Grant manifest unstable identities—hard to predict. The ending is a troubled one.

Hitch's lovers pass over the usual stage of "getting to know you." In *Spellbound* (1945), two strangers move quickly to an irresistible embrace, an impetuosity seldom seen in 1930's Hollywood romances.

mised by their erotic vested interests. Is it possible for a lecherous judge to dispense impartial justice? Can an infatuated attorney disbelieve his client's innocence? *The Paradine Case* has a troubled ending: Mrs. Paradine, the accused, admits to the stunned barrister that she is guilty, leaving him with his reputation tarnished and a hurt but loyal wife.

Then we have *Notorious,* whose plot deals with an American federal agent named Devlin (Cary Grant). He falls in love with Alicia Huberman (Ingrid Bergman), the daughter of a former foreign agent. In the opening scene, we see a different Ingrid Bergman at a party in Miami. Drunk and promiscuous, she is driven home by Cary Grant. There is obviously romantic electricity as Hitchcock short-circuits the reserved image of the noted Swedish actress. Another romantic se-

In *Notorious,* Ingrid Bergman meets Cary Grant at a Miami party. Her slatternly ways and dress suggest spiritual imprisonment. Later, in a Rio de Janeiro hotel, they both embrace, as love unlocks her prison door.

quence takes place on a hotel balcony in Rio de Janeiro. Since the Motion Picture Production Code prevented any long continuous kissing, the director circumvented it by having interrupted kissing, with Grant and Bergman nibbling at one another's lips and ears as they discuss preparations for dinner. Interestingly enough, *Under Capricorn* again portrays Bergman as a guilt-ridden, heavy-drinking woman. Her three roles for Hitchcock are revealing studies of unstable, highly vulnerable women whose beautiful surfaces conceal a need for men to come to their rescue and to make them more complete. Feminist film criticism would uncover not a few relevant insights into the male psychology underlying these portrayals of decentered women.

Directors are successful to the extent that they control the making of a film. This is especially true of authors who have gained the authority to make the final cut in the editing room. Among world-class directors, Hitchcock ranks close to Chaplin in terms of directorial autonomy. I see an anomaly in a powerful director such as Hitchcock being dominated in fantasy by pretty (mostly blonde) women whom he regards in his celluloid fantasies as subordinate and unstable, women who seem desperately to cry out not for complementarity, but for masculine domination. Clues abound to make this interpretation worthy of further discussion.

The Grace Kelly films extend the gallery of Hitchcock's women by giving us an American woman of class and breeding, as contrasted with Joan Fontaine's Britishness and Ingrid Bergman's Swedishness. In three successive films, Kelly became progressively amorous: coolly married but interested in another man (Robert Cummings) in *Dial M for Murder;* kittenish and playful with her fiancé (James Stewart) in *Rear Window;* and, finally, passionate in an embrace with an ex-cat burglar, Robie (Cary Grant), on the Riviera in *To Catch a Thief.* In the third film Kelly plays Frances Stevens, who sets alluring romantic traps for Robie. Hitchcock uses double entendre in referring to her jewels and her breasts ("Here, hold them"). When Kelly and Grant embrace, the fireworks display outside their room reaches a climax. (In *North by Northwest,* Hitch has further recourse to Freudian symbolism: the audience sees Cary Grant and Eva Marie Saint, now married, in their pajamas and embracing in a Pullman compartment of a train which rushes through a tunnel. Thus is romantic consummation piquantly suggested.)

The best of Hitchcock's films reveal an unmistakable psychospiritual viewpoint. Noteworthy are his three classic horror entries which blend explicit sexual themes and subtle religious allusions: *Vertigo, Psycho,* and *Frenzy.* Each film has a single word title that signifies psychic decenteredness, or indeed, some personality disorder. More revealing, however, to my mind, is that publicity posters featured each film as "Hitchcock's *Vertigo,*" "Hitchcock's *Psycho,*" "Hitchcock's *Frenzy.*" We know that the Master of Suspense could be a prankster and a practical joker. Could he not also play psychological tricks with his images, sounds, and credit titles? Like any good mystery writer, he left clues for the inquiring mind, for the perceptive sleuth. Why, we may ask, did he deliberately plant teasing clues about his own inner life, the "trials of conscience" mentioned in an interview with a fellow Jesuit alumnus? Why did he imprint on the celluloid frames of these three unsettling films psychological fingerprints which fused sexual and religious references unique to Hitchcock?

Vertigo, Psycho, and *Frenzy* merit a comparative analysis to identify common elements. They have no strong hero or heroine with whom the audience can identify. The audience can feel only a certain solidarity of remorseful pity for the woman victims, all killed by obsessive men who see them as objects, not as feeling subjects with their own wills and destinies. The abnormal behavior seems to spring from infantile behavior. In *Vertigo,* Midge (Barbara Bel Geddes) is clearly a mother figure and even refers to the traumatized Scottie Ferguson as a "child." In *Psycho,* Norman Bates's domineering mother is completely internalized in his psyche. In *Frenzy,* Bob Rusk lives with his mother (no father or siblings in evidence); we presume they live alone and that, as a bachelor, he is all she has. If we accept the immature development of the three fantasy-possessed protagonists, we have an interesting common bond.

The essential melodramatic plot has aspects of tragedy in all three films. There is no public challenge, no historical background, no "wrong-man" or love-on-the-run theme to engage our interest. The plot is intensely private, an intrapsychic drama. In each sexual horror film, one question remains unanswered and opaque at the end: What are the dark forces that motivate this attractive, rather intelligent man to be overdetermined, to move in a self-destructive orbit as he relentlessly pursues attractive women upon whom he becomes fixated? These handsome men perform bizarre actions which are, without any doubt, sexually compulsive in character. Let us briefly look at each of the three films from the vantage point of the irresistible nature of impossible love, a fatal type of instant falling in love based on pure animal attraction.

In *Vertigo,* acrophobic Scottie Ferguson (Jimmy Stewart) is requested by a well-to-do college chum, Elster, to serve as his private eye and account for the doings of his beautiful blonde wife, Madeleine (Kim Novak). Having rescued her from a suicidal drowning under San Francisco's Golden Gate Bridge,

In *Psycho*, shuttered light imprisons Janet Leigh in her lunch hour tryst with a married man. Infatuated, she robs $40,000. Legally guilty, is she morally culpable, anymore than the psychically determined Norman in the last scene?

Scottie falls in love with her. She is the descendant of the Spanish Doña Carlotta who committed suicide after going mad. There is no personality center to either Scottie or Madeleine. Both are different from Midge, a no-nonsense woman with predictable middle-class aspirations. Madeleine dies (seemingly) in a fall from a mission tower. Scottie is depressed. Later, he meets Judy (Kim Novak dressed down and with dark hair). He tries to make her over into Madeleine, but Judy *is* Madeleine.

In *The Films of Alfred Hitchcock*, Robert A. Harris and Michael S. Lasky write: "If *Rear Window* explored the realm of the voyeur, *Vertigo* unravelled what essentially was a man obsessed with making love to the simulacrum of a dead woman. Though technically not necrophilia, still it qualifies, in a moral and psychological sense. It is distasteful to term it as such, I know, but Scottie's uncontrollable maniac passion occupies the last two-thirds of the film."[1] He has Judy rearrange her hair and dress style to resemble Madeleine. In Catholic moral thought, Scottie would be sinfully guilty of adulterous intentions, for whenever he made love to Judy, he would be imagining Madeleine, who was another man's wife. Hitchcock understood the complex moral levels of subjective guilt involved in this film because when Grace Kelly left to become the princess of Monaco, he felt a void. She had made three consecutive box-office hits with him: *Dial M for Murder, Rear Window,* and *To Catch a Thief.* His search for a replacement led him to Tippi Hedren. Was this the Judy/Madeleine doppelgänger theme in his life? Some critics feel it was. The parallel is provocative, especially in light of Spoto's revelation in *The Dark Side of Genius* about Hitchcock's obsession for Tippi Hedren.

In effect, Scottie Ferguson is in love with one woman, not married but single and eminently available. His fascination, however, is based on her unavailability: first, because she was thought to be married to a friend (Elster); second, because she was thought to be dead; and third, because she could be resurrected physically but not spiritually. In short, the dressed-down Kim Novak was believed to be different from the dressed-up Kim Novak, even though she was both Madeleine and Judy, the same person. Moreover, Madeleine/Judy was the mistress of Scottie Ferguson's friend, Elster. She posed as Elster's wife to deceive Scottie into thinking that she had fallen from the church tower, when, in actuality, it was the corpse of Elster's murdered wife that fell. A fascinating and complex plot!

Underneath the illusions, disguises, and amorous projections, nothing morally wrong is taking place—except in the fevered imagination of the vertiginous detective. At bottom, Scottie has been in love with only one woman; she is someone's mistress, but she is available. *Vertigo* deals with the violation of a triple taboo (notice the mystical three again) against desire: (1) a married woman (who really is not); (2) a dead woman (who really is not); and (3) a substitute woman (who really is not). From a Catholic moral and theological standpoint, although there is nothing objectionable here with things as they are, intention is tantamount to the deed. (What you intend is what you get, at least on the spiritual tally sheet.) The Catholic influences in this film are as important as in *Psycho,* where Marion Crane's passion and Norman Bates's psychic disorder greatly attenuate the moral gravity of their crimes. *Vertigo* is a veritable hall of mirrors with infinite reflections of subtly changing angles of moral and theological perceptions.

Then we have *Psycho.* Hitchcock called it a "fun film," but we know that he was given to remarks that were quotable but not meaningful or expressing his real thought.[2] In the case of Marion Crane (Janet Leigh) and Norman Bates (Anthony Perkins), we have contrasting cases of deviance. The former commits theft, the latter commits murder. Both crimes are sexually motivated. Recall that Marion wants to marry Sam Loomis (John Gavin), who needs money for a divorce. As for Norman, he is terribly conflicted. His possessive mother forbade him to become involved with women, even though she herself had an illicit lover. The film has two interlocking triangles. It is ironic that Norman, imprinted by a sexual ethic of *noli tangere* ("don't touch"), is the avenger of those women who violate that strict puritanical code. It is he who kills his mother, her lover, and Marion.

The symbolism in the film is important and has manifest Freudian overtones. At the risk of far-reaching overinterpretation, I suggest that Hitchcock was probably aware of the sexual connotation in the names of Marion Crane (i.e., clearly a bird symbol but perhaps an allusion to an "erection" device) and Norman (i.e., Master Bates). Second, the motel is the modern inn for highly mobile tourists and traveling professionals. It is a convenient trysting place, economical and anonymous. (Marion Crane does not sign her real name in the office ledger—she signs "Marie Samuels"; recall that Sam is the name of her lover.)

The Bates Motel is a countersign to the Bates mansion, a Victorian residence with its proper gingerbread facade and dark secrets. I have suggested that the three-story house is an architectural allegory for Freud's three-level analytical model of the psyche: the id (the basement of libidinal desire, with orgasm as the symbol of death), the ego (the ground floor of public ingress and egress, the connection with the outer world of civilized contacts), and the superego (the third floor of parental orders and influences). Norman lived in the attic, an escapist fantasyland above the dynamics of authority, social interaction, and especially encounters with women (see Chapter IX, "Techniques of Expressionism"). The stuffed birds in the motel office suggest sexual desire, for their protruding beaks are evident phallic symbols. In certain subcultures of America, "bird" refers to a man's genitals (unlike in England, where it is a slang expression which refers to a woman). On the wall is a picture of a nude woman modestly wrapping her arms around her body in a protective gesture; Marion is seen with one arm similarly gripping her other arm in a subconscious posture of self-defense. There is a larger framed picture of Susanna and the Elders, those two "dirty old men" from the Old Testament who publicly accused a woman of solicitation when she refused their proposition to lie with them. They had spied on her taking a bath and their lust was kindled. When Marion undresses in her motel room, Norman removes this picture on the adjoining back-office wall to engage in voyeurism, looking at her through the peephole. This triggers his inner conflict: Master Bates versus Mother Bates who resents the feminine engine of erection, Crane, Marion!

The religious symbols in *Psycho* are less immediately obvious than those in *Vertigo* and *Frenzy,* but they are there. I mentioned the reference to Susanna and the Elders. In the penultimate scene, the psychiatrist enters a room to speak to Marion's sister Lila (Vera Miles), Sam Loomis, and the police chief. A long shot shows him enter the room: on the wall at the left is a cross. Later, in medium shot, it is revealed as a wall lighting fixture, but the first scene clearly shows a cross symbol. (In all interpretations of subliminal embedments, no irrefutable evidence can be adduced either to prove or disprove completely the hypothesis.)

I mentioned in Chapter I, "The Man Behind the Director," that Hitchcock is pointing beyond facile scientism to awesome mystery. As confirmation of this, the final scene is pathetically touching as it shows Norman in a cell with an insane smile on his face as his mother speaks in a voice-over.

This scene undercuts the rational explanation of the psychiatrist. The film text obliges me to look beyond Hitch's mischievous remark about *Psycho* being a "fun" film. The horror is too great and the linkage of sex and religion points to a biographical subtext made up of crises with origins in a Jesuit Catholic upbringing and the relaxed moral atmosphere following World War I. Norman Bates's world is comprised of his Victorian home, with its repressive memories, and the motel, with its contemporary bathrooms, beds, and Gideon Bibles in the drawers. Again, religion and sex are linked, at least implicitly.

In *Frenzy,* the protagonist, Richard Blaney (Jon Finch), is a "wronged man," framed by his buddy Bob Rusk (Barry Foster), a lecherous rapist and killer. Hitchcock seems to suggest that Rusk is a human pollutant, represented by the ugly effluvia floating along on the Thames. (In the opening scene, a politician addresses a crowd about environmental pollution; suddenly, a naked female body drifts up onto shore, murdered—choked with a fraternity tie.) In the scene when Rusk rapes Brenda (Barbara Leigh-Hunt), Blaney's ex-wife, she strategically submits and sublimates the attack by reciting a psalm. He garrotes her with his tie; around her neck is a gold cross on a chain. Why this emblematic detail? And why the black trunk-coffin with its strap binders in the discernible form of a cross outlined on the top? The religious symbolism is unmistakable, although subtle.

I believe that Hitchcock, once overregulated in terms of educational, religious, and family discipline, gradually deregulated his life, not in terms of outward profession or family conduct, but in terms of moviemaking in Hollywood. A leap forward in his career and sexual consciousness occurred when David O. Selznick brought him to the world's film center. There he had large budgets, his choice of actors, and the pick of the best screenwriters. But he also had access to beautiful women as fantasy objects in terms of romantic bonding. True, Hitch had used subjective camera work before; however, in Hollywood he became more psychoanalytically aware of how to exploit close-ups, camera angles, and reaction shots of fright and horror reflected in the eyes of the players. Thus, he progressed in learning how to cement identification with his own emotional states through the more expressive stars at his disposal in Hollywood.

Hitchcock's mature films (1951–1976) support a valuable observation shared with me at Universal Studios in 1978 by Albert Whitlock, Hitch's British-born special-effects supervisor. He told me that Hitchcock had a penchant for "impossible loves," that he fell in love with such major actresses as Ingrid Bergman, Grace Kelly, and Tippi Hedren. (It is clear that he was also partial to Vera Miles, Eva Marie Saint, and Kim Novak.) It is remarkable how blondes feature in his canon of films. It is even more remarkable that the principal women victims in *Vertigo, Psycho,* and *Frenzy* are all blonde. "Blood and blondes"; they die violently, these women who cannot fulfill the exalted, indeed "impossible" expectations of their anguished admirers and predatory pursuers.

That the eye is the chief gateway of the senses, and especially of sexual temptation, is a closely held belief among Catholics and would have been impressed on Hitchcock. Recall the earlier mention of the Jesuit rule regarding modesty of the eyes: downcast and never directly meeting the gaze of a woman. *Champagne* (1928) ends with a lecherous stare by a mustachioed man looking at a woman (Betty Balfour) through the champagne glass he is draining. This finale is disturbing and discounts any good feelings audiences desired to carry away, especially couples dating.

Similar striking images return in 1945 with *Spellbound,* when Hitchcock used the power of the eye and its role in sexual attraction. Not only are irresistible looks featured in the film when Constance looks meltingly at Dr. Edwardes, but the dream sequence designed by Salvador Dali uses eyes.[3] A woman goes about with large scissors and cuts drapes on which are painted huge eyes, thus recalling, for the perceptive film buff, Dali's use of the eye-cutting razor in *Un Chien Andalou* of Luis Buñuel. In *The Paradine Case,* we have the lecherous look of Charles Laughton's Judge Horfield. In *Strangers on a Train,* we have the furtive exchange of glances at the amusement park between Anthony Bruno and Miriam Haines, his prospective murder victim. She already is accompanied by two men, neither of whom is her husband, and yet she flirts with a third man, a total stranger. Her glasses fall to the ground when she is strangled, and we see the frightening act distortedly reflected in the broken lenses. She will never flirt again with those eyes.

Rear Window is the greatest entertainment or art film ever dedicated to the theme of the eye as all-searching and omnipresent. Jimmy Stewart's Jeff first uses the naked eye, then binoculars, and finally, the telescopic lens. He compensates for his physical immobility by the technical extension of vision. The lens enables him to go where he physically cannot. Critics see this film as a form of self-reflexivity in which the director portrays his role as visionary extraordinaire. In each apartment viewed by Jeff and the audience is an example of a film genre: murder, romance, the family, musical comedy, and loneliness. In Munich in 1924, Hitchcock learned about the adroit use of the "unchained" camera by German directors, such as F. W. Murnau, who was shooting the classic *The Last Laugh.* In *Faust,* Murnau had the camera take the spectator from heaven to earth in a dazzling use of the traveling camera. The eye of the audience became disembodied. Hitchcock saw the possibilities and capitalized on them in *Rear Window* and, subsequently, in *Vertigo, Psycho, The Birds,* and *Frenzy.* The last-named picture uses a solemnly mournful back-tracking shot which takes the spectator from the apartment door (behind which a rape and murder has occurred) out to the street.

It is in *Psycho* that the eye plays a crucial role: the eye of the audience entering the hotel room at noon in Phoenix and witnessing a tryst; the shaded eyes of the highway patrolman who frightens Marion Crane as she sleeps in her car; the Peeping Tom eye of Norman Bates looking at Marion undressed; the lifeless eye of Marion, lying in the shower as her blood rinses down the drain; the cowlike eyes of Norman/ Mother with their empty glazed stare denoting madness and a subhuman state. The eye is the window of the soul, not only for spiritual writers but also for Hitchcock. More often than not, to see is to want, to want is to will, to will is to do. In a world where curiosity and the sensational are paraded unashamedly before the public's eye, the risk is that we will be inclined to want, to will and to do what we see.

Motion picture photography heightens desire for some

through the magnified image even more than textual or abstract knowledge. In Hitch's case, however, the information is folded deftly into the frames so that the reflective viewer who sees the film three times, as Hitch recommends, reaps a rich dividend beyond the mere sensation of thrills and excitement. This is exceptionally the case with *Psycho,* which deals with vision and desire in strong opposition to parental and societal taboos. (We recall Scottie Ferguson's triple violation of similar taboos in *Vertigo.*) Norman acts out the mother (superego) on the third floor of the Victorian house. It is to the basement (id) that he carries her skeleton. (Recall that, disgusted by her waywardness, he had poisoned her and her lover with strychnine.) Norman leaves and enters through the foyer on the ground floor to attend to the motel, which is his escape into another world of spontaneous human contacts. There he has created his own theater of fantasies, a peephole (symbolically hidden under a painting of Susanna and the Elders).

The scenes before, during, and after the voyeurism are heavily laden with erotic allusions and religious symbols. If the beaks of the stuffed birds are phallic symbols, then the knife must also be seen as one. Certainly in *Psycho* this allusion is unmistakable, for Norman, disguised as his mother, has whet his sexual appetite for Marion in the previous scene of voyeurism. The internalized mother forbids this desire. At the point where Marion has reconciled her internal conflict, taking an ego stand by resolving to return the money (thus bridging id with superego), she is victimized by a person who is caught between the schizoid cross-pressures of superego (mother figure) and id (Norman).

Except in the *The 39 Steps,* the knife is generally wielded by women to redress an unfair relationship of dependency upon a man. In *Blackmail,* a woman protects her virginity by stabbing in self-defense, but she is left with guilt. In *Sabotage,* the husband, Verloc, appears to run himself onto the dinner knife held by the nervous wife, obviously contemplating avenging her young brother's untimely death caused by Verloc's timebomb. In *Dial M for Murder,* the wife stabs her attacker. In *The Wrong Man,* the delicatessen owner's burly wife fearlessly brandishes a knife when threatened by the robber's gun. She taps for help; her husband responds and subdues the thief. If women stab, men strangle (*The Lodger, Strangers on a Train, Frenzy*). Is Uncle Charlie (Joseph Cotten) in *Shadow of a Doubt* a strangler? The camera repeatedly calls attention to his hands, as William Rothman conclusively establishes.[4] We wonder, recalling that the often unbalanced killers of women are stranglers. Sexual excitement is implicit in many stories of strangling, and we can presume that knifings by women signify a revenge through a reverse phallic assault. In *Sabotage,* Sylvia Sidney enters the movie theater before killing her husband and sees the Disney animated cartoon in which Cock Robin is killed by an arrow. The scene, one of jealousy and unrequited love, resonates strongly in her.

Hitchcock's view of sex is linked to its irrepressible power to redraw the boundaries of reality, thus leading the impulsive person into dangerous thoughts and actions, much as the moth is drawn to the flame. One French psychoanalyst sees in Hitchcock's films a Freudian pattern wherein men often have psychotic tendencies with the ego at the service of the id, whereas women are portrayed as neurotics with the ego in tense conflict between the superego and the id.[5] In short, women are different types of souls in suspense in Hitchcock's work than are men. In *Psycho,* Marion Crane responds to a double social-sexual aggression, that of the insolent "millionaire," who flirts with her and from whom she steals $40,000, and her lover Sam, who meets her sexual needs clandestinely because he is married and cannot yet afford a divorce. (Here we have a foreshadowing of Marnie's sexually induced thievery.) While Marion must flee to avoid the distasteful fragment of a reality which she cannot confront (neurosis), Norman denies reality completely in order to construct an alternate, seemingly better, reality (psychosis).

Where does biography end and filmography begin in Hitchcock's oeuvre? Hard to say. It is facile, even presumptuous, to read too much into such films as *Psycho* and *Vertigo,* but autobiographical references cannot be dismissed out of hand with regard to the absence of father figures and the presence of possessive mothers—*Strangers on a Train, North by Northwest, Psycho, The Birds, Marnie,* and *Frenzy.* (Even in *Vertigo,*

Scottie's friend Midge "mothers" him as a child.) Maternal possessiveness triggers anxiety and infatuation, tendencies of a virtually irresistible kind. Sexual curiosity and desire, recurrent themes, are matched by repetitious, at times compelling, allusions to religion—some explicit (priests, nuns, the Sacred Heart, crosses, and churches), some implicit (conscience, guilt, remorse, retribution, and sacrificial victimhood).

Why did a directorial genius again and again yoke erotic desire and religious symbolism together? Why are his morose themes both artfully and convincingly presented? Why the recurring Catholic and Jesuit references: meliorism, *agere contra,* the innocent victim theme, and—not to be overlooked—the detection of the growth and decline in character through retracing in the light of the principle of beginning, middle, and end?

Hitchcock's trials of conscience are neither those of an abnormal person nor those of the average person. His mind and imagination were exceptionally advanced, constantly at work seeking new connections and novel twists to his pet topics. We cannot forget that he was an unusually sensitive artist dealing with what are, essentially, underground themes, discreetly handled: incest (*Shadow of a Doubt*), sacrilege (*I Confess*), voyeurism (*Rear Window, Psycho*), necrophilia (*Vertigo*), sex-related aberration (*Marnie*), and acquaintance rape (*Frenzy*). Nevertheless, Hitch's earnest search for a personal, coherent view of the cosmos is no different from that of any believer of any religion who must face the mounting complex discontinuities of a shrinking world with expanding technologies, information, and population pressures.

There seems to be an ambivalent inheritance Hitchcock carried with him from his Catholic upbringing. On the one hand, there was the undeniable conditioning process, the tendency to react automatically to please parents, teachers, clergy, and authority figures in general.[6] On the other hand, there was the belief, deeply rooted in church teaching, that sex is a significant aspect of life but must be integrated within a framework of relationships of trust so that anticipation in reason and liberty replaces immediate instinctual satisfaction. The joy of sex is in the pursuit, not the capture, which may explain Hitchcock's subtle suggestions that marriage is more constraint and obligation than mutual attraction and consensual sharing.

Until the changes in the church introduced by Vatican Council II in the 1960s, Jesuit spirituality was relatively privatized, largely based on a personal relation to Christ, a life of prayer, and apostolic activity conducted a respectful distance from people, especially women. (One nationally known Jesuit speaker and university president, after fifty years in the order, stressed loneliness as the Jesuit ideal in a touching prayer he had composed.) Would Hitch have affirmed such a prayer, although a husband and father? Probably! Even in Hollywood he was aloof from the colony of celebrities, only accepting invitations to industry events, celebrations, and tributes. People reacted differently to Hitchcock when they met him in person than when he was seen in publicity appearances or in his cameo roles. Generally, people either liked or disliked him immediately. He held strong opinions and had inflexible expectations. For instance, Paul Newman was a houseguest of the Hitchcocks during the production of *Torn Curtain*. Spontaneously, he rose from the dinner table and went to the refrigerator for a bottle of beer. Hitchcock bristled at his taking such license. The two of them did not get along on the set except in terms of professional collaboration. In the same way, Jesuits tend to evoke definite reactions from people; there is seldom any fence-sitting. One generally takes a stand immediately—for or against. Holding uncompromising positions and with a clear sense of purpose, Hitch did not court companionship or cultivate support groups. Consequently, he was often by himself, just as he once was at Saint Ignatius College, not a joiner, nor an athlete, nor committed to extracurricular activities.

I mention this because of Hitch's tender treatment in *Rear Window* of Miss Lonelyhearts. He understood that character and portrayed her in a compassionate way. Moreover, a study of Hitchcock's films reveals how, in reaction shots, people are often kept isolated from one another on different planes. This stylistic point is revealing, for, to my mind, film was definitely a part of Hitch's personal retreat into privacy. His genius lay in translating the varied products of fantasy from the screen of his imagination onto the larger twenty-five-foot by forty-foot screen. Close observation of many of his films confirms that his notion of personal intimacy was often remote, a product of yearning rather than experience, definitely more a physical pull of infatuation than a magnetic compatibility in trusting romantic friendship. In *Spellbound,* Gregory Peck and Ingrid Bergman keep a longing distance between them: the audience is treated to exaggerated, soulful looks and faces which light up suddenly in amorous joy. Missing are the scenes of playful courtship, of "getting to know you," as in Frank Capra's movies. In this regard, Hitch's Hollywood period lacks the middle ground of companionate love found in *The 39 Steps* and *Young and Innocent,* two early British films entirely free of Hitch's later preoccupation with Freud's libidinal drives. I submit that Hitchcock's early experiences of austerity, rein- forced by a Jesuit education, created in him a receptivity for a more relaxed atmosphere following World War I in Eng- land.

Something very similar also occurred with the effect of childhood Jesuit education on James Joyce and Luis Buñuel. Both they and Hitchcock were raised in a patriarchal world, subject to a program of religious asceticism and strict educa- tional discipline. Though from different national origins, each artist experienced a type of strict ideal found in the Catholic and Jesuit traditions. Their art owes no small debt to the creative reaction caused by such a training. Of course this was common with people of superior endowments and not necessarily with the bulk of Jesuit graduates.

There is a psychospiritual connection yoking the religious upbringing of Joyce, Buñuel, and Hitchcock with their sexual candor and concern. Their artistic vocation led all three to create a personal synthesis of secular and religious values which integrated the biological, psychological, and social horizons of this world while respecting the all-encompassing mysteries which are referred to by such terms as the occult, the esoteric, and the supernatural. To my mind, Hitch was even more effective than Joyce or Buñuel in demythologizing the physical world and creating an awesome sense of the occult and the supernatural, that which lies in the other world beyond memory, fantasy, desire, and dreams. Hitch often used the camera as an emotional X-ray and, at times, as the eye of God. He used a sense-drenched medium as a dramatic trampoline to make audiences accept as believable the invisible psychospiritual dynamics of the deep human self.

If sexuality had been bracketed as a subject to be treated with sufficient seriousness at home, at school, and within the larger culture of his childhood milieu, Hitch would have later made a sustained effort for not only intellectual coherence, but also personal integration. As with so many religious educational environments, however, the sexual and the sacred were kept at arm's length. There is no evidence that, at Saint Ignatius College, sex was ever demeaned or presented as intrinsically evil. Probably, the celibate life, especially as a part of a religious vocation, was stressed as the "higher" way. Thus, like many adolescents riding the crest of a new wave of mores and sexual attitudes, Hitch had to bring sexuality into his conscious mind and incorporate it into the convictions he carried away from his previous schooling. We should not be surprised at his fascination with Freudianism, which rules many of his pictures from *Spellbound* (1945) through *Psycho* (1960). With *The Birds* (1963), there is a different tack—not Freudian, more Jungian, and clearly within the dynamic of the original spirit of the Ignatian *Exercises* with its primacy of charity over sin and division. In his own way, Hitch had to integrate forward to incorporate in his life the novel experiences that were breaking on the shores of world consciousness following his graduation in 1913. This was no light task for a fourteen-year-old lad to grapple with, keeping in mind the practical and personal consequences of Horace's maxim: "You may drive out Nature with a pitchfork, yet she still will hurry back."

To do Hitchcock full justice, we cannot let our memory dim those tender scenes of affectionate couples and playful courtships: *The 39 Steps, Rebecca, Mr. and Mrs. Smith, The Man Who Knew Too Much, The Birds* and, in *Family Plot,* his last film, the cozy couple represented by Bruce Dern and Barbara Harris. Hitch bracketed neither sexuality nor the sacred, for his searching mind trusted confidently that both were complementary secrets that were integral parts of a single mystery which encompassed the human race. Thus,

In *The Lady Vanishes* (1938), Naunton Wayne and Basil Radford are seen as overt homosexuals with a Tyrolean housemaid as comic relief. Hitch was broad-minded about untypical types. Ironically, he cast such popular stars as Cary Grant and Jimmy Stewart in flawed roles. ("Things are not as they seem!")

interlaced with his bold erotic scenes and sexual references are undeniable religious motifs inculcated by his Catholic mentors: death, guilt, remorse, and the haunting questions about the ultimate meaning of our wondrously strange condition as kings and queens in exile—souls fallen, then redeemed, but while here on our earthly pilgrimage, ever in suspense.

Notes

1. Robert A. Harris and Michael S. Lasky, *The Films of Alfred Hitchcock* (Secaucus, N.J.: Citadel Press, 1976), p. 189.
2. Hitch would be somewhat more revealing when he trusted the interviewer, as in the case of François Truffaut, Richard Schickel, and John O'Riordan, the young alumnus of his alma mater, Saint Ignatius College.
3. Harris and Lasky, Ibid., p. 122.
4. William Rothman, *Hitchcock: The Murderous Gaze* (Cambridge: Harvard University Press, 1982), pp. 196–197, 204–207, 218, 225, 238–239.
5. Raymond Bellour, "Psychoses, Neuroses, Perversion," *Camera Obscura: A Journal of Feminism and Film Theory*, Vols. 3/4, pp. 114 ff.
6. See the pertinent article by a French psychologist, at the time a Jesuit, Louis Beirnaert, "The Problem of Conditioning in the Church," *Cross Currents*, Vol. 12 (Fall 1962), pp. 433 ff.

CHAPTER XIV

Confession: Secular and Sacred

From an early "age of reason" (about seven years), Hitch was required to give a daily, detailed account of his activities to his mother in her bedroom. Donald Spoto quotes Hitchcock: "It was something she always had me do. It was a ritual. I always remember the evening confession." Later, as a train boy at Saint Ignatius, Hitch was obliged to stand in line with his classmates and go to confession once a week. This ritual was often a thoughtless routine for confessor and penitent alike. "Bless me, Father, for I have sinned. It's been one week since my last confession." For preteenage boys and those slightly older, it could be a mechanical obligation and one taken for granted. As an adult, Hitch, with typical wit, parodied the mindless habits such a weekly duty could lead to. He had the penitent say, "I killed my mother." The priest replied, "How many times, my son?"

Beneath the slightly irreverent irony was a deep, abiding awareness of the wisdom underlying the Church's sacramental practice of the rhythm of private confession and the psychological need to admit one's transgressions as an antidote to haunting guilt. Is it possible that a young boy, given to the fear-inspiring routine of confessions, would learn the art of dissimulation, that is, the avoidance of full disclosure? If he made witty, slightly irreverent remarks about confession, nevertheless he had a strong urge to rid himself of guilt. Hitch's attitude toward confession can best be gleaned from his British and American films. Let us look more closely at this self-revealing artist whose work treated both secular and sacred confession.

I Confess (1953) is, of course, the emblematic case study of

Roman Catholic confession. A priest, Fr. Logan (Montgomery Clift), once in love with a pretty woman, replaces his dead brother (a World War II victim) as a seminarian. The spiritual motivation is never developed; the reason is internal and sentimental. However, Clift's countenance and bearing resemble those of the cleric in the moving Robert Bresson film, *The Diary of a Country Priest,* based on the novel by Georges Bernanos. In that film, we have a deeply interiorized curé so attuned to divine inspiration that the sins of the parishioners and townspeople weigh heavily on him.

Hitch's film is more melodramatic, combining religion and romance with suspense and mystery in a rather convincing way. The murder plot is involved, but not the love affair. The actors cannot carry the heavy freight of the encumbered plot, but Clift lifts it higher than the rest of the cast. Hitch disliked Clift's Method acting, but his role was enhanced by a brooding mien, a distant look, and a mystical sense of sacerdotal solemnity. As a cult figure (due to his tragic, early death), Clift's presence is paying a never-ending dividend that Hitch could not have expected.[1] The film deserves the triple viewing that Hitch said was necessary for fuller enjoyment.

There are three confessions in the film: two by the villain, Otto Keller (O. E. Hasse), and a public one in the street by his wife, Alma (Dolly Haas). She is shot as a consequence and dies in the arms of the priest, who gives her absolution. Critics, including Spoto, have pointed out that "Alma," the name of Mrs. Hitchcock, was not a coincidence. She is the savior of the maligned priest, jeered by the Quebecer bystanders outside the courthouse after his acquittal. Bresson's *Diary of a Country Priest* ends with the saintly priest's dying words: "All is grace!" Curiously, *I Confess* ends with the murderer and his wife both dying in what Catholics consider a state of sanctifying grace, destined for a face-to-face vision of God.

A curious providential cover of supernatural mystery hangs over this movie. It is, basically, an insider film; its total comprehension escapes not only non-Catholics, but many believers, including some priests. *I Confess* hinges on Hitch's profound sense of irony in the sense that a priest implicates himself legally as a major suspect in a first-degree-murder charge by the very act of removing the weight of eternal damnation from the actual killer. The paradox is based on the crucial distinction in Catholic spirituality between the natural and the supernatural. Hitch was stressing the precarious spiritual condition of four souls in suspense, faced not only with this-worldly threats of loss of reputation, imprisonment, and possible execution, but also the pains of eternal damnation in the life to come. This subtext was operative for the Jesuit-trained director but not immediately shareable with the mass public in terms of dramatic images conveying theological distinctions meaningful to insiders.

Motion pictures use secular confessional scenes as a dramatic device: witness Frank Capra's classic films such as *Mr. Deeds Goes to Town, Mr. Smith Goes to Washington,* and *Meet John Doe.* In real life people unburden themselves for purposes of psychological release and social communication. Seldom in the history of film, however, do we have themes involving sacramental confession. Thus, it is unusual to have a "sex idol" such as Montgomery Clift dispensing the absolution of the Catholic church to Alma and Otto Keller by means of a trinitarian blessing, "in the name of the Father, the Son, and the Holy Spirit." This formula, incidentally, Hitch heard dozens of times from his Jesuit confessors during his three years at Saint Ignatius College. Confession was done by classes as a routine obligation at least biweekly.

What *I Confess* offers, in contrast to many other examples of secular confession in Hitch's filmology, is an effective form of reconciliation. The faith of the two penitents is sealed by Fr. Logan's granting an unconditional warranty to reconciliation with God, so different from the type of indiscreet public confession which does not lead to personal transformation or deep conversion of one's life. Let us look at the need to confess, whether sacramentally or due to some compulsion to achieve a lightness of feeling. In Lancashire, England, there is a saying about the "big Catholic," one who doesn't go to church but will beat up any man in a pub who criticizes the pope. A similar inconsistency is found in those non-Catholics who shun the idea of confession to a priest but bare the details of their intimate lives to anyone they might casually meet, say, in a tavern or on a train. The need to confess is imperious, and

Hitch shows this time and again before and after *I Confess* (e.g., in *Strangers on a Train*, Bruno Anthony confesses in this way when he discloses to Guy Haines his murderous hatred for his own father; Guy too utters his deep resentment for his philandering wife: "I could strangle her").

Hitch's early films were seldom sensitive to the internal forum where the shadows of guilt banish the sunshine of peace. Take *The Pleasure Garden* (1926). In his first complete feature, Hitch dealt with murder and the danger of easy options in civilized lands and the South Seas but not with the mordant pangs of conscience or haunting black clouds of guilt. Later, in *Downhill* (1927), he failed to convince the audience of the authenticity of the guilt felt by those responsible for the plight of the innocent schoolboy (Ivor Novello) who was ostracized unjustly for nobly assuming the punishment of a guilty classmate. Hitch brilliantly captured in concrete superimpositions the sensitive fears of the lad (for Hitch himself had all the fears); the father's unforgiving position implants guilt and projects it. There is an un-ambiguous happy ending, unlike in his mature Hollywood features.

In *The Lodger* (1926), "Avenger" Drew (Ivor Novello) intends to make retribution for his sister's death by killing the mass murderer whom the law seeks to punish and eliminate. Maurice Yacowar, with unfailing perception, identifies the germ of Hitch's penchant for seeing beyond deed to intent as a measuring rod for allocating guilt.[2] *The Lodger* contains three guilty parties who are without remorse or conscience: Drew, the vigilante boarder; the policeman, Joe, who has Drew falsely arrested; and the mob, which tries to kill Drew. Guilt is pervasive and recognized eventually. Joe saves Drew from the mob when the real culprit is caught. Meanwhile, Hitch has cut to the roots of passion, self-interest, and rash judgment. This moral, all-seeing analysis would mark all of Hitch's later work.

Other than guilt, Hitch's fears have to do with being the odd man out: *The Lodger* (Joe loses out), *Champagne* (the Boy may still lose out), *The Manxman* (Philip Quillian loses out) and, later, the triangles in *Rich and Strange, Sabotage, Notori-ous, North by Northwest,* and *Frenzy*. In Hitchcock's British period, one discerns in the director an anarchic sense of insecurity that created anxiety and a preoccupation with the relaxation of those moral norms he knew as a child.

It is of striking interest that Hitch's silent films did not address the question of self-judgment as mediated by the transcendental referee of conscience.[3] *Blackmail,* considered Britain's first sound film, suggests conscience in an oblique way. The murdered artist had left a painting called "The Laughing Jester." It is the sight of this painting being carried as evidence into the police station that startles the guilty couple. Since the fiancé, a detective, shirked his duty in order to cover up his lover's slaying of the painter, their reaction to the accusing finger being pointed at them by the painted clown is really not a pang of conscience but a frisson of fear at the thought of being found out. Similarly, six years later, *Sabotage* also alludes to a lack of inner peace rather than to a guilt which would be accountable before a higher, invisible tribunal of other-worldly justice.

A remarkable instance of guilty conscience, easily over-looked, is the case of the blackface minstrel drummer in that memorable scene from *Young and Innocent* (1937). In a spectacular sweeping, uncut, overhead-crane shot, Hitch-cock's camera moves suspensefully 145 feet across a large hotel ballroom to a point six inches away from the twitching eyes of the villainous drummer. We now know who the murderer is. As if he feels our eyes on him, his uncontrollable guilt moves him to collapse and, when awakened, to confess his crime. It is not only a sensational scene technically but also a dramatic instance of irrepressible remorse and the need to confess. All three British films point the way to the more explicit treatments of confession, mostly secular, in Hitch-cock's later Hollywood period. Consider the years 1940 to 1947, when Hitch was under contract to David O. Selznick. Of the ten films that he directed for the producer of *Gone with the Wind,* I regard three as having Catholic or Jesuit relevance.

Take *Suspicion,* a film which ends on a strongly ambiguous note. Is Cary Grant intent on killing his wife, Joan Fontaine? Or is she oversensitive and paranoid? No answer is given; as a result, we, the audience, can only speculate. Hitch's version is more fascinating than the novel on which it was based: there the reader knew that the wife was eventually murdered. Conscience has a glimmering presence because of the tender, Oscar-winning performance of Joan Fontaine, looking in the last scene like a frightened sparrow. Men tend to feel empathy for her and transfer it to Cary Grant's screen persona with its legacy of trustworthy playfulness. However, many women in the audience can never feel secure with the character as delineated in the screenplay. Will conscience make such a coward of Johnny Aysgarth that he will protect his wife? While Hitch keeps us guessing, male psychology is inclined to give him another chance, and female psychology feels there is too much at stake.

As for *Shadow of a Doubt,* it is concerned with conscience *and* genes. True, we are confronted with lives in suspense, but not, to my mind, with souls in suspense. Such critics as François Truffaut have identified the religious vein of original sin that runs throughout the plot. There is a moral parallelism between niece Charlie (Teresa Wright) and her Uncle Charlie (Joseph Cotten), for she shares in the dark side of her favorite uncle. The parallelism goes beyond the mere similarity of their names. The main characters seem driven by a fatalistic blind force over which they have little control. The dramatic interest is there, but it has more of the elements of a Greek tragedy than those of a Shakespearean play.

As for *Notorious,* there is growth in the moral development of the protagonists, the FBI agent Devlin (Cary Grant) and the undercover plant Alicia Huberman (Ingrid Bergman). Each unstable in his or her love for the other, the lead characters achieve a happy ending, free of conscience pangs. However, Hitch obliges the audience to stay behind as the lovers drive away. Even if Claude Rains' fate is deserved, his authentic love for his legal wife stirs our conscience about the rightness of it all, and that is what Hitchcock intended with this final scene. The other Selznick efforts entertained audiences with situations of imperilment that did not directly affect the soul in its precarious state of suspension between time and eternity.

As an independent producer of *Rope, Under Capricorn,* and

In *Notorious,* Nazi Claude Rains plots with jealous mother (Leopoldine Konstantin) to poison his traitorous wife, Ingrid Bergman. Another instance of Hitch's dependent mother-son relations, reflecting his childhood.

Stage Fright, Hitch was primarily concerned with technical experimentation and his newfound freedom. In *Rope,* we meet Professor Rupert Cadell (Jimmy Stewart), a college teacher of philosophy who advocates the Nietzschean principle that those in the "superman" category are not restricted by the conventional rules regarding lying, infidelity, and even murder. Cadell is surprised that his two students, acting on the Nietzschean logic he had taught in class, assumed the attribute of supermen and committed a murder merely for the thrill of it. He says, "You've given my words meaning I never dreamed of." (Nietzsche's principles are believed to have influenced the racial supremacist views of Adolf Hitler and the Third Reich.) *Under Capricorn* seeks to examine not guilt feelings, but the present consequences of a past crime. In *Stage Fright*'s opening scene, Richard Todd is established as innocent, when in actuality he murdered the husband of his mistress (Marlene Dietrich). Hitch tried with these three films to expand the lexicon of cinema more than to deepen understanding of the spiritual crises of conscience in the main characters. In this sense, the three films fall below the artistic level and moral profundity of his later films. Nevertheless, they merit greater study and appreciation.

It is noteworthy that in Hitchcock's work with Warner Bros. there is a psychospiritual realism not evident in his later Paramount pictures, which were much more successful both in a critical and in a commercial sense. A word about each of the four Warner features: *Strangers on a Train, I Confess, Dial M for Murder,* and *The Wrong Man.*

Strangers on a Train (1951) ends on the same note as did *Blackmail* and *Sabotage.* Tennis-playing Guy Haines (Farley Granger) has married a senator's daughter after a mentally disturbed socialite, Bruno Anthony (Robert Walker), has killed the former's first wife. Although Haines never intended to commit the exchange murder, nevertheless, he feels somewhat implicated. Hitch shows this in a comic way in the last scene: on a train, Haines becomes visibly uneasy at the sight of a clergyman who wishes to strike up a conversation.

The scene is humorously ironic à la Hitchcock. There is, however, a more subtle interpretation. The conventional view has it that Guy wishes to avoid, at all costs, another strange meeting such as his first one with Bruno. But keep in mind Hitch's generalized fear of priests. Moreover, there is a question of conscience, for Guy's second, happier marriage would not have been possible without Bruno's slaying of the first wife. The director's subtlety allows us to muse about possible interpretations. In any event, Guy Haines is, and will remain, a soul in suspense.

I have already discussed at length *I Confess,* a Warner Bros. production and a study of five souls in suspense: the priest, his earlier love, her present husband, and the dead sacristan and his saintly wife.

In *Dial M for Murder,* Hitch's third film made at Warner Bros., it is not clear that Margot Wendice (Grace Kelly) will ever have complete interior peace of mind after having killed the murderous agent contracted by her sinister playboy husband (Ray Milland), who jealously wanted her out of the way. In the early part of the film, Margot's dresses change in color from bright red to somber black (as noted elsewhere in this book). Not only has she been accused, but she has herself stabbed another human being. Never has there been a better application of the three-dimensionality of film than the scene in which "Margot, her outstretched arm grasping for the scissors, seems to thrust her arm out of the screen almost pleading with the audience to place the scissors in her hand."[4] Knowing full well the chemistry of human nature, Hitch lures us into a moral trap, thus simulating those situations in which conscience is put to sleep. Yes, Margot Wendice killed in self-defense, but the death of another human cannot be treated as mere animal sacrifice. There must be some misgivings, even in an act of justifiable homicide.

As for *The Wrong Man,* another Warner's film, the conscience issue is in the forefront of the film, followed by the subplot of the mental breakdown of Manny Balestrero's afflicted wife, both already discussed at length.

The Paramount films *The Trouble with Harry, To Catch a Thief* and *The Man Who Knew Too Much* earned money for the studio and the director, while *Rear Window* and *Vertigo,* also successful, won the distinction of becoming film classics. In none of these Paramount films do I find the stirrings of conscience, the clear judgment calls of that inner voice I designate as the transcendental referee.

A stunning suspense-thriller, *Rear Window* deals largely with opportunism, instinct, passion, habit, and people leading lives of quiet desperation. We, the audience, share Jimmy Stewart's voyeurism and also the dread of what might happen to him once he is discovered by the wife murderer (Raymond Burr). Seen from the perspective of conscience, the film yields some interesting new insights into the ways in which the director can manipulate the mass audience. Hitchcock understood the classic rhetorical principle of the sophists, "Make the worst argument seem the best." (The Jesuits have often been accused of preaching that the end justifies the means.) Such reference books as *The New World Dictionary* gives as a meaning of the term *Jesuit* "one who is a crafty schemer; cunning dissembler; casuist"—in short, one with no serious conscience or scruples. Such allegations must be carefully weighed!

To Catch a Thief has been called "Hitchcock's Champagne," bubbly-bright and intoxicating in terms of its visual luxury and romantic seductiveness. Like the film's characters, we allow our critical judgment as well as our consciences to be lulled into a suspension of disbelief and are never disappointed in our two-hour occupancy of the moral limbo Hitch creates for Cary Grant and Grace Kelly.

The Trouble with Harry is a serious theological tract on the inevitability of death, even when it is a sunlit satire about simple, likable Vermont folk. If conscience tries to move us to think about, or even glance at, life beyond the grave, those who shun the thought of death are not likely to see conscience as a foreshadowing of any eventual Divine Judgment. *Vertigo,* that superbly crafted, psychospiritual classic, deals with an altered state of consciousness, seriously aberrant, with a paralysis of conscience as grave as the psychotic infatuation of Jimmy Stewart's Scottie Ferguson. This last and greatest of the director's Paramount films testifies to Hitchcock's ability to entertain, provoke deep thought, and stir audiences emotionally and imaginatively, but (at least in his Paramount period) to avoid any serious grappling with that thin-voiced but persistent monitor of morals we call conscience.

The Universal period was marked by *Psycho* and *The Birds,* two classic Hitchcock films with heavy accents on pathological behavior (private disorder) and cosmic retribution (social disorder). We definitely are in the realm of the First Week of the Ignatian *Exercises,* with some oblique references to Christ in terms of innocent female victims with bloody stigmata. From *Marnie* through *Family Plot,* Hitch becomes talkative; someone observed that he felt there was a pathology of late-twentieth-century Western civilization and a turning away from deeds (visually shareable) and words (often untestable, as in the case of unfulfilled promises). In this regard, it is worth mentioning that Ignatius of Loyola spoke more sparingly as he grew older, believing that deeds counted so much more than words, which he trusted less and less. If

Hitch's early British films were charming and novel, his last Universal films had heavy and complex plots. *Marnie, Torn Curtain,* and *Topaz* are loquaciously leaden and lack the golden visual highlights of *Rear Window, North by Northwest,* and *Psycho.*

We must wonder about the psychoreligious development from Hitchcock's most splendid period (*Rear Window* through *The Birds*) to his lesser works (*Marnie* through *Family Plot*). The characters seem either overwhelmed by circumstances to which they are hardly equal or afflicted by deep accidental childhood or adult trauma. In the first category, we have *Rear Window, I Confess, The Wrong Man, North by Northwest,* and *The Birds.* In the second are *Vertigo, Psycho, Marnie,* and *Frenzy.* The other films do not give us true trials of conscience, but rather characters with no preoccupation with eternity. The young Hitchcock would have heard the Latin expression often used in Jesuit schools and seminaries, *Quid ad aeternitatem?* ("what has that to do with eternity?"), which could apply to such romance-action melodramas as *To Catch a Thief, The Man Who Knew Too Much, Torn Curtain,* and *Topaz.* I would bracket *The Trouble with Harry* and *Family Plot,* as both are of subtle, highly ironic theological importance, but not in terms of three-dimensional characters trying to sort out the complexity of good and evil influences operating on them.

I disagree with those critics who believe that such films as *The Trouble with Harry, Vertigo, North by Northwest, Psycho, The Birds, Marnie,* and *Frenzy* fare better on the screen than in theoretical discussion. Hitch was not only an intellectual artist but also a religious artist, and he excelled in dealing with altered states of consciousness. The aforementioned films deal with constraints on human freedom: phobias and avoidance of concerns regarding death, traumas, cultural conditioning, family crises, role automatism, man as nature's greatest predator, sexual stigmas, and treatment of women as compelling and unchaste pleasure objects. Yet in none of these films is conscience a critical factor.

Take *North by Northwest.* There is unquestionably character growth by Roger O. Thornhill and moral conversion by Eve Kendall. However, the development is catalyzed externally. Thornhill becomes progressively aware of perfidy—the political deceit of Vandamm and his agents and the romantic betrayal by Eve. When Eve is denounced by Thornhill at the auction, her conscience is piqued by his barbed words. He later learns of her conflict of interest and senses that she chose patriotism over passing pleasure. It is not the private prick of guilt but the public scourge of shame that catalyzes her conversion.

It is an overlooked aspect of Hitch's cinematic genius that he was an eloquent and constant analyst of the three basic psychospiritual responses to which humans are heir: shame, guilt, and anxiety.[5] Guilt is curiously present in many films (*Blackmail, Sabotage*) and conspicuously absent in others such as *North by Northwest*. Neither Vandamm nor the Professor has any scruples or moral misgivings. They are exclusively operational machines programmed for preordained results. As for Thornhill and Eve, she is other-directed and susceptible to shame, while he is still less a moral being, acting reflexively out of pain and pleasure ("Who is with me? Who is against me?"). He has more charisma and courage than character and conscience. Thornhill is the archetypal product of a consumer society which stresses survival, the calculus of self-interest that obviously motivates him in the film's earlier scenes.

The question Hitch leaves unanswered is, Will Thornhill abandon advertising—the "permissible lie"? Recall that while dangling from Mt. Rushmore, Eve calls her husband-to-be a "liar"—gratuitously, with no provocation, no contextual logic or motivation. Why? Is it a clue from the director that America's destiny is linked with Roger O. Thornhill's courage to refuse to be an accomplice in an occupation which pays dividends at the external level but subverts the trust that human communication rests on?

Notes

1. In *The Dark Side of Genius,* p. 341, Donald Spoto describes Hitch's underside in force-feeding Clift's alcohol habit at a party at the director's Bel Air home. I mention this to stress Clift's vulnerability, which shines through in *I Confess.*

2. Yacowar. *Hitchcock's British Films,* pp. 39–40.
3. Neil Hurley, "Conscience, the Transcendental Referee," in *Theology Through Film* (New York: Harper and Row, 1969), pp. 57–73.
4. See Harris and Lasky, *Films of Alfred Hitchcock,* p. 164.
5. David Riesman shed much light on these psychological reflexes in *The Lonely Crowd* (Chicago: University of Chicago Press, 1953). There he contrasted three character types: (1) the "tradition-directed," ruled by shame; (2) the "inner directed," guided by guilt; and (3) the "other directed," impelled by anxiety regarding what, in a fad-conscious, changing world, is acceptable at the moment.

CHAPTER XV

The Emotional Seesaw of Suspense

In *The Lady Vanishes,* Iris Henderson (Margaret Lockwood) discusses her pending marriage of convenience to a nobleman with two girlfriends. All three are scantily dressed. Iris stands on a table in a slip. She is a far cry from the Iris who passes through the crucible of doubt and social rejection. She knows she has seen Miss Froy (Dame May Whitty) and insists on it. No one else confirms her testimony; in fact, the Hitchcockian devilish-type villain (Paul Lukas) insinuates that she is not well. (She was earlier hit on the head with a flowerpot.) In an underappreciated scene we see her caught between the villain and the playful musician Gilbert (Michael Redgrave), at this time a doubter also. Each has her in a firm grasp. Even more important, however, is her dress—a white sweater, a dark blouse and skirt, and a flowing broad scarf with her initials within a circle—IH. Those of us raised as Catholics can infer a sacerdotal allusion for the circle, and her movements at times give the impression of *IHS,* the abbreviation of the Greek meaning "Jesus Christ Savior." (The popular interpretation years ago was "I Have Suffered".) Hitch would have seen this IHS on the back of the priest's chasuble. Actually, Iris's wardrobe appears to be a cross between that long flowing robe (the chasuble) and the officiating priest's scarf (called a stole). Standing as a prisoner between Redgrave and Lukas, she reminds the reflective Catholic scholar of a wisp of a Christ figure. Add the presence of the fake nun who converts, and we have an example of growth in all directions. *The Lady Vanishes* features the principle of meliorism—she becomes less shallow and leaves her fiancé for Gilbert, who also grows morally.

The *Exercises* can be compared to a symphony with a harmonic line of melody consisting of meditations (e.g., "Life of Christ"). Beneath this musical flow of biblical themes is an alternating rhythm made up of an emotional double beat of consolation and desolation. Of course, each retreatant experiences it in a different way and at different times. The retreat director is trained to orchestrate this rhythmic alteration to help retreatants to recognize the good and evil spirits at work in their psychic lives, influencing them either toward or away from Godward choices and habits of conduct. In the spirit of the *Exercises,* I would maintain, Hitchcock also places great importance on consolation and desolation as key indicators for interpreting personal betterment and character transformation. The difference is that the Master of Suspense used enlarged moving images within an entertainment formula, whereas Ignatius invited the retreatant to use the imagination as both projector and screen.

Allowing that Hitch brilliantly employed oblique cinema metaphors instead of thematic religious references, we can also recognize traces of Ignatian meliorism in *The 39 Steps.* It is obvious that the protagonist, Richard Hannay (Robert Donat), is quickly depressed to find that his reputation and life are at stake. An innocent victim, Hannay fortuitously meets Pamela (Madeleine Carroll), who is a critical catalyst in his moral growth regarding chivalry, duty, romance, and sex.[1] There is growth in all directions, thanks to Hannay's courage, moral stamina, resourcefulness, and, yes, even cunning. Recall that marvelous scene of humor and suspense where Hannay wins over the common people at a political rally. So convincing are his utterances that the crowd warms up to such spontaneous platitudes as, "Everybody gets a square deal and a sporting chance."

In this respect, Maurice Yacowar plumbs the moral depths of this superb entertainment, acknowledging "the growth of the Donat and Carroll characters to be able to adjust to and handle the unruly upsets of their lives."[2] I concur with Yacowar that order and harmony emerge from the discontinuity and chaos sprinkled throughout the plot. With him, I also reject the assumption of biographer John Russell Taylor that it is unnecessary to interpret "the film's being an allegory

Robert Donat and Madeleine Carroll in *The 39 Steps*. The scene alludes to the mythological River Styx, flowing over Hades (home of the dead).

of good and evil."[3] After the audience shares with Pamela and Hannay the roller-coaster ride of anxiety, imperilment, suspicious distance from each other, and continual suspense, it is relieved and ultimately inspired as the film closes where it began—in the Palladium.

When he is trapped by the police, Hannay's fertile intuition impels him to hurl a surprise question at Mr. Memory on stage: "What are the thirty-nine steps?" Bound by rigid role conditioning, the unfree Mr. Memory spurts out the secret plans he has memorized regarding an advance type of aircraft—plans which he will convey to a foreign enemy. In an instant, Hannay is a hero instead of a lonely, hunted man. As earlier in the political rally, Hannay exhibits an admirable degree of extemporaneous inventiveness. He not only exonerates himself, but deservedly seals the love of his formerly fickle partner, Pamela, and achieves the gratitude of the nation for his patriotic service. A subtle irony accompanies Hannay's ingenious ability to overturn the subversive plot of the four-fingered villain, Mr. Jordan. At the rally, Hannay envisioned "a world from which suspicion, cruelty and fear have been forever banished." Note the negative emotions which are rarely banished from a vintage Hitch movie.

There is a remarkable emotional balance as fragile as it is tender in the final scene, where the elegant Pamela puts her black-gloved hand into the handcuffed hand of Hannay. A haunting, metaphorical, almost mystical, meaning colors the joining of the velvet glove with the steel manacle, a contrast representing the rhythm of our emotional lives, for the handcuff symbolizes the negative emotions of loneliness and constraint, while the lady's smooth glove betokens positive hope, assurance, and loving companionship. The binary rhythm of consolation and desolation runs throughout *The 39 Steps,* as it also makes up the dynamic subtext of the Ignatian *Exercises.* Hitchcock's film suggests a subtle ambiguity, characterizing the couple as souls in suspense, but less so than before they met.

If we understand the Ignatian rules of emotional suspense, now gloom and desolation, now hope and consolation, Hitch's films gain in enjoyment when seen in terms of positive and negative feelings. His fascinating variations of plot and character can best be described by these three categories:

(1) The normal human situations of mixed motivation, troubled conscience, and swings from anxiety and fear toward contentment and security, then back again. Examples would include *The Lodger, The Ring, Young and Innocent, Notorious, Rear Window,* and *The Birds.*

(2) The less ordinary, but nonetheless recurring, situations of people limited in terms of responsibility and free choice due to childhood traumas, psychospiritual blockage, and family or environmental conditioning (e.g., *Vertigo, Psycho, Marnie,* and *Frenzy*).

(3) The less common examples of high moral character, inspirational behavior, and even saintly conduct usually the result of heroic imagery inculcated in the person so that,

despite legal, institutional, and social injustices he or she bravely faces unfounded accusations and undeserved penalties involving loss of reputation, prison, and even execution (*Murder!, I Confess, The Wrong Man,* and let us not forget the martyred anti-Castro agent Juanita in *Topaz*).

The reader should recognize how these categories would apply more readily to Hitchcock's work than to that of such world-class directors as Griffith, Chaplin, Renoir, Ford, Bergman, or Fellini, to name a few. It is interesting that, in his finest suspense melodramas, he kept returning to the same pattern of alternating emotional valences. In this genre, Hitch was at home and earned his unparalleled reputation. He experimented with other film types, such as *Juno and the Paycock, Waltzes from Vienna, Jamaica Inn,* and *Under Capricorn.* Critics and audiences, as a rule, were far from enthusiastic about such films. Thus, Hitch returned time and again to his forte, raising the crime melodrama to unprecedented heights of entertainment, at times even high art, and, I would add, spiritual awareness.

In my years of research on Hitchcock, I have been struck by his exceptional ability to avoid simplification of character. I mentioned earlier that he departed from the Victorian formula of good versus evil—favored by Charles Dickens, D. W. Griffith, Charles Chaplin, and Walt Disney—who would fix characters so unalterably that sympathy could never cross over to antipathy or vice versa. Thus, villains would rarely convert, nor would heroes or heroines reveal moral blemishes. Hitch's way of portraying character was to mingle good and evil, allowing likable human traits in villains and occasional lapses of character in the personalities that represent the angels of our better nature.

In *Notorious,* Devlin (Cary Grant) is really neither likable nor admirable; Ingrid Bergman's Alicia evolves from an angry, drunken woman to a courageous patriot; Claude Rains' villain, Sebastian, elicits considerable sympathy from us in the final scene. The film is a major advance in Hitch's ability to delineate psychospiritual forces in the lives of characters who are not the stock cardboard types ordinarily seen in crime or action plots. In such a film, Hitch was doing what a retreat director in the Ignatian *Exercises* does—namely, eliciting reactions from those undergoing an emotional or mental experience and challenging them to sort it out in terms of right and wrong. Recall the last scene of *Notorious*: Cary Grant and Ingrid Bergman are escaping from the Nazi trap in which she was slowly dying of poison. That makes us, obviously, feel good. However, Hitch focuses his camera on the cornered Claude Rains, whose love for his wife (Bergman) compromised his total dedication to the cause of the Third Reich's overseas activities. As he turns to walk up the stairs, we notice his stern-faced mother flanked by two determined Nazi partisans. In a sense, Hitch is impelling the audience to think out at a deeper level what has been transpiring on the silver screen. The images speak for themselves. Hitch neither makes a comment nor editorializes. Cary Grant slams the car door and locks it, a grim gesture equivalent to a decree of execution for a man who, obviously, wanted to escape and take his chances in America. The film closes with the camera lingering on the back of the forlorn, virtually condemned man. Hitch has switched our attention, perhaps even our sympathy.

Having made three-day Ignatian retreats, the young Alfred would have been familiar with one particular dramatic contemplation to ferret out the roots of self-interest in making the Election. In Jesuit circles, the contemplation is known as "The Three Classes of Men," each faced with a decision of how to dispose of a large sum of money, honestly acquired, but posing a challenge to conscience and inner peace in the light of God's greater glory and service to one's neighbor. The first group does nothing and keeps the money. The second group compromises by keeping a portion of it and disposing of the rest on behalf of worthy causes. The third group, convinced that the money is not necessary but only useful, makes a decision of total sacrifice on behalf of charity and philanthropy. Following Ignatius' counsel, the retreat master stresses that the criterion is inner peace, aligning one's existential call to inner harmony with God's will as recognized in biblical reflection, prayer, and guidance from an experienced counselor. In *Notorious* Hitch troubled the audience's peace—its eager search for the happy ending.

The young Hitch would have been repeatedly exposed to

reminders of the need for inner peace and a calm conscience, for confession and a review of one's life in order to reform it. This dynamic would have occurred in anecdotes, sermons, exhortations, and lessons in religion class. He would have heard such graphic analogies as the tree in the crowded forest that drops its lower limbs to gain strength to grow taller and reach the sunlight denied the smaller trees. Without question, he would have known of the incident of Ignatius challenging a fellow student—the young, athletic bon vivant Francis Xavier—with the biblical axiom, "What doth it profit a man to gain the whole world and suffer the loss of his soul?" (It is no coincidence that this text is used in *The Manxman* to shed light on a tragic decision made by a friend whose human respect—based on false loyalty—compromises a woman who does not truly love the friend whom she marries.)

As a soul in suspense, Hitch was a master at portraying similar suspense in his characters. By that I mean the wide arc experienced emotionally by persons who do not fully understand the spectrum of unintended consequences flowing from either short-sighted, altruistic motives (e.g., *The Manxman*), or precipitous decisions based on romance (*The Lodger*). This latter film aptly illustrates the sticky-wicket choices in life where the trade-offs are closely matched in terms of advantages and disadvantages, thus making for open-ended pessimism.

Self-interest, often cloaked in the guise of rationalization, is a powerful, recurring example of mixed motivation in the lives of Hitchcockian characters. One sees it very clearly in the double bind of a detective in love, willing to compromise his responsibilities as a law officer for the sake of his beloved, as do the slightly tainted police officers in *The Lodger* (1926), *Blackmail* (1929), and *Sabotage* (1936). Indeed, there are numerous such mercurial shifts in mood and atmosphere in a Hitchcock film, but especially distinctive is the consistently recognizable dualism at work in characters who can rise or decline in moral performance.[4]

We all experience hellbroth situations of conflicting allegiances where public duty or responsibility clashes with the interest of the individual. We are squarely in the heart of the Ignatian test case of "The Three Classes of Men," with the compromised choice of the second group sacrificing justice, honesty, and virtue for one's own interest rather than the good of a neighbor or God's greater glory. Hitchcock referred to the role of self-interest as tainting justice and besmirching the legal process.

From the writer James Bridie, Hitch learned to point the audience to the imminent future of the characters as portrayed in the final scene. *Notorious* is a prime example of Hitch's ability to have the audience continue to think about the characters beyond the film, giving them life on the screen of the audience's imagination. Certainly, the anguished protagonists in *Vertigo, Psycho, Marnie,* and *Frenzy* have destinies which could go in different directions. The ethical and religious concerns subtly etched into these films have an unusual, if not unique, character in the history of cinema.

Having seen examples of mutable motivation with ups and downs of moral performance, let us now study Hitch's masterly treatment of conflicted personalities with serious freewill impediments arising through parent/child conditioning, constraining psychic blockages, and compromising external situations involving threats of economic failure, reputation, or the loss of a lover. Sometimes, the references are to sudden panic (*Foreign Correspondent, Torn Curtain, The Birds*), urban crowds (*Rich and Strange, Sabotage, North by Northwest, Topaz*), or angry mob behavior (*The Lodger, Lifeboat, I Confess*). These films deal with individuals in conglomerate situations where rationality declines so that, metaphorically, $2 + 2 = $ not 4 but 3. Undoubtedly, Hitch learned from Fritz Lang, whose classics *M* and *Fury* highlighted the subhuman falling off of reason and conscience of people in crowds.

Add to these case studies Hitchcock's films about the limitation of free will through psychic complexities ranging from neurosis, psychosis, and childhood trauma to lunacy: *The Wrong Man* (manic-depressive), *Vertigo* (latent necrophilia and obsession), *Psycho* (schizophrenia), *North by Northwest* (compulsive opportunism, mendacity, and general amoral behavior), *The Birds* (maternal possessiveness), *Marnie* (kleptomania with roots in childhood sexual trauma), *Frenzy* (implied Oedipal mother complex linked to retarded development). These films point to impediments to the full exercise of human liberty.

In these motion pictures of psychic instability, there is usually a spiritual subtext. Hitch definitely is interested in direction upward and downward in answer to such questions as, Why do people drift from civilized norms? Why do the ideals of youth become blunted? Why do people fail to develop the rich promise of their potential? We recognize Rule No. 333 of the Ignatian *Exercises*: the significance of retracing one's life in terms of beginning, middle, and end. Without denying free will or God's help, Saint Ignatius invokes the enemy of human nature as a factor in his spiritual strategy. Notice he avoids the suggestive scare images taught in catechism classes—the Devil, Satan, Lucifer, and the Demon. His descriptor is more realistic and less mythical, insinuating a strategic counterplayer, a vigorous competitor, an unscrupulous rival, who is opposed to the divine image latent in humans. Certainly, the sense of evil in Hitch's films is pervasively dark and became intensified as his career went on. The subtext of his tragedies and "wrong-man" pictures owe not a little to the Jesuit manual of spirituality, which comports with the premise of modern game theory, building on the most pessimistic assumption—that your adversary is stronger than you imagine and could win all. Not many directors of mysteries or thrillers feature diabolical-looking villains such as Hitch used in *Champagne, The Lady Vanishes, Saboteur, Strangers on a Train, Vertigo, North by Northwest, Frenzy,* or *Family Plot.* His cast of evil personalities consists of more than mere lawbreakers and points to an alliance with a higher malevolent force. I strongly commend this point to the attention of the loyal Hitchcock fan.

In *Blackmail,* Hitch plants a conscience teaser—a painting of a laughing clown that appears three times during the film. The picture was done by the murdered artist. It has a neutral look when we first see it. The second time it is seen after the murder, it appears to be accusatory. In the final scene, the portrait mocks the couple who go free, but now must live with the nagging doubt of some ultimate other-worldly sentence. (It is noteworthy that Hitchcock used the laughing clown in

The Wrong Man, where it appears as a picture on the wall during a quarrel between Manny and his wife.)

Hitch's ironic touches suppose a larger context of psycho-spiritual reality, invisible but real. Take the scene in the bank in *Shadow of a Doubt.* Henry Travers is the teller; he gives bills to Uncle Charlie (Joseph Cotten), at whose side stands Teresa Wright. There are two signs referring to national defense, promoting the sale of Liberty Bonds. Hitch seems to suggest that there is an enemy within, not an Axis power or nation-state adversary, but a mass murderer of another stripe than Hitler. In the last scene (of Uncle Charlie's funeral), the preacher says, "He was one of us." There's the "shadow of doubt" about the compartmentalized view of good versus evil, as if iniquity did not have roots in each of us.

Lifeboat shows the spiritual underside of democracy—"us" versus "them"—forgetting we are "them" in terms of spiritual roots in humanity as souls in suspense. Hitch invariably lent a touch of compassion, strength, and goodness to villain types. *Fas est doceri ab hoste* ("one can learn even from one's enemies"). There are unforgettable scenes riveted in my memory of revelations of tenderness, private sorrow, or a higher awareness of solidarity:
—the blackmailer falling from the dome of the British Museum (*Blackmail*);
—the grieving Peter Lorre holding in his arms the fatally shot Cicely Oates (*The Man Who Knew Too Much*);
—the anxious transvestite acrobat afraid of the police, and letting go of the trapeze bar to fall to his death (*Murder!*);
—the farm wife remaining behind in *The 39 Steps* to face her stern husband's ire after she helps Robert Donat to safety;
—the pained look on Oscar Homolka's face in *Sabotage* when imagining Picadilly Circus being bombed;
—the Nazi submarine captain, Willi (Walter Slezak), beaten to death by the Allied survivors (*Lifeboat*);
—Claude Rains' odd man out at the end of *Notorious;*
—the fright on the face of the unfaithful wife being strangled by Robert Walker in *Strangers on a Train;*
—Kim Novak with a nosegay of flowers in the cemetery

visiting a Spanish grandam's grave in a mystical flight of identity (*Vertigo*);
—Tippi Hedren's Marnie exhausted from past recollections as she is helped by Sean Connery (*Marnie*);
—Janet Leigh counting the stolen funds in *Psycho* following her resolve to return to Phoenix;
—Tippi Hedren's stigmatized body in *The Birds;* and
—Barbara Harris's final wink into the camera in *Family Plot.*
These are reflections on the screen of the man looking through the camera's rear window.

As for the rare persons with hardly any ego agenda, we have truly memorable case studies. There is Norah Baring in *Murder!* (1931); she is unjustly accused and bears herself regally despite an unfriendly press, public indignation toward her, a split jury, and the gloom of women's prison. We are not informed, either overtly or through indirection, what her ruling motive is for such saintly behavior. In *I Confess* (1953), Fr. Logan is a martyr in attitude if not in fact. The presence of many crucifixes, crosses, statues, the church altar with candles, and the outdoor Way of the Cross—all highlight his religious inspirational sources (largely themes from the Third Week of the *Exercises*). In *The Wrong Man,* Henry Fonda's Manny Balestrero says the rosary to the Virgin Mary and prayers to the Sacred Heart of Jesus. (Both are devotions with which Hitch would have been very familiar.)

Hitchcock gives us a God-like view of human moral dilemmas in terms of inner emotional harmony and an untroubled conscience. We are in a typical human predicament of mixed emotions and choices regarding reputation (pride), security (peace), and future happiness (a happy ending). The heart of the Ignatian *Exercises,* I believe, is the core of Hitchcock's unique artistic power as director—the intersection of the universal dynamic of good versus evil in terms of our personal consciences contending with the consolation and desolation caused by our outer world of relationships.[5] The reader can decide regarding Hitchcock's power to touch mystical depths.

Hitch's oeuvre supports Karl Rahner's commonsense observation that "most good people make important decisions

pretty much by using the Ignatian logic, only less consciously
and with a greater possibility of error. They choose, not on
purely rational and objective grounds, but according to what is
suitable to them, what fits in with their basic feeling about
themselves, what corresponds to their fundamental personal
orientation."[6]

I cite three examples from Hitch's films to prove the
meliorism of a character, a change of heart away from
acquiescence in evil or compromise in wrongdoing. First,
Alma (Dolly Haas), the wife of the murderous sacristan (O. E.
Hasse) in *I Confess,* protests the innocence of the priest as he
leaves the courtroom, legally acquitted, but roughly re-
proached by the angry crowd. She is then shot by her husband
who confesses to the exonerated priest as he lies dying. The
mixed emotional state of the wife is matched, some critics
aver, by the impure motives of Fr. Logan. In *The Films of
Alfred Hitchcock,* Robert A. Harris and Michael S. Lasky write:
"The transference-of-guilt idea still looms large as a concur-
rent question. Michael Logan feels guilty because Otto has
killed a man he himself would have liked to kill."[7] Can we
judge the intentions of Fr. Logan. I do not see any internal
evidence that we can.

Second, in *Psycho,* Janet Leigh's Marion Crane sits munch-
ing a sandwich, attending to Norman Bates's (Anthony
Perkins) maniacal monologue that gives her a standard for
judging her own behavior, her own conscience, her own
future. She stands up to excuse herself and states emphatically
that she will return to Phoenix the next morning. Again, we
see a phototropic movement of the spirit—toward the light.

Third, in *Marnie,* the title character becomes attached to a
steeplechase horse, Forio. When he breaks his leg, she
reluctantly shoots him. A catharsis ensues, for she cannot
steal again. When Mark sees her reaching into the vault for
packets of money, he challenges her in a loud voice to take
them, but she hesitates and remains immobile.[8] I see the
death of Forio playing a sacrificial, redemptive role. It
certainly purges Marnie's misanthropy and phallic vengeful-
ness.

Psycho is a splendid case study where we have three slices of
life. One is that of the rationally scientific analysis by the

The very last image in *Psycho* shows the retrieval of the sunken car with Marion's stolen money. Rising from the muddy water, the curved bumper suggests a perverse smile.

psychiatrist. (Hitch would seem to discount this view by the cross emblem discernible in the shadowy distant wall lamp.) The second view shows Norman Bates in a restraining jacket with a fixed gaze into the camera, defying us to judge. Again, Hitch seems to undercut the pat professional explanation we have just heard. Third, "The End" appears over the scene of Marion's car being extracted from the bog. The whole thrust of this scene raises more questions of what will happen later. Enveloped in layers of mystery, *Psycho* leaves us with three large question marks:

(1) Legally, will the late Marion Crane be exonerated from theft by the authorities, thanks to a fragment of a note found by Sam Loomis?

(2) Where does psychic illness end and spiritual or moral responsibility begin?

(3) Can we bracket life in such watertight compartmental-

ized terms that biblical truths are excluded so as to disallow the possibility of moral innocence in a case involving a heinous crime? Did not the notorious "Son of Sam" claim to be obedient to higher voices in the same way that Norman Bates is presented to be under the complete sway of his dead mother's influence?

Hitchcock's films have theological suspense, as do the Ignatian *Exercises*. In both instances consolation and desolation recur in a seesaw fashion and point to an interplay of intra- and extrapsychic forces. Often Hitchcock leaves us with the unresolved happy ending. Consider *Sabotage*: Will Sylvia Sidney one day be incriminated? In *Suspicion,* will Cary Grant attempt to kill his wife, Joan Fontaine? In *Vertigo,* will James Stewart become totally unhinged mentally, or will his friend Midge put him back together again? In *Marnie,* will Tippi Hedren and Sean Connery make it? And finally, in *Frenzy,* will the "wrong" man recover from the personal blows and the murders of two important women in his life?

We Hitchcock fans see the suspenseful action and rising romantic curve, but are we fully conscious of how the protagonists' wills are guided toward melioristic and morally laudatory decisions? Study Hitchcock's wronged persons to see how, for example, Roger O. Thornhill in *North by Northwest* is not per se a morally good person, although he is a victim in danger of losing his life. He himself admits that his initials spell "rot." We note that his middle initial aptly symbolizes moral vacuity. This extraordinary Hollywood entertainment embodies the key principles of the Ignatian *Exercises,* for Thornhill (a Calvary symbol) grows steadily in character from a "liar" for profit to a loyal patriot and a man who finds a rich romance that otherwise would have passed him by. This picaresque suspense-thriller directly descends from similar moral parables of personal, romantic, and socio-political meliorism—*The 39 Steps, Young and Innocent, Saboteur,* and *Notorious.*

If films imitate life, it is because in both, human beings ride on rivers of feeling. Emotions clearly affect human decisions and conduct. Hitch's films recognize this and sway audiences to identify at times with villainy. We root for Bruno Anthony in *Strangers on a Train* to retrieve the fallen cigarette lighter from the sewer grate; we share in *Psycho* the anxiety of Norman Bates when Marion Crane's car stops momentarily from sinking into the bog; many of us feel relieved when the rapist-murderer Bob Rusk retrieves his tie clasp from the stiff, dead fingers of his latest victim in *Frenzy*. This psychological shock of recognition has a spiritual valence as well, and is an integral part of Jesuit education, spiritual guidance, and the retreat apostolate. Moreover, it is an added but unacknowledged ingredient in the negative surprise element that a reflective fan would relish. Hitch aimed deliberately at a strategy of subliminals and subtle subplots, recognizing that motion picture photography permits a far wider range of implications and oblique meanings than the still photograph. This is a point which has received scant treatment in film theory regarding the role of the implicit in motion picture art, entertainment, and its power to convey indirect propaganda and covert ideology.

As with other entertainers and artists, Hitchcock understood that audiences were attracted to themes of violence, crime, and sexuality. The Bible, the Ignatian *Exercises,* and Shakespeare's plays treat disorder more than harmony, peace, and tranquil love. As with the Bible and Shakespeare, Hitch used deviance, disorder, and dread to stamp the imagination of the audience with artistically unforgettable and spiritually profound lessons—turning points in human lives that are Godward. Hitch's canon of fifty-three films rejects the two-story theology which Christian thinkers had traditionally developed by hermetically sealing off divine action from the profane times and places where the vast majority of people pass their lives.

Hitchcock shows female examples: *Murder!*, *The 39 Steps, Young and Innocent, The Lady Vanishes, Notorious, Spellbound, I Confess, Psycho,* and *Marnie.* Take Tallulah Bankhead (*Lifeboat*). She grows romantically and spiritually, losing all her prized possessions *acceptingly.* Her detachment substantiates Karl Rahner's interpretation that, after finding God's peace there must be external experiences which mediate divine assistance. The link is not photographable, to be sure, and yet there is evidence of results—of melioristic behavior.[9] We see that the triple viewing suggested by Hitchcock yields a spiritual dividend of religious fear and supernatural shock, provided the viewer has the key to understanding the pattern. I thus conclude that there is a parallel between the director's axiom that things are not as they seem and the Ignatian strategy for discerning the personally felt but publicly invisible ebb and flow of desolation and consolation in our lives as they relate to our spiritual progress—the beginning, middle, and end. The results are photographable, but the complex web of causes and influences can only be inferred. Thus the formula of fright and delight informing the work of the Master of Suspense has the indelible impress on it of his three years under the English "Jays," and must be seen as more than a form of sensational entertainment. Beneath the seductive and shocking surfaces of his brilliant images is a graphic picture of souls in suspense, struggling for equilibrium on an emotional seesaw.

Notes

1. I am indebted to a perceptive article by Charles Silet, "Through a Woman's Eyes: Sexuality and Memory in *The 39 Steps*," in *A Hitchcock Reader*, Marshall Deutelbaum and Leland Poague, eds. (Ames: Iowa University Press, 1986), pp. 109– 121.
2. Yacowar, *Hitchcock's British Films*, p. 182.
3. Taylor, *Life and Times*, p. 179.
4. Neil Hurley, "The Mutability of Motivation: Hitchcock's Films," *Theology Today*, Vol. 30, No. 3 (October 1978), pp. 326–328.
5. Karl Rahner, "The Ignatian Process for Discovering the Will of God in an Existential Situation," in *Ignatius of Loyola—His Personality and Spiritual Heritage, 1556–1956: Studies on the 400th Anniversary of His Death*, Friedrich Wolf, ed. (St. Louis: Institute of Jesuit Sources, 1977), pp. 280–293. The summation was made by Harold E. Weidman of a longer English translation of W. J. O'Hara found in Karl Rahner, *The Dynamic Element in the Church* (New York: Herder and Herder, 1964), pp. 84–170.
6. Rahner, "Ignatian Process," p. 288.
7. Harris and Lasky, *Films of Alfred Hitchcock*, p. 161.
8. This scene strongly resembles the last one of a psychoanalytic thriller, *Blind Alley* (1939), a quality "B" movie. A cop killer

(Chester Morris) hides from the police in the office of a psychiatrist (Ralph Bellamy), who unlocks the traumatic secrets of his childhood. When the police lay siege to the building, the gunman points his gun at an exposed cop, but finds he cannot pull the trigger. The psychic burden has been therapeutically lifted.

9. Rahner, "Ignatian Process," p. 285.

CHAPTER XVI

Summary

Hitchcock's vaunted perfectionism resonates with the themes of the last chapter: *agere contra,* meliorism, and the *magis.* Moreover, inscribed in his work are recurrent Catholic and Jesuit codes, emblems, and symbols. These are manifest as early as *The Pleasure Garden,* develop through *Rich and Strange,* continue on into his early Hollywood period with *Mr. and Mrs. Smith,* to reach a crescendo of inspiration in the 1950s with such dark, brilliant classics as *Strangers on a Train, Rear Window, Vertigo,* and *North by Northwest.* The twilight of his career saw a deepening of his psychospiritual concerns in *Psycho, The Birds, Marnie, Torn Curtain, Topaz, Frenzy,* and *Family Plot.* In these seven pictures are references to guilt, retribution, redemption, death, and even hell. Cruciform postures, Pietà scenes, infernal symbols of fire and flame, and cross icons are woven together in mystery-thriller plots which trail off into mystical inconclusiveness. There is a striking correspondence between the open-ended pessimism of Hitch's film signature and that of the Jesuit manual of formation, the Ignatian *Exercises.* Both Hitch's canon of films and the meditation strategy of the Four Weeks are marked by a strong sense of the power of evil, not only in terms of supernatural powers, agencies, and forces that are not photographable, but also in terms of the thwarted purpose of personal and family lives as well as of communities and nations.

In his illuminating study, *Artistic Expression,* Vytautas Kavolis makes a relevant comment: "The image of a disharmonious universe seems likely to generate anxiety regarding man's relationship with his surroundings."[1] In the case of

Hitchcock and the *Exercises,* the images used are those of disequilibrium and a precarious relationship with God. It is significant that in the First and Third Weeks the human form is shown as distorted and wounded. Similarly, in Hitchcock's films, we have recurrent instances of misperception, delirium and nightmares, and references to abnormal states of consciousness ranging from neurosis through psychosis and even insanity. On the other hand, we also find in the Second and Fourth Weeks of the *Spiritual Exercises* a complementary tendency toward realistic representation intimating a belief in a constructive, even caring, principle in the cosmos against which the evil powers cannot prevail. In Hitch's three darkest movies—*Vertigo, Psycho,* and *Frenzy*—there is a slight opening toward the future and a possible healing. In short, Hitchcock does not slam the door in a fatalistic way. So, too, the Ignatian *Exercises* seeks to restore a lost equilibrium through the principle of *agere contra.* The meliorism we see in many of Hitchcock's characters is due to effort, courage, and a fortuitous romance that ripens into a transformational love leading to a greater sense of responsibility and community or national redemption (e.g., *The 39 Steps, Saboteur, North by Northwest, The Birds,* and *Marnie*).

In the Jesuit *Exercises,* it is clear from the outset that Ignatius of Loyola sees each human soul as a field of spiritual combat in which supernatural forces compete for victory—those celestial forces from God doing battle with infernal ones from the Devil. Although the individual is free, the underlying strategies used by each of the rivals (the good spirit, the evil spirit) are not self-evident to those souls in suspense who are on the emotional seesaw of desolation and consolation. However, the strategies are discoverable. Spiritual guidance by a trained director using conversion, a turning toward the light, and the subsequent cathartic practice of confession. This process, invisible but felt, is the foundation of the shared belief of Ignatius and Hitchcock in the axiom, "Things are not as they seem."

I believe this has relevance for understanding Hitch's filmology. Let us address one striking example, hitherto unrecognized: the compassion with which Hitch treats a number of evil characters. We have memorable portraits of

In *Notorious* (1945), Claude Rains watches Ingrid Bergman and Cary Grant escape. The camera leaves them to compel our sympathy for the non-hero's fate as "loser."

villains who, along the way, become capable of very touching human gestures, sudden caring attitudes and even complete moral turnabouts. Take the hired assassin, Abbot (Peter Lorre), in *The Man Who Knew Too Much* (1934). A menacing man with an ugly scar on his forehead, Abbot barks more than he bites and unexpectedly melts in tender grief over the death of his sister, a woman of dour countenance. Or, take the soft-spoken and reluctant saboteur, Verloc (Oscar Homolka), in *Sabotage*. We find him sympathetic. That holds true also for his contact, René, who supplies the explosives. A kindly looking, philosophical man, he comments to Verloc, "We all have crosses to bear." In *Notorious,* Sebastian (Claude Rains) truly loves his wife (Ingrid Bergman) but is left behind in the final scene when her American lover (Cary Grant) rescues her from certain death by poisoning. Hitch's camera discounts the happy ending for the audience, who must directly experience what the escaping lovers do not see. Sebastian looks forlorn and quietly desperate. He turns to face his mother and his disappointed Nazi colleagues. Hitch's camera dollies forward as Sebastian turns his back to us, giving us the impression that we are pushing him into an indescribable trap in which perhaps death could be a relief. No other director could engineer the transfer of identification from one character to another, sometimes even within the short span of time it takes to glimpse a given character.

Psycho stands, to my mind, as the unsurpassed study in the rhetoric of identification—anchoring the audience's partisan interest in a deviant person whose crime we almost sanction because of a sympathy which clouds our judgment. After Marion Crane (Janet Leigh) embezzles $40,000 from her employer, Hitchcock gives us the first point-of-view scene, showing her in a car suddenly startled by recognizing her employer crossing the street. We, too, are instinctively anxious, irrationally hoping that she will not be observed. As for Norman Bates (Anthony Perkins), our sympathies lie wholly with him and never more so than when he visits the scene of the crime to cover up what we believe at the time to be a vindictive knifing by his deranged mother. I agree with those critics who feel that Hitchcock not only identified keenly with such romantic stars as Cary Grant, Jimmy Stewart, and Gregory Peck, but also with a number of less sympathetic types such as Sean Connery as Mark Rutland in *Marnie* and Alec McCowen as Inspector Oxford, a man who must eat the unappetizing meals prepared by a well-meaning wife.

Understanding the mutability of human motivation, Hitch did not give his audiences readymade superheroes or the Victorian villains of a Charles Dickens novel. In this respect, he never fitted easily into the Hollywood mold. Even in *Frenzy,* the rapist and murderer (Barry Foster) looks up to return the greeting of his smiling, white-haired mother as she gazes out of her window. Within the easily recognizable realm of day-to-day pedestrian reality, Hitchcock makes us aware of the spiritual combat, the tissue of tempting opportunities to deviate from idealism and to indulge in self-interest. In the chapter, "The Emotional Seesaw of Suspense," we examined carefully the many instances when Hitch showed us how we could become different persons at different times. The notion of the doppelgänger, borrowed from the Expressionism of the German silent cinema, also resonates with Christian doctrine as found in Scripture.

The fact that Ignatius stresses two contrary psychospiritual streams of influence on each one of us lays the foundation for the alternative selves each of us can become by deliberate choice or uncaring default. The finesse of Hitchcock lies in his being not only a Master of Suspense, but also (without discounting his talents as an entertainer and artist) a master of spiritual combat. In fact, there are mystical overtones in his finest films, as the reader will agree if the effort is made to study with a clear horizon the final scenes of *Vertigo, Psycho, The Birds,* and *Frenzy.* These are, indeed, stark finales, brimming with apocalyptic significance, if not for the community, then at least for the individual. The scenes stay with us, crying out for resolution and a respect for mystery in the cosmic sense of the word. This is his open-ended pessimism.

In Hitchcock's films, we seldom find the unalloyed Hollywood happy ending—that is, one without any hint of further challenges, moral lapses, or recurrence of villainy. Hitchcock inclines toward the troubled happy ending (*Champagne, The Manxman, Blackmail, Sabotage, Notorious, Strangers on a Train,* and *Topaz*). Jesuit spirituality affirms the classic Catholic tradition of a constant spiritual combat in which vigilance and moral effort are indispensable. Where Hitchcock reveals his quintessential Catholic sensibility, is in films that touch on First Week themes of the *Exercises.* Consider the references to human frailty and inconstancy of motivation: *The Ring, Champagne, The Skin Game, Suspicion,* and *Dial M for Murder.* Or take the question of moral descent and hellish corruption: *Downhill, Easy Virtue, Suspicion, Rope, Vertigo,* and *Frenzy.*

The metaphysical consideration of original sin and the downward resourcelessness of the human character is highlighted in *Shadow of a Doubt, Under Capricorn, The Trouble with Harry, Psycho,* and *Topaz.* Finally, we have the example of innocence betrayed, with a haunting semblance of Christlikeness: *The Lodger, Murder!, I Confess,* and *The Wrong Man.*

Obviously, Hitchcock directed entertainments which were rich in characterization and insights regarding romance, patriotic valor, and moral education through mistakes made by infatuation, desire, and greed. Even when his films were not specifically Catholic or Jesuit, Hitchcock strongly colored them with a distinctive depth of psychological expression: *The Man Who Knew Too Much, Secret Agent, Young and Innocent, The Lady Vanishes, Rebecca, Foreign Correspondent, Lifeboat, Spellbound, The Paradine Case, To Catch a Thief,* and *Torn Curtain.*

It is fitting we end with Hitchcock's last film, *Family Plot.* There is a very interesting scene in which Bruce Dern and Barbara Harris unexpectedly careen downhill in a car without brakes. The car comes to a stop in a field after knocking down a crudely constructed cross. The cross is not a subliminal; it is photographically established. I talked with the scriptwriter, Ernest Lehman, about this scene. He mentioned that, at the Cannes Film Festival, several French critics thought this had symbolic meaning. Lehman went back and mentioned it to Hitch, whose answer was simply that one of the property men had put it up. Attribution of intent is never easy unless the creators wish to claim intentionality. The scene of the crash includes an unambiguous cross. I incline toward drawing a connection between the harrowing experience that the couple have and the crashing against the cross as a prelude to a difference in their attitude. Hitch insinuates clearly a link between suffering and growth—meliorism.

Implicit in the filmology of Alfred Hitchcock is an oblique but dramatically discernible relationship to an Absolute Director for whom Hitch is a skilled, intensely earnest, but imperfect surrogate. Like Shakespeare, Hitch has created characters with lives of their own, thus allowing art to imitate life. Whereas Shakespeare used linguistic metaphors, Hitchcock used visual analogues for the larger drama of life. In a sense, both were using the dramatic device of the play within the play to prick conscience. In a way, before both artists, Ignatius of Loyola used the life of Christ in a subtly psychological rearrangement to stir up deep feelings in the retreatant, to provide a grim look at his or her personal Way of the Cross and the will to courage, to produce a personal resurrection, that happy ending which critic Parker Tyler called "the last laugh."[2] If Ignatius of Loyola made active participants of those willing to undergo his *Spiritual Exercises,* so too Shakespeare and Hitchcock reached out through the multiple levels of meaning in their entertainments to pull the audience into the plot and induce the shock of recognition. All three men were aware of a higher Spectator for whom we earthly players are performing.

To quote D. H. Lawrence, "Never trust the artist. Trust the tale." This I have done with a view to demonstrating that reflected in Hitchcock's motion picture creed is the imprint of the Catholic-Jesuit vision received in England during three critically impressionable years. This vision is essentially one of balanced realism and restless perfectionism. Hitch's work has, by and large, left criticism limping. He has left us with brilliantly dark images, but always surrounded by an aura, however faint, of light. As Al Whitlock perceptively testified, he had "all the fears," but the religious fears seemed to predominate. The stocky, cocky Jesuit student who wrote hundreds and hundreds of times "A.M.D.G." at the top of his lessons and exams folded into the frames of his films a message of meliorism—that growth depends on counteracting evil—*agere contra.* Is it rash to attribute to Sir Alfred Hitchcock, the words of James Joyce, a fellow Jesuit alumnus: "You allude to me as a Catholic . . . now you ought to allude to me as a Jesuit"?

Notes

1. Vytautas Kavolis, *Artistic Expression: A Sociological Analysis* (Ithaca: Cornell University Press, 1968), p. 117.
2. Parker Tyler, *The Hollywood Hallucination* (New York: Simon and Schuster, 1970), pp. 169 ff.

APPENDIX I

Interview with Alfred Hitchcock,
by John O'Riordan

[The following telephone interview was given by Hitchcock in 1972 to John O'Riordan, a student of the present Saint Ignatius College (Upper School), Middlesex, England. The introductory paragraphs, as well as the text of the interview, were written by O'Riordan.]

An illusory aura of glamour, excitement, and intrigue surrounds the dwindling U.S. film industry today. It is conscious of diminished prestige, haunted by the long shadows of the golden age of yesterday and engaged in a desperate fight to remain solvent. Few personalities remain unaffected by the pressing economic considerations which seem to dictate totally the quality of films today, a situation arising from the remarkable predominance of television over all other comparable forms of communication media.

Alfred Hitchcock has remained true to his ideals and is acclaimed today as a film genius, a master of suspense pictures, a tradition of the cinema. This old Ignatian, now engaged in a new feature production in Los Angeles, kindly consented to a transatlantic telephone interview, and I began by asking him to tell of his school experiences . . .

O'RIORDAN: Now, you attended Saint Ignatius College, back in 1910. To what degree, if any, did this association with the Jesuits influence your later life?

HITCHCOCK: Well, I suppose I was probably too young to realize it at the time, but the type of education that they provided more or less shapes the mind into given reasoning powers and so forth. The method of punishment, of course, was highly dramatic because the form master would tell the pupil of his wrongdoing and he would

289

have to go before the priest and it was left to the pupil to decide when to go, and he would keep putting it off and then he would go at the end of the day to a special room where there would be a priest or a lay brother who would administer the punishment—like sort of, in a minor way, going for execution.

OR: Looking back, do you think that was a good thing or a bad thing?

H: I think it was a bad thing, because it was unpleasant. You see, it was not like they give boys the cane in other schools. This was a rubber strap. If by chance you had gone as bad as to be sentenced to, shall we say, twelve, you would have to spread it over two days because each hand could only take three strokes, as it became numb.

OR: You had this Jesuit schooling. Would you regard yourself today as a religious person?

H: "Religious," that is a pretty wide term. It is a question of one's behavior pattern, and a claim to be religious rests entirely on your own conscience, whether you believe or not. A Catholic attitude was indoctrinated into me. After all, I was born a Catholic, I went to a Catholic School, and I now have a conscience with lots of trials over belief.

OR: I have heard that you were rather good at geography. Would you have ever considered yourself to be an academic student?

H: Well, I had my own hobbies in that sense. I was very fond of shipping and took a great interest. In fact, around the age of ten or eleven, I had at home a map of the world with little flags on it, rather in the manner they used to mark out the war, and each little flag represented a ship at sea, and I would follow *Lloyd's Daily Register* and move each flag, which represented a ship, around the world.

OR: What attracted you to geography, though?

H: Oh, I think it's just a matter of imagination. For example, one of my greatest crazes was reading *Cook's Continental Timetables,* and I used to do the Trans-Siberian railway journey many times.

OR: At that time, what ambitions did you have?

H: I don't think I had any future ambitions, because I was preoccupied. I think my ambitions did go towards the theater because, even in those days, I was a first-nighter and devotee of film itself. I didn't read fan magazines, I used to read trade papers and there used to be a bookshop just off Leicester Square, near the Leicester Galleries, and upstairs they had all kinds of American trade magazines as well. There was *Motion Picture Daily, Motion Picture Herald,* then we had what was known in those days as *Cinematograph Lantern Weekly,* and there was *The Bioscope.* My favorite was the English *Cinematograph.* I think that's now dead, but one could follow all the latest films long before they appeared to the public.

OR: How did you become involved with the film industry in a professional way?

H: Well, at that time I was working for a cable company. I had some engineering training after I left Saint Ignatius, and I did some time at the School of Engineering and Navigation. I worked in the Estimating Department and then asked to be transferred to the Advertising Department. I went to the University of London in the evening for art classes, so that I became a designer of advertisements. I did the drawings, and the advertising manager would write the copy for them. Following my trade paper information, I learned that the Americans were opening a studio at Islington, so what I did was to find out what film they were going to make first and then I submitted a sample of what we knew then as "Art Types." In other words, in a silent film they needed titles, and usually they were illustrated. So you see, the work of an art title was not entirely different from the laying out of an advertisement, with words and the illustration. I had a sample made up and I took it along to the Paramount—it was called the Famous Players—Lasky, in those days. The point was, I had this whole thing made up and designed and showed it to them. I didn't simply go along and say, "I would like to do the titles in your films." I took a sample along, and of course I got the job. I left the engineering firm and went into the studio, into the Editorial Department. In those days they didn't have producers, they had a scenario department, and under the chief scenario were the writers who came from America, and being in that department and designing the titles, I also at the same time learned to write scripts.

OR: Did you ever really imagine that you would become a film director eventually?

H: Not at all. As a matter of fact, when the Americans closed the studio they left it to be a rental studio, and an English company came in, and by this time I was going to get the job as assistant director, until they said to me: "We need a writer for this film. Do you know one?" I said: "Yes. I can do it. I'll show you a sample of a script that I have written." It was a story that I didn't write for money or anything, I just wrote it as an exercise and the story was an adaptation and they read this script. So I got the job. Then my friend, the art director who was coming on to the same picture, told them he was unable to come, so they said to me, "What about the art direction on this picture—designing the sets?" I replied, "I can do that as well." Within a couple of years, I wrote the scripts, became art director and the production manager on half a dozen pictures. Well, then all of a sudden the director told the producer that he didn't need me anymore, there was some politics involved or something like that going on, and I was asked by the producer, a man called Mike Hawthorn, how would I like to direct a picture. I said it had never occurred to me; I was very happy doing the job I was doing. I went on to Germany. They were all silent films you see, and I had a writer of the script with me, and I made my first film as director in Germany, in Munich.

OR: I know you did a lot of early films in the 1920s and you were employed on many different pictures. Now, I believe you met your future wife, Alma Reville, at about this time?

H: Yes, she was with the American company. She was a cutter, editor, and script girl at the same time. In those days the film was put together by her, and then the director and the scenario editor would organize it. She did what we call the "rough cut." That's where I met her in 1923. She had been in the business since 1916, long before me.

OR: I have noticed that you always make at least one personal appearance in your films. How did this start off?

H: It started off when I was doing the third picture as a director. The first two were done in Germany; the third one was made in London at the studio in Islington and it was called *The Lodger* by Mrs. Bella Lamb, and we were doing the scene in the newspaper office and I made one of these personal appearances.

OR: It seems that you specialize particularly in suspense. Why is this so?

H: That's an English thing, you know. The English have always been fascinated by crime, and in those days they had some very interesting criminal cases, and the English have always been much more interested in that sort of thing than any other country. I suppose the nearest would be France, but in America, for example, the suspense sort of thriller in its form of literature was second-class literature, not first.

OR: Why do you think that was so?

H: I don't know, but the English, you could name so many— Collins, he was quite brilliant, and Conan Doyle, and then you came up to Agatha Christie today.

OR: You once said your love of films was far more important to you than any considerations of morality. Now, in view of this, would you find it morally acceptable to direct a film like the recent production called *The Devils*?

H: I wouldn't touch that sort of thing. As a matter of fact, in the last film I made (it was called *Frenzy*) I had an occasion to have a scene in it with a nude body of a dead girl tucked away in a sack of potatoes, and the murderer knew that clutched in her hand was an incriminating piece of evidence, a piece of jewelry. So I had this scene where he had to get on the truck and get this body out. Now, obviously, pulling this nude body out of the truck could be, you know, unnecessarily unpleasant, but I had a bikini of potatoes made which was wrapped around the girl's middle. So he is scraping away at the potatoes to bring the body out. The audience were never allowed to see the full body, because when he got to her hands they were both crossed covering her breasts. I went to a tremendous amount of trouble to avoid bad taste. A film like *The Devils* has got religion in it, and I have never gone in for that.

OR: Actually, what has motivated you into creating over fifty films? I mean, it is quite a remarkable number.

H: Well, I don't know, it's just hard work and naturally it is harder for me, because it isn't as though I can make it on any subject, because the public—with my name in films—are looking for suspense and the thriller element.

OR: Have you ever thought of branching out and doing a comedy film, perhaps?

H: I put the comedy in the films. In *Frenzy,* for example, a lot of the comedy is between the chief inspector on the case and his wife, which normally would be elements of the case in the Scotland Yard office, which is so much a cliché that I take situations like that and turn them into comedic ones.

OR: From all the films you have done, which film did you enjoy making most of all?

H: One of them! I have enjoyed several of them, but one I made years ago, called *Shadow of a Doubt,* that was made in 1942. There was the beloved uncle of a family in a small town who comes to visit them. [He] apparently is well-to-do and everybody adores him, and what they don't know is that he is a criminal on the run for having murdered several widows, taking place before the film opened. They did the tremendous suspense of this very nice—mother and father and three children, and in there is their uncle, whom they all love, right in the middle of them. So the suspense is, will they ever find out what he really is? In fact, the younger daughter found it out. He tried to kill the daughter to keep her mouth shut. It was made in a small town in northern California. It was written by Thornton Wilder, a famous American playwriter, and we shot it all in the real town.

OR: You say this is the most enjoyable one you have filmed. Which was the most challenging?

H: *The Birds,* because of the technical problems involved. The main problem was what we call a double printing job, in other words, we had these scenes of people being attacked by birds, children running onto the street and birds swooping down on them. We photographed the children alone, and we filmed the birds against the same background and put the two together.

OR: Have you any idea which you would particularly like to develop into a film some time in the future?

H: Well, no. I have always had an idea that I would like to do a film during twenty-four hours in the life of a city, say London or New York. I would take it right through to the following dawn, to cover all the facets of the city. The only film made on those lines was a documentary on Berlin, made by a man called Ruttman. That was documentary, not carrying any story line.

OR: For a total of five years you appeared regularly on television. How do you compare the medium of television to that of cinema?

H: Totally different. The economics of television are such that there are tremendous production limitations of television. You don't spend quite the same money as on films, and the shooting of television has to be very rapid. In other words, when you are filming a piece of film you hope to get on the screen, you cut off about two minutes a day, whereas in television you have to get at least nine minutes a day. Totally different approach. You can't do anything cinematical—it would cost too much money. But I did enjoy the television shows very much. You know, I used to do a half-hour show in two days, and I shot a one-hour show in five days.

OR: What would you like your epitaph to be?

H: "HE JUST FINISHED THE LAST REEL IN TIME."

APPENDIX II

Letter from Fr. Albert V. Ellis, S.J.

In 1979 the late Fr. Albert V. Ellis, S.J., was almost ninety years old when he graciously sent the author the following letter. It was, to quote Fr. Ellis, "written *gladly* in the hospital" after his second blood transfusion. The letter is full of many random but vivid memories which should be further verified. It conveys a feeling, understandably positive, regarding Jesuit piety, discipline, and morale in the same era in which Master Alfred spent four years of his youth at Saint Ignatius College, Stamford Hill, outside of London. Written in a stream-of-consciousness style, the letter is self-explanatory. A word is necessary, however, about four Latin terms used by Fr. Ellis in his salutation, in the final paragraph, and in his final words of affection:

P.C. = Pax Christi = "Peace of Christ"

Bis dat qui cito dat = "Who gives quickly gives, indeed, a double gift"

O.P.I. = *Oremus pro invicem* = "Let us pray for each other"

Tuus in corde Christi = "Yours in the Heart of Christ" (this Latin phrase is a reference to the Jesuit devotion to the Sacred Heart of Jesus).

> Bridge House
> 27 McKinley Road
> Bournemouth
> BH4 8AG
> 4/6/81

Dear Fr. Hurley, P.C.

You honour me too much! But, I'll muster my *own memories* about the *regime* at *St. Ignatius*! Alfred *Hitchcock* must have been 2, 3 or 4 forms below me & I doubt if I ever heard his name. Fr. Bill

Donovan, S.J. (at Bridge House now) would know more, being 2 classes behind me. But routine must have been the same, even for Hitchcock. Forgive my scrappy itemization!

1. I was a scholarship (bursary) boy with other bright lads (!) in IIB beginning in Sept 1911 nearly 12 yrs old—about 24 in my class.

2. 8:45 a.m.: Boys' Mass—in the big church—large attendance even of "train boys" i.e. from a distance (day schools normally began at 9:00 a.m.). (During Holy Week, the Passion was read in English during the Mass.) Boys trooped into Mass as they arrived— Morning Prayer, Our Father, Hail Mary, Creed, Morning Offering, after Mass.

3. Boys filed out (*genuflecting* before the Blessed Sacrament, as usual), across the playground to various classrooms.

4. Each class had its *own* room & altar of Our Lady (flowers, candlesticks). Except for science, drawing, woodwork, the class stayed in this same room for all subjects. But, I remember Mr. Mabbs (alleged agnostic lay science master) teaching us in our own IIB room, the beginnings of botany: monocotyledon, dicotyledon, chlorophyll, rose family, keeled pea family, etc. From the start in IIB "by heart" tasks set daily for homework included parts of "Penny Catechism"; Latin grammar; lyrics from Palgrave's Golden "Treasury," Parts I, II, III, IV (editor a brother of a famous [ex-S.J.] ambassador, Jewish); Fr. Kingdon, S.J.'s Latin Grammar; Siepman's French. Daily drill in these items, very rapid in 2nd & 3rd form where we were seated two by two as "Romans v. Carthaginians" (score books kept by the two class leaders aiming at "victory"). Opponent was expected to *correct* his neighbour. Very keen! Victory was celebrated with extra play.

4 [*sic*]. *Continuity* & "solidarity" was helped enormously not only by the form's semi-permanent classroom (with its own Lady Statue decorated and lit up especially in May & during the Junior Sodality's weekly class fervorinó) but the "permanent" class master scholastic or priest whom one got to *know* as a person, not a mere "stand-offish" lecturer. His desk was on a rostrum, sliding black-boards fixed on the wall behind his chair. Moreover, at the beginning & end of his sessions, he knelt & said a short prayer, e.g. "Grant, we beseech Thee, O Lord, that all our intentions, actions, etc." [*Spiritual Exercises*] Very often the form master (if a scholastic) moved up *with* his class especially from II to III or III to IV—an enormous help. A devil you know is better than one you don't know. Cybernetics, communication! human relations can get more positive reaction than learning. The scholastics would often tuck up their S.J. gowns & play football in the playground with the boys: a

short, white-headed priest did, too. Examples of dedicated boyish
S.J.'s make good sermons!

5. *Religion*. As new pupils in a new world we were taught to begin
every theme with A.M.D.G. with a cross above it [*Ad majorem Dei
gloriam* = "For the greater glory of God"] & end it with L.D.S.
[*Laus Deo Semper* = "Praise to God forever"]—a good introduction
to the meaning of a new life. The daily catechism drill was
sometimes supplemented by a short talk by the scholastic, e.g. on
devotion to the Sacred Heart. The footballer-priest formed a Junior
Sodality for IIIrd & IVth forms and gave us a Friday p.m. talk after
which we could go (if we wished—no *compulsion*) to Confession in
the church with the other classes. This priest also encouraged
Saturday Holy Communion & arranged for a simple breakfast @
three pence (Old Style). Senior sodalists naturally enlarged the
number. An annual 3-day "Retreat" by one of the priests was kept
up. Fr. Corti, S.J., the astronomer helped to *widen our outlook*! Fr. R.
Mangan, S.J., especially impressed me by his talk on *death*: "Don't
be afraid of dying—just face up to it. When you get into bed at night
push your feet down—though it may be cold for your toes! Say to
yourself: 'Well, one day I shall be *carried out* like this, am I ready
now? O my God, I am sorry, etc.' " A frightening practice to
suggest to 14 year olds, but very tranquillizing in action. Recommended!!! Against the horrors of the 1914–18 holocaust (more
than 20 million dead) & total involvement, conscription, etc. of the
nations—the Four Last Things became *very real*.

Boys even from other parishes naturally took part in the Corpus
Christi open air processions: the footballer priest, Fr. T. McAvoy,
S.J., organized a huge public procession through the town in
honour of Our Lady—the statue was guarded unobtrusively by 4
professional boxers! Tiny Tommy McAvoy walked up & down
rallying the singing: "Arm! Arm! for the struggle approaches! . . .
St. George be our patron in the battle. . . . "

Being a parishioner elsewhere myself, I could not attend all
Stamford Hill functions & celebrations (Church guilds, clubs or
combined with College activities) but I remember a "College
concert" held at St. Ann's Convent in St. Ann's Road, probably in
aid of their orphanage: the footballer-priest sang the "Queen of the
Earth," a popular song in honour of Our Lady: 3 or 4 scholastics
sang the "round," "Peter Piper picked a peck of pickled peppers" &
"The Baby on the Shore." Tommy Breen & another lad did a tap
dance. Fr. Holmes, S.J. (who ran our weekly singing classes and had
some splendid trebles in the choir) must have arranged other items.
He used to take his treble soloists to sing to the dying in St. Joseph's

Hospice-Hackney, also to distinguished country houses and for a holiday at Stonyhurst College: both left St. Ignatius College early (4th form?) but Jack Banfield became a priest S.J. & his brother George a lay brother S.J. Probably like Hitchcock they were too artistic to be academic.

The annual Prize Distribution in the Tottenham Town Hall was quite a big public show—in 1914 it included a serious short dramatic sketch depicting the Kaiser's declaration of war. Reggie Dunn's father (an old soldier) contributed a cornet solo; there were songs & choruses also & the pick of all the senior & junior Elocution prize competitors.

All these 5 pages so far have been written "currente camelo" (as Paddy is alleged to have said). At this point I shall try to indicate their relevance to your main thesis. I *think* I saw the Hitchcock name in St. Ignatius Church reserving seats as so many parents did: "bench rents" to help the church (but *chairs* then). In any case the family ran a shop not far off, in London district.

Having lived myself in or about London & with Londoners for years I seriously believe that every normal Londoner of the "middle" or working class (esp. shopkeepers & assistants) is as sharp as a needle & never shy though he may *not be academically minded.* Much too restless! *Imagination!* (Presumably Hitchcock was not deaf & dumb even mentally!) He could not have been *impervious* to S.J. influences but *possibly* (I've no idea) rebellious or a passive resister like Brother George Banfield, S.J., as a boy. R.I.P.

That S.J. system certainly succeeded 70-plus years ago though the college only opened, I think, 10 years or so before with unfinished buildings. It is difficult to imagine now how so many things favored the S.J. system of education then, even in many minor details. . . .

As you see, I have written all this as soon as possible, presuming "speed is of the essence." *Bis dat qui cito dat.* Moreover, I have some kind of internal hemorrhage liable to cramp my style, so its now or never. So forgive my lack of form! O.P.I.!

Tuus in corde Christi,
A. V. Ellis, S.J.

APPENDIX III

Letter to Alfred Hitchcock from the Author
(with background explanation)

I am especially indebted to cinematographer Lenny South, who felt strongly that I should have an interview with Hitchcock. He believed Hitch would want to meet me after reading three articles I had written on his work in *America* (the Jesuit weekly),[1] *The New Orleans Review* (the quarterly published at the Jesuit University, Loyola of the South),[2] and *Theology Today* (Princeton University).[3] South, at the time, did not know what Donald Spoto later told me in his apartment in West Greenwich Village, New York, namely, that Hitch's secretary, Peggy Robertson, was under strict orders (as were the security officers at the Universal Studio gate) not to admit any priest to see the director. This is curious, for Hitchcock did have friends who were Jesuits, as mentioned earlier. My only explanation is that Hitchcock had received a letter I sent in 1978 to his home in Bel Air requesting an interview. Whether this letter put the Master of Suspense on guard, I cannot say. What is certain is that Lenny South's persistent efforts to secure me an interview were in vain. Disappointed and perplexed, South was apologetic for not obtaining the interview, for he strongly believed that my point of view would prove interesting to Hitchcock.

My articles on Hitch were not so pointed as the topics outlined in the following letter, in which I draw a parallel with James Joyce, making reference to the "hangman God" of Joyce's religious education as described in *The Portrait of the Artist as a Young Man*. What I would have learned of substantive value from an interview with Hitchcock will remain a question mark. In general, he was reserved, except with certain trusted people, such as François Truffaut, Richard Schickel (the *Time* film critic), and Charles Champlin (the *Los Angeles Times* film critic).

My hypothesis is that Hitchcock did not want any probes regarding either religious matters or moral and theological inquiries into his work. Nevertheless, he did enjoy a long and cordial friendship with Fr. Tom Sullivan, S.J., of Loyola Marymount University (Los Angeles). Donald Spoto did not interview Fr. Sullivan, who has described a humorous and friendly Hitchcock—in short, a personality that never appears as such in Spoto's book. Fr. Sullivan was an exceptional source, for he established that Hitchcock could be friendly with Jesuits. If Alfred Hitchcock refused to see me, it was because he undoubtedly perceived me as an investigative reporter, a stranger with an agenda that he could not control. (Hitchcock as a director believed in control; very little spontaneity was allowed during the shooting of his films.) It is understandable that he wanted to protect his privacy. I do know that Donald Spoto was met with cautious reserve by close members of Hitchcock's crew, probably for the same reason I and Lenny South never heard from Hitchcock's office regarding our request for an interview.

The following letter was mailed to Alfred Hitchcock at his home in Bel Air, Beverly Hills, on April 28, 1978. At the time I was an assistant professor in the Department of Communications at the Jesuit university called Loyola of the South in New Orleans, Louisiana. The original letter was never returned.

Dear Mr. Hitchcock:

I am doing an extensive study of your film signature. In addition to the enclosed, articles will appear in an anthology, *Religion and Cinema,* and in the Fall issue of *Theology Today.* I shall eventually send you copies.

I recognize three patterns in your work, hitherto unexplored:

(1) "Meliorism"—people grow (usually together) in crisis—a theme of struggle and salvation which is found in the *Spiritual Exercises* of St. Ignatius. Admitting no conscious influence, I wonder if such retreats left their mark as with Stephen Hero in James Joyce's *Portrait of the Artist as a Young Man.* Did you experience the "Hangman God" of which Joyce wrote?

(2) Only two types of character seem to remain immutable, i.e. fixed in their ways: the devout protagonist of *I Confess* and *The Wrong Man* (played by rebel types, Clift and Fonda) and the Central European spies and agents of your intrigue films. This suggests that in a democracy people are changeable—except for saintly types. The dread forces of good and evil express themselves in *I Confess* and *The Wrong Man* but are mastered heroically and with apparent supernatural help. *Vertigo* and *Psycho* leave us perplexed by evil's force, whereas *The Birds* and *Marnie* offer some hope (but there is the possibility of more "feathery thunder" and more traumatized ghetto girls).

(3) The German "Expressionism" which reflects unseen forces with which we must cope. Your nine months at UFA undoubtedly had an influence, but Ignatian spirituality as communicated by Jesuits is very expressionistic, suggesting dark forces and therapy through love, commitment, and greater insight.

I plan a book on these thoughts since your work reflects the three patterns indicated. I would appreciate an interview at your convenience in July or August. My questions would center on recollections of Jesuit experiences, your attitudes toward democracy and its terror and splendor, and, finally, your indebtedness to the silent German cinema. I have a hypothesis that out of *The Wrong Man* comes a new direction in your work and would hope to study this film and the five successive films up to *Torn Curtain.*

Respectfully yours,
Neil P. Hurley, S.J.

Enclosures

1. Neil P. Hurley, "Inside the Hitchcock Vision," *America* (June 12, 1976), pp. 512–514.
2. Neil Hurley, "Hitchcock's Fearful Persuasion," *New Orleans Review,* vol. 7, no. 3 (Summer 1980), pp. 190-193.
3. Neil Hurley, "The Mutability of Motivation: Hitchcock's Films," *Theology Today* (October 1978), pp. 326–328.

APPENDIX IV

Alfred Hitchcock's Honorary Ph.D. Address at Santa Clara University, Santa Clara, California, 1963

May it please Your Excellency, Very Reverend Father Rector, members of the faculty, guests, and fellow classmates. First of all I must apologize for arriving too late for exams. In a period of our history when we are becoming concerned with educational "drop-outs," you are witnessing a new phenomenon—the "drop-*in*." For I have not only missed exams, I seem to have missed quite a bit more—*including* Theology one-ten. (Theology 110: The Sacrament of Matrimony, two-unit senior elective.)

I might say here that the university won Mrs. Hitchcock's undying admiration when she learned that one of the requirements for graduation was matrimony. How you managed this before going co-educational, I'll never know!

The thought of my being an honorary Doctor of Humane Letters is an awesome one. I must only assume that this is the same degree that was conferred on Dr. Jekyll.

And yet, there is logic to my being here today. Santa Clara University was founded one hundred and twelve years ago to produce well-rounded men. If I do not qualify as well rounded, I would like to see the man who does.

I do hope the university will make it clear at once that this degree was not conferred merely to enhance my television program. You see, people are likely to misunderstand, since the surest way of achieving a large audience in television is to have a doctor on your show. However, I doubt if these robes can ever be used as surgical gowns. For one thing, the color is not likely to inspire confidence. (Dressed in the scarlet red robe of the regents.)

It is also open to question as to whether a Doctor of Letters, humane or otherwise, would ever say, "The Birds *Is* Coming."

Fortunately there is no serious evidence that my appearance here is being protested. Not by the National Association of Teachers of English or even the National Association for the Prevention of Cruelty to Animals. I have detected one dissident element, but its suggestion of "Hitchcock Go Home" has been so subtle as to be completely inoffensive. I refer to your recent production called "Bye-Bye Birdie."

As you might suspect, I have an unusual interest in gravestones, and I am reminded of the delightful epitaph that marks the resting place of a great Irish scientist. It describes Robert Boyle as "The Father of Chemistry and the Uncle of the Earl of Cork." It is this same happy mixture of learning and family ties, of brain and blood, which I see reflected here on this Commencement morning.

A Commencement is a most peculiar occasion. The students sit quietly for perhaps the first time in four years, each holding his breath lest someone tap him on the shoulder and announce that a mistake has been made.

There is also an unaccustomed stillness among the faculty. They, poor dears, are exhausted from their labors of trying to put old wine into new bottles. Education has been defined as "leading out," but these people know it is "stuffing in," and hard work at best.

The third group present are the parents. You truly deserve to be here. For college tuitions being what they are, I suspect that you have bought a fair fraction of this place. But you are also strangely quiet, perhaps wondering if that child of yours is wearing a square hat because his head is now shaped that way.

Someone must be brought into this tomblike silence to provide the sound and fury. This brings us to the Commencement speaker. He is supposed to draw a line under an entire college education and add everything up. He must attempt to tidy up all the loose ends of these four years. Furthermore, he must have the temerity to think he can, in one brief moment, provide an inspiring flash, some magic touchstone which will send the graduate out to slay dragons and defeat giants. This is preposterous. In the first place, the Giants are never going to be foolish enough to get on the same baseball field with you again. (May 13, 1963—Buck Shaw Stadium—San Francisco Giants 4, Santa Clara Broncos 6.)

But even if I had the fantastic intellectual equipment to provide all the answers, you might be sorry you asked the questions. Perhaps you know this story which T. S. Matthews tells in his recent book: "It was decided to link up all the computing machines in the world, and by pooling their mechanical brains, it was hoped that some fundamental questions could be answered. The link-up was duly made, and when all was ready, the President of the United States asked the first great question: 'Is there a God?' . . . For several minutes there was such a silence all over the world that the only sound was the whirring and clicking of the massed computers. Then the answer came back: 'There is now.' "

As I mulled over what might prove helpful this morning, by way of encouragement, I thought of another epitaph. This is from Charles Wallis' book, *Stories on Stone,* a most satisfying collection of epitaphs. The one I would like to quote is cut on a tombstone in Girard, Pennsylvania:

> *In Memory of*
> Ellen Shannon
> Aged 26 years
> Who was fatally burned
> March 21st 1870
> By the explosion of a lamp
> filled with "R. E. Danforth's
> Non-Explosive
> Burning Fluid."

Today, standing here among you, I keep thinking of another kind of fire than that which was provided by Mr. Danforth's remarkable fluid. It is the fire a good university lights in the minds of men.

I know some of you are taking refuge in the definition which claims that education is what remains after you've forgotten all the facts you learned in college. Though it sounds similar, I much prefer another definition: that an education is what you have left after you have lost everything that can possibly be taken away from you.

I am sure you are taking a great deal more away from here than you think. One of Harvard's early presidents used to say that a man got a great deal out of Harvard if he just came and "rubbed his shoulders against the buildings." This may be sufficient for honorary degrees, but I imagine Father Donohoe has expected rather more at Santa Clara. So have these professors. Do not underestimate what they may have given you, what lights they may have kindled. These innocent-looking men have records—all of them. Academic records. Among them are several accomplished pyromaniacs. They are forever setting hidden fires—sometimes with delayed fuses.

Although I have not been so privileged, I can say that you have been fortunate to study here. Being a Jesuit university, Santa Clara represents the oldest and largest education system in America. Those of us who are outside its walls know Santa Clara as a good university. We know it as a place which is dedicated to lighting the lamps of the human intellect.

This week I examined the university catalogue, curious to see what courses I had skipped. (By the way, there was one requirement for my degree. The faculty insisted that I have a reading knowledge of English.) In the catalogue I found courses in Inorganic Chemistry, Advanced Propulsion Systems, and Experimental Psychology of Perception, but nowhere did I find a mention of humor. No "Advanced Humor." Not even "Humor One and Two." I know full well that this has not been a neglected subject on this campus. However, if there is a point I can make today, it is the importance of a sense of humor. The need for humor in one's work.

I labor in a business and among people who can be very serious about what they're doing. I might say that the genre of stories I deal with is *deadly* serious. For me, the only way to treat these stories is with humor. Without this approach, a story like *Psycho* would be a documentary, and so harsh as to be almost unbearable.

I also like to keep a sense of humor *while working*. One should approach my type of work with a kind of hand-rubbing glee. A kind of pleasure as I contemplate whether it would be best to have the detective fall down the elevator shaft or backward out the window.

All of you will not be fortunate enough to spend your lives committing murder, on film or otherwise, but I do hope that you can keep your work well flavored with the saving salt of humor.

Dr. Willis R. Whitney, founder and for thirty-two years the director of the General Electric Research Laboratory, must have been involved in projects which were also deadly serious. Yet they say of Dr. Whitney that he used to visit every scientist in his private laboratory at least once a week. Always his greeting was the same: "Are you having any fun today?"

Every job you will hold and every task that will be assigned to you will be important, I know. Many will seem to be matters of life and death. I hope you will remember that Tragedy and Comedy are but two sides of the same coin. If you can step back from your work, you may not only catch sight of some amusing irony, but you may be able to return to the task with some fresh insight as well.

Remember that of all the creatures on this earth, only man has an intellect which gives him an immeasurable potential, and yet only to man has God given the gift of laughter. I believe that the latter was meant to compensate for the awesome responsibilities of the former.

Fellow members of the Class of 1963, I shall not hold you here much longer, for you have proved your right to go. There are bonds, I believe, some of which you may not realize, that will tie you to this place forever.

I can tell by your laughter and your smiles that *you* are "having fun today." My wish for you on this Commencement morning is that you will continue having fun in everything you do. You have much to gain and the risk is small. After all, as Sir Max Beerbohm observed: "Of all the countless folk who have lived before your time on this planet, not one is known in history or in legend as having died of laughter."

As for this honor which has been conferred upon me: I hope you will accept the sincere thanks of a grateful if somewhat tardy student. This means a great deal to me. So, when you next see my image flickering on your television screen, if I loom a bit larger, it will not mean that I have gained weight—blame it on the righteous puff of pride.

APPENDIX V

Letter to the Author from Fr. Thomas Sullivan, S.J., a Friend of Hitchcock

The Jesuit Community
Loyola Marymount University
18 July 1986

Dear Neil:

Sorry for this long delay in responding to your good letter; I've been out of town—Eureka and such colorless places, but getting a job done.

So you are still working on the book; I thought I had missed it. Will these help?

I met Hitch first at RKO when he was working on *The Paradine Case* in 1947—nearly forty years ago. I was just ordained and working at Loyola University here in Los Angeles. I was much impressed meeting the great Hitch; I am sure he was not, but he was very gracious. Shortly afterwards, we had several luncheons together on Bellagio Road; there I met Alma, who was always sweet and hospitable. It was Hitch who introduced me to Anita Colby, who had just made the cover of *Time* and tagged "The Face." Both were Catholic and very gracious—at least to this priest.

Over the years I took a number of Jesuit priests to the various studios where Hitch worked and he was always pleasant with them—often ignoring me to talk with them.

I recall once—perhaps it was at Paramount—I walked on the set with some friends and without a pass. It was between shootings and Hitch was not there. In a few minutes the crew began to return and some of the cast. A security man came up to me and said, "Sorry Father, this is a closed set, you'll have to go." Just then Hitch walked on; I turned to him and said that they were throwing me out. Hitch said, "If you leave, so do I." And the security man

309

disappeared. That's not to make me some kind of hero; just to make the point that Hitch did not hate all priests.

We had many meals together over the years, at his home, at Perino's, at his villa in the Santa Cruz mountains. After dinner at the villa, Alma would go up to her room; Hitch and I would have a night-cap, talk script or anything from Marconi to macaroni. Incidentally, one of his neighbors up there in Palo Alto was Sam Taylor, his lawyer and great friend. . . .

I've said Mass at his home many times, although he was no great church-goer. When his grandchildren visited Rome, I set up a Papal audience for them. But I have heard that he never requested an audience for himself. Methinks the Pope scared him. . . .

What I'd like you to read is the speech we wrote for Hitch when we gave him our honorary doctorate at Santa Clara 1961 or 62. . . . At the graduation exercises that day in the Santa Clara Mission gardens, Hitch was most gracious to dozens of Jesuits—and he was most pleased with the honorary doctorate. . . .

Anyhow, Neil, hope this fragment helps a bit. Incidentally, the studio showed me *Psycho III* a few weeks ago—not worth seeing. The producer, that evening, said he would go to confession to me immediately after the screening!

Oh, here is a thought. At one point, years ago, Hitch sent $5000 to his school in London; he may have done it twice, showing some affection for his alma mater (grammar school). He sent the check through my office for tax reasons; hence my knowledge of it. But it does show some interest and affection for his former priest faculty.

I'm off, Neil. Sorry this is so brief; hope it helps. Incidentally, there is no reason for using my name at all. Hitch and Alma are gone; and I am ready to go any time. We only live twice and the best is yet to come. That was my thesis at Hitch's funeral.

In Christo,
Fr. Tom Sullivan, S.J.

APPENDIX VI

Letter to the Author from Fr. Robert Goold, a Student at Saint Ignatius College in Hitchcock's Time

Nazareth House
162, East End Road
East Finchley
London N.2.
12th October, 1981

Dear Father Hurley,

My apologies for the delay in answering your air mail letter concerning the schooldays of Alfred Hitchcock. I have been unwell but am now able to deal with correspondence.

The Annual Dinner of the Old Ignatian Association—the Old Boys of St. Ignatius College, Stamford Hill in North London—takes place next month and I have asked the Hon. Secretary if he could enclose a note asking for any information especially of the present addresses of Hitchcock's classmates—they may know. Such classmates would now be at least in their 80's so I am not very hopeful at the moment.

I myself am 78 years of age. I went to St. Ignatius College when I was 9 years of age, starting in the lowest Form (Prep.) so could not be a classmate. My memory does recall my first term (Christmas Term) at the college—with good reason, as the following incident will reveal. I was one of the boys (all ages) who "took Soup" at midday, in "The Soup Room" to supplement my midday sandwiches. We would buy a book of tickets for that week, enabling us to go every day. I was terribly shy, having come straight from Convent School and had been at St. Ignatius barely 8 weeks. And so I cannot say if Hitchcock was with us in the Soup Room. I did not know him.

On this occasion I recall coming out into the playground for our midday "break," with five or six of my companions at table. Suddenly, one yelled out, "Look Out! Here comes 'Cocky,' " and they all scattered. I, a new boy, found myself facing a much bigger boy with smiling eyes that fascinated me like a snake. He was wearing knickerbockers that buttoned just below the knee, with a heavy tweed of the same material jacket with a belt. In those days the style was known among grown-ups as "a shooting jacket"; so this was a junior version. I was wearing a sailor suit of those days.

This boy who had been called "Cocky" came towards me; with 2 companions spread-out fan-wise. They quickly came upon me; seized my arms and frog-marched me to the entrance to the stoke-hole in the cellar of St. Ignatius' Church which adjoined our playground. I was hustled into this cellar; the boy they called "Cocky" holding my shoulders from behind; his companions holding my wrists and twisting them. Once inside and the door shut, they acted quickly. "Cocky" took down my trousers (and I found out afterwards) had with a quick movement and a large safety-pin fastened a small "Jumping-Cracker" firework to my shirt tail at the back. It was only a small cracker for it went off only three times. Having lit the firework, the 3 boys dashed up the stairs into the playground; leaving me considerably scared with this cracking firework at my shirt tail. I fell over, as my trousers were around my ankles.

Fortunately, I was not burnt. I managed to unpin the cracker, restore my clothes to decency, and scurry away up the steps to the playground, hoping I would not be caught by the Playground Duty Master in a forbidden place.

As you see, I cannot say that my tormentor was Alfred Hitchcock, only that the other boys called him "Cocky." I had been at the school only a few weeks, so knew hardly any of the boys except the few in my class; I was so young, only nine years of age.

If I hear anything more at the Annual Dinner in November I will let you know and send the names and addresses. I myself was Hon. Secretary of the Old Boys' Association some fifty years ago but do not recall Hitchcock's name on my list. By then he could have been in America making films.

Yours sincerely,
Robert Goold

Interview with Janet Leigh, by Tom Weaver

(Printed with the courteous permission of Tom Weaver)

WEAVER: Exactly how did you become involved on *Psycho?*

LEIGH: Mr. Hitchcock sent me the book and said that he would like me to play Marion Crane. He said that the script was not quite finished and there would be some changes—they would not change the fact that Marion got killed, but there *would* be changes in the character. The *movie* Marion would not be quite as mousy; in the book she was really quite plain, and Hitchcock didn't intend to do that. He wanted the love scenes between the characters of Marion and Sam to be very realistic. I read the book and I could *see* what was there, and just the idea of working with Hitchcock was enough for me.

W: How *did* you enjoy working with Hitchcock?

L: I *loved* him—just adored him. He was obviously the most prepared director—after I *did* get the script and I was signed, I went to meet him and he showed me how every shot in the picture was already worked out.

W: *Psycho* was made quickly and inexpensively with TV technicians. How did you adjust to the more rapid pace?

L: I loved it. The sophistication of the equipment had progressed by that time, so things didn't take so long. It's very difficult to "sustain" a character when you're waiting, forever it seems, between shots. So I absolutely adored it.

W: In your book you wrote that Hitchcock promised to let you

313

alone and allow you to shape your own performance. *Did* he provide you with much in the way of direction or guidance?

L: If I needed it. But as long as what I did fit into his camera and fulfilled the piece of his picture I was supposed to fulfill, he let me pretty much alone. If I didn't come up to it—in other words, if there was more he needed—or if I went *beyond* it and should do *less,* he would tell me. But I was pretty much on my own.

W: Much has been recently written about the "dark side" of Hitchcock's personality, but you never seemed to be on the receiving end of any of this.

L: Nope. I assume that that is true. I can't say yes or no. I can only talk about what was with me. He couldn't have been better with me. One *funny* thing I recall is that he was trying to determine which dummy of Mother to use in the film, and so periodically when I would come back from lunch and I'd walk into my trailer on the set, there would be this apparition there—a dummy of Mother. There were various forms of Mother; I don't know whether he was gauging the volume of my screams or *what* [laughs], but I'm sure I had *some*thing to do with the decision as to which Mother was used in the climax!

W: Both Vera Miles and John Gavin got a dose of Hitchcock's displeasure.

L: I never worked with Vera Miles. I was done by the time that she started, and I only had that one opening scene with John Gavin. I remember John had a little trouble in the love scene—it just wasn't as passionate as Hitchcock wanted—but I don't know firsthand whether or not John and Hitchcock had any subsequent run-ins.

W: The bathroom and shower scenes were well ahead of their time. Were you pleased with the history-making opportunity, or did you go in with misgivings?

L: I had no misgivings whatsoever. *None.* I knew how hard Hitchcock had worked and how he had manipulated the censors' office to get certain things *in*to the picture. He would put outrageous things in the script *knowing* that the censors would tell him there was no way that he'd be allowed to do them; and then Hitchcock would say, "Okay, then I'll give *that* up, but I *have* to have *this*"—the things he had actually wanted all along.

W: Is it *really* true that *Psycho* has turned you off on taking showers?

L [ingenuously]: Uh huh—it *is* absolutely true. I'm a scaredy-cat [laughs]! I won't even take a *bath* in a hotel unless I can face *out,* even if I have to have my back to the faucets. It just scares me—I never thought about it before *Psycho,* but you are absolutely defenseless in that situation.

W: Did Hitchcock actually try to inveigle you into doing that shower scene in the nude?

L: This is *b.s.* There have been so many myths about that shower scene, and I've tried to put them to rest every time they've come up. What some people forget is that we had the Hays Office in those days—there was censorship. There was no *way* we could do it in the nude—no possible way! There *couldn't* have been a nude model, because it would not have been allowed in the picture. The only time that they used a stand-in for me was when Tony Perkins pulled the body out of the bathroom. Hitchcock said there was no sense in my doing that; no one could see who was wrapped up in that shower curtain, so there would be no purpose served by me getting dragged and bumped around in that scene. But getting back to what I was saying, those people don't realize what the censorship restrictions were like at that time, as compared to today. Today, of course, there'd be no fuss at all about a person doing a scene like that in the nude. But at that they show you everything. I think the new horror films are not as good. Your imagination is much stronger than anything that they could graphically depict.

W: Do you see many new horror films?

L: No.

W: Did you see the sequels to *Psycho*?

L: I saw *Psycho II.* I haven't seen *III* yet—I *want* to see *III*, because Tony Perkins directed it, but so far I just haven't been able to. I didn't think very highly of *Psycho II;* it left nothing to the imagination. As I said earlier, what your mind conjures is *so* vivid that nothing can match it.

W: In your opinion, what would Hitchcock have thought of these sequels?

L [looking heavenward]: Hitch, I hope I'm saying it right—here goes: I think he would have just been *revolted*. That type of film is just so contrary to what he believed in, which was suspense and mystery, imagination, and titillation. And there's none of that in *Psycho II*.

W: Was there ever any talk about working with Hitchcock again after *Psycho*?

L: No. After the impact that *Psycho* had, you couldn't have Marion Crane in another Hitchcock picture—you just couldn't! Because no matter what role I played, it still would have been Marion Crane. So it just couldn't be.

W: If by some stretch of the imagination you had been offered a role in a new *Psycho* film, would you have accepted it?

L: No—and Jamie [her daughter, Jamie Lee Curtis] didn't either. She was offered a part in *Psycho II* [the Meg Tilly role].

W: If you had to be remembered for just one film, would you want it to be *Psycho*?

L [laughs]: I don't know if I have a choice!

W: But isn't it unflattering for a star to be best-remembered for a supporting part?

L: If you think about it, the rest of the picture, after Marion's been killed, is about trying to *find* Marion. So Marion is really there the whole time, even though you only saw her for *x* number of minutes. Also, one picture does not a star make, and one picture does not a career make. For an actress to be remembered at all is *very* flattering.

APPENDIX VIII

Telephone Interview with Albert Whitlock, Special Effects Supervisor and Matte Artist for The Birds, Topaz, and Frenzy

(The author initiated the call on February 14, 1988)

HURLEY: Hello Al! Thanks for your letter! I found it very interesting.

WHITLOCK: Hello, Father! You may have found my letter a bit strange, because I mentioned Barrie's *Peter Pan*. Of course, Hitch knew Barrie. The analogy of death in *Peter Pan* was something Hitchcock avoided. I noticed he never wanted to think about it. It seems to me that *Peter Pan* "smacked at" [alluded to] real death in a way that Hitch did not deal with it.

H: That's curious, Al. In the book I'm finishing there will be several stills with cemetery scenes—*To Catch a Thief, The Trouble with Harry, Vertigo,* and *Family Plot.* In fact, I have one from that last film: it shows Hitch sitting in his director's chair, looking at an open grave. I'm sure he thought of death with reluctance and fear. You go back a long time with Hitch, don't you Al?

W: Yes, I do. My first picture with him was *The Man Who Knew Too Much* for Gaumont-British. Michael Balcon was the producer. Ivor Montagu was the associate producer.

H: Some critics feel that it was the end of his apprenticeship. He gave signs in this film of becoming the genius of mystery and suspense that later would represent his international image.

W: I would say definitely he was known throughout the world— certainly, on the sets and around the studio. Of course, I was

317

physically on the set, but lower than the dust beneath his dolly wheels, you might say. But, yes, we talked about him quite a bit. Remember, I started with Hitch in 1934, but still recall glowingly the experiences of those days. Those of us who worked for him were constantly impressed with his quips, his ideas on how to shoot a scene, and the way he dealt with people in the cast and the crew. Was he a world celebrity, you ask? I can only say that by 1934 he was getting excellent coverage in the British press, and, I'm sure in Europe and America as well.

H: Certainly, his subsequent films enhanced his reputation—*The 39 Steps, Secret Agent, Sabotage,* and *The Lady Vanishes.*

W: That's right. In our later years in Hollywood, Hitch liked to reminisce about the "old days" when we worked with low budgets at such quaint studios as Islington [Gainsborough] and Shepherd's Bush. I'd remind him of a story or an incident which he had forgotten, but which he recognized as something typical of what he might have said or done. He enjoyed such moments of recollection.

H: I noticed you didn't say the "*good* old days" in referring to the 1930s in England.

W: Well, it was not all uphill. We lacked resources and Hitch sought greater independence—and eventually found it.

H: Memory does have a way of making the past look rosier. You know, Al, I once interviewed Glen MacWilliams, an American cinematographer who worked many years in England and later was the cameraman on *Lifeboat.* He told his agent, Myron Selznick, about Hitch—insisting that no director in the Hollywood of the thirties was his equal. Myron's curiosity was piqued.

W: That sounds true. Hitch was very innovative. When they pulled a picture off the shelf that Balcon hated, he became surprised that Hitch made it into a success. I refer to *The Lodger,* released in 1926. Balcon called Hitch into his office at Islington and expressly told him that he was a "national asset," and that he was all right!

H: I know that Balcon was earlier impressed with what Hitch did with *The Pleasure Garden* in Munich in 1925. He "back-stopped" director Gordon Cutts, who evidently had problems in meeting deadlines. Balcon appreciated Hitch's talent and economy. It stood the young associate director in good stead.

W: Hitch showed great promise at an early age. He looked even younger.

H: Al, what did you actually do during the filming of *The Man Who Knew Too Much?*

W: I was the youngest person on the set—"gofer" and general factotum.

H: How did Hitch and Balcon get along?

W: Not well at all! In his later years, Hitch never had kind words for Balcon. There was mutual professional respect, but some tension. You must keep in mind that Hitch made a great deal of money for Gaumont-British.

H: I understand from a well-documented book, *Hitchcock and Selznick,* that Balcon provided what he termed "ballasts" in the persons of Ivor Montagu as associate producer and Charles Bennett as script doctor. That was on *The Lodger,* an earlier silent film.

W: Yes, Hitch certainly needed a scenarist and additional help, especially with regard to a script and scheduling, but the finished film was a unique product because of him. He had a special gift for involving audiences. His career proved that.

H: What Hitch added was a style that was not manifest in terms of the plot action or character dialogue. It's something you feel but can't describe. I personally believe that he was interested in the esoteric, not necessarily the satanic, but that something mysterious that goes beyond the senses.

W: It's interesting you say that. I'll never forget talking with him on the set of *The Birds.* He turned to me and emphatically said, "Al, this is *not* a science fiction picture." I looked at him, and said, "What kind of picture is it then, Hitch?" He didn't say a word, but just walked away. You know, Father, it's the only film I ever worked on with him that I had the distinct impression he wasn't sure of how the film would work out or where it was going. In fact, the reviews I read really didn't understand the film and didn't give it the praise that it really enjoys today.

H: That's true of *Sabotage* [1936], *The Trouble with Harry* [1956], *The Wrong Man* [1957]. I personally find some mystical moments in *The Birds*. When I say esoteric, I mean spiritual, and that can include dark forces as well as those of light and love.

W: Let me tell you a story he once shared with me. I've not ever seen reference to it in print.

H: Please do.

W: Well, we were at lunch once at Universal in his sanctum sanctorum and talking about zeppelins. It was at the time of my working on the film, *Hindenburg*. Hitch thought back to an incident in World War I. A bomb dropped a short way from his home in Leytonstone. He said it was a bakery three doors away, but it really was Potter's Bar, some way off. Hitch's memory lapsed at times.

H: That happens to a number of us.

W: It seems that Hitch's mother was a "stout-little lady," Hitch's words verbatim. She and a visiting aunt sought protection with the boy Hitch under a kitchen table. Apparently, his mother was a very devout woman—she kept making the sign of the cross, not once or twice, but repeatedly. There, on her knees, she just kept crossing herself. After a time, the aunt stood up, left the room and began to boil water for tea. When Mrs. Hitchcock heard the water boiling, she gave the following command from under the table: "Mine's two lumps!"

H: I like that—that's typically English! Of course, Hitch was very aware of how human beings were prisoners of habits and automatic responses. In the book, I give a number of examples—Mr. Memory in *The 39 Steps* is one case. Any other memories?

W: Well, Hitch differed from other directors and film executives in wanting to go beyond mere melodrama. He thought it was too limited a situation in itself. He actually said to me: "Melodrama, Al. They don't understand it." It is my contention that he went beyond it.

H: Well, I know that Gary Cooper turned down the role for *Foreign Correspondent* [1940] because he didn't like that kind of genre film, sort of pulpy melodrama. As a result, Joel McCrea got the part. Hitch raised the spy thriller to an unprecedentedly high level of critical appreciation. Hollywood didn't really see beyond the crime-suspense form to his genius and art. Selznick particularly had trouble seeing Hitch's unique way of treating suspense- melodrama.

W: Well, Hitch felt that many producers did not really understand melodrama in the way he did. He admitted plot was important and also character development, but for him the psychological moments were very important—the mood, the mannerisms, and facial reactions that would touch an audience.

H: He certainly drew audiences into the screen to identify with his main characters. *Psycho* is brilliant that way. Of course, some critics feel he did too much with inanimate objects—a key, a glass of milk, an orchestra cymbal, a dinner knife, a tie clasp, whatever.

W: Yes, he did more of that than other celebrated directors, didn't he?

H: Other associates have stressed his knack for coloring such objects with the emotions of the person handling or using the object. If such a lifeless object was an indispensable instrument for the execution of a plot or a plan, then the audience could be made to feel that emotional relation with the object as if it were part of its own life. We know that Aristotle placed plot over character, but I believe that in Hitch's case he believed the key to audience identification was the changing mood of a character, whether good or evil. Hitch guided the audience to follow even a negative character, such as Claude Rains in *Notorious*.

W: I know that Hitch deepened his understanding of the role of characters in a film. For years he tended to see them as products of their earlier training and life experience. That was very different from my experiences with Walt Disney, who never looked backward but always toward the future. He was an optimist.

H: Disney's films could be dark, often expressionistic. Take *Snow White and the Seven Dwarfs*. Very interesting point about Hitch's preoccupation with the past, Al.

W: Hitch did change, however. You have heard of the Scottish screenwriter James Bridie haven't you?

H: Yes, he worked on *Under Capricorn.*

W: And, before that, on *The Paradine Case.* Well, his belief was that you build interest in audience involvement with the characters. He told Hitch, "After you have left the theater, you must think, what will the characters be doing in three weeks' time?" That impressed Hitch, I know. This covers my point that Hitch went beyond simple melodrama.

H: In other words, the audience would wonder, What would the characters be doing in the future? His characters are, generally left in the last scene with doubt, suspicion, monotony, or nagging anxiety. Recall Claude Rains in *Notorious* or Farley Granger in *Strangers on a Train.* The past weighs on them and will color their futures. Interesting personal insight there, Al. Did Hitch resent actors, whom he called "cattle"?

W: Not really. Of course, he favored the camera and editing; that was moviemaking for him; but no, he appreciated good acting—say, a Cary Grant, a Jimmy Stewart, a Grace Kelly. He did not have much tolerance for actors who were eager to be directed. He felt that professionals should know what they were doing. There was one American actor, on *Topaz,* who was quite upset because Hitch never said anything, good or bad, about this actor's performance. He told me how concerned he was. He wanted advice, some encouragement, anything. I told him that Hitch had seen all his films, even his screen tests, and had approved him because he was confident that he could do the job. If he chose you, then he knew you were capable. Of course, Hitch did spend more time with actresses and that would make male stars wonder. He didn't like "Method" acting and told one such actor tersely, when asked what his motivation should be, "The money." He trusted actors, but would intervene if he saw something wrong.

H: Do you feel, Al, that Hitch did better work with scarce resources than with the Hollywood stable of stars, the big budgets and sets; in general, the broad-based support of large organizations?

W: Hard to say, really. He could do both well. He really needed independence and worked toward that.

H: There's a new book, *Hitchcock and Selznick,* which argues that each needed the other—that, in Hitch's case, he needed control, supervision, and correctional guidance. Is this true?

W: I really don't know this and feel that the opposite is true. He became his own producer to avoid supervision, but accepted heavy criticisms from above—i.e. *Topaz*—because he *feared* authority. People like Michael Balcon and Selznick made Hitch feel uncomfortable. He liked to innovate, to set himself challenges, to break new paths. Several films were not fully understood upon their release. Hitch was ahead of his time.

H: I know critic Andrew Sarris was virtually alone in his defense.

W: Hitch was certainly ahead of many critics. You know, for *Frenzy* he had a big budget, but instead of shooting a lavish production, he chose to be realistic. I didn't like *Frenzy*. He was out of touch with contemporary England. It looked different from some previous films.

H: I agree, coming after *Torn Curtain* and *Topaz.*

W: Those two pictures were not up to his potential.

H: Was Hitch better as what is called a minimalist, you know, working close to a preconceived notion of what he wanted instead of asking, "How much do I have to spend, or can I spend?"

W: Yes, I would say that Hitch did what he wanted to that way. If it was a working-class film, then he would give it that look. I know that, in *Frenzy,* he shocked audiences with several bold scenes; that last scene was particularly grisly. The angry "wrong man"—Jon Finch, the actor—thinks he's found his friend and murderer—Barry Foster—in bed and has a crank handle with which he intends to beat him bloody. It turns out that the body in the bed is the latest female victim. Alma Hitchcock complained to her husband that he had gone too far.

H: It was a frightening scene, all right, and Hitch went ahead and shot it.

W: You know, as an afterthought, many of us thought that the casting in *Frenzy* should have been reversed. The villain, Barry

Foster, should have played the falsely accused man, and Jon Finch, not an easily likable person in real life, should have done the murderer's role. Incidentally, Finch died young in a motorcycle accident.

H: Reverse roles? That would have been interesting!

W: Yes, I really think that the picture would have been stronger if that reversal had taken place, as suggested by Peggy Robertson.

H: I once told Frank Capra, a close friend of Hitch, about the first rape scene in *Frenzy*. Critics missed the religious significance. The victim was the ex-wife of Jon Finch. Barry Foster is looking for a kinky sex partner; she runs a legitimate matrimonial bureau and tries to send him away. He becomes aggressive and subdues her by force. The close-up shows her with a gold cross on a chain around her neck. During the struggle, she quietly recites a psalm. We see her bosom slightly revealed. She instinctively—in a reflex gesture of modesty—covers it. It's a wonderful touch! Capra sat up and his eyes gleamed as I related the episode. His imagination was fired by admiration for this Hitch touch.

W: Yes, but, it seems to me, the more important thing in this scene is his switch to the subjective, to make the audience experience being victim and so to exonerate Hitch from an inexcusably brutal scene.

H: Interesting! Al, you worked on the artwork for the prison scene in *Frenzy*.

W: Yes, I did, Father. Hitch always worked from sketches and then shot the scene. He wanted visuals even before the actual shooting.

H: It's a vital scene, I recall. Jon Finch must escape, so he injures himself by falling down a cast-iron staircase. He goes flying through the air, dangling horizontally. Very dramatic! Al, you worked on both the early economical British pictures and later, in Hollywood, on the more expensive productions.

W: Yes, I did. I wanted to come to America. Our industry was really controlled by American and other interests. Besides, I met so many Americans in England and I liked them. Working with Hitch was an experience.

H: You did copy reproductions of modern paintings for Hitch, too.

W: Yes, I once did a Raoul Dufy and a Vlaminck. Hitch asked me to do them so I worked six very long Sundays to complete them. On the Vlaminck, I had to use a palette knife to smear the impasto to just the right thickness. The Dufy had interesting transparent color and figures, not wanted, showed through, not easy to reproduce. It's interesting—Hitch invited me and art editor Henry Bumstead to his ranch in Santa Cruz. Upon arriving, Hitch went out of his way to show me the Dufy over his mantelpiece. He was a perfect host; so was Alma. We had a lovely evening, very relaxing.

H: I understand that both preferred to entertain at home and were not part of the extravagant Hollywood social scene.

W: They did eat out often and would be seen socially that way.

H: Were you interviewed by Donald Spoto for his book, *The Dark Side of Genius?*

W: Well, I was quoted by him in the back of the book. The book is well written.

H: And thoroughly researched, too.

W: I didn't like the book at all. It's not a Hitchcock I recognize. Nor did Joan Fontaine, who was interviewed in England. Referring to the Spoto book, she said Hitch was, at times, inclined to blue humor, but she found him to be a gentleman.

H: I know that Lenny South felt the same way. He worked with Hitch and Robert Burks from 1951 on and did the last film, *Family Plot.* He was disappointed with the book, and although he spoke with Spoto, he told me that he avoided any lengthy interview sessions or invitations to dine.

W: Well, I know that Hitch was not particularly fond of Spoto; they met and talked. He was scornful once in talking about Spoto, saying that he overintellectualized and saw *too* much hidden meaning.

H: Several close friends of Hitch, including crew members, missed a larger picture of Hitch—one that would include other aspects of his character.

W: Definitely! There were too many facets to his character to concentrate only on the dark side of his personal life. In the case of genius, complexity must be respected.

H: Maybe there will be a book dealing with the lighter aspects. Thank you for an enlightening interview, Al.

W: You're welcome, Father. Good luck with the book!

Bibliography

Books

Bogdanovich, Peter. *The Cinema of Alfred Hitchcock*. New York: Museum of Modern Art, 1962.
Valuable interview material with incisive comments by the author; well illustrated.

Brill, Leslie. *The Hitchcock: Romance: Love and Irony in Hitchcock's Films*. Princeton, N.J.: Princeton University Press, 1988. Brill holds that Hitch's romantic melodramas are, in the strict sense, comedies, that offer that "last laugh" that refuses to be defeated, and, in a religious sense, is a secular adaptation, as the late critic Parker Tyler held, of the Resurrection. I personally believe that *The Trouble With Harry* has a more spiritual subtext than Brill allows for. This apart, however, the work is original and exciting, with revealing references to recurring motifs, such as arches, and themes of questing, descent, and ascent—ancient literary references to be found in Virgil, Dante, and Shakespeare. He upgrades *I Confess* and *The Wrong Man,* but, misses, I feel, the biographical subtexts in *Vertigo* and *Psycho*. Can the person be so stringently separated from the filmmakers? One wonders.

Deutelbaum, Marshall, and Leland Poague, editors. *A Hitchcock Reader*. Ames: Iowa State University, 1986.
A splendid anthology of critical essays which confirm Hitchcock's towering position in world cinema history. Although the reader will not find many religious allusions (e.g., Hitchcock's Catholic/Jesuit formation, numerology, spatial geometry, and Christ figure transfigurations), nonetheless there are significant psychological discussions of men-women relationships, the occult, deviant behavior, and hidden symbolic meanings. This volume incorporates recent feminist criticism, Marxist theory, and linguistic analysis. Of the twenty-five essays, I recommend these: Thomas Hyde (*Spellbound*); Robert Stam and Roberta Pearson (*Rear Window*); Robin Wood ("On Male Desire and

Anxiety"); James McLaughlin (*Shadow of a Doubt*); Marian Keane (*Vertigo*); Raymond Ballour (*Psycho*); and Leland Poague (*Psycho*).

Douchet, Jean. *Alfred Hitchcock*. Paris: Editions de l'Herde, 1967.
Very strong analysis of the transcendental aspect of Hitchcock's genius in terms of magic, the occult, and metaphysical dread.

Durgnat, Raymond. *The Strange Case of Alfred Hitchcock*. Cambridge: MIT Press, 1974.
A survey of Hitchcock criticism and his films; often insightful but at times opinionated in terms of a strong rejection of some very popular films.

Fallaci, Oriana. *The Egotists: Sixteen Surprising Interviews*. Chicago: Henry Regnery, 1963.
In her interview with Hitchcock, this noted Italian reporter expresses her personal distaste for the director as formal and cold. I suspect that Hitch did not feel at ease with her. He expressed emotion in his films, through preconception and studied techniques, not in interviews where he was not in control.

Gloege, James Cornelius. "River of Feeling." Master's thesis, University of Southern California, 1968. Pp. 29 ff.
A highly original thesis on the role of emotion in entertainment films. The examples from directors such as Hitchcock lend credence to the author's interpretation.

Harris, Robert A., and Michael S. Lasky. *The Films of Alfred Hitchcock*. Secaucus, N.J.: Citadel Press, 1976.
An excellent overview of Hitchcock's work with plot synopses, many pertinent illustrations, and intermittent original insights.

Higham, Charles, and Joel Greenberg. *Hollywood in the Forties*. New York: Coronet, 1970. Pp. 21, 31, 46, 98–99, 105, 156. Paperback.

Leff, Leonard J. *Hitchcock and Selznick: The Rich and Strange Collaboration of Alfred Hitchcock and David O. Selznick in Hollywood*. New York: Grove/Weidenfeld, 1988.
A detailed study of a celebrity producer and a world-class director: Selznick, who preferred strong plots, logical dialogue, and rationally motivated action, and Hitchcock, who believed in

camera movement, montage, and subliminal manipulation of audience feelings.

LeValley, Albert J., editor. *Focus on Hitchcock*. Englewood Cliffs, N.J.: Prentice-Hall, 1972.
An indispensable anthology for any appreciation of Hitchcock. The editor's superb introduction will excite anyone just becoming acquainted with Hitch's work. With a theological sensibility, André Bazin, a leading French critic, tried to tease out of Hitchcock observations on his inner life, the source of that great river of emotion which ran from scenes of healing and reconciliation to scenes of darkness and near despair (e.g., *Psycho*, *Vertigo*, *Frenzy*).

Modleski, Tania. *The Women Who Knew Too Much*. New York: Methuen, 1988. This is a penetrating study of the director's fascination, indeed even obsession, with the theme of female psychology. Surrounded by beautiful women, Hitch was liked by them, but, undoubtedly, would liked to have been taken more seriously in a romantic sense. This study is a key to a better understanding of his attraction to such stars as Ingrid Bergman, Grace Kelly, and Tippi Hedren.

Perry, George. *The Films of Alfred Hitchcock*. New York: E. P. Dutton, 1965.
An excellent collection of still photographs from the films of the Master of Suspense.

Phillips, Gene D. *Alfred Hitchcock*. Boston: Twayne Publishers, 1984.
A handy overview of Hitchcock's life and work, with many relevant comments by the author, a Jesuit priest.

Rahner, Karl, S.J. *The Dynamic Element in the Church*. New York: Herder and Herder, 1964.

————. *Spiritual Exercises,* translated by Kenneth Baker, S.J. New York: Herder and Herder, 1965.
Rahner is considered by many Protestant and Catholic theologians to be the most penetrating systematic thinker since the Dominican priest Thomas Aquinas, who was called the Angelic Doctor.

Rebello, Steven. *Alfred Hitchcock and the Making of Psycho*. New York: Dembner (Distributed by W.W. Norton), 1990. A long overdue micro-analysis of a film that, at the time of its release, was underappreciated by many serious film critics and Hitch scholars, who now accept it as a horror classic, and not just a cult picture. What Hitch folded into this film, at times deliberately, at times through unconscious creative inspiration, is awesome. Rebello points us to further analysis—spiritual as well as *psycho* "logical."

Robinson, David, editor, with Ann Lloyd. *Movies of the Fifties*. London: Orbis Publishing, 1982. Pp. 174 ff. Interesting observations about the films influenced by Hitchcock.

Rothman, William. *Hitchcock: The Murderous Gaze*. Cambridge: Harvard University Press, 1982. A brilliant and indispensable research tool for understanding why Hitchcock made the camera the star over and above actors, writers, producers, and composers, even though he respected all of these as essential contributors to a collective product. Rothman has been criticized for indulging in overinterpretation, but by and large his musings provoke the reader's reflection, always a desideratum. The first three films, discussed in terms of Hitch's visual genius, deal with the "wrong person" theme (*The Lodger, Murder!, The 39 Steps*). The last two films analyzed treat the "doubling effect," what the Germans call *der Doppelgänger* (*Shadow of a Doubt, Psycho*). The judicious reader will discover the power of the unvoiced image and how Hitchcock created mood, particularly with regard to guilt transfer, moral ambiguity, mutable motivation, and the key passions of love, hate, and lust.

Sarris, Andrew. *Confessions of a Cultist*. New York: Simon and Schuster, 1971. Pp. 84–86, 141–144, 268–272. Perceptive remarks by the *Village Voice*'s film critic and staunch proponent of that auteur theory which the work of Hitch validates as much as any director in film history.

Scanlon, Ross. "Drama as a Form of Persuasive Communication." Ph.D. dissertation, Cornell University, 1937. A penetrating academic analysis of how theatrical and film types of drama can make use of rhetoric and aesthetics, certainly a distinctive characteristic of Hitchcock's work.

Spoto, Donald. *The Art of Alfred Hitchcock*. New York: Hopkinson and Blake, 1976.
An illuminating study of Hitchcock with stress on literary references that are parallel to Hitch's concern. Also valuable is the list of recurring motifs, such as trains, birds, parent-child relationships, and food. The analyses of *Vertigo* and *Family Plot* are particularly well done.

――――. *The Dark Side of Genius: The Life of Alfred Hitchcock*. Boston: Little, Brown, 1983.
This highly controversial study appeared despite efforts to suppress it; family, friends, colleagues, and admirers of Hitchcock in the Hollywood-Beverly Hills area found the book in poor taste. One could say that the research was partial, although well founded. There were many Hitchcocks, depending on the relationship and the mercurial moods which the Master of Suspense experienced and, happily, translated to the screen in terms of entertainment and, very often, high art. However regrettable this study may seem to those who knew Hitch, the book cannot be overlooked. Spoto chose to study a little-known side of the Master of Suspense. Complementary things could have been added by Spoto, had he been granted interviews with such close associates of Hitch as Leonard South. Not only had South worked with Hitch since 1951 (*Strangers on a Train*), he also directed the photography on *Family Plot* (1976). He purposely avoided being interviewed by Spoto, as he recounted to me, because he did not feel comfortable with Spoto's intentions.

Taylor, John Russell. *Hitch: The Life and Times of Alfred Hitchcock*. New York: Pantheon Books, 1978.
In his introduction, the author goes directly to the "Hitchcock Enigma," namely, why did the director become a "machine for making movies"? The thesis is stated in the epilogue: Hitch "actually made himself into a film, at once subject, object and medium." Taylor prudently makes the reservation that Hitchcock's films alone cannot be used as an easy key to unlock the secrets of his character. In averring that films were for Hitchcock "the weapon a timid man uses to bring a hostile environment under control," the author brings to mind the credo of James Joyce in *A Portrait of the Artist as a Young Man*: "I will try to express myself in some mode of life or art, as freely as I can and as holy as I can, using for my defense the only arms I allow myself to use, silence, exile, and cunning." This authorized biography is

interesting but has been amply complemented, if not surpassed, by the work of Spoto, Yacowar, Rothman, and numerous perceptive essayists.

Thomson, David. *Movie Man*. New York: Stein and Day, 1967. Pp. 125–131.
The screen character of Cary Grant is discussed, thus shedding light on Hitchcock's principal male star.

Truffaut, François, with Helen G. Scott. *Hitchcock*. New York: Simon and Schuster, 1967.
A unique source for insights on filmmaking; the 472 photographs are an aid to the parry and thrust which takes place between an admiring questioner, Truffaut, and a cinema genius, Hitch, who, as always, replies guardedly.

Tyler, Parker. *The Hollywood Hallucination*. New York: Simon and Schuster, 1970. Pp. 168–189.
Not much has been written about Hitchcock's compromise to commercialism and the star system. Chapter 8 treats the false "happy endings" to which Hollywood was inclined. Psychological manipulation is one thing, but tampering with original stories is another. Tyler, a brilliant critic, discusses *Suspicion*. To Hitchcock's credit, he made the ending sufficiently ambiguous to please the audience and also to sow seeds of doubt that the character played by Cary Grant might, at some future date, commit murder.

Wood, Robin. *Hitchcock's Films*. London: A. Zwemmer, 1965.
This book contributed to the awakening of many Hitch fans to the hidden meanings in pictures that were appreciated only in terms of their entertainment surfaces and which, when first released, were not adequately analyzed. Some scholars differ with Wood, but the reader will profit from his provocative aperçus.

Wood, Robin. *Hitchcock's Films Revisited*. New York: Columbia University Press, 1989. Wood has gone back to up-date and add cogent insights to his previous readings of Hitch masterpieces, such as *Rear Window*, *Vertigo*, and *Psycho*. Wood is an indispensable authority on the Master of Suspense.

Yacowar, Maurice. *Hitchcock's British Films*. Hamden, Conn.: Archon Books, 1977.

An excellent treatment of the early silent and sound films made in England, several of which were scripted and edited by Alma Reville, Hitchcock's wife.

Articles and Interviews

Allen, Tom. "Hitchcock's Half-Century Grin." *America,* Vol. 134, No. 290 (April 3, 1976).

"Ascetic Sadist." *Time,* Vol. 43, No. 94 (January 31, 1944).

Bellour, Raymond. "*Marnie,* une lecture." *Revue d'Esthetique,* Vol. 20, Nos. 2-3 (April-September 1967).

———. "Ce que savait Hitchcock." *Cahiers du Cinéma,* No. 190 (May 1967).

———. "*Les Oiseaux*: analyse d'un séquence." *Cahiers du Cinéma,* No. 219 (1969). Mimeo, British Film Institute, Educational Advisory Service.

———. "Psychoses, Neuroses, Perversion." *Camera Obscura: A Journalism of Feminism and Film Theory,* Vols. 3/4, pp. 104–134.

Champlin, Charles. "Murders Turn Hitchcock On." *Los Angeles Times,* January 19, 1973.

Domarchi, Jean. "Le Chef d'Oeuvre Inconnu." *Cahiers du Cinéma,* No. 39 (October 1954), pp. 33–38.

Douchet, Jean. "La Troisième Clé de Hitchcock." *Cahiers du Cinéma,* Nos. 99, 102 (1959).

———. "Hitch et Son Public." *Cahiers du Cinéma,* No. 113 (1960).

Durgnat, Raymond. "To Catch a 'Hitch.' " *Quarterly Review of Film Studies,* Vol. 8, No. 1 (1983), pp. 43–48.

Dynia, Philip. "Alfred Hitchcock and the Ghost of Thomas Hobbs." In Richard Dyer MacCann and Jack Ellis, eds., *Cinema Examined,* New York: E. P. Dutton, 1982, pp. 23–37.

French, Philip. "Alfred Hitchcock: The Film-maker as Englishman in Exile." *Sight and Sound,* Vol. 54, No. 2 (1985), pp. 116–122.

Giacci, Vittorio. "Alfred Hitchcock: Allegory of Ambiguous Sexuality." *Wide Angle,* Vol. 4, No. 1 (1980).

Hardison, O. B. "The Rhetoric of Hitchcock's Thrillers." In W. R. Robinson, ed., *Man and the Movies,* Baton Rouge: Louisiana State University Press, 1967, pp. 137–152.

Higham, Charles. "Hitchcock's World." *Film Quarterly,* Vol. 16, No. 2 (1963), pp. 3–16.

Hitchcock, Alfred. "Much Ado About Nothing?" *The Listener* (a BBC talk given in London, March 10, 1937), p. 448.

———. "Hitchcock's Comments on *Frenzy*" (taped lecture in Arthur Knight's class, April 27, 1972). Los Angeles: University of Southern California, Doheny Library Film Research Center.

Hodenfield, Chris. "Mu-u-u-u-rder by the Babbling Brook." *Rolling Stone Magazine,* July 29, 1976, pp. 38ff.

Houston, Penelope. "The Figure in the Carpet." *Sight and Sound,* Vol. 34, No. 4 (1963), pp. 159–164.

Hurley, Neil. "Inside the Hitchcock Vision." *America,* June 12, 1976, pp. 512–514.

———. "The Mutability of Motivation: Hitchcock's Films." *Theology Today,* Vol. 30, No. 3 (October 1978), pp. 326–328.

———. Book Review of Joan Fontaine's *No Bed of Roses. America,* January 13, 1979, pp. 18–19.

———. Book Review of John Russell Taylor's *Hitch. America,* March 17, 1979, p. 224.

———. "Christ-Transfigurations in Film: Notes on a Meta-Genre." *Journal of Popular Culture,* Vol. 13, No. 3 (1980), pp. 427–433.

———. "Hitchcock's Fearful Persuasion." *New Orleans Review* (Summer 1980), pp. 190–193.

————. "The Hitchcock Romance." *Daily Variety,* December 7, 1988, p. 20 (a review of Leslie Brill's book of the same title with my remarks on *The Trouble with Harry*).

Jhirad, Susan. "Hitchcock's Women." *Cinéaste,* Vol. 13, No. 4 (1984), pp. 30–33.

Kane, Lawrence. "The Shadow World of Alfred Hitchcock." *Theatre Arts,* Vol. 33, No. 4 (1949), pp. 32–40.

Kracauer, Siegfried. "Hollywood's Terror Films: Do They Reflect an American State of Mind?" *Commentary* (August 1946), pp. 132–160.

Lambert, Gavin. "Hitchcock and the Art of Suspense." Part 1, *American Film,* Vol. 1, No. 4 (1976), pp. 16–23; Part 2, Vol. 1, No. 5 (1976), pp. 60–67.

MacShane, Frank. "Stranger in a Studio: Raymond Chandler and Hollywood." *American Film,* Vol. 1, No. 7 (May 1976), pp. 54ff.

Miller, Gavin. "Hitchcock Versus Truffaut." *Sight and Sound,* Vol. 38, No. 2 (1969), pp. 82–88.

Monaco, James. "The Cinema and Its Double: Alfred Hitchcock." *Take One,* Vol. 5, No. 2 (1976), pp. 6–8.

Poague, Leland. "Hitchcock and the Ethics of Vision." In William Cadbury and Leland Poague, eds., *Film Criticism: A Counter Theory,* Ames: Iowa State University Press, 1982, pp. 91–155.

Rothman, William. "How Much Did Hitchcock Know?" *Quarterly Review of Film Studies,* Vol. 5, No. 3 (1985), pp. 383–392.

Sarris, Andrew. "Alfred Hitchcock: Prankster of Paradox." *Film Comment,* Vol. 10, No. 2 (1974), pp. 8–9.

Schickel, Richard. "We're Living in a Hitchcock World, All Right." *New York Times Magazine,* March 3, 1957, pp. 17ff.

Silver, Alain. "Fragments of a Mirror: The Use of Landscape in Hitchcock." *Wide Angle,* Vol. 1, No. 3 (1976), pp. 52–61.

Stam, Robert. "Hitchcock and Buñuel: Desire and the Law." *Studies in the Literary Imagination,* Vol. 16, No. 1 (1983), pp. 7–27.

Take One. "Alfred Hitchcock: A Friendly Salute." Vol. 5, No. 2 (1976). Special Hitchcock number.

Thomson, David. "The Big Hitch." *Film Comment,* Vol. 15, No. 2 (1979), pp. 26–29.

Truffaut, François. "Un Trusseau de Fausses Clés." *Cahiers du Cinéma,* No. 39 (October 1954), pp. 45–52.

Westerbeck, Colin L., Jr. "The Hitchcock Touch." *Commonweal,* Vol. 96, No. 429 (August 11, 1972).

Wide Angle, Vol. 4, No. 1 (1980). Special Hitchcock number.

Wollen, Peter. "Hitchcock's Vision." *Cinema* (Cambridge), No. 3 (1969), pp. 2–4.

Wood, Robin. "Hitchcock, Alfred." In Christopher Lyon, ed., *Directors/Filmmakers: The International Dictionary of Films and Filmmakers,* Vol. 2, Chicago: St. James Press, 1984, pp. 259–263.

Film Reviews
(in sequence according to release date)

"*The Lodger.*" Roger Manvell, *Sight and Sound,* Vol. 19, No. 9 (January 1951), pp. 377–378.

"*Blackmail*: The Opening of Hitchcock's Surrealist Eye." Harry Ringel, *Film Heritage,* Vol. 9, No. 2 (Winter 1973–1974), pp. 17–23.

"Mirth, Sexuality and Suspense: Alfred Hitchcock's Adaptation of *The Thirty-Nine Steps.*" *Literature/Film Quarterly,* Vol. 3, No. 3 (1975), pp. 232–239.

"The Lady Vanishes." Alan Stanbrook, *Films and Filming,* Vol. 9, No. 10 (July 1963), pp. 43–47.

"Notorious." David Bardwell, *Film Heritage,* Vol. 4, No. 3 (Spring 1964), p. 96.

"Strangers on a Train." Henry Hart, *Films in Review,* Vol. 11, No. 6 (June/July 1951), pp. 36–38.

"Strangers on a Train." Richard Winnington, *Sight and Sound,* Vol. 21, No. 1 (August/September 1951), pp. 21–22.

"I Confess." Hilda Black, *American Cinematographer* (December 1952), pp. 524–525; 546–547.

"I Confess." Robert Kass, *Films in Review,* Vol. 4, No. 3 (March 1953), pp. 148–150.

"I Confess." David Fisher, *Sight and Sound,* Vol. 23, No. 1 (July/September 1953).

"The Wrong Man." Ken Gay, *Films and Filming,* Vol. 3, No. 7 (April 1957), p. 26.

"The Wrong Man." Veronica Hume, *Films in Review,* Vol. 8, No. 1 (January 1957), pp. 33–34.

"The Wrong Man." Penelope Houston, *Sight and Sound,* Vol. 26, No. 4 (Spring 1957), p. 211.

"Rear Window." Dirwent May, *Sight and Sound,* Vol. 24, No. 2 (October/December 1954), pp. 89–91.

"Rear Window." Steve Sondheim, *Films in Review,* Vol. 5, No. 8 (October 1954), pp. 427–429.

"Rear Window." Ernest Boreman, *Films and Filming,* Vol. 1, No. 2 (November 1954), p. 18.

"Rear Window." Comments by Alfred Hitchcock. *Take One,* Vol. 2, No. 2 (1969), pp. 18–20.

"*Vertigo.*" Jeremey Browne, *Films in Review,* Vol. 9, No. 6 (June/July 1958), pp. 333–335.

"*Vertigo.*" Derek Conrad, *Films and Filming,* Vol. 4, No. 12 (September 1958), p. 25.

"*Vertigo.*" Penelope Houston, *Sight and Sound,* Vol. 27, No. 6 (Autumn 1958), p. 319.

"*Vertigo.*" Francis M. Nevins, Jr., *Journal of Popular Culture,* Vol. 11, No. 2 (Fall 1968), pp. 321–331.

"*North by Northwest.*" Dai Vaughan, *Sight and Sound,* Vol. 28, Nos. 3, 4 (Summer/Autumn 1959).

"*North by Northwest.*" Peter Baker, *Films and Filming,* Vol. 5, No. 12 (September 1959), p. 25.

"*North by Northwest.*" *Film Quarterly,* Vol. 14, No. 2 (Winter 1960), p. 62.

"*Psycho.*" Shirley Conover, *Films in Review,* Vol. 11, No. 7 (August/September 1960), pp. 426–427.

"*Psycho.*" Peter Baker, *Films and Filming,* Vol. 6, No. 12 (September 1960), p. 21.

"*Psycho.*" Peter John Dyer, *Sight and Sound,* Vol. 29, No. 4 (Autumn 1960), pp. 195–196.

"*Psycho.*" Ernest Callenbach, *Film Quarterly,* Vol. 14, No. 1 (Fall 1960), pp. 47–49.

"*The Birds.*" Ernest Callenbach, *Film Quarterly,* Vol. 1, No. 4 (Summer 1963), pp. 44–46.

"*The Birds.*" Comments by Alfred Hitchcock. *Take One,* Vol. 1, No. 10 (1968), pp. 6–7.

"*Marnie.*" William Johnson, *Film Quarterly,* Vol. 18, No. 1 (Fall 1964), pp. 38–42.

"*Marnie.*" Ian Cameras and Richard Jefferey, *Movie,* No. 12 (Spring 1965), pp. 21–24.

"Marnie." Peter Bogdanovich, *Cinema,* Vol. 2, No. 3 (October/ November 1964), p. 49.

"Topaz." Michael Walker, *Movie,* No. 18 (Winter 1971), pp. 10–13.

"Frenzy." Stanley Kauffmann, *New Republic,* July 8, 1972, pp. 22–34.

"Family Plot." Andrew Sarris, *Village Voice,* April 19, 1976.

"Family Plot." M. Kasindorf and P. D. Zimmerman, *Newsweek,* July 14, 1975.

The Pleasure Garden (1925)
PRODUCER: Michael Balcon, Erich Pommer. SCREENPLAY: Eliot Stannard, from the novel by Oliver Sandys. DIRECTOR OF PHOTOGRAPHY: Baron Ventimiglia. ASSISTANT DIRECTOR: Alma Reville. STUDIO: Emelka at Munich, Germany. LEADING PLAYERS: Virginia Valli (Patsy Brand), Carmelita Geraghty (Jill Cheyne), Miles Mander (Levet), John Stuart (Hugh Fielding).

The Mountain Eagle (1926)
PRODUCER: Michael Balcon. SCREENPLAY: Eliot Stannard. DIRECTOR OF PHOTOGRAPHY: Baron Ventimiglia. STUDIO: Emelka at Munich. LOCATION WORK: Austrian Tyrol. LEADING PLAYERS: Bernard Goetzke (Pettigrew), Nita Naldi (Beatrice), Malcolm Keen (Fear O'God), John Hamilton (Edward Pettigrew). (Released in the U.S. as *Fear O'God*)

The Lodger: A Story of the London Fog (1926)
PRODUCER: Michael Balcon. SCREENPLAY: Alfred Hitchcock and Eliot Stannard, based on the play by Mrs. Belloc-Lowndes. DIRECTOR OF PHOTOGRAPHY: Baron Ventimiglia. SETS: C. Wilfred Arnold and Betram Evans. EDITING AND SUBTITLES: Ivor Montagu. ASSISTANT DIRECTOR: Alma Reville. STUDIO: Islington. LEADING PLAYERS: Ivor Novello (the lodger), June (Daisy Bunting), Marie Ault (Mrs. Bunting), Arthur Chesney (Mr. Bunting), Malcolm Keen (Joe Betts).

Downhill (1927)
PRODUCER: Michael Balcon. SCREENPLAY: Eliot Stannard, from the play by Ivor Novello and Constance Collier (under pseudonym of David Lestrange). DIRECTOR OF PHOTOGRAPHY: Claude McDonnell. EDITING: Ivor Montagu. STUDIO: Islington. LEADING PLAYERS: Ivor Novello (Roddy Berwick),

Ben Webster (Dr. Dowson), Robin Irvine (Tim Wakely), Sybil Rhoda (Sybil Wakely), Lillian Braithwaite (Lady Berwick). (Released in the U.S. as *When Boys Leave Home*)

Easy Virtue (1927)
PRODUCER: Michael Balcon. SCREENPLAY: Eliot Stannard, from the play by Noël Coward. DIRECTOR OF PHOTOGRAPHY: Claude McDonnell. EDITING: Ivor Montagu. STUDIO: Islington. LEADING PLAYERS: Isabel Jeans (Laurita Filton), Franklin Dyall (M. Filton), Eric Bransby Williams (the correspondent), Ian Hunter (plaintiff's counsel), Robin Irvine (John Whittaker), Violet Farebrother (Mrs. Whittaker).

The Ring (1927)
PRODUCER: John Maxwell. SCREENPLAY: Alfred Hitchcock and Alma Reville. DIRECTOR OF PHOTOGRAPHY: Jack Cox. ASSISTANT DIRECTOR: Frank Mills. STUDIO: Elstree. LEADING PLAYERS: Carl Brisson (One-Round Jack Sander), Lilian Hall Davis (Nelly), Ian Hunter (Bob Corby).

The Farmer's Wife (1928)
PRODUCER: John Maxwell. SCREENPLAY: Alfred Hitchcock, from the play by Eden Philpotts. DIRECTOR OF PHOTOGRAPHY: Jack Cox. ASSISTANT DIRECTOR: Frank Mills. EDITING: Alfred Booth. STUDIO: Elstree. LOCATION WORK: Wales. LEADING PLAYERS: Lilian Hall Davis (Minta Dench), Jameson Thomas (Samuel Sweetland), Maud Gill (Thirza Tapper), Gordon Harker (Cheirdles Ash).

Champagne (1928)
PRODUCER: John Maxwell. SCREENPLAY: Eliot Stannard. DIRECTOR OF PHOTOGRAPHY: Jack Cox. STUDIO: Elstree. LEADING PLAYERS: Betty Balfour (Betty), Gordon Harker (her father), Theo von Alten (the mysterious passenger, her guardian), Jean Bradin (her fiancé).

The Manxman (1929)
PRODUCER: John Maxwell. SCREENPLAY: Eliot Stannard, from the novel by Hall Caine. DIRECTOR OF PHOTOGRAPHY: Jack Cox. ASSISTANT DIRECTOR: Frank Mills. STUDIO: Elstree. LEADING PLAYERS: Carl Brisson (Peter Christian), Malcolm Keen (Philip Quillian), Anny Ondra (Kate).

Blackmail (1929)
PRODUCER: John Maxwell. SCREENPLAY: Alfred Hitchcock,
Benn W. Levy, and Charles Bennett, from the play by Bennett.
DIRECTOR OF PHOTOGRAPHY: Jack Cox. SETS: Wilfred C.
Arnold and Norman Arnold. EDITING: Emile de Ruelle. LEAD-
ING PLAYERS: Anny Ondra (Alice White), Sara Allgood (Mrs.
White), John Longden (Frank Webber), Charles Paton (Mr. White),
Cyril Ritchard (the artist), Donald Calthrop (Tracy, the black-
mailer). (Joan Barry recorded the dialogue for Miss Ondra.)

Juno and the Paycock (1930)
PRODUCER: John Maxwell. SCREENPLAY: Alfred Hitchcock
and Alma Reville, from the play by Sean O'Casey. DIRECTOR OF
PHOTOGRAPHY: Jack Cox. SETS: Norman Arnold. EDITING:
Emile de Ruelle. STUDIO: Elstree. LEADING PLAYERS: Sara
Allgood (Juno), Edward Chapman (Captain Boyle), Sidney Morgan
(Joxer), Marie O'Neill (Mrs. Madigan).

Murder! (1930)
PRODUCER: John Maxwell. SCREENPLAY: Alma Reville, from
the play *Enter Sir John* by Clemence Dane (pseudonym of Winifred
Ashton) and Helen Simpson. DIRECTOR OF PHOTOGRAPHY:
Jack Cox. SETS: John Mead. EDITING: René Harrison. STUDIO:
Elstree. LEADING PLAYERS: Herbert Marshall (Sir John Me-
nier), Norah Baring (Diana Baring), Phyllis Konstam (Dulcie
Markham), Edward Chapman (Ted Markham), Esme Percy (Handel
Fane). (Hitchcock directed a lost version in German. Called *Mary,*
it starred Alfred Abel and Olga Tchekowa in the leading roles.)

The Skin Game (1931)
PRODUCER: John Maxwell. SCREENPLAY: Alfred Hitchcock
and Alma Reville, from the play by John Galsworthy. DIRECTOR
OF PHOTOGRAPHY: Jack Cox, assisted by Charles Martin.
EDITING: René Harrison and A. Gobett. STUDIO: Elstree.
LEADING PLAYERS: Edmund Gwenn (Mr. Hornblower), Jill
Esmond (Jill), John Longden (Charles), C. V. France (Mr.
Hillcrest), Helen Haye (Mrs. Hillcrest), Phyllis Konstam (Chloe),
Frank Lawton (Rolfe).

Rich and Strange (1932)
PRODUCER: John Maxwell. SCREENPLAY: Alma Reville and
Val Valentine, from a story outline by Dale Collins. DIRECTORS
OF PHOTOGRAPHY: Jack Cox and Charles Martin. SET:

C. Wilfred Arnold. MUSIC: Hal Dolphe, conducted by John Reynders. EDITING: Winifred Cooper and René Harrison. STUDIO: Elstree. LOCATION WORK: Marseilles, Port Said, Colombo, Suez. LEADING PLAYERS: Henry Kendall (Freddy Hill), Joan Barry (Emily Hill), Percy Marmont (Commander Gordon), Betty Amann (the "princess"), Elsie Randolph (Elsie). (Released in the U.S. as *East of Shanghai*)

Number Seventeen (1932)
PRODUCER: Michael Balcon. SCREENPLAY: Adapted by Alfred Hitchcock from the play and novel by Jefferson Farjeon. DIRECTOR OF PHOTOGRAPHY: Jack Cox. STUDIO: Elstree. LEADING PLAYERS: Léon M. Lion (Ben), Anne Grey (the young girl), John Stuart (the detective).

Waltzes from Vienna (1933)
PRODUCER: John Maxwell. SCREENPLAY: Adapted by Alma Reville and Guy Bolton from the play by Bolton. SETS: Alfred Junge and Peter Proud. MUSIC: Johann Strauss the Elder and Johann Strauss the Younger. STUDIO: Lime Grove. LEADING PLAYERS: Jessie Matthews (Rasi), Edmund Gwenn (Strauss the Elder), Fay Compton (the countess), Frank Vosper (the prince). (Released in the U.S. as *Strauss' Great Waltz*)

The Man Who Knew Too Much (1934)
PRODUCERS: Michael Balcon and Ivor Montagu. SCREENPLAY: A. R. Rawlinson, Charles Bennett, D. B. Wyndham-Lewis, Edwin Greenwood, from an original concept by Wyndham-Lewis and Charles Bennett. ADDITIONAL DIALOGUE: Emlyn Williams. DIRECTOR OF PHOTOGRAPHY: Curt Courant. SETS: Alfred Junge and Peter Proud. MUSIC: Arthur Benjamin, directed by Louis Levy. EDITING: H. St. C. Stewart. STUDIO: Lime Grove. LEADING PLAYERS: Leslie Banks (Bob Lawrence), Edna Best (Jill Lawrence), Peter Lorre (Abbot), Nova Pilbeam (Betty Lawrence), Pierre Fresnay (Louis Bernard).

The 39 Steps (1935)
PRODUCERS: Michael Balcon and Ivor Montagu. SCREENPLAY AND ADAPTATION: Charles Bennett and Alma Reville, from the novel by John Buchan. DIRECTOR OF PHOTOGRAPHY: Bernard Knowles. SETS: Otto Werndorff and Albert Jullion. COSTUMES: J. Strassner. MUSIC: Louis Levy. EDITING: Derek N. Twist. STUDIO: Lime Grove. LEADING PLAYERS: Made-

leine Carroll (Pamela), Robert Donat (Richard Hannay), Lucie Mannheim (Annabella Smith), Godfrey Tearle (Prof. Jordan), Peggy Ashcroft (The Crofter's Wife), John Laurie (The Crofter), Helen Haye (Mrs. Jordan), Wylie Watson (Mr. Memory).

Secret Agent (1936)
PRODUCERS: Michael Balcon and Ivor Montagu. SCREENPLAY: Charles Bennett, from Campbell Dixon's play inspired by W. Somerset Maugham's "Ashenden" detective series. ADAPTATION: Alma Reville. DIALOGUE: Ian Hay and Jesse Lasky, Jr. DIRECTOR OF PHOTOGRAPHY: Bernard Knowles. SETS: Otto Werndorff and Albert Jullion. COSTUMES: J. Strassner. MUSIC: Louis Levy. EDITING: Charles Frend. STUDIO: Lime Grove. LEADING PLAYERS: Madeleine Carroll (Elsa Carrington), John Gielgud (Edgar Brodie/Richard Ashenden), Peter Lorre (the General), Robert Young (Robert Marvin), Percy Marmont (Caypor), Florence Kahn (Mrs. Caypor), Lillie Palmer (the maid), Charles Carson ("R").

Sabotage (1936)
PRODUCERS: Michael Balcon and Ivor Montagu. SCREENPLAY: Charles Bennett, from Joseph Conrad's novel *The Secret Agent.* ADAPTATION: Alma Reville. ADDITIONAL DIALOGUE: Ian Hay, Helen Simpson, and E. V. H. Emmett. DIRECTOR OF PHOTOGRAPHY: Bernard Knowles. SETS: Otto Werndorff and Albert Jullion. MUSIC: Louis Levy. COSTUMES: J. Strassner. EDITING: Charles Frend. STUDIO: Lime Grove. LEADING PLAYERS: Sylvia Sidney (Mrs. Verloc), Oscar Homolka (Verloc), John Loder (Ted Spenser), Desmond Tester (Stevie), William Dewhurst (Mr. Chatman), Martita Hunt (his daughter). (Released in the U.S. as *A Woman Alone*)

Young and Innocent (1937)
PRODUCER: Edward Black. SCREENPLAY: Charles Bennett and Alma Reville, based on the novel *A Shilling for Candles,* by Josephine Tey. DIRECTOR OF PHOTOGRAPHY: Bernard Knowles. SETS: Alfred Junge. MUSIC: Louis Levy. EDITING: Charles Frend. STUDIOS: Lime Grove and Pinewood. LEADING PLAYERS: Derrick de Marney (Robert), Nova Pilbeam (Erica), Percy Marmont (Colonel Burgoyne), Edward Rigby (Will), Mary Clare (Erica's aunt), John Longden (Kent), Basil Radford (Uncle Basil). (Released in the U.S. as *The Girl Was Young*)

The Lady Vanishes (1938)
PRODUCER: Edward Black. SCREENPLAY: Sidney Gilliatt and Frank Launder, from the novel *The Wheel Spins,* by Ethel Lina White. ADAPTATION: Alma Reville. DIRECTOR OF PHOTOGRAPHY: Jack Cox. SETS: Alec Vetchinsky, Maurice Cater, and Albert Jullion. MUSIC: Louis Levy. EDITING: Alfred Roome and R. E. Dearing. STUDIO: Lime Grove. LEADING PLAYERS: Margaret Lockwood (Iris Henderson), Michael Redgrave (Gilbert), Dame May Whitty (Miss Froy), Paul Lukas (Dr. Hartz), Googie Withers (Blanche), Cecil Parker (Mr. Todhunter), Linden Travers (his mistress), Mary Clare (the Baroness), Naunton Wayne (Caldicott), Basil Radford (Charters), Catherine Lacey (the "nun").

Jamaica Inn (1939)
PRODUCERS: Erich Pommer and Charles Laughton. SCREENPLAY: Sidney Gilliatt and Joan Harrison, from the novel by Daphne du Maurier. ADDITIONAL DIALOGUE: J. B. Priestley. ADAPTATION: Alma Reville. DIRECTORS OF PHOTOGRAPHY: Bernard Knowles and Harry Stradling. SPECIAL EFFECTS: Harry Watt. SETS: Tom N. Morahan. COSTUMES: Molly McArthur. MUSIC: Eric Fenby, directed by Frederic Lewis. EDITING: Robert Hamer. LEADING PLAYERS: Charles Laughton (Squire Humphrey Pengallan), Leslie Banks (Joss Merlyn), Marie Ney (Patience Merlyn), Maureen O'Hara (Mary, the Merlyns' niece), Emlyn Williams (Harry), Wylie Watson (Salvation), Robert Newton (Jem Traherne).

Rebecca (1940)
PRODUCER: David O. Selznick. SCREENPLAY: Robert E. Sherwood and Joan Harrison, from Daphne du Maurier's novel. ADAPTATION: Philip MacDonald and Michael Hogan. DIRECTOR OF PHOTOGRAPHY: George Barnes. SETS: Lyle Wheeler. MUSIC: Franz Waxman. EDITING: Hal C. Kern. STUDIO: Selznick International. LEADING PLAYERS: Joan Fontaine (the second Mrs. de Winter), Laurence Olivier (Max de Winter), Dame Judith Anderson (Mrs. Danvers), George Sanders (Jack Favell), Nigel Bruce (Major Giles Lacey), Gladys Cooper (Mrs. Lacey), C. Aubrey Smith (Colonel Julyan), Florence Bates (Mrs. Van Hopper), Leo G. Carroll (the doctor).

Foreign Correspondent (1940)
PRODUCER: Walter Wanger. SCREENPLAY: Charles Bennett and Joan Harrison. ADDITIONAL DIALOGUE: James Hilton

and Robert Benchley. DIRECTOR OF PHOTOGRAPHY: Rudolph Mate. SPECIAL EFFECTS: Lee Zavitz. SETS: William Cameron Menzies and Alexander Golitzen. MUSIC: Alfred Newman. EDITING: Otto Lovering and Dorothy Spencer. ASSISTANT DIRECTOR: Edmond Bernoudy. STUDIO: United Artists. LEADING PLAYERS: Joel McCrea (Johnny Jones/Huntley Haverstock), Laraine Day (Carol Fisher), Herbert Marshall (Stephen Fisher), George Sanders (Herbert Folliott), Albert Basserman (Van Meer), Robert Benchley (Stebbins), Eduardo Cianelli (Krug), Edmund Gwenn (Rowley).

Mr. and Mrs. Smith (1941)
PRODUCER: Harry E. Edington. STORY AND SCREENPLAY: Norman Krasna. DIRECTOR OF PHOTOGRAPHY: Harry Stradling. SETS: Van Nest Polglase and L. P. Williams. MUSIC: Roy Webb. SPECIAL EFFECTS: Vernon L. Walker. EDITING: William Hamilton. STUDIO: RKO. LEADING PLAYERS: Carole Lombard (Ann Krausheimer Smith), Robert Montgomery (David Smith), Gene Raymond (Jeff Custer), Philip Merivale (Mr. Custer), Lucile Watson (Mrs. Custer), Jack Carson (Chuck Benson).

Suspicion (1941)
SCREENPLAY: Samson Raphaelson, Joan Harrison, and Alma Reville, from the novel *Before the Fact,* by Francis Iles (pseudonym of Anthony Berkeley). DIRECTOR OF PHOTOGRAPHY: Harry Stradling. SPECIAL EFFECTS: Vernon L. Walker. SETS: Van Nest Polglase, assisted by Carroll Clark. MUSIC: Franz Waxman. EDITING: William Hamilton. ASSISTANT DIRECTOR: Dewey Starkey. LEADING PLAYERS: Joan Fontaine (Lina McLaidlaw), Cary Grant (Johnny Aysgarth), Sir Cedric Hardwicke (General McLaidlaw), Nigel Bruce (Beaky), Dame May Whitty (Mrs. McLaidlaw), Isabel Jeans (Mrs. Newsham).

Saboteur (1942)
PRODUCERS: Frank Lloyd and Jack H. Skirball. SCREENPLAY: Peter Viertel, Joan Harrison, and Dorothy Parker, from an idea by Alfred Hitchcock. DIRECTOR OF PHOTOGRAPHY: Joseph Valentine. SETS: Jack Otterson. MUSIC: Charles Previn and Frank Skinner. EDITING: Otto Ludwig. STUDIO: Universal. LEADING PLAYERS: Robert Cummings (Barry Kane), Priscilla Lane (Patricia Martin), Otto Kruger (Charles Tobin), Alma Kruger (Mrs. Van Sutton), Norman Lloyd (Fry, the saboteur).

Shadow of a Doubt (1943)
PRODUCER: Jack H. Skirball. SCREENPLAY: Thornton Wilder, Alma Reville, and Sally Benson, from a story by Gordon McDonnell. DIRECTOR OF PHOTOGRAPHY: Joseph Valentine. SETS: John B. Goodman, Robert Boyle, A. Gausman, and L. R. Robinson. COSTUMES: Adrian, Vera West. MUSIC: Dimitri Tiomkin, directed by Charles Previn. EDITING: Milton Carruth. STUDIO: Universal. LOCATION WORK: Santa Rosa, California. LEADING PLAYERS: Joseph Cotten (Charlie Oakley), Teresa Wright (Charlie Newton), Patricia Collinge (Emma Newton), MacDonald Carey (Jack Graham), Henry Travers (Joe Newton), Hume Cronyn (Herb Hawkins), Wallace Ford (Fred Saunders), Edna May Wonacott (Ann Newton).

Lifeboat (1943)
PRODUCER: Kenneth MacGowan. SCREENPLAY: Jo Swerling, from a story by John Steinbeck. DIRECTOR OF PHOTOGRAPHY: Glen MacWilliams. SPECIAL EFFECTS: Fred Sersen. SETS: James Basevi and Maurice Ransford. MUSIC: Hugo Friedhofer, directed by Emil Newman. COSTUMES: René Hubert. EDITING: Dorothy Spencer. STUDIO: Twentieth Century-Fox. LEADING PLAYERS: Tallulah Bankhead (Constance Porter), William Bendix (Gus), Walter Slezak (Willy), Mary Anderson (Alice MacKenzie), John Hodiak (Kovac), Henry Hull (Charles Rittenhouse), Heather Angel (Mrs. Higgins), Hume Cronyn (Stanley Garrett), Canada Lee (George "Joe" Spencer).

Spellbound (1945)
PRODUCER: David O. Selznick. SCREENPLAY: Ben Hecht, from the novel *The House of Dr. Edwardes,* by Francis Beeding (pseudonym of Hilary St. George Saunders and John Palmer). ADAPTATION: Angus MacPhail. DIRECTOR OF PHOTOGRAPHY: George Barnes. SPECIAL EFFECTS: Jack Cosgrove. SETS: James Basevi and John Ewing. MUSIC: Miklos Rozsa. COSTUMES: Howard Greer. EDITING: William Ziegler and Hal C. Kern. DREAM SEQUENCE: designed by Salvador Dali. PSYCHIATRIC CONSULTANT: May E. Romm. STUDIO: Selznick International. LEADING PLAYERS: Ingrid Bergman (Dr. Constance Petersen), Gregory Peck (John Ballantyne), Leo G. Carroll (Dr. Murchison), Norman Lloyd (Garmes), Rhonda Fleming (Mary Carmichael), Michael Chekhov (the old doctor).

Notorious (1946)
PRODUCER: Alfred Hitchcock. ASSOCIATE PRODUCER: Barbara Keon. SCREENPLAY: Ben Hecht, from a theme by Hitchcock. DIRECTOR OF PHOTOGRAPHY: Ted Tetzlaff. SPECIAL EFFECTS: Vernon L. Walker and Paul Eagler. ASSISTANT DIRECTOR: William Dorfman. SETS: Albert S. D'Agostino, Carroll Clark, Darrell Silvera, Claude Carpenter. COSTUMES: Edith Head. MUSIC: Roy Webb, conducted by Constantin Bakaleinikoff. EDITING: Theron Warth. STUDIO: RKO. LEADING PLAYERS: Ingrid Bergman (Alicia Huberman), Cary Grant (Devlin), Claude Rains (Alexander Sebastian), Leopoldine Konstantin (Mrs. Sebastian), Louis Calhern (Paul Prescott).

The Paradine Case (1947)
PRODUCER: David O. Selznick, from the novel by Robert Hichens. ADAPTATION: Alma Reville. DIRECTOR OF PHOTOGRAPHY: Lee Garmes. SETS: J. MacMillan Johnson and Tom Morahan. COSTUMES: Travis Banton. MUSIC: Franz Waxman. EDITING: Hal C. Kern and John Faure. STUDIO: Selznick International. LEADING PLAYERS: Gregory Peck (Anthony Keane), Ann Todd (Gay Keane), Charles Laughton (Judge Horfield), Alida Valli (Mrs. Paradine), Ethel Barrymore (Sophie Horfield), Charles Coburn (Simon Flaquer), Louis Jourdan (André Latour).

Rope (1948)
PRODUCERS: Sidney Bernstein and Alfred Hitchcock. SCREENPLAY: Arthur Laurents, from the play by Patrick Hamilton. ADAPTATION: Hume Cronyn. DIRECTORS OF PHOTOGRAPHY: Joseph Valentine and William V. Skall. COLOR CONSULTANT: Natalie Kalmus. SETS: Perry Ferguson. MUSIC: Leo F. Forbstein's interpretation of Francis Poulenc's "Mouvement Perpetuel No. 1." COSTUMES: Adrian. EDITING: William H. Ziegler. STUDIO: Warner Bros. LEADING PLAYERS: James Stewart (Rupert Cadell), John Dall (Shaw Brandon), Farley Granger (Philip), Sir Cedric Hardwicke (Mr. Kentley), Joan Chandler (Janet Walker), Constance Collier (Mrs. Atwater), Edith Evanson (Mrs. Wilson), Douglas Dick (Kenneth Lawrence), Dick Hogan (David Kentley).

Under Capricorn (1949)
PRODUCERS: Sidney Bernstein and Alfred Hitchcock. SCREENPLAY: James Bridie, from the novel by Helen Simpson. ADAP-

TATION: Hume Cronyn. DIRECTOR OF PHOTOGRAPHY: Jack Cardiff, with the assistance of Paul Beeson, Ian Craig, David McNeilly, Jack Haste. SETS: Tom Morahan. MUSIC: Composed by Richard Addinsell and conducted by Louis Levy. EDITING: A. S. Bates. COSTUMES: Roger Furse. COLOR CONSULTANTS: Natalie Kalmus and Joan Bridges. STUDIO: M-G-M at Elstree. LEADING PLAYERS: Ingrid Bergman (Henrietta Flusky), Joseph Cotten (Sam Flusky), Michael Wilding (Charles Adare), Margaret Leighton (Milly), Cecil Parker (governor), Dennis O'Dea (Corrigian).

Stage Fright (1950)
PRODUCER: Alfred Hitchcock. SCREENPLAY: Whitfield Cook, from two stories by Selwyn Jepson, "Man Running" and "Outrun the Constable." ADAPTATION: Alma Reville. ADDITIONAL DIALOGUE: James Bridie. DIRECTOR OF PHOTOGRAPHY: Wilkie Cooper. SETS: Terence Verity. MUSIC: Leighton Lucas, conducted by Louis Levy. EDITING: Edward Jarvis. STUDIO: Elstree. LEADING PLAYERS: Marlene Dietrich (Charlotte Inwood), Jane Wyman (Eve Gill), Michael Wilding (Inspector Wilfred Smith), Richard Todd (Jonathan Cooper), Alastair Sim (Commodore Gill), Dame Sybil Thorndike (Mrs. Gill), Kay Walsh (Nellie), Patricia Hitchcock (Chubby Bannister).

Strangers on a Train (1951)
PRODUCER: Alfred Hitchcock. SCREENPLAY: Adapted by Raymond Chandler and Czenzi Ormonde from the novel by Patricia Highsmith. ADAPTATION: Whitfield Cook. DIRECTOR OF PHOTOGRAPHY: Robert Burks. SPECIAL EFFECTS: H. F. Koene Kamp. SETS: Edward S Haworth and George James Hopkins. MUSIC: Dimitri Tiomkin, conducted by Ray Heindorf. COSTUMES: Leah Rhodes. EDITING: William H. Ziegler. STUDIO: Warner Bros. LEADING PLAYERS: Robert Walker (Bruno Anthony), Farley Granger (Guy Haines), Ruth Roman (Ann Morton), Leo G. Carroll (Senator Morton), Patricia Hitchcock (Barbara Morton), Laura Elliot (Miriam Haines), Marion Lorne (Mrs. Anthony), Jonathan Hale (Mr. Anthony), Norma Varden (Mrs. Cunningham).

I Confess (1952)
PRODUCER: Alfred Hitchcock. ASSOCIATE: Barbara Keon. SCREENPLAY: George Tabori and William Archibald, from Paul Anthelme's play, *Our Two Consciences*. DIRECTOR OF PHOTOG-

RAPHY: Robert Burks. SETS: Edward S. Haworth and George James Hopkins. MUSIC: Dimitri Tiomkin, conducted by Ray Heindorf. EDITING: Rudi Fehr COSTUMES: Orry-Kelly. TECHNICAL CONSULTANT: Rev. Paul LaCouline. STUDIO: Warner Bros. LOCATION WORK: Quebec. ASSISTANT DIRECTOR: Don Page. LEADING PLAYERS: Montgomery Clift (Father Michael Logan), Anne Baxter (Ruth Grandfort), Karl Malden (Inspector Larrue), Brian Aherne (Willy Robertson), O. E. Hasse (Otto Keller), Dolly Haas (Alma Keller), Roger Dann (Pierre Grandfort).

Dial M for Murder (1953)
PRODUCER: Alfred Hitchcock. SCREENPLAY: Alfred Hitchcock, from Frederick Knott's play. DIRECTOR OF PHOTOGRAPHY: Robert Burks. Color by WarnerColor. Shot and released in Naturalvision 3-D. SETS: Edward Carrère and George James Hopkins. MUSIC: Dimitri Tiomkin. COSTUMES: Moss Mabry. EDITING: Rudi Fehr. STUDIO: Warner Bros. LEADING PLAYERS: Ray Milland (Tony Wendice), Grace Kelly (Margot Wendice), Robert Cummings (Mark Halliday), Anthony Dawson (Swann/ Lesgate), John Williams (Inspector Hubbard).

Rear Window (1954)
PRODUCER: Alfred Hitchcock. SCREENPLAY: John Michael Hayes, from a novella by Cornell Woolrich. DIRECTOR OF PHOTOGRAPHY: Robert Burks. TECHNICOLOR CONSULTANT: Richard Mueller. SPECIAL EFFECTS: John P. Fulton. SETS: Hal Pereira, Joseph MacMillan Johnson, Sam Comer, and Ray Mayer. MUSIC: Franz Waxman. EDITING: George Tomasini. COSTUMES: Edith Head. ASSISTANT DIRECTOR: Herbert Coleman. STUDIO: Paramount. LEADING PLAYERS: James Stewart (L. B. Jeffries), Grace Kelly (Lisa Fremont), Wendell Corey (Tom Doyle), Thelma Ritter (Stella), Raymond Burr (Lars Thorwald), Judith Evelyn (Miss Lonelyhearts), Ross Bagdasarian (the composer), Georgine Darcy (Miss Torso), Jesslyn Fax (the sculptress), Irene Winston (Mrs. Thorwald).

To Catch a Thief (1955)
PRODUCER: Alfred Hitchcock. SECOND UNIT DIRECTOR: Herbert Coleman. ASSISTANT DIRECTOR: Daniel McCauley. SCREENPLAY: John Michael Hayes, from David Dodge's novel. DIRECTOR OF PHOTOGRAPHY: Robert Burks. TECHNICOLOR CONSULTANT: Richard Mueller. SECOND UNIT

PHOTOGRAPHER: Wallace Kelley. SPECIAL EFFECTS: John P. Fulton. PROCESS PHOTOGRAPHY: Farciot Edouart. SETS: Hal Pereira, Joseph MacMillan Johnson, Sam Comer, and Arthur Krams. MUSIC: Lynn Murray. EDITING: George Tomasini. COSTUMES: Edith Head. STUDIO: Paramount. LOCATION WORK: the Mediterranean coast of France. LEADING PLAYERS: Cary Grant (John Robie), Grace Kelly (Frances Stevens), Jessie Royce Landis (Jessie Stevens), Brigitte Auger (Danielle Foussard), John Williams (the insurance inspector).

The Trouble with Harry (1956)
PRODUCER: Alfred Hitchcock. SCREENPLAY: John Michael Hayes, from John Trevor Story's novel. DIRECTOR OF PHOTOGRAPHY: Robert Burks. SPECIAL EFFECTS: John P. Fulton. TECHNICOLOR CONSULTANT: Richard Mueller. SETS: Hal Pereira, John Goodman, Sam Comer, and Emile Kuri. MUSIC: Bernard Herrmann. EDITING: Alma Macrorie. COSTUMES: Edith Head. STUDIO: Paramount. LOCATION WORK: Vermont. LEADING PLAYERS: Edmund Gwenn (Captain Wiles), John Forsythe (Sam Marlowe), Shirley MacLaine (Jennifer), Mildred Natwick (Miss Gravely), Mildred Dunnock (Mrs. Wiggs), Jerry Mathers (Arnie), Royal Dano (Alfred Wiggs), Philip Truex (Harry).

The Man Who Knew Too Much (1956)
PRODUCER: Alfred Hitchcock. ASSOCIATE PRODUCER: Herbert Coleman. SCREENPLAY: John Michael Hayes and Angus MacPhail, from a story by Charles Bennett and D. B. Wyndham-Lewis. DIRECTOR OF PHOTOGRAPHY: Robert Burks. TECHNICAL CONSULTANT: Richard Mueller. SPECIAL EFFECTS: John P. Fulton. SETS: Hal Pereira, Henry Bumstead, Sam Comer, and Arthur Krams. MUSIC: Bernard Herrmann. ("Que Será, Será" and "We'll Love Again" by Jay Livingston and Ray Evans; "Storm Cloud Cantata" by Arthur Benjamin and D. B. Wyndham-Lewis, reorchestrated by Bernard Herrmann and played by the London Symphony Orchestra under Herrmann's direction.) EDITING: George Tomasini. COSTUMES: Edith Head. ASSISTANT DIRECTOR: Howard Joslin. STUDIO: Paramount. LOCATION WORK: Morocco, London. LEADING PLAYERS: James Stewart (Dr. Ben McKenna), Doris Day (Jo McKenna), Daniel Gélin (Louis Bernard), Brenda de Banzie (Mrs. Drayton), Bernard Miles (Mr. Drayton), Christopher Olsen (Hank McKenna), Reggie Malder (the assassin).

The Wrong Man (1957)
PRODUCER: Alfred Hitchcock. ASSOCIATE PRODUCER:
Herbert Coleman. SCREENPLAY: Maxwell Anderson and Angus
MacPhail, from Maxwell Anderson's *True Story of Christopher
Emmanuel Balestrero.* DIRECTOR OF PHOTOGRAPHY: Robert
Burks. SETS: Paul Sylbert and William L. Kuehl. MUSIC: Bernard
Herrmann. EDITING: George Tomasini. ASSISTANT DIREC-
TOR: Daniel J. McCauley. STUDIO: Warner Bros. LOCATION
WORK: New York City. TECHNICAL CONSULTANT: Frank
O'Connor, District Attorney, Queens County. LEADING PLAY-
ERS: Henry Fonda (Christopher Emmanuel Balestrero), Vera
Miles (Rose Balestrero), Anthony Quayle (Frank O'Connor),
Esther Minciotti (Mrs. Balestrero).

Vertigo (1958)
PRODUCER: Alfred Hitchcock. ASSOCIATE PRODUCER:
Herbert Coleman. SCREENPLAY: Alec Coppel, replaced by
Samuel Taylor; from the novel by Pierre Boileau and Thomas
Narcejac, *D'entre les morts,* published later as *Sueurs froides.* DIREC-
TOR OF PHOTOGRAPHY: Robert Burks. SPECIAL EFFECTS:
John P. Fulton. SETS: Hal Pereira, Henry Bumstead, Sam Comer,
and Frank McKelvey. TECHNICOLOR CONSULTANT: Richard
Mueller. MUSIC: Bernard Herrmann, conducted by Muir Math-
ieson. EDITING: George Tomasini. COSTUMES: Edith Head.
ASSISTANT DIRECTOR: Daniel J. McCauley. TITLE DE-
SIGNS: Saul Bass. DREAM SEQUENCE: John Ferren. STUDIO:
Paramount. LOCATION WORK: San Francisco, Santa Cruz, San
Juan Bautista. LEADING PLAYERS: James Stewart (John Fer-
guson, also called "Scottie"), Kim Novak (Madeleine Elster/Judy
Barton), Barbara Bel Geddes (Midge Wood), Tom Helmore
(Gavin Elster), Henry Jones (the coroner), Raymond Bailey (the
doctor), Ellen Corby (manager, McKittrick Hotel), Konstantin
Shayne (Pop Liebl), Lee Patrick (a neighbor).

North by Northwest (1959)
PRODUCER: Alfred Hitchcock. ASSOCIATE PRODUCER: Her-
bert Coleman. SCREENPLAY: Ernest Lehman. DIRECTOR OF
PHOTOGRAPHY: Robert Burks. TECHNICOLOR CON-
SULTANT: Charles K. Hagedon. SPECIAL EFFECTS: A. Arnold
Gillespie and Lee Leblanc. SETS: Robert Boyle, William A. Horning,
Merrill Pye, Henry Grace, and Frank McKelvey. MUSIC: Bernard
Herrmann. EDITING: George Tomasini. TITLE DESIGNS: Saul
Bass. ASSISTANT DIRECTOR: Robert Saunders. STUDIO:

M-G-M. LOCATION WORK: New York City, Long Island, Chicago, Rapid City. LEADING PLAYERS: Cary Grant (Roger Thornhill), Eva Marie Saint (Eve Kendall), James Mason (Philip Vandamm), Jessie Royce Landis (Clara Thornhill), Leo G. Carroll (The Professor), Philip Ober (Lester Townsend), Josephine Hutchinson ("Mrs. Townsend," actually Vandamm's sister), Martin Landau (Leonard), Adam Williams (Valerian), Doreen Lang (Maggie).

Psycho (1960)
PRODUCER: Alfred Hitchcock. SCREENPLAY: Joseph Stefano, from Robert Bloch's novel. DIRECTOR OF PHOTOGRAPHY: John L. Russell. SPECIAL EFFECTS: Clarence Champagne. SETS: Joseph Hurley, Robert Clatworthy, and George Milo. MUSIC: Bernard Herrmann. TITLE DESIGNS: Saul Bass. EDITING: George Tomasini. ASSISTANT DIRECTOR: Hilton A. Green. COSTUMES: Helen Colvig. STUDIO: Paramount. LOCATION WORK: Arizona, southern California. LEADING PLAYERS: Anthony Perkins (Norman Bates), Janet Leigh (Marion Crane), Vera Miles (Lila Crane), John Gavin (Sam Loomis), Martin Balsam (Milton Arbogast), John McIntire (Sheriff Chambers), Lurene Tuttle (Mrs. Chambers), Simon Oakland (the psychiatrist), Frank Albertson (Cassidy), Vaughn Taylor (Mr. Lowery), Mort Mills (the policeman), Patricia Hitchcock (Caroline).

The Birds (1963)
PRODUCER: Alfred Hitchcock. ASSISTANT TO MR. HITCHCOCK: Peggy Robertson. SCREENPLAY: Evan Hunter, from the short story by Daphne du Maurier. DIRECTOR OF PHOTOGRAPHY: Robert Burks. SPECIAL EFFECTS: Lawrence A. Hampton. SPECIAL PHOTOGRAPHIC ADVISOR: Ub Iwerks. BIRD TRAINER: Ray Berwick. SETS: Robert Boyle and George Milo. SOUND CONSULTANT: Bernard Herrmann. ELECTRONIC SOUNDS: Remi Gassman and Oskar Sals. ASSISTANT DIRECTOR: James H. Brown. ILLUSTRATOR: Albert Whitlock. CREDITS: James S. Pollak. EDITING: George Tomasini. STUDIO: Universal. LOCATION WORK: Bodega Bay, San Francisco. LEADING PLAYERS: Tippi Hedren (Melanie Daniels), Rod Taylor (Mitch Brenner), Jessica Tandy (Mrs. Brenner), Suzanne Pleshette (Annie Hayworth), Veronica Cartwright (Cathy Brenner), Ethel Griffies (Mrs. Bundy), Charles McGraw (Sebastian Sholes), Ruth McDevitt (Mrs. MacGruder), Elizabeth Wilson (waitress at the Tides Café).

Marnie (1964)
PRODUCER: Alfred Hitchcock. ASSISTANT TO MR. HITCH-
COCK: Peggy Robertson. SCREENPLAY: Jay Presson Allen, from
Winston Graham's novel. DIRECTOR OF PHOTOGRAPHY:
Robert Burks. SETS: Robert Boyle and George Milo. MUSIC:
Bernard Herrmann. EDITING: George Tomasini. ASSISTANT
DIRECTOR: James H. Brown. STUDIO: Universal. SECOND
UNIT LOCATION WORK: Maryland. LEADING PLAYERS:
Tippi Hedren (Marnie Edgar), Sean Connery (Mark Rutland),
Diane Baker (Lil Mainwaring), Louise Latham (Bernice Edgar),
Martin Gabel (Strutt), Alan Napier (Mr. Rutland), Mariette
Hartley (Susan), Bruce Dern (the sailor), Edith Evanson (the
cleaning woman), S. John Launer (Sam Ward).

Torn Curtain (1966)
PRODUCER: Alfred Hitchcock. ASSISTANT TO MR. HITCH-
COCK: Peggy Robertson. SCREENPLAY: Brian Moore. DIREC-
TOR OF PHOTOGRAPHY: John F. Warren. SETS: Frank Arrigo.
MUSIC: John Addison. EDITING: Bud Hoffman. ASSISTANT
DIRECTOR: Donald Baer. STUDIO: Universal. LEADING
PLAYERS: Paul Newman (Michael Armstrong), Julie Andrews
(Sarah Sherman), Lila Kedrova (Countess Kuchinska), Wolfgang
Kieline (Gromek), Ludwig Donath (Professor Lindt), Tamara
Toumanova (the ballerina), David Opatoshu (Mr. Jacobi), Mort
Mills (the farmer), Carolyn Conwell (the farmer's wife).

Topaz (1969)
PRODUCER: Alfred Hitchcock. ASSISTANT TO MR. HITCH-
COCK: Peggy Robertson. SCREENPLAY: Samuel Taylor, based
on Leon Uris's novel. DIRECTOR OF PHOTOGRAPHY: Jack
Hildyard. SETS: John Austin, Alexander Golitzen, and Henry
Bumstead. SPECIAL PHOTOGRAPHIC EFFECTS: Albert Whit-
lock. STUDIO: Universal. LEADING PLAYERS: Frederick Staf-
ford (André Devereaux), Dany Robin (Nicole Devereaux), Claude
Jade (Michele Picard), Michel Subor (François Picard), Michel
Piccoli (Jacques Granville), Philippe Noiret (Henri Jarré), John
Forsythe (Michael Nordstrom), Karin Dor (Juanita de Cordoba),
Per-Axel Arosenius (Boris Kusenov), Sonja Kolthoff (Mrs.
Kusenov), John Vernon (Rico Parra), Roscoe Lee Browne (Philippe
Dubois), Don Randolph (Uribe), Tina Hedstrom (Tamara
Kusenov), John Roper (Thomas), Anna Novarro (Carlotta Men-
doza), Lewis Charles (Pablo Mendoza).

Frenzy (1972)
PRODUCER: Alfred Hitchcock. ASSISTANT TO MR. HITCH-
COCK: Peggy Robertson. SCREENPLAY: Anthony Shaffer, from
Arthur LaBern's novel, *Goodbye Picadilly, Farewell Leicester Square.*
DIRECTOR OF PHOTOGRAPHY: Gil Taylor. SPECIAL PHO-
TOGRAPHIC EFFECTS: A. Whitlock. SETS: Simon Wakefield.
ART DIRECTOR: Bob Laing. ASSISTANT DIRECTOR: Colin
M. Brewer. EDITING: John Jympson. MUSIC: Ron Goodwin.
ASSOCIATE PRODUCER: William Hill. PRODUCTION DE-
SIGN: Syd Cain. STUDIO: Pinewood, London. LEADING PLAY-
ERS: Jon Finch (Richard Blaney), Barry Foster (Bob Rusk), Barbara
Leigh-Hunt (Brenda Blaney), Anna Massey (Babs Milligan), Alec
McCowen (Inspector Oxford), Vivien Merchant (Mrs. Oxford),
Billie Whitelaw (Hetty Porter), Clive Swift (John Porter), Felix
Forsythe (Bernard Cribbins).

Family Plot (1976)
PRODUCER: Alfred Hitchcock. ASSISTANT TO MR. HITCH-
COCK: Peggy Robertson. SCREENPLAY: Ernest Lehman, from
Victor Canning's novel, *The Rainbird Pattern.* DIRECTOR OF
PHOTOGRAPHY: Leonard J. South. PRODUCTION DE-
SIGNER: Henry Bumstead. SET DECORATIONS: James W.
Payne. FILM EDITOR: J. Terry Williams. SOUND: James Alexan-
der and Robert L. Hoyt. COSTUMES: Edith Head. MUSIC: John
Williams. SPECIAL EFFECTS: Albert Whitlock. UNIT MAN-
AGER: Ernest B. Wehmeyer. FIRST ASSISTANT DIRECTOR:
Howard G. Kazanjian. SECOND ASSISTANT DIRECTOR:
Wayne A. Farlow. SCRIPT SUPERVISOR: Lois Thurman. MAKE-
UP: Jack Barron. PRODUCTION ILLUSTRATOR: Thomas J.
Wright. TITLES AND OPTICAL EFFECTS: Universal Title.
LEADING PLAYERS: Karen Black (Fran), Bruce Dern (George
Lumley), Barbara Harris (Blanche Tyler), William Devane (Adam-
son), Ed Lauter (Maloney), Cathleen Nesbitt (Julia Rainbird),
Katherine Helmond (Mrs. Maloney), William Prince (Bishop).

Select Hitchcock Cameo Appearances

The Lodger: Hitchcock's back is seen at a newsroom desk, and later he is one of a crowd at the arrest of the alleged killer.

Blackmail: Reads a newspaper in the subway while being pestered by a small boy.

Murder!: A street pedestrian.

The 39 Steps: A passerby on the street.

Young and Innocent: An awkward news photographer outside a courtroom during a murder trial.

The Lady Vanishes: A passerby in the London railroad station.

Rebecca: Waits outside a telephone booth for George Sanders to finish a call.

Foreign Correspondent: A pedestrian who walks past the American reporter, Joel McCrea.

Mr. and Mrs. Smith: Again, a pedestrian who walks past the male lead, Robert Montgomery.

Saboteur: A curious bystander at a newsstand.

Shadow of a Doubt: Declares a full house in a poker game on a moving train.

Lifeboat: Is pictured in contrast ("before" and "after") in a fat-reducing advertisement in the newspaper being read by William Bendix.

Spellbound: Leaves an elevator in a New York City hotel.

Notorious: A guest drinking champagne at a party.

The Paradine Case: Carries a large cello case.

Rope: In the opening scene, Hitchcock is crossing the street.

Under Capricorn: Seen first as one of many listeners at a state function and later on the stairs of the government house in Australia.

Stage Fright: Passes Jane Wyman and looks back at her as he overhears her talking to herself.

Strangers on a Train: Boards a train while clumsily carrying a heavy double bass.

I Confess: Crosses at the top of an outdoor stone staircase in Montreal.

Dial M for Murder: As part of a college reunion photograph in Grace Kelly's apartment.

Rear Window: Humorously winds a clock.

To Catch a Thief: Sits next to Cary Grant on a country bus.

The Trouble with Harry: A pedestrian who walks past the outdoor art exhibit of John Forsythe.

The Man Who Knew Too Much: Glimpsed in an outdoor marketplace in Marrakech.

The Wrong Man: The prologue is narrated by the unseen Hitchcock.

Vertigo: Crosses a street in San Francisco.

North by Northwest: Runs to catch a bus but is left standing after the driver shuts the door in his face.

Psycho: Stands outside of the realty office in Phoenix, wearing a wide-brimmed hat.

The Birds: Passes Tippi Hedren as he leaves a pet shop, walking two dogs on a leash.

Marnie: Leaves a room in a hotel.

Torn Curtain: Holds a baby in his lap in a hotel lobby.

Topaz: Sits in a wheelchair at an airport.

Frenzy: A spectator at a political rally on the Embankment in London.

Family Plot: Forms a very distinctive silhouette on the frosted glass door of the Registry of Births and Deaths.

Index

About the Author

Father Neil P. Hurley, S.J., is President-Founder of INSCAPE, dedicated to "edutainment," adding delight by insight. He received his B.S. in Accountancy from Fordham University, worked as an accountant for Price, Waterhouse & Co. and received his M.A. and Ph.D. in Political Science from Fordham University and his Licentiate in Philosophy from Bellarmine College in New York. He spent four years at the State University of Innsbruck (Austria) and was ordained a Jesuit priest there in 1959. He studied spirituality for a year at Oude Abdij at Drongen, Belgium. He has done post-doctoral work at NYU Graduate School of Business Administration and at the Florida State University in Religion and Media.

Fr. Hurley spent twelve years in Chile with a Social Action and Research team of Jesuits at the Bellarmine Center in Santiago. He conducted three international seminars on the possibility of linking twenty universities in the hemisphere by space communications. Returning to the US in 1975 after a three-month sabbatical in India, Fr. Hurley taught as an adjunct professor at Florida State University, Fordham University, Loyola-Marymount University and was an associate professor at Loyola University in New Orleans. Fr. Hurley has lectured at the Quaker World College, Notre Dame University, and the University of Southern California (Cinema-TV School).

"Hitch" in scarecrow pose for his light comedy TV mystery show.